HOPE

Prevails

Insights from a Doctor's

Personal Journey through Depression

DR. MICHELLE
BENGTSON

"As a counselor, I have read many books on depression, but I have never read a book that deals with the spiritual aspect of healing as thoroughly as does *Hope Prevails*. Dr. Bengtson draws from her own personal journey as well as her professional experience. I highly recommend this book for anyone who has tasted the pain of depression or knows a friend who is depressed."

—**Gary Chapman**, PhD, author of *The 5 Love Languages*

"There are many fine, worthy, and insightful books written about depression, but in my view, Dr. Bengtson's trumps them all."

—**Marilyn Meberg**, Women of Faith speaker and author of *Constantly Craving*

"I often see the long-term and devastating effects of the hard to define, hard to leave behind ravages of depression. It seeks to wear down and wear out our hope. When longing to help another caught in despair, I'm acutely aware of how inadequate I am to help them, realizing that Christian platitudes and casual verses only serve to make those suffering from depression feel more alone or misunderstood. In *Hope Prevails*, Dr. Michelle Bengtson provides some profound wisdom for us all. By sharing her own journey of recovery, Michelle offers a breakthrough approach that focuses on the spiritual component of recovery as a means to overcome. This book finds the crossroads between treatment and faith. What you hold in your hand is a rare gift. It's hard to find a person who will be so honest about his or her own struggle in order to help you with yours. It's a double blessing when that person also possesses the expertise, experience, and grace to meet your needs. I recommend this book, and this woman, to those caught in the trap of depression. There is hope and it does prevail."

—**Jan Greenwood**, pastor of Pink (Gateway Women) at Gateway Church in Southlake, Texas, and author of *Women at War*

"Nowhere else have I found an author speak to the difficulty of depression with this level of specific explanation, insight, and hope. In *Hope Prevails*, Dr. Michelle Bengtson unfolds a deeply personal narrative that speaks both to cause and antidote. She balances the truths of depression with a chord of hope, tethering us to both the love and the power of God. On those days when you're tired and weary and feel like you just can't keep going, this book is like having a girlfriend right there with you. A girlfriend who just happens to be a trained and certified mental health professional who relies on Scripture to equip you with the tools you need to overcome."

—**Jo Ann Fore**, author of the award-winning *When a Woman Finds Her Voice*

"In my thirty years as a practicing psychotherapist, I've never read a book that suggests more helpful and concrete ways of overcoming depression as *Hope Prevails*. This book goes a major step beyond what therapy accomplishes by helping us maintain our hope. Dr. Bengtson's own struggle with depression is carefully woven into her well-credentialed research on its causes and etiology. Then she leaves us with a powerful prescription for finding relief and peace. The message is clear and never loses its power. I'm grateful for this book and the many who will get relief reading it and following her prescriptions. And, how helpful to those with someone in their life dealing with depression."

—**Pat Wenger**, MA, LPC, MFT

"*Hope Prevails* is a treasure trove of Scripture, music, and medicine for the soul. This book shares truth upon truth for anyone encountering depression. It is a very important work that should be held in the highest regard in any family library. Most of all, it is honest. Michelle genuinely opens up a window of her heart, revealing her own darkest hours in order to shine a light of hope for you and me. If you or anyone you love touches even the fringe of depression, I highly recommend this work as a key doorway to your journey toward joy, peace, and the full life you can have in Christ."

—**Jennifer Strickland**, author of *Beautiful Lies*, inspirational speaker, and founder of URMore.org

"Dr. Bengtson exposes the lies and opens our eyes to the truth about depression! I loved this book! Like a sweet friend walking with us in our darkest days, with experiential wisdom and tender compassion, Dr. Bengtson exposes the lies and reveals the truth about depression and what keeps us trapped in physical, emotional, and spiritual bondage. If you are ready to finally break free, your Rx is waiting. Take Michelle's hand and allow her to offer you the hope your soul is longing for."

—**Patty Mason**, author of *Finally Free: Breaking the Bonds of Depression without Drugs* and founder of Liberty in Christ Ministries

"It is one thing to have clinical expertise and knowledge; it is entirely something different to have a story. Dr. Michelle Bengtson weaves these all together, on a foundation of her deep and tested faith, to give a response, or more accurately a weapon against, this monster called depression. Reading this book gives the clear awareness that you are not alone and you are not defeated. More than her book, Michelle's life shouts, 'Hope Prevails!'"

—**Bob Hamp,** founder and director of Think Differently Counseling, Consulting and Connecting and author of *Think Differently, Live Differently*

"Dr. Michelle Bengtson's enlightening book, *Hope Prevails*, provides a master blueprint for overcoming negative thoughts and toxic emotions. Targeting a generation who feels lost and hopeless, this book provides meaningful help to everyone who has endured unexpected heartache, pain, or trauma. *Hope Prevails* offers effective answers on how to overcome loss and reach for a life brimming with peace, joy, and limitless dreams. Reading this book will drastically improve your life."

—**Tracey Mitchell,** TV host, preacher, and author of *Downside Up*

"It's very likely that you or a loved one has experienced the effects of depression: profound sadness, lack of energy, loss of joy. You may have found yourself wishing for the honest counsel of a wise woman or a close friend, even a special therapist. Someone who would understand what you are going through without you having to find the words. Someone who has a special kind of wisdom and guidance to share. Through *Hope Prevails*, Dr. Bengtson relates to the reader as a caring friend while providing professional insights formed by years of education, training, and experience as a neuropsychologist. She attends to the spiritual aspects of healing from depression and interprets frequently used depression treatment techniques within the context of a close relationship with God. Dr. Bengtson sprinkles personal knowing alongside professional knowledge to deliver sound teachings and recommendations from the perspective of a 'helper' who has had her own battles against depression, has grabbed hold of God's promises, and has realized joy in him. She delivers inspired love and understanding of her own and through that shows God's love for those who are in despair. She is *that* friend, maybe not one you know personally but one whose words can comfort and guide you just as powerfully toward a fulfilled relationship with God, the Healer."

—**Laura Patke,** PsyD, licensed psychologist

"Everyone who suffers or knows someone who suffers from depression needs to read this book. If I had read it twenty-three years ago, I never would have attempted suicide!"

—**anonymous reader**

"It is a unique position to be both the doctor and the depressed patient. Those dual experiences offer rare insight into the nuances of a very difficult journey. Dr. Michelle Bengtson has written a wonderful, hope-filled book for those who suffer from depression and for those who love them. Because she's been in the place of the patient, her compassion abounds. Because she has been in the place of the doctor, her knowledge is spot-on. Because she is a lover of God, her book offers practical, spiritual hope for anyone who is searching. I encourage you to read it! It will make you better, no matter your situation."

—Jan Silvious, author of *Fool-Proofing Your Life*
and *Same Life, New Story*

"Dr. Michelle Bengtson sent this ball over the fence! *Hope Prevails* is the most helpful and practical thing I've read on dealing with depression! A compassionate work from someone who's been through the struggle personally. This is a must-have resource for anyone struggling with depression or for those who know someone who is. Armed with Scripture, Dr. Bengtson gives step-by-step strategies for combating the lies of the evil one. Hope is on every page!"

—K. Douglas Brown, associate pastor of family ministries
at Metropolitan Baptist Church, Oklahoma City,
and author of *Shotgun Rider: Restoring
Your Passion for the Ministry Trail*

"If you or a loved one are walking through the valley of depression, be encouraged that you are not alone. Dr. Michelle Bengtson has provided a powerful resource to help you on your journey toward hope. It is a personal and positive book, as you learn from Dr. Bengtson's own story as well as her practical knowledge in the field. I love how she shares a prescription, a prayer, and a playlist at the end of each chapter to give you an extra boost of strength. *Hope Prevails* is a must-read for every person who struggles with depression."

—Karol Ladd, author of *Thrive, Don't Simply Survive*

"It is refreshing to have a board-certified neuropsychologist acknowledge the spiritual component of depression, but it is even more impressive that Dr. Bengtson would be willing to share her own journey through the fog of despair. Her personal insights are invaluable for those who are struggling with what is often described as '*the common cold of mental illness.*'"

—Dr. Neil T. Anderson, founder and president emeritus of Freedom
in Christ Ministries and author of *Overcoming Depression*

HOPE
Prevails

Insights from a Doctor's
Personal Journey through Depression

DR. MICHELLE
BENGTSON

Revell
a division of Baker Publishing Group
Grand Rapids, Michigan

Published by Revell
a division of Baker Publishing Group
P.O. Box 6287, Grand Rapids, MI 49516-6287
www.revellbooks.com

Printed in the United States of America

Library of Congress Cataloging-in-Publication Data
Names: Bengston, Michelle, author.
Title: Hope prevails : insights from a doctor's personal journey through depression / Dr. Michelle Bengston.
Description: Grand Rapids : Revell, 2016. | Includes bibliographical references.
Identifiers: LCCN 2016009953 | ISBN 9780800727079 (pbk.)
Subjects: LCSH: Depressed persons—Religious life. | Depression, Mental—Religious aspects—Christianity.
Classification: LCC BV4910.34 .B46 2016 | DDC 248.8/625—dc23
LC record available at https://lccn.loc.gov/2016009953

Published in association with MacGregor Literary Agency.

16 17 18 19 20 21 22   7 6 5 4 3 2 1

Contents

Contents

Dedication

You would likely not even be reading this book were it not for the love and encouragement of Margie Houmes. Margie was not just a spiritual mother. She was a prayer warrior, and my biggest cheerleader. She believed in me when I didn't believe in myself and taught me the most about who I am as a daughter of the Most High God.

Margie lived out her faith like no one else I've ever met. Simple conversations with Margie turned into praise and worship celebrations of Jesus. With the love of Jesus, Margie always found the wallflower of a room and made them feel like a celebrity. Margie always jokingly finished our conversations with, "When you become famous, don't forget us little people," to which I replied, "I could never forget, Margie, for I am one."

Sadly, Margie was killed in a head-on collision the day before Mother's Day, not long before I completed this manuscript. I had sent Margie a Mother's Day card thanking her for the influence she had on my life and for the kingdom. Through her death, I was fortunate to see the impact Margie had on the lives of thousands. Though she considered herself a "little person" and was one of the most humble people I've ever met, her faith was as big as a mountain and her influence for the kingdom even greater. I don't know if she read that card before she began dancing with her almighty Savior in heaven, but this is my chance to say thank you to her publicly for forever positively changing the direction of my walk with Christ.

My hope and prayer for every reader of this book is that you too at some point will have a Margie Houmes in your life and that you will know just how much you are loved and valued as a child of the Most High God.

Foreword

Some people rip through life as if their hair were on fire. Others sit fearfully on the sidelines hoping not to catch sparks. Then there are those who don't care one way or the other. They say, "Bring it on . . . or not . . . whatever."

Many people don't fight external hair fires or indifference to life. Instead, they are the silent majority who trudge through their days with an internal pain carefully hidden behind cheerful competence. However, known only to the mask holder is the fear of mask slippage. Such slippage threatens to reveal deep shame, fear of rejection, and horror at being truly seen. Actually, those responses may be indicators of an undiagnosed depression: the sense that somehow "I can't make life work. I feel desperate and not sure I even care about anything anymore."

Here is the good news about mask slippage. When the mask slips or drops, there is no more pretending you have your ducks in a row. There is the freedom to admit you never liked those ducks anyway. In fact, you don't care if you ever see them again. In case you see yourself in any of these descriptions and would love to not only find relief from your pain but also gain an understanding of that pain, I suggest you read *Hope Prevails* by Dr. Michelle Bengtson.

The book title is your first clue to the book's message. There is always hope in spite of the degree of inner pain you are experiencing.

Dr. Bengston is a board certified neuropsychologist. Although a highly trained and specialized doctor in brain-behavior relationships, she makes this vulnerable and compelling opening statement in her book: "I see patients in my office every week with mental health disorders, including depression. I diagnose their condition and make treatment recommendations. Yet all my education and experience didn't protect me from succumbing to this devastating condition myself."

She goes on to say, "I've written this book because I've been there." When someone of Dr. Bengtson's professional stature and training tells me depression can hit and debilitate anyone at anytime, I take notice. I also take heart. She says, "I'm writing today from where I stand, the other side of depression's valley. I encourage you to persevere. You will not always feel this way. There are brighter days ahead."

There are many fine, worthy, and insightful books about depression, but in my view, Dr. Bengtson's trumps them all. She does not underestimate the value of medication, therapy, exercise, and wise food choices. But in her words, "Only when I started to understand what depression does to us spiritually, as well as what it cannot do, . . . did I finally begin to experience the chains of depression falling off."

Each chapter of the book concludes with a recommended playlist of music that was uplifting and encouraging to her. She believes that listening to praise and worship music helped her hold on when her grip was shaky.

To those of us frail human beings who suffer from a shaky grip, or to those who seriously fear not making it through life, God says he will never leave us. We will make it. This book will underscore that biblical truth over and over again. Our first step of making it to the other side of the valley of depression may well be falling into the competent and compassionately written words of this God-honoring book: *Hope Prevails*.

Marilyn Meberg
Women of Faith speaker and author of *Constantly Craving*

When the Whole World Is Laughing but You

"For I know the plans I have for you," declares the Lord, "plans to prosper you and not to harm you, plans to give you hope and a future."

Jeremiah 29:11

They say a person needs just three things to be truly happy in this world: someone to love, something to do, and something to hope for.

Tom Bodett

I know how you feel. Really, I do. I see patients in my office every week with mental health disorders, including depression. I diagnose their condition and make treatment recommendations. Yet all my education and experience didn't protect me from succumbing to this devastating condition myself.

Professionally, I am a board-certified neuropsychologist with lots of degrees and alphabet soup following my name. I am trained in identifying and treating mental health disorders, and I've worked in the field for over twenty years. I know that physiological problems can contribute to depression, and sometimes medication is necessary and helpful in treating it. Difficult life circumstances can usher it in, and sometimes therapy and counseling are also necessary and helpful.

Despite my professional experience, I too have suffered in this valley. I was sad and irritable and constantly felt defeated. My greatest shock came when I tried the same treatment suggestions I typically offered my patients—and they didn't work. I tried medication, I participated in therapy, I ate right and exercised dutifully, and I even prayed and claimed healing. For me those things weren't enough.

Only when I started to understand what depression does to us spiritually, as well as what it cannot do, and then started cooperating with God did I finally begin to experience the chains of depression falling off.

I wrote this book to share what worked for me and what can help you. Part of what I realized during my dark journey is that this condition affects us physically, emotionally, and spiritually. The traditional treatments I tried didn't address the spiritual side of depression. Without addressing this aspect, and without treating the *whole* person, my healing was suboptimal.

Few books discuss what depression does to us on a spiritual level. That is the emphasis of this book. While I will address what depression is, where it comes from, and ways to treat it, I will also share what it does to us spiritually and how that perpetuates the problem. There is hope that comes from realizing how depression affects us spiritually and what it cannot do to us on a spiritual level.

I've written this book because I've been there. I know what depression is. I know the shame that tags along with depression like a pesky younger sibling. I know the pain it brings and how it feels to believe no one understands. If someone hasn't gone through this journey themselves, then they can't completely understand. I tried many of the tools and techniques that mental health professionals suggest. Some I have recommended to my own patients. Some helped, but they weren't sufficient. At least they weren't for me. Not until I realized how depression is perpetuated on a spiritual level and addressed the spiritual issues did I start to walk out of the valley.

I've written this book to walk alongside you. In my pain, I desperately longed to have someone walk alongside me—someone who understood the depths of my despair. I needed more than anything to know I wasn't alone and that I wasn't worthless because I struggled. I want you to know you are not alone. You may feel alone at times, as I did. But someone does understand. I've been there. Our circumstances surrounding the season of depression may be different, but the pain involved is the same.

I've written this book to help dispel some of the myths and lies about this condition that make it difficult to see the proverbial light at the end of the tunnel. I've read a library of books about this topic but never found one that helped me understand it from a spiritual perspective. The enemy of our soul thrives on keeping us in darkness and unable to live in the fullness of all God created us to be.

I've written this book to offer hope. In the midst of my battle, hope was elusive. I wasn't sure I would survive. Actually, I wasn't sure I wanted to survive. But hope—the belief in a purpose, the belief in something better—can make all the difference. Without hope, what reason do we have to get up in the morning? With hope, we want to move forward, press on, get to the other side, and then share with others what we have learned to offer them hope during their times of trial.

Listening to praise and worship music helped me to hold on when it seemed my grip was failing. At the end of each chapter, I include a recommended playlist of music that was uplifting and encouraging to me in the hope that you too will be encouraged. Just to get you started, you might benefit from listening to the following:

"Healing Begins," Tenth Avenue North, © 2010 by Reunion Records

"Worn," Tenth Avenue North, © 2012 by Reunion Records

"You Are I Am," MercyMe, © 2012 by Fair Trade/Columbia

"You Are My Strength," Hillsong Live, © 2010 by Hillsong Church T/A Hillsong Music Australia

"Shoulders," For King & Country, © 2014 by Word Entertainment LLC

"Nearness," Bethel, © 2015 by Bethel Music

"I Feel His Love," Laura Hackett Park, © 2014 by Forerunner Music

At the end of each chapter, I also offer a "doctor's prescription" ("Your Rx")—questions for you to ask or steps for you to take to help you find healing from your depression. Of course, I won't know if you follow the prescription, but I trust that you are tired of feeling the way you do and want help. I want to walk through this journey with you, and I'm confident that one day you will be in a position to do the same for someone else.

Hope Prevails,
(Dr.) Michelle Bengtson

A Letter
to My Depressed Self

Dear One,

I know you are in pain. You feel as if you can't sink any lower and that no one understands. But I do. I've been there.

I'm writing today from where I stand, the other side of depression's valley. I encourage you to persevere. You will not always feel this way (Ps. 30:5). There are brighter days ahead (Job 11:17; Prov. 4:18).

I've learned a few important lessons during the journey out of depression that I want to share with you. So grab my hand or that of a trusted loved one and hang on. Hang in there until you see the first glimmers of dawn.

Everyone faces resistance of some kind in their life, but not all push through the fear and the pain. You can, and I promise you will be so grateful that you did! The first step is always the hardest. Then your success in that step will fuel the next. You will ultimately look back and be thankful, not necessarily for the challenges but that they showed you what a strong team you and God are together (Rom. 8:31) and how he is such a faithful provider (Phil. 4:19).

While I'm intimately acquainted with the loneliness you feel, I promise you are not alone (Heb. 13:5). You cannot see clearly through the searing tears that sting your eyes, but from the other side I'm able to see how God was with you every second of every minute of your despair (Ps. 121).

I've always hated the expression "what doesn't kill us makes us stronger." I know that in the valley there are days you just wish it would kill you so that your pain would end. But from this side looking back, I can see that good really can come from your pain (Rom. 8:28).

You will appreciate joy, which offers so much more than happiness ever will (Acts 13:52; Gal. 5:22–26; James 1:2–4). You will savor peace instead of worry and dread (Phil. 4:6–7). You will relate to others with a knowing compassion that nothing can imitate (2 Cor. 1:4). You will know God more deeply and intimately than you ever dreamed possible after clinging to him in your darkest nights and begging him to reveal himself to you (Pss. 23; 30:3; 56:8; Isa. 30:19–21; 40:1–3; 43:1–3; Matt. 11:28–30; James 1:2–5).

I know some days your faith is weak and your hope is dim. Even Jesus felt despair when he cried out, "My God, my God, why have you forsaken me?" (Matt. 27:46). But the truth is God entrusted Jesus with his most important assignment on earth. You too have good work to do that God has divinely purposed for you (Jer. 29:11; John 15:16; Eph. 2:10), and you are a partaker with Christ of a heavenly calling (Heb. 3:1, 14).

I know life is hard and you get frustrated because you don't see enough progress fast enough. You need to know that is because, just like Jesus, you have an enemy who seeks to steal, kill, and destroy (John 10:10). But God is greater than any foe who rises against you (1 John 4:4). God has promised that with him you are victorious (1 Cor. 15:57) and you are more than a conqueror (Rom. 8:37; Eph. 3:20; Phil. 2:13; 4:13). He is pleased that you simply love and trust him and want to know him more (Ps. 147:11).

My heart grieves for you because today you wonder where you fit in or if you even fit in at all. That is another lie from the enemy because he doesn't want you to celebrate your ultimate destiny. Oh, my dear, you not only fit in but are also accepted in the beloved (Eph. 1:6). God has already promised that you are a citizen of heaven (Eph. 2:6, 19; Phil. 3:20; Col. 1:12) and a joint heir with Christ (Rom. 8:17; Gal. 4:6–7).

Some days you feel unworthy, like you don't measure up. But we all feel that some days. Those are lies from the enemy, who seeks to demean you and devalue you. Your enemy knows the Word of God better than you do. But God's truth says that you are a loved child of God (John 1:12; Rom. 8:14–17; Gal. 3:26, 28; 4:6–7; 1 Thess. 5:5), you are a new creation in Christ (2 Cor. 5:17; Gal. 2:20; 1 Pet. 1:3, 23), and you are a friend of Jesus (John 15:15). Jesus makes you worthy (2 Thess. 1:11–12).

There are times when you feel like God is angry with you. That is another lie from the enemy. God is for you, not against you (Rom. 8:31). God is not distant and angry. He loves you completely (1 John 4:16). He wants to lavish his love on you (1 John 3:1) because he is your heavenly Father and you are his child. Every earthly father has his flaws, but your heavenly Father is perfect (Matt. 5:48), and he offers you more than any earthly father ever could (Matt. 7:11).

My desire is that you will know how much God loves you (John 17:23; 1 John 4:10) and how he is your greatest encourager (2 Thess. 2:16–17). He loves you with an everlasting love (Jer. 31:3) and rejoices over you with singing (Zeph.

3:17). He considers you his treasured possession (Exod. 19:5), and he will never stop doing good things for you (Jer. 32:40). If you delight in him, he promises to give you the desires of your heart (Ps. 37:4), the very same desires he instilled in you (Phil. 2:13).

Many days you feel like a failure. Dear one, Jesus was the only perfect one to ever live. All of us are failures in comparison to him. The good news is that through Jesus's death on the cross, he took our imperfection on himself, so now when God looks at you, he sees a child who is redeemed and forgiven (2 Cor. 5:18–19; Eph. 1:7; 4:24; Col. 1:13–14; 1 John 2:12). God considers you a saint (1 Cor. 1:2; Eph. 1:1; Phil. 1:1; Col. 1:2). You are chosen of God, holy and dearly loved (Col. 3:12; 1 Thess. 1:4). There is no failure in falling down—only in choosing not to get back up and press on. God has said that our job is to believe (Heb. 11:6), and when we do that, we have pleased him.

You look at the tasks ahead of you and think you aren't good enough for the job. Would it surprise you to know that is another lie from the enemy? With God's help, all things are possible (Matt. 19:26). When you feel tired and weak, remember that God will give you the strength to do anything he wants you to do (Isa. 40:31; Phil. 4:13). Cling to him, because his right hand will hold you up (Ps. 63:8).

My heart longs for you not to worry about how you will manage to meet all your needs. You carry a load that is too heavy for you. On this side I see how much easier it is when you give your burdens to God and take his easier yoke in exchange (Matt. 11:30). You wear yourself out striving— striving to be good enough so that others will like you and so that God will love you. But he already does. Nothing you could do will make him love you more or less. Every- thing good comes from God (James 1:17). He has already promised to provide everything you need (Matt. 6:31–33). He rewards those who earnestly seek him (Heb. 11:6)—and you are doing that, so be gentle with yourself. If you do your part and believe, he will do his part and provide!

Your recent days have been dark, and you've wondered if this is God's plan for you. Oh, dear one, that isn't so. It is God's desire that you prosper and be in health (3 John 1:2). You wonder if you will ever get out of this valley of depression and if the tears will ever stop. Better days are ahead (Ps. 107:43; Prov. 4:18), though perhaps you cannot see them yet. God will wipe away every tear from your eyes, and he will remove all the pain you've endured (Rev. 21:3–4).

"Hope deferred makes the heart sick, but a longing fulfilled is a tree of life" (Prov. 13:12). The enemy has deferred your hope, but it's time to reengage your hope and believe the Lord is going to restore what the enemy has taken from you (Joel 2:25).

Take hold of hope and believe that a great outcome will result from the challenges you are currently going through (Rom. 8:28). As a result of your hope, you will experience a strengthening of your faith. When you are tested, don't let your faith falter. Keep it strong based on all the above promises God has given you. Guard against falling prey to doubt and unbelief. The enemy is looking for a door opened even a tiny crack so he can come back in and whisper more lies to you.

You will rise up out of this pit (Rom. 6:4–5), and when you do, you will share the good news with the brokenhearted, grieving, and poor who will need the encouragement of one who has walked through depression and survived (2 Cor. 1:4).

You will experience the Lord's favor as he comforts you in your sadness, exchanges your ashes for a crown of beauty, takes your mourning and gives you joy, and takes your spirit of despair and replaces it with praise (Isa. 61:1–3). You will stand firm in the Lord and experience his never-ending joy (1 Thess. 3:8–9). Trust, surrender, hope, and do not fear. Let God take it from here. I am praying that you will have eyes to see, ears to hear, and a heart that believes (Prov. 20:12). You will continue to hear from the Lord, so take your desire to go deeper with him into intimate, focused praise and worship, casting your cares on him because he cares for you (1 Peter 5:7). Proclaim his Word over yourself and over your life. You do not have to defend yourself to other people, but proclaim God's many promises for you (Ps. 68:11) and defend yourself to the enemy, who has been trying to steal, kill, and destroy. Remember, you and the Lord are a majority (1 Sam. 17:45).

Don't believe for a minute the enemy's lie that you will have to live with depression forever. God wants for you to enjoy good health, body and soul (3 John 1:2). No weapon formed against you will prosper (Isa. 54:17).

It's my prayer for you that "the God of hope will fill you with all joy and peace as you trust in him, so that you may overflow with hope by the power of the Holy Spirit" (Rom. 15:13). God is not through with you. He has plans for you, plans for a hopeful future (Jer. 29:11). You can look into the future with bright eyes at all those things you previously dreamed. God gave you those dreams, and they are yours (Eph. 3:20). God is going to bring you out of this desperate place, and when he does, you will have such hope to share with others (Ps. 81:10).

You are loved,
Me (and God)

1

This Thing Called Depression

I will be glad and rejoice in your love,
for you saw my affliction
and knew the anguish of my soul.

Psalm 31:7

I had some experience in dealing with people who have mental illness and depression, but I didn't see the signs in myself. I couldn't ask for help because I didn't know I needed help.

Clara Hughes

I want to ask you a few questions. No one will know your answers, so answer with complete honesty. The truest answer is likely the one you find yourself thinking, "But I wouldn't want her to know . . ." Believe me, I've thought that very same thing myself—many times.

- Do you ever look around you and it seems as if the whole world is laughing but you?
- Have you ever gone to sleep one night and awoken the next morning to find your joy, your enthusiasm, or your motivation has disappeared?
- Do you hear others speak of joy and think, "I've no idea what joy feels like"?
- Does it ever feel as if you live in a state of "constant overwhelm"?
- Do the simplest tasks require more effort than you can muster?
- Would you or those close to you consider you a "glass half empty" kind of person?

If you answered yes to any of these questions, it's possible you are experiencing or have experienced symptoms of depression.

Depression presents in various ways depending on the individual, but the common thread is that it's always emotionally painful. Perhaps the description of depression to which I could most relate is that "it's like drowning, except you can see everyone around you breathing" (author unknown).

Many experience depression, don't recognize it for what it is, and would be loath to admit it even if they did. Denial never means something doesn't exist or didn't happen, just that the pain of recognizing it seems to outweigh the potential benefit of being vulnerable and seeking help. Sometimes it's difficult to answer the question "What's wrong?" when we can't first answer the question "What's right?"

For the longest time I didn't want to admit to myself, or to anyone else, that I struggled with depression. My mother suffered with it the majority of her adult life. Her mother and her sister succumbed to it for years as well, although they didn't recognize it for what it was or call it depression.

Sometimes it's difficult to answer the question "What's wrong?" when we can't first answer the question "What's right?"

Growing up, I lived in a home where depression abounded, yet I never heard that term. It was as if depression was a way of life. My mother suffered from depression, yet I chalked up her way of interacting to her personality, thinking to myself, "That's just the way she is." So when depression reared its ugly head in my own life, I didn't initially recognize it for what it was. Denial doesn't mitigate the experience; it just dampens our ability or our willingness to proactively seek change or get help. Sadly, it prolongs our misery.

What Is Depression?

In psychiatry, depression falls under the classification of a "mood disorder." It's considered a condition of general emotional dejection and withdrawal during which one experiences a greater degree of sadness or sadness that lasts longer than what is reasonably warranted given the circumstances. It often results in decreased energy, stamina, or functional activity. Depression can present in a wide range of severities and is expressed in different ways depending on the age, gender, ethnicity, personality, upbringing, and circumstances of the person suffering.

In any given year, approximately 18.8 million American adults suffer from a depressive disorder,[1] and at some point in their lives, about one out of four Americans will experience depression.[2] If we broaden the scope, at least 350 million people globally live with depression.[3] In the United States, only 29 percent of all persons with depression reported contacting a mental health professional last year,[4] and in some countries, as few as one out of ten receive effective treatment.[5] Nearly twice as many women as men are estimated to be affected by a depressive disorder each

Depression is the leading cause of disability worldwide.

year.[6] These figures translate to more than 9 million women in the United States each year suffering from this devastating condition.[7] If you are not one of them, you know one of them! Depression is the leading cause of disability worldwide.[8]

The incidence of depression is increasing. Depression often begins in the early middle-age years and is also fairly common among the elderly. It's sometimes a reversible cause of cognitive changes in seniors. It's also increasingly common in children and youth. Over half of youth diagnosed with depression experience a recurrence within seven years.

Everyone experiences feelings of sadness at times, but generally this is a fleeting emotion that resolves itself relatively quickly. Depression, however, interferes with daily functioning for weeks or longer.

Symptoms of Depression

Some of the most common symptoms of depression include:

- feeling sad, blue, down, or numb
- irritability or agitation
- difficulty concentrating
- feeling worthless, helpless, and/or hopeless
- feeling guilty
- indecisiveness
- decreased energy or motivation

- decreased interest in previously enjoyed activities
- decreased social interaction
- crying
- sleep disturbance
- appetite disturbance
- unintentional weight gain or loss
- aches and pains that do not improve with treatment
- excessive use of alcohol or other substances (including prescription medication)
- thoughts of suicide

There are a myriad of other associated symptoms. Most sufferers will experience a subset of symptoms, and the severity varies from person to person. Depression affects people in different ways. Men and women display symptoms of depression differently. Children with depression present much differently than adults with the same condition. Older adults suffering from depression also present differently and often with less obvious symptoms. They may be reticent to admit to sadness or grief, and their presentation may be masked by other medical conditions.

How depression is experienced and the degree to which it affects one's functioning is very personal in nature. Consider it like this: you and I could both see a physician and receive a diagnosis of allergies, yet your symptoms may include congestion and cough while mine might entail a runny nose, itchy eyes, and hives. While our symptoms vary, our diagnosis is the same. The same is true with depression in that we can both suffer but present with different symptoms. If not treated effectively, depression can result in devastating life consequences such as broken relationships, divorce, job loss, physical illness, personal injury, or suicide.

Often symptoms of depression are masked by external behaviors used to cope with internal feelings. For example, addictive behaviors such as drinking, overeating, or excessive spending can begin as an effort to cope with the underlying symptoms of depression, including sadness, loneliness, or irritability. Angry outbursts can mask feelings of rejection or embarrassment frequently experienced during a depressive episode. Even traits that appear to be more socially desirable, like perfectionism, drivenness, people pleasing, or peacekeeping, can be subconscious coping styles for managing the discomfort depression produces.

As a medical professional, I've found that many misunderstand depression. Those who don't suffer from it or haven't had a loved one deal with the ache from it have a hard time grasping the personal depth to which depression cuts or the devastating sense of loss and sadness that accompany it. Those who have not experienced it for themselves will frequently be either ignorant of depression's presence or in denial of it.

The majority of books written on the subject, as well as many treating practitioners, ignore the spiritual side of depression. The spiritual battle is the reason more people aren't effectively treated and why individuals frequently experience recurrence after treatment. Treatment, then, if it's to be truly helpful, cannot ignore this aspect. I endeavor to shed light on this spiritual battle to equip you to fight this war more effectively.

Now that you have a better understanding of what depression is, the next chapter discusses one of the biggest secrets impacting the church today.

Your Rx

1. Reread the list of the most common symptoms of depression. Put a check mark next to each one you've experienced

for more than two weeks to determine if depression may be a factor in this current season for you. If you aren't sure, do not fret. Only a physician, psychologist, or therapist can diagnose with certainty, yet reviewing the list will give you an indication and start you in the right direction.

2. In your preferred version of the Bible, look up the following verses: Psalms 31:7; 34:17–18; 54:4. Then write them on index cards and place them where you will see them frequently. I encourage you to read each of these passages aloud three times daily, committing them to memory. The Bible tells us that faith comes by hearing, and at this point in your journey through depression, it will help for you to hear God's promises as you recite them aloud to yourself.

My Prayer for You

Father, you know the battle I've fought. You recall the days when the only prayer I could offer for myself was a whispered, feeble "Help." During those days, I depended on the prayers of others to carry my needs to your throne. It is my privilege and honor to come before your presence now, Father, on behalf of the one reading these words. You know every unspoken need. You know there is fear you won't hear or answer because the pain hurts too bad or has gone on so long. Father, lift up this precious one. Your Word tells us in Psalm 18:30 that your way is perfect and that you are a shield to all who trust in you. Sometimes, Father, we have to borrow on the faith and trust of others who are just a step or two ahead of us in the journey. I trust you that your way is perfect and that you will show your love, your perfect way, to this one you love. Father, you will do as you promised in Isaiah 41:13. I trust you will take this one by the hand and lovingly say, "Do not be afraid. I will help you." Thank you, Father, for your great love for us, that you care for us, and that you hear and long to answer every prayer. In Jesus's name, amen.

Recommended Playlist

"Need You Now," Plumb, © 2012 by Curb Records

"Hold On," MercyMe, © 2012 by Fair Trade

"Healing Has Begun," Matthew West, © 2010 by Sparrow Records

"Walls," Cody Carnes, © 2012 by Gateway Create Publishing

"Song of Solomon," Jesus Culture, © 2012 by Jesus Culture Music

"Steady My Heart," Kari Jobe, © 2012 by Sparrow Records

"Hands of the Healer," John Waller, © 2009 by Reunion Records

"Always Enough," Casting Crowns, © 2009 by Reunion Records

"Because He Lives," Matt Maher, © 2015 by Essential Records

"Everything Falls," Fee, © 2009 by Ino/Columbia

"You Stand," Gateway Devotions, © 2014 by Gateway Create Publishing

2

You Are Not Alone

For I wrote you out of great distress and anguish of heart and with many tears, not to grieve you but to let you know the depth of my love for you.

2 Corinthians 2:4

Alone we can do so little; together we can do so much.

Helen Keller

I'm here to tell you the secret is out: even Christians get depressed. Unfortunately, Christians are often the ones who most feel they must hide their pain and pretend that nothing is wrong. We go to church each weekend with a smile plastered on our faces and an "I'm fine" on the tip of our tongues. All the while we tell ourselves:

"If they knew the truth, they would think I'm pathetic."
"If they knew how much I really do not have my act together, they would think I'm incompetent."

"If they knew how desperately alone and unhappy I really feel, they would think something is wrong with me."

This line of thinking can make depression worse and more difficult to overcome.

When you experience despair daily, and it seems no matter what you try, things don't get better, it becomes easier for you to accept that your feelings are "normal," that this is your fate.

But hope prevails! I say this not just because I am a doctor but because I've been there. The thoughts suggested above mirror my experience through multiple bouts of depression. I hope and sincerely pray that by reading these pages you will feel comforted and you will know you are not alone.

Unfortunately, Christians are often the ones who most feel they must hide their pain and pretend that nothing is wrong.

Depression does not have to become a permanent way of life. There is hope. Jesus has offered "inexpressible joy" (1 Peter 1:8 NKJV), which must be the absolute opposite of depression. The Bible offers a wealth of promises for those who suffer through the torrent of depression. Matthew 5:4 promises, "Blessed are those who mourn, for they will be comforted." Psalm 126:5 promises, "They who sow with tears will reap with songs of joy." We have access to the God of all comfort (see 2 Cor. 1:3–4).

During my darkest days, when I truly could not fathom a time in the future when I would not suffer the gut-wrenching despair of my depression, I clung to the promises found in Scripture. Verses such as Isaiah 51:11 provided me with the hope that no one else could offer: "Those who have been ransomed by the LORD will return. They will enter Jerusalem singing, crowned with everlasting joy. Sorrow and mourning will disappear, and they will be filled with joy and gladness" (NLT). Oh, how I wanted to be overcome with joy and gladness.

Can you relate? Is that how you feel?

After a particularly devastating period in my life, when depression clung to me like a spider web that you just can't shake loose, I could appreciate the value of the trial. I remember telling a friend, "I don't ever want to go through anything that painful again. Honestly, I wouldn't voluntarily choose to endure such pain, nor would I wish it on anyone. But now that I'm on the other side, I can see how even in the midst of such pain God was there. And truly, he used even pain for my good. For that I am thankful."

Still, there were days I wasn't sure I could go on. Or that I even wanted to. Days when I begged God to take the depression from me. Days when I literally could not pray anything other than a tearfully whispered, "Help." But after the sorrow and mourning disappeared, I had a new appreciation for 1 Peter 4:12–13, which says, "Dear friends, don't be surprised at the fiery trials you are going through. . . . Instead, be very glad—for these trials make you partners with Christ in his suffering, so that you will have the wonderful joy of seeing his glory" (NLT).

You may be reading this and thinking, "That's all well and good for her, but she doesn't know what I've gone through." Or perhaps you are reading this and thinking, "If one more person tells me another Bible verse and thinks that will make me feel better, I'll scream." Can I tell you something? I thought those very same things! I was tired of even trying, and I was sick of crying. I tried to smile on the outside, but on the inside I felt like I was dying. And I just wanted it to stop.

I had been a Christian since I was seven years old. I had memorized hundreds of verses by the time I graduated from high school. When I was in the throes of depression, a friend said I needed to "snap out of it." As if it was yesterday, I remember thinking, "She has no idea what I've been through. If she did, she would understand why I feel the way I do and why I can't just snap out of it." And I remember getting frustrated to the point of being angry when fellow Christians would quote Bible verses to try to make me feel better. I felt like all they were doing was giving me platitudes, which, in my mind, just proved to me they had no idea what I was going through.

Time to Be Honest

If you are reading this book right now, I suspect one of two things is true. Either you struggle with depression, or you love someone who does. I wish I could sit right beside you and hold your hand. Sometimes when we hurt so badly, we don't necessarily want anyone to say anything; we just need a warm embrace or a knowing touch that speaks more than words. Quite possibly, if we were sitting together right now, if I put my hand on your shoulder and gave you a glance that conveyed, "I understand," tears might start to flow. Maybe as you read this you are trying to hold back the tears. Let them come. Don't try to hold them back. You don't need to pretend anymore.

Do you remember the questions I asked you in chapter 1? I wanted you to feel free to give answers that rang true in your deepest core. If you want freedom from depression, you have to decide you are ready to dispel some myths and lies and replace them with truth—God's truth. That includes the lies you unknowingly allowed yourself to believe about yourself, the lies you may have believed about others, and those you've let others believe about you. So if you read something in these pages that causes a tear, let it run. Feel it. Ask yourself, "What prompted that?"

You might also think, "I'm afraid if I let myself cry I might never stop." Those were once my exact words to a therapist. I promise that healing your hurts will dry your tears. Don't deny yourself the feeling and pretend it doesn't exist. If you do, it will resurface later only stronger and probably at a less opportune time.

So often, unfortunately, we feel shame attached to our plunge into depression, as if the devastation of that period of darkness isn't enough suffering. I experienced that too on multiple levels. I felt ashamed because I was the doctor who was "supposed to have all the answers." If I had the answers for other people, why couldn't I prevent myself from falling down the slippery slope into the valley? I have friends who are always cheerful and peppy, while for years it seemed like a black cloud followed me everywhere. I didn't want to be like that, and I repeatedly asked the question, "What is wrong with me?" I tried so many of the treatment suggestions I prescribed for my own patients, and yet they weren't enough to stop up the flood of tears or produce a rainbow that I could appreciate.

Once I became aware of the spiritual aspects of depression, the curtain was pulled back and I found new ammunition to fight the battle.

I'm going to be honest with you. I never found one magical cure-all. I did, however, through my years of professional practice and years of personal struggle, come to realize that there are several factors at play during bouts of depression that affect us spiritually and perpetuate our ordeal. Once I became aware of the spiritual aspects of depression, the curtain was pulled back and I found new ammunition to fight the battle. Then, just like with a good deal at a favorite store or restaurant, I couldn't keep it to myself. I don't want anyone to suffer one more minute if I can offer help.

The circumstances that led to our struggles with depression may be different, but there is hope. There are things that depression does to us on a spiritual level, but by the grace of God, there are also things that God will not allow depression to do. We will explore some of the lies and myths that influence our experience of depression. "Then you will know the truth, and the truth will set you free" (John 8:32).

Often we lose perspective and need the guidance of someone who can understand our situation and knows the appropriate course of action. Especially when traversing the valley of depression, we can struggle with indecision and decreased drive and motivation. If you were to see a doctor for a physical illness, they might prescribe a medication to help you. If you came to see me in my office for depression, I would give you a prescription of treatment suggestions. Just as your physician can't force you to take the prescribed medication, I can't force you to take my recommendations. Jesus didn't force the lame man by the pool to follow his commands (see John 5:1–15). The man wanted healing badly enough to do as Jesus suggested. That was the implied question Jesus asked. It was not so much "Do you want to get well?" but rather "Are you willing to do what it will take to get well and stay well?"

Are you ready to exchange your despair for an abundant and full life? Are you ready to get well? In the next chapter, we will discuss where depression comes from. Once we know where depression comes from, we can be strategic in avoiding the traps that have previously lured us in.

Your Rx

1. Prayerfully consider and answer the question, "Have I allowed myself to feel shame because I've suffered with depression?" Then take that shame to God in prayer, telling him you want to exchange it for his perfect perspective of you. You are not your depression, and shame does not come from God. It comes from the enemy, who wants to keep you stuck in the valley.

2. Ask yourself this question: "Am I willing to do what it will take to get well and stay well?" If the answer is anything but a firm yes, then ask God to reveal to you what is standing in the way. Ask him to help you surrender to his leading.

3. Look up the following verses: Psalm 126:5; Isaiah 51:11; Matthew 5:4; 2 Corinthians 1:3–4. Then write them on index cards and place them where you will see them frequently. Read each of these passages aloud three times daily, committing them to memory.

My Prayer for You

Father, my heart is heavy for the one reading this book right now. And I know that your heart is inclined to this precious child of yours as well. Your Word says in 3 John 1:2 that you desire for us to enjoy good health and for all to go well with us. I know that is your desire for me and for the one reading along, so I ask you to grant a fresh revelation to us so that we may exchange darkness and despair for good health. Romans 8:1 says, "There is now no condemnation for those who are in Christ Jesus," so, Father, I ask that you will remove any vestiges of shame or embarrassment that this dear one has felt as a result of suffering from depression and being misunderstood or maligned by those who have never experienced its wrath. I know, Father, that you understand our pain and our sorrows because Isaiah 53:3 tells us that Jesus "was despised and rejected by mankind, a man of suffering, and familiar with pain." Father, I thank you that you understand our pain and offer hope. Infuse this dear one with an extra measure of faith and hope in you for brighter days ahead. Because of your Son and his sacrifice for us, amen.

Recommended Playlist

"Before the Morning," Josh Wilson, © 2009 by Sparrow Records

"Blessings," Josh Wilson, © 2013 by Josh Wilson

"You Make Me Brave," Bethel, © 2014 by Bethel Music

"I Can Feel You," Bethel, © 2013 by Bethel Music

"Strong Enough," Matthew West, © 2010 by Sparrow Records

"We're Not Alone," Elevation Worship, © 2013 by Essential Worship

"Shoulders," For King & Country, © 2014 by Word Entertainment LLC

"You Satisfy My Soul," Laura Hackett, © 2012 by Forerunner Music

"Jesus, Hold Me Now," Casting Crowns, © 2009 by Reunion Records

"You're Not Alone," Owl City, © 2015 by Republic Records

3

The Underlying Causes
of Depression

Why, my soul, are you downcast?
  Why so disturbed within me?
Put your hope in God,
  for I will yet praise him,
  my Savior and my God.

                    Psalm 42:5

But with the slow menace of a glacier, depression came on.
No one had any measure of its progress; no one had any plan
for stopping it. Everyone tried to get out of its way.

                    Frances Perkins

After a patient has been diagnosed with depression, the first question that patient usually asks is, "What caused it?"

Many things contribute to depression and much emphasis is put on answering the question, "What caused it?" or "Where did it come from?" I frequently answer patients by saying, "For any particular individual, we may never fully know." Is that frustrating? Hear me out. Often by the time someone comes to my office or goes to their general practitioner, multiple contributors have impacted their current situation.

Much as we don't see a clogged drain before it backs up, we often don't recognize the initial signs of anxiety, depression, cancer, heart disease, and many other conditions for what they are. Until enough signs and symptoms add up to a situation warranting concern, we don't recognize a problem exists. We don't seek help, often for months or years. Then we often don't recall the initial warning signs. We may not remember if or when our sleep, diet, or exercise patterns became irregular. Or we may have forgotten about the stress we previously endured for a time at work, home, or other places.

Sometimes knowing the exact answer to "Why?" may not be as important as answering "What do we do about it?" Still, it can be helpful to know potential causes of depression in order to lessen the chances of experiencing it again in the future.

It's Chemical

The symptoms associated with depression, for many, can be traced back to the chemical makeup of the brain. The brain contains many chemicals, called neurotransmitters, that help transport information from one part of the brain to another. Monoamines, which are mood-related chemicals, include dopamine, norepinephrine, and serotonin. These particular neurotransmitters help regulate sleep, appetite, sexual interest, emotions, and reactions to stress. Many individuals who suffer from depression have lower levels of monoamines in their brains. Yet different symptoms of depression are experienced depending on the varying levels of chemicals and hormones. This helps explain why, for example, some individuals with depression experience insomnia or a loss of appetite while others sleep or eat excessively. This is also why one person may respond to a medication differently than someone else being prescribed the same medication.

Studies indicate that our thoughts affect our neurotransmitter production, which then directly influences our physical experience of a situation. Imagine you are home alone late at night watching a movie when you hear a rattle of the doorknob. When you hear the unexpected sound, you think, "I don't know what that is—maybe it's a thief." The thought signals to your brain that there is an emergency, and as a result, your brain produces excess chemicals such as cortisol, which is used in an emergency to help with fight or flight. Your body then reacts to the increased chemical production. Your heart rate increases as your blood flows away from your digestive track and into your limbs so you can react quickly. So while our chemical makeup can impact our mood, our thoughts can impact our chemistry.

It's Genetic

Genetics can play a large role in our experience of depression. Research suggests that approximately 40 percent of individuals with depression suffer as a result of a genetic link. An individual is three to five times more likely to experience depression if a relative has suffered from depression.[1]

Even if there is a genetic predisposition for certain medical and emotional conditions in your family history, that does not mean you will necessarily succumb. Think, for example, about alcoholism. Having an alcoholic parent or grandparent may increase your risk of being predisposed to alcoholism yourself, but not everyone with an alcoholic relative becomes an alcoholic.

It's Secondary

Physiology and medical disorders such as thyroid disease, diabetes, or stroke can also contribute to depression. I encourage those who experience symptoms of depression for a prolonged period of time to see their physician and undergo a routine medical physical to rule out physiological contributors to their mood.

Sometimes vitamin deficiencies, such as low vitamin D, can contribute to depressed mood, fatigue, and lack of energy. Thyroid dysfunction is often associated with symptoms of depression, including lethargy, irritability, and indecisiveness. Low blood sugar and insulin resistance often lead to similar symptoms. Many individuals who suffer from cancer, a heart attack, a head injury, or a stroke may also develop symptoms of depression. It's not within the scope of this book to list every possible medical condition that can contribute to symptoms of depression. It's important, however, to be aware that such relationships exist so you can explore these potential factors with your physician.

It's Reactionary

Environmental factors and stress are also frequent contributors to depression. When we are raised around family members who suffer from mental health conditions such as depression, we can be susceptible to their influence and mimic their negative or depressed responses to situations because of their modeled behavior.

Major life changes can contribute to depression, yet the depression may not start right at the time of change or crisis but rather be experienced weeks or months later as a delayed response.

Stress can also contribute to depression, whether good stress or bad stress. Our bodies react chemically in the same way whether we are going through the death of a loved one or the birth of a new baby, whether we are sitting in a traffic jam late for a very important meeting or being given a raise for a job well done.

Am I saying that chemical imbalance, genetics, medical conditions, and environmental factors cause our depression? Yes and no.

It's Spiritual

While all of the above contribute to depression, there are also spiritual roots. The next several chapters focus on the spiritual aspect because unless we treat the underlying roots of depression, we cannot expect to rid ourselves of it permanently.

All people, Christian or not, have a spiritual nature. It's the way God made us. We also have an enemy who is a spirit, and we are susceptible to his attacks. Peter warned, "Your enemy the devil prowls around like a roaring lion looking for someone to devour" (1 Peter 5:8). Paul said that we stand in the middle of a war between two opposing kingdoms. "For we are not fighting against flesh-and-blood armies, but against evil rulers and authorities of the unseen world, against mighty powers in this dark world, and against evil spirits in the heavenly places" (Eph. 6:12 NLT). The enemy isn't only concerned with strong-arming Christians. He seeks to separate believers and nonbelievers alike from God (see Eph. 2:1–2). Both Christians and non-Christians often unknowingly open the door to the devil by the things they do, say, or believe, allowing the "roaring lion" to enter and wreak havoc in their lives.

This is where spiritual roots to depression start, but it's not where they end. In Scripture, the enemy is referred to as the father of lies, incapable of telling the truth (John 8:44). When we succumb to the enemy's influence, we often unconsciously agree with the lies he feeds us, lies that do not align with God's truth. And he builds lie upon lie until our view of ourselves, the people around us, and the world we live in becomes as bent as a tree in a hurricane. God described this situation in Hosea. He said, "My people are destroyed for lack of knowledge" (Hosea 4:6 KJV).

Lest you become worried or concerned about information you lack or about the presence of a shadowy spiritual enemy, I encourage you not to take on that fear. Fear is just another tool of this enemy. "For God hath not given us the spirit of fear; but of power, and of love, and of a sound mind" (2 Tim. 1:7 KJV). Take courage and rejoice because God's Word reminds us, "You, dear children, are from God and have overcome them, because the one who is in you is greater than the one who is in the world" (1 John 4:4).

The common outcome of depression is usually a lack of peace and joy. We have a very real enemy who seeks to steal our joy and kill our peace. John 10:10 says, "The thief comes only to steal and kill and destroy." In his Word, however, God promises to make our joy full: "I have told you this so that my joy may be in you and that your joy may be complete" (John 15:11). God sent Jesus so that we could live an abundant life. The verse above about the thief has a second half to it. Jesus does not leave us with loss, death, and destruction but gives us a promise. The entire verse reads like this: "The thief comes only to steal and kill and destroy; I have come that they may have life, and have it to the full" (John 10:10).

Do you want some good news? You are not the primary cause of your depression. Neither are your genetics or your situations. The thoughts that lead to your depression are not your thoughts. They are thoughts offered to you by the enemy that you've come into agreement with. The enemy aims to keep us in a state of bondage and despair under a canopy of heaviness and oppression. Our enemy influences us primarily through our thoughts during situations in our lives. Unintentionally, we allow the enemy access to interfere with our thoughts. A direct correlation exists between our thoughts and our physical and emotional well-being.

Proverbs 23:7 reminds us, "For as he thinketh in his heart, so is he" (KJV).

We often unknowingly give the enemy permission to influence our lives. But 1 John 4:4 reminds us that the one who is in us is greater than the one who is in the world. James 4:7 tells us to resist the devil and he will flee. We have the authority and the ability to close the door and eliminate the influence of the enemy.

My experience of depression had a spiritual root. Since coming to understand the impact of spiritual roots on depression, I cannot recall an instance of dealing with a depressed person, professionally or personally, when a spiritual root was not evident to me. This is an area, though, that is largely unaddressed by the medical profession, or even by many churches. Not many people are asking about spiritual roots. There is not much contemporary discussion of it. It's also hard to discern these spiritual influences within ourselves. Unlike the onset of a physical ailment such as a stomachache or a toothache, which is acute and demands our attention, the lies of the enemy slide undetected into our thoughts, and then into our emotions and choices, and eventually into the core of who we are. Only later does their destructive power emerge as they bring on an illness like depression.

You are not the primary cause of your depression.

My Own Story

Let me share some of my own story to help you see what I mean. Looking back, I can see all of the above-mentioned contributors to my depression experience. My first known personal acquaintance with depression came when postpartum depression rapidly overwhelmed me following my first son's birth. During the postpartum period, hormones are erratic, so a chemical imbalance was undoubtedly a contributor.

After the postpartum depression resolved and I settled into parenthood and lived through what could be thought of as the normal period of sleep deprivation, I remained fatigued and moody beyond what was reasonable. My physician wisely ran tests, which revealed a thyroid disorder. This physiological condition affected my mood, energy, motivation, and outlook.

My mother, aunt, and grandmother all suffered with depression, so a genetic component was a feasible factor. Although I did not suffer with depression as a child, my mother was depressed most of my childhood years. She modeled behavior and a mentality that colored my perception of the world. I thought her experience was normal. So while a genetic predisposition was likely a factor, modeling within the home was also at play.

Throughout my life, I endured difficult circumstances and many trying events that each could have impacted my thoughts, attitudes, beliefs, and mood. They included:

- multiple childhood surgeries and rehabilitation
- the premature death of my father when I was young
- years of graduate school
- multiple moves
- caring for a parent and a spouse with cancer
- a miscarriage
- a life-threatening illness

Do I think my family's history of depression, my parent's modeling in the home, the birth of my children, or any of my difficult life circumstances *caused* my depression? No. But I did before I understood the spiritual contributors to depression. Now I look at those experiences and situations as the seeds of depression. How I responded would either provide fertile ground for those seeds to flourish or choke out the seeds before they took root.

Having a greater understanding of our enemy and how he operates, I now clearly recognize the roots of my depression. This is my hope for you as well. God said his people are destroyed because of lack of knowledge (Hosea 4:6). Each week in my office I see how true this is. We are destroyed when the enemy knows more about the roots of our depression than we do. We cannot fight effectively until we understand what we are fighting and have the weapons to engage in battle.

My depression had many spiritual roots. Hindsight gave me fresh revelations about these roots. Very early in my life, I experienced a life-threatening illness, which resulted in multiple surgeries and hospital stays (during a time when parents weren't allowed to stay with their young children). The enemy took advantage of that time and offered up lies:

"You aren't safe."

"You are abandoned and alone."

"No one cares about you."

"You can't trust others to be there for you."

"You need to be prepared to fend for yourself."

As a child, I didn't know any better at the time, and I fell for his deception and responded in ways that aligned my perspective with his dishonest manipulation and opened the door to the spirits of rejection, abandonment, fear, doubt, unbelief, and even a poverty mind-set. This was a spiral staircase going down because the enemy used that wrong thinking to convince me of more lies that interfered with my health, my mind, and my heart.

After my illness, physical disfigurement remained. I was too young to realize I was different from others, but the enemy knew he could use the situation to his advantage. Children teased me about my physical deformity, called me names, and isolated me at recess and in gym class. Even a Girl Scout troop leader made me a mockery to my peers by emphasizing my physical limitations to motivate the rest of the troop. Each time I heard the enemy's lying whisper. At the time, I did not know it was the enemy and his lies:

"No one likes you because you're different."

"You'll never be as good as they are."

"Nobody will love you the way you are."

As a naïve child, I readily believed the enemy's lies. In my heart, I watered the soil to let those seeds take root. An unloving spirit firmly planted itself in the core of my belief system and colored my perception of myself, others, and God. It was then difficult for me to fully appreciate the Father's unconditional and complete love for me, making it impossible for me to love myself or others fully. We cannot give what we do not have.

Living with a depressed mother, feeling I wasn't good enough, and subconsciously fearing rejection and abandonment, I spent decades of my life trying to compensate for my perceived flaws by trying to be perfect in other areas. Never considered good enough for athletic pursuits, I focused my efforts on academics. Unfortunately, even in that area I agreed with the enemy: "Anything short of perfection is failure and unacceptable." And again peers took their jabs at me, this time because I excelled. Again the enemy taunted, "It doesn't matter what you do. You'll never measure up, and you'll never be accepted or acceptable."

I believed the lies of the spirit of self-hatred, causing me to hate anything that represented imperfection in myself and believing others and God did too. After allowing years of derogatory statements by others to pierce my heart, I listened to the taunts of the spirits of self-hatred, self-rejection, self-condemnation, self-pity, self-bitterness, self-resentment, and unforgiveness. I even began to punish myself.

God's Word declares, "How beautiful on the mountains are the feet of those who bring good news, who proclaim peace, who bring good tidings, who proclaim salvation, who say to Zion, 'Your God reigns!'" (Isa. 52:7). Unaware of what the Word said, rather than agreeing with God's truth and seeing my feet as beautiful, I looked at my physical deformity and hated it. I rejected that imperfect part of myself and "punished" that foot by never letting it take the first step as a way of acknowledging that its imperfection made it and me inferior.

I also lived much of my life agreeing with the spirit of fear rather than believing God's truth: God did not give me the spirit of fear, but instead he gave me power, love, and a sound mind (2 Tim. 1:7). When my father died suddenly and unexpectedly during my adolescent years, my first thought was wrapped up in fear: "What do I have to do to help support the family?" The enemy taunted me with, "If God would take your father, what makes you think he won't take your home, your finances, and the rest of your family?" Believing that lie just further entrenched fear in my life. I reacted with the belief that I couldn't trust God and could depend only on myself. That was a very lonely and depressing place to live.

After decades of agreeing with the enemy's characterization of me rather than believing what God said, I lived under the weight of the spirit of heaviness. I frequently woke in the morning feeling covered by a blanket of oppression, followed by days lived in despair and feelings of hopelessness. Those days were often governed by my feelings instead of by God's truth. But feelings are not reliable. Our feelings are the outward manifestation of the thoughts we believe.

When we feel fearful, worried, or anxious, those emotions are the outward representation of what we have believed (e.g., "Something bad is going to happen," "I can't trust God to take care of me," "God's Word is true for others but not for me," etc.). When we feel angry, we behave in ways that are consistent with what we have believed to be true (i.e., "I've been wronged," "Others have intentionally hurt me," "I have to protect myself," etc.). When we feel sad, blue, or depressed, our emotions are a representation of the conscious or subconscious thoughts we have believed (i.e., "I'm not good enough," "I don't deserve better than this," "I'm always rejected," etc.). For many years I accepted the lie that "I'll probably always feel this way." Do any of these sound familiar?

Our feelings are the outward manifestation of the thoughts we believe.

Stress, anger, and the belief that our situation will never change (hopelessness or helplessness) can all lead to varying degrees of depression. The Bible talks about oppression and a spirit of heaviness, which is depression. Typically, I find that many spirits work together to exacerbate the effects. In my own life, I know the spirit of heaviness was a propelling force in my spiral down to depression's valley. I also agreed with the lies presented to me through guilt, self-hatred, and self-pity that contributed to bitterness, anger, and a rejection of myself. I was unaware of the invisible war waged against me, but I was also unaware of what God's truth said about me, making me an easy, defenseless target. I find this to be true of many of my patients as well.

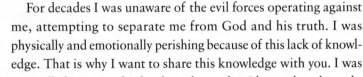

For decades I was unaware of the evil forces operating against me, attempting to separate me from God and his truth. I was physically and emotionally perishing because of this lack of knowledge. That is why I want to share this knowledge with you. I was compelled to write this book to share what I learned so that others can experience the abundant life Jesus promised. In the next few chapters, we will uncover what the enemy does to make us depressed and keep us there. Then we will explore what, by God's grace, God won't allow the enemy to do to us.

You wouldn't be reading this book right now if you or a loved one didn't struggle with at least shadows of a spirit of heaviness and depression. Breaking the emotional chains of depression that weigh us down under that spirit of heaviness is a process. God's Word reveals to us in Isaiah 61:3 that one of the keys in that process is to offer God our praise. It's hard to remain beaten down and oppressed when we are praising the Lord. If you continue to praise him as you read this book and do the recommended exercises at the end of each chapter, he will meet you where you are!

Are you ready to learn the enemy's tactics to keep you under the blanket of heaviness?

Your Rx

1. Look up the following verses: Psalm 42:5; Jeremiah 29:11; John 15:11; 1 John 4:4. Write them on index cards and place them where you will see them frequently. Read each of these passages aloud three times daily, committing them to memory.

2. List the potential chemical, genetic, medical, and environmental conditions in your life that may have had a role in your depression.

3. Prayerfully ask the Lord, "Father, what lies of the enemy have I believed that contribute to my depression and detract from my ability to live life fully?" Write down his response to you. Then pray, "Father, show me your truth. Give me the faith to believe your truth rather than the lies that seem true." Record what he reveals to you.

My Prayer for You

Father, your Word says in Isaiah 54:17 that no weapon formed against us will prevail. I thank you that you give us so much grace when we make mistakes and when we believe lies that are not in agreement with your truth. I thank you that you show us so much mercy and that you've led this dear child of yours to read these pages in an effort to exchange despair for gladness. Father, I pray that your Holy Spirit will minister to this person's heart and bring a fresh revelation of your truth. I thank you, Lord, that no matter what exists in our genetic inheritance, no matter what difficult circumstances we encounter, and no matter what the enemy plots to harm us, you are bigger and greater than all of it and that it's your desire for us to be in health and to live life to the full. Because of the hope we have in Jesus, amen.

Recommended Playlist

"While I Am Waiting," John Waller, © 2007 by Reunion Records

"We Will Not Be Shaken," Bethel, © 2015 by Bethel Music

"Our God Reigns Here," John Waller, © 2011 by City of Peace Media Inc.

"Begin Again," Jason Gray, © 2014 by Centricity Music

"Cover Me," Zach Neese, © 2011 by Gateway Create Publishing

"We Won't Be Shaken," Building 429, © 2013 by Essential Records

"Nearness," Bethel, © 2015 by Bethel Music

"Break the Chains," John Waller, © 2014 by Label Me Not

4

Recognize You Have an Enemy

The thief comes only to steal and kill and destroy; I have come that they may have life, and have it to the full.

John 10:10

We will never achieve the levels of peace, joy, and effectiveness to which we are called if we are being influenced by evil in certain compartments of our lives.

Robert Morris

The previous chapter revealed that there are many potential contributors to depression and that frequently a combination of factors turns a case of the blues or a subjective feeling of sadness into depression. Regardless of the cause, and while everyone's experience is unique, depression has some fairly predictable spiritual consequences.

When we consider depression, we think of how it impacts our emotional and mental functioning. But if we don't arrest the downward spiral, over time it swells from affecting our emotional and mental functioning to negatively impacting our bodies and our spiritual health. In short, depression affects our entire being.

Depression hurts in so many ways, and the pain and emotional turmoil, to a very large degree, can feel like a broken heart. Scripture attests to this: "A happy heart makes the face cheerful, but heartache crushes the spirit" (Prov. 15:13).

Let's look at what the enemy does to us through depression.

Depression Turns Us into Someone We Don't Recognize

After eleven years of marriage, I became pregnant with our first child. My husband and I were both so excited, as were the grandparents—who I suspect had almost given up on the idea of receiving grandchildren from our union. My mother was especially ecstatic, as this would be her first grandchild from either my brother or me. I had imagined for years what it would be like to bring a baby into this world and to be a mother. I had all sorts of expectations for our life as a family. But when depression descended, those expectations dissipated like a dream upon waking, and even this wondrous time of life took on a gray, cheerless tone.

After a healthy pregnancy and a fairly routine labor and delivery, we brought our son home from the hospital. I felt like the happiest mother who ever lived. Shortly afterward, however, I didn't recognize myself anymore. It was as if I had gone to bed one night a happy mother of a newborn and woken up the next day feeling devastated, like I had lost everything. Even when the baby wasn't crying, I was.

I had no idea why I was crying. Nor could I stop. Tears sprang from nowhere. I loved this sweet baby. I was so happy to finally be a mother, yet all I could do was cry. I'm not talking about the little sniffle that follows the predictable sad ending of a chick flick. I lapsed into uncontrollable weeping in response to trivial events like knocking a paper off the countertop—or nothing in particular. I wasn't in pain. It couldn't yet be attributed to weeks of newborn-induced sleep deprivation. I was not yet overwhelmed with the daily schedule of caring for an infant. I didn't know why I was crying, and nothing helped to stop the tears. I tried sleeping when the baby slept. I made sure I ate well. I took the baby in his stroller for daily walks to get my exercise. Warm showers only signaled to my body that it was time to nurse. Nothing helped.

There wasn't much I could say for certain during that time. I only knew this wasn't how it was supposed to be. I had brought home a precious, healthy, beautiful baby boy. I couldn't have asked for more, but it seemed I couldn't feel worse. This wasn't anything like I had expected. I knew I should be happy, but I just couldn't find my happy place.

I was ill equipped and began to feel not only devastated but also like a personal failure. I hadn't seen any of my friends go through anything like this. And it certainly didn't look like any of TLC's programming about babies and motherhood. This situation was so much harder than nine months of pregnancy or labor and delivery, and it wasn't improving.

My mother called to check on us one evening during one of my frequent crying spells. When she asked what was wrong, I gave her the same tearful response I gave anyone who asked: "I don't know. I just can't stop crying." After a few more questions, she identified my tormenter and explained that I was suffering from postpartum depression. She made me promise to hang up the phone with her and immediately contact my physician.

It helped a little to know what I was dealing with, to have a name for it. But that knowledge alone wasn't enough to rid me of the despair I felt. That would be like knowing a hurricane is coming and expecting that knowledge to be enough to repair the damage sustained in its wake. I had heard of postpartum depression before, but I couldn't relate to it in my childless years. All I knew was that I no longer felt like myself.

Depression can turn us into a person we don't recognize. Sometimes the transformation happens seemingly overnight, as in my case after the birth of my son. For others depression slowly infiltrates daily life over weeks or months or years, like when you step onto a scale for the first time in a while and think, "When did I put on thirty pounds?" Depression can take you from the person you used to be and turn you into someone your spouse, your kids, and your friends don't understand, leaving them to wonder, "What happened?"

We see in his writings that David experienced the same thing and lamented to God about his state of despair: "But LORD and King, help me so that you bring honor to yourself. Because your love is so good, save me. I am poor and needy. My heart is wounded deep down inside me" (Ps. 109:21–22 NIrV). Yet David went on to share hope. "He heals the brokenhearted and binds up their wounds" (Ps. 147:3). That is God's commitment to us. While we may feel broken and wounded in our despair, God promises to heal those places in us.

The Truth about How God Sees Us

While depression can turn us into someone we don't recognize, it can help to remember that Jesus sees us not only as we are but also as we can be. Jesus is God, and God is and was and always will be (see John 1:1–3). So God in his omniscience knew our entire future before we took our first breath, and our fall into depression comes as no surprise to him, nor does our journey out of this desert land. Furthermore, the Bible tells us, "Before I formed you in the womb I knew you, before you were born I set you apart" (Jer. 1:5). God knows where we started out, and he knows who we are and what our struggles are. He knows how his redemptive power can transform and restore us. When God looks at us, he sees the righteousness of Jesus. We are told in 2 Corinthians 5:21, "God made him who had no sin to be sin for us, so that in him we might become the righteousness of God."

While depression can turn us into someone we don't recognize, it can help to remember that Jesus sees us not only as we are but also as we can be.

My go-to verse for comfort is Jeremiah 29:11: "'For I know the plans I have for you,' says the LORD. 'They are plans for good and not for disaster, to give you a future and a hope'" (NLT). While God sees us in our season of pain, he also knows that he has so much better in store for us after we make it through depression's dark tunnel and arrive on the other side.

Often during periods of depression, we don't admit to others how we really feel, and we pretend to be happier than we are. In their book *The Cure*, John Lynch, Bruce McNicol, and Bill Thrall note, "All masks are the product of pretending something in our lives is true, even if experience denies it."[1] Jesus looks past the masks we put on for the rest of the world to see us as we truly are, even as we try to hide the guilt, shame, and utter despair we feel. He doesn't see our faults. He doesn't see the things others don't like in us. He doesn't see those parts of us we don't like in ourselves. No. Instead, he sees a wounded child who needs the shelter of his wing and the comfort of his healing touch so that we can assume our rightful place as his heir. He wants to take our pain, our "ashes," and exchange them for beauty.

During my darkest days, I found hope in Isaiah 61:1–3:

> The Spirit of the Sovereign LORD is on me,
>> because the LORD has anointed me
>> to proclaim good news to the poor.
>
> He has sent me to bind up the brokenhearted,
>> to proclaim freedom for the captives
>> and release from darkness for the prisoners,
>
> to proclaim the year of the LORD's favor
>> and the day of vengeance of our God,
>
> to comfort all who mourn,
>> and provide for those who grieve in Zion—
>
> to bestow on them a crown of beauty
>> instead of ashes,
>
> the oil of joy
>> instead of mourning,
>
> and a garment of praise
>> instead of a spirit of despair.
>
> They will be called oaks of righteousness,
>> a planting of the LORD
>> for the display of his splendor.

This passage reminds us it's always God's desire to comfort his children, heal the brokenhearted, give us joy for our sadness, and show us the path to freedom.

Depression Contributes to Loneliness

Depression destroys our foundation and contributes to loneliness. My postpartum depression hit like a tsunami. I had no idea that depression would be a consequence of giving birth. I felt so alone. I didn't personally know anyone who had suffered with postpartum depression, so I was unprepared and isolated. I began to believe the lies that I was alone in my suffering and that there was something wrong with me. I was embarrassed to talk about it.

I feared there was something inherently flawed about me that was making me suffer this devastation to my sense of well-being. I felt ashamed. I didn't have the wherewithal to consider that if I was too embarrassed or ashamed to talk about my experience, perhaps others were too. In my quietness, I suffered alone. Now I realize I wasn't really alone. Isaiah 43:2 promises, "When you pass through the waters, I will be with you; and through the rivers, they shall not overflow you. When you walk through the fire, you shall not be burned, nor shall the flame scorch you" (NKJV).

Did you hear what that said? Did you hear the warning? The verse doesn't say we won't go through difficult times. It doesn't say we won't feel as if we are drowning or go through times so intense that they are like walking through fire. Oh no! It warns us about *when* we will go through trials. We are implicitly promised that we will go through difficult times, destructive times, painful times, times that will change the landscape of our lives forever. But we will not go through them alone. God promises his presence with us the entire time. When we go through difficult times, we will not suffer alone because God will be with us.

Have you ever seen the devastating effects of a flood? Floods destroy. This verse in Isaiah took on personal meaning for me when we experienced our own flood.

We bought a home several years back. It wasn't fancy, but we loved it. When we moved in, we gave fresh paint to every wall and decorated. We filled every room with furniture. Shortly thereafter, we went away for a week. When we returned, it was midnight and our two young ones were sleeping in the car. We unfastened their seat belts, and my husband and I each carried one in our arms. We walked into our house to find it covered from one end to the other with water. The entire week we were away, a toilet overflowed and flowed and flowed. Six inches of water blanketed the entire house. It soaked the carpets and swelled the drywall. It damaged the furniture and destroyed everything stored at ground level. Our front door sat somewhat sheltered from the road, so no one saw the water seeping out the front door or around the foundation. Even if they had, they would not have known how to reach us, for we had just recently moved in and were still strangers to the neighbors.

In my naïveté, I thought, "Give it six weeks and we'll be back to normal." Well, this was one time when naïveté benefited me. The flooring had to be replaced. Most of the drywall had to be cut out and replaced. At one point, we could stand at one end of the house and look between the exposed studs and see all the way to the opposite end of the house. The flood ruined our floors, our walls, our furniture, and our cabinets. Our home was a mess. What was previously a place of refuge and comfort became a place of frustration and despair. Contractors spent months tearing out the damage, putting up new walls, and painting, laying new flooring, and installing new cabinets and fixtures. A year later, our house still wasn't back to normal; the rebuilding process seemed unending. It was dirty and dusty, and it left us crying out, "When will this be over?"

God's Word tells us that rivers may roar, but they will not overflow us. It tells us that we will walk through fire, but we will not be burned or scorched. Because of God's great love, these hard times won't destroy us, although during periods of depression, we might feel as if they will. I certainly did. Because of his love, God promises to be with us during our most difficult times—during periods of depression. We must hold tight to that promise as our feet get wet and our backs get hot. God is here to hold on to us and walk every step with us. The secret to this verse is to accept that difficult circumstances will happen while remembering that we are not alone in our adversity. We have an enemy who would like to paralyze us in fear with the rivers, floods, and fires of our lives. Instead, we must take God at his Word and believe that what he tells us is truth and applicable to our concerns.

The depths of depression can feel so very lonely, like no one cares and no one understands. And at times, it may feel like not even God cares. During the darkest days of my depression, I felt completely alone. I cried out to God from the privacy of my bedroom, "You promise that you will never leave us or forsake us, but I feel all alone! Where are you?" In those periods of despair, I had to choose to believe God and trust in his promises rather than my feelings. I ultimately found comfort not in people or possessions but in the truth of God's Word. One of the verses that spoke so strongly to me, and I hope it will bless you as well, is 2 Corinthians 4:17: "These troubles and sufferings of ours are, after all, quite small and won't last very long. Yet this short time of distress will result in God's richest blessing upon us forever and ever!" (TLB).

Depression Causes Us to Focus on Feelings Rather Than on Truth

I used to think that feelings are neither right nor wrong; they just are. But feelings are capricious and can't be trusted. They are also strong and compelling. The enemy uses our feelings against us. He uses the despair and the loneliness we feel during periods of depression to convince us of the lies he whispers in our ears. "Your God says he will never leave you, but where is he now? If he was really here, you wouldn't feel so lonely!" In those times, we must cling to the truth of God's Word. God cannot and will not lie. "God is not like people, who lie; he is not a human who changes his mind. Whatever he promises, he does; he speaks, and it is done" (Num. 23:19 GNT).

The enemy, however, is the master deceiver. He makes his career out of lying. "From the very beginning he was a murderer and has never been on the side of truth, because there is no truth in him. When he tells a lie, he is only doing what is natural to him, because he is a liar and the father of all lies" (John 8:44 GNT). It's important to know God's Word, to study and learn it, so that when we are tempted to trust our feelings, the Holy Spirit will remind us of truth so we will not be deceived by the enemy's lies. We are told of this in John 14:26: "But the Advocate, the Holy Spirit, whom the Father will send in my name, will teach you all things and will remind you of everything I have said to you." But the Holy Spirit cannot remind us of the verses we have not read.

In some of my darkest days, I cried out to him through my tears, "God, I know you say in your Word that you will never leave us or forsake us, and I want to believe that, I do, but where are you now? I hurt, physically and emotionally. I feel so alone. If you are really there, why can't I feel you?" I thought I was doing all the right things. I regularly attended church, had my morning devotions, and read God's Word. Yet none of that seemed to make a difference. Time has a way of giving perspective.

He promises he won't ever leave us, but he won't force us to stay in his presence either.

I am an achiever by nature—a doer. I have a very driven personality. Yes, I was having my morning devotions, but truthfully, I was not really having much of a quiet time per se. My surroundings were quiet, but my heart and mind were not.

Even as I read my devotion or the Scripture for the day, my mind jumped ahead to my schedule or plans or problems of the day. And if time was running short and I needed to head off to work, I would cut short my time in prayer. The time I cut short was the time I spent listening to God.

God was gentle in his correction, as he helped me to see the error in my thinking. He had not left me, but my lack of attention was not conducive to recognizing his presence or the gift of comfort he offered. He tenderly showed me this one morning as I reread a familiar story about another woman who had difficulty setting aside her to-do list to be still in his presence:

> She had a sister called Mary, who sat at the Lord's feet listening to what he said. But Martha was distracted by all the preparations that had to be made. She came to him and asked, "Lord, don't you care that my sister has left me to do the work by myself? Tell her to help me!"
>
> "Martha, Martha," the Lord answered, "you are worried and upset about many things, but few things are needed—or indeed only one. Mary has chosen what is better, and it will not be taken away from her." (Luke 10:39–42)

The Lord showed me that we can be lonely when we are too busy to take time to rest in his presence and listen to him. His Word is true. He promises he won't ever leave us, but he won't force us to stay in his presence either. We need to spend time with him and in his Word so we know his truth and can use it to combat our feelings.

Satan uses three primary tactics to perpetuate our depression, affecting us to such a degree that we no longer recognize ourselves. He seeks to kill our joy, steal our peace, and destroy our identity. We feel alone in our pain and focus on our feelings rather than on God's truth. The enemy's key motivation in the life of a Christian is to thwart our effectiveness in glorifying God and blunt our ability to share the good news with others who would trust in God. We are warned in John 10:10, "The thief comes only to steal and kill and destroy," but then it goes on to give us great hope, as Jesus promises, "I have come that they may have life, and have it to the full."

In the pages ahead, I'll share with you how the truth of that verse manifests itself within the experience of depression—what depression does to us spiritually. We will reflect on how the enemy kills our joy, steals our peace, and seeks to destroy our identity. Then we will uncover what, by the grace of God, depression cannot do to us. The enemy seeks to keep us in the storm of depression, but God is so good that he doesn't allow the enemy to determine our worth, dictate our destiny, or separate us from God's love. In fact, we can take solace in knowing that what the enemy intended to harm us, God will use for good (see Gen. 50:20). That's what I call "godly revenge." Take heart, my friend. No matter how bad you feel right now, hope prevails!

Your Rx

1. Consider what you were like before you encountered depression. What has changed that makes it difficult to recognize that old you? What would your friends or family identify as changes? Choose one thing consistent with either the old you or the person you would like to become and take a step of faith toward that new version of you. Perhaps you used to enjoy a daily walk, a bike ride, or artwork. Pick an activity and strive to incorporate it into your life. Or maybe you used to enjoy spending time with friends but have let some of your friendships fade. You could send a text message, email, or call one friend just to touch base.

2. Look up the following verses: Psalm 147:3; Isaiah 43:2; 61:1–3; Jeremiah 1:5; John 10:10. Write them on index cards and place them where you will see them frequently. Read each of these passages aloud three times daily, committing them to memory.

3. Make a list (for your eyes only) of the things you like about yourself (e.g., "I don't like others to hurt," "People share their problems with me because I won't tell others," "I do what I say I'll do," etc.) Then each morning as you stand in

your bathroom getting ready for the day, look at yourself in the mirror and proclaim over yourself those characteristics or traits you like (e.g., "I am compassionate," "I am trustworthy," "I am reliable," etc.). Remember, faith comes by hearing. If depression has turned you into someone you don't recognize, it's time to start listening to the truth about who you are.

My Prayer for You

Father, you are no stranger to pain, and I take comfort in knowing that you weep when we weep—that is how much you care for your children. I pray, Father, that you will enfold this one in your mighty strong arms of love. In our darkest hours, sometimes it can be hard to recognize ourselves, but you know every hair on our heads. You know when we sleep, and you know when we wake. And you know our greatest need. Comfort your child now, Father, in a way that only you can, for in your Word you say that you came to give not only life but abundant life. Breathe life back into this despairing heart, I pray. I thank you that we can stand on your promises and know that you will be faithful to your Word. In Jesus's name, amen.

Recommended Playlist

"Greater," MercyMe, © 2014 by Fair Trade/Columbia

"God, I Look to You," Bethel, © 2014 by Bethel Music

"Your Great Name," Natalie Grant, © 2010 by Curb Records

"Whom Shall I Fear?" Chris Tomlin, © 2013 by sixstepsrecords/ Sparrow Records

"The Hurt and the Healer," MercyMe, © 2012 by Fair Trade

"You Will Never Leave Me," Sidewalk Prophets, © 2011 by Word Entertainment LLC

"Even This Will Be Made Beautiful," Jason Gray, © 2014 by Centricity Music

"Beauty Will Rise," Steven Curtis Chapman, © 2009 by Sparrow Records

"Who I Am," Blanca, © 2015 by Word Entertainment LLC

"Strong Enough," Matthew West, © 2010 by Sparrow Records

"Here in Your Presence," New Life Worship, © 2006 by Integrity/ Columbia

5

Recover Your Joy

Those who plant in tears
will harvest with shouts of joy.

Psalm 126:5 NLT

Real joy is not found in having the best of everything, but in
trusting that God is making the best of everything.

Ann Voskamp

The enemy uses three primary tactics against us. According to John 10:10, he steals, kills, and destroys whatever opposes his kingdom of darkness. In the case of depression, he swoops in and steals our joy.

Our enemy purposes to build his kingdom of darkness while denigrating God's holy kingdom. In stealing our joy, the enemy diminishes our enthusiasm for all things. Worse yet, he takes from us that which attracts others to us and thus to God, making us less effective in drawing others to God, the giver of joy. Yet despite the enemy's lies, God's Word affirms that we can experience joy even in the midst of our troubles. "When troubles of any kind come your way, consider it an opportunity for great joy" (James 1:2 NLT). For many years, while I was depressed, that is what I wanted, but I didn't know how to access it. Maybe that is where you are now.

We can't know if David were to see a doctor today if he would receive a diagnosis of depression, but he certainly experienced a crisis of joy. He begged God to return joy to him: "Restore to me the joy of your salvation, and make me willing to obey you" (Ps. 51:12 NLT).

During those times when we lack joy, hoping for better days presents a challenge. Depression feels like a heavy curtain that is hard to pull back, obscuring the sunshiny day outside. We have been forewarned of such times: "Friends, when life gets really difficult, don't jump to the conclusion that God isn't on the job. Instead, be glad that you are in the very thick of what Christ experienced. This is a spiritual refining process, with glory just around the corner" (1 Peter 4:12–13 Message). I treasure how the New International Reader's Version reveals in verse 13 the hope God gives for a return of our joy: "Then you will have even more joy when Christ returns in glory." I want that. Do you?

In my darkest days, as illness stole my physical health, I struggled to string coherent sentences together. Dehydration drained my energy like a sieve. One day lapsed into another. I barely knew the day of the week, and I could only guess the date.

On most days I suffered alone in the house while the children attended school and my husband worked at the office. But the Lord and I had frequent conversations. I searched for answers—answers I knew only he could provide. In the deepest recesses of my heart, those places I had tried to hide even from him, I sensed God had been waiting a long time for me to begin asking the hard questions.

I felt weak and frail. I was petite to begin with, then illness stole a third of my body weight and left my arms and legs tattooed with rainbow-colored bruises in different stages of healing. During this time, physical illness beat me down and left me despairing. Some days I had to borrow other people's hope because it felt like mine had run dry.

I was tethered to my bed by IVs, which kept me hydrated and fed, and lessened my pain. I could do little from my bed other than sleep, listen, or read. I devoured numerous books about joy, and to be honest, I disliked most of them. Several books talked about the importance of being grateful. I interpreted them to say I lacked gratitude and a thankful attitude and therefore my joy remained deficient. Like it was my fault. One more thing for me to feel ashamed of. I had yet to learn it was difficult to be depressed and truly grateful at the same time.

I saw nothing pretty about me. I detested my reflection in the mirror, nor did I like what I saw in the mirror to my soul. Did God love even me? If so, why? I didn't have much to offer him. The unloving spirit continued to rear its ugly head, disallowing me to love myself or receive God's love, then leaving me unable to truly love others.

Despite my feelings, I prayed every day of my illness. Among other things, I always prayed for three things:

1. For God to help me have a more accurate perspective of him
2. For God to help me understand how he viewed me and to replace my image of myself with his image of me
3. That God would show me what joy was and that he would give it to me abundantly as he promised in Scripture

The Lord knew the true condition of my heart. He started revealing that, while I was thankful, there was a depth and breadth of things he had given me, done for me, and provided me that I was only dimly recognizing, much less thankful for. For example, I didn't acknowledge the windows in my sick room that allowed glimpses of nature. My convalescent room was air-conditioned and provided relief from the sweltering Texas summer heat. I rested in a double bed that was much easier to navigate than the king-sized bed on risers in the master bedroom. In comparison to the rest of the world, I was a rich woman. In many ways, I had more than I needed.

I must admit to you that I did not come to this conclusion quickly. There were many things I wanted and more I thought I needed. While I kept my eyes on those things, I struggled to acknowledge all the blessings I had overlooked. I took so much for granted, including my health—to the point that I previously worked a hundred hours a week and expected my body to give more.

I can't really tell you what ultimately cracked my defenses. I think it was just finally an act of desperation. Desperation makes us willing. I so desperately wanted this intangible thing called joy. I wasn't even sure I knew what joy was. I just knew I didn't have it. I sensed it was something amazing, and it was something I urgently desired. So I was willing to pray for it daily.

My transformation started slowly. I found a fresh journal and labeled it "Gratitude Journal." Day after day I recorded one, or two, or sometimes three or more things and thanked God. I began with the very obvious things like my family, career, house, and car. Not terribly profound, but it was a start. Each morning when I awoke, before my mind could spring ahead to the day, I immediately thanked God for whatever blessings came to mind.

Rather than keeping my eyes on my problems, I consciously praised God for who he was and what he had done in my life. A pivotal change occurred when I determined to thank him in advance for his answers. I trusted God to hear my prayers and be faithful to answer them and thanked him before I saw the physical outcome. I focused on keeping my eyes on him. Doing so helped me maintain a joy-producing perspective rather than a joy-defeating perspective, consistent with Proverbs 23:7: "For as he thinks in his heart, so is he" (NKJV).

The Greek philosopher Epictetus said, "He is a wise man who does not grieve for the things which he has not but rejoices for those which he has."[1] We must choose to focus on our blessings. If we focus on what we don't have or what we wish we had, life will always feel incomplete. Zig Ziglar, a well-respected Christian motivational speaker, said, "The more you are grateful for what you have, the more you will have to be grateful for."[2]

The Quest for Joy

As I talked to more and more people, I realized I was not alone in my quest for joy. I heard one person after another confess, "I'm not sure I know what joy is." Many admitted, "I've spent more of my life depressed than not depressed." Countless others shared, "This is just the way I am. If I've been this way most of my life, there is little hope of that changing now." Some went so far as to conclude, "This must be my cross to bear," as if depression is some kind of spiritual assignment from God.

I too had previously entertained the lies coming from the spirits of despair, doubt, unbelief, and self-pity. My heart ached for those who shared their suffering with me. It aches for you, because I know how desperation feels. I don't want anyone to endure that darkness. You may be thinking those same words right now: "I'm not sure I know what joy is."

The best way I can describe joy is like a fullness in your heart, like an inner contentment despite outer circumstances. Kay Warren, wife of Rick Warren, the pastor at Saddleback Church in suburban Los Angeles, suggests, "Joy is the settled assurance that God is in control of all the details of my life, the quiet confidence that ultimately everything is going to be all right, and the determined choice to praise God in all things."³ She describes joy as "a settled conviction about God. It's a quiet confidence IN God. And joy is a determined choice to give my praise TO God.⁴

It must be underscored that joy is a gift from God. It's not something we earn or conjure up. Jesus said, "If you keep my commands, you will remain in my love, just as I have kept my Father's commands and remain in his love. I have told you this so that my joy may be in you and that your joy may be complete. My command is this: Love each other as I have loved you" (John 15:10–12). Romans 15:13 also conveys that joy is a gift: "May the God of hope fill you with all joy and peace as you trust in him, so that you may overflow with hope by the power of the Holy Spirit." But while these verses reveal the truth that joy is a gift bestowed on us by God, they also point out that we have a role to play if we want to thrive in that gift.

So what do we do when the enemy has stolen our joy?

Whenever we find that we have come into agreement with anything that is not of God, especially the lies of the enemy, the Bible says we must recover ourselves. Recognizing our need for help is the first step in initiating change. We must recognize that we have cooperated with the enemy, listened to and agreed with his lies, and given in to his temptations. Then we must repent to God and, if necessary, to others. Repenting removes the enemy's right to interfere with our lives. We must renounce and reject the lies of the enemy and in their place receive God's love, forgiveness, peace, and joy.

Seek God's Presence

Perhaps you've experienced joy but aren't experiencing it now and don't know how to regain its fullness in your heart. When we feel disheartened and desire to take back that which the enemy has stolen from us, our first line of defense must be to intentionally spend time in God's presence, just as David encouraged: "You make known to me the path of life; you will fill me with joy in your presence, with eternal pleasures at your right hand" (Ps. 16:11).

David knew how to tap into a greater measure of joy: "Surely you have granted him unending blessings and made him glad with the joy of your presence" (Ps. 21:6). I love how the Message translation of the Bible recounts David's agonizing pleas to God because I relate to such desperation and desire for change.

> I'm feeling terrible—I couldn't feel worse!
>> Get me on my feet again. You promised, remember?
> When I told my story, you responded;
>> train me well in your deep wisdom.
> Help me understand these things inside and out
>> so I can ponder your miracle-wonders.
> My sad life's dilapidated, a falling-down barn;
>> build me up again by your Word.
> Barricade the road that goes Nowhere;
>> grace me with your clear revelation.
> I choose the true road to Somewhere,
>> I post your road signs at every curve and corner.
> I grasp and cling to whatever you tell me;
>> GOD, don't let me down!
> I'll run the course you lay out for me
>> if you'll just show me how." (Ps. 119:25–32)

Healing and restoration come when we get so close and personal with Jesus that no one can come between us. In God's presence there is fullness of life and joy. This suggests that we must do our part first and then God will do that which only he can do. James 4:8 explains that we must draw near to God and then he will draw near to us. If we desire joy, the first move is for us to spend time in God's presence. But *we* make the first move.

I was a busy woman, with the weight of my family's livelihood as well as the livelihood of several staff members on my shoulders. I attended church, prayed, even participated in a women's Bible study, yet it took a life-threatening illness for me to begin to appreciate the joy that can only come from spending time in God's presence. During my illness, I drew near and felt so close to him that I didn't want to do anything but cocoon in his presence. I did not watch television, even my favorite indulgences like *Survivor*. I didn't want to play games, even with my family. And I certainly didn't want to run errands or do chores!

Being in God's presence may take different forms and be experienced in a variety of ways, individual to each person. Personally, it usually begins by preparing my heart to worship. I do that by making sure I have confessed and asked for forgiveness of any known sin. Then I play quiet instrumental praise and worship music to calm my mind and release the constricting concerns of the day. Somehow, the more tranquil the music is, the more I feel it. I also soften the volume of my own voice. I want to hear what God desires to share with me instead of dragging out, again, my tattered list of worries, concerns, and needs.

When I asked others about their experience of seeking God's presence, they all noted the importance of getting quiet and waiting to hear or sense what God wants to say. I have one friend who describes the experience as embracing the quiet long enough to realize it's not quiet at all. God is there with us, and he has things to show and tell us all the time. The longer we pay attention— through stillness, walking, writing, reading the book of nature or the Bible itself—the more we turn aside and pay attention to what God is saying and doing in the most ordinary of moments, the easier we feel his presence and hear his voice.

During my prolonged convalescence, I was at a particularly low point emotionally and unable to do much for myself physically. I could not get up and go to work. I was unable to care for my family. Even showering and dressing took more energy and effort than I could summon. While my physical body longed for relief from the excruciating pain, my emotional state plummeted from the daily toll of the pain and the isolation. The change in my abilities took with it my esteem and my identity.

I spent hours alone, although not really alone. I prayed for what seemed like hours. Where one prayer left off, the next began. It was a time in my life that I despised, yet, unexpectedly, at the same time cherished.

I hated my weakened state and being unable to do all the things I was accustomed to doing. I lamented being dependent on others for help. My self-image as a strong, independent woman seemed to belong to a memory of a former life. During this time, I clung to God with every ounce of my being.

The longer I remained in this condition, the more I appreciated the extended time I had in God's presence. I valued the opportunity to sit, listen, and learn more intently than I ever had before. I appreciated the stillness and the quiet, for I could hear God's voice more clearly.

Every Scripture verse seemed to jump off the page as if it was speaking directly to my heart's cry, as if it had been written just for me. I began to savor each one like a piece of chocolate. I wrote verses on Post-it notes and put the notes up in my room as reminders of God's warnings, promises, comforts, and admonitions to me. I taped the notes on my bedposts, lamp shades, closet doors, dresser drawers, and even my IV pole. Having the visible reminder of his Word encouraged me. I saw how he had carried others through difficult times in the past. His Word assured me that he could and does still act in such amazing ways today.

David prayed for the ability to continually stay in God's presence: "One thing I have asked of the LORD, and that I will seek: that I may dwell in the house of the LORD [in His presence] all the days of my life. . . . Do not hide your face from me, do not turn Your servant away in anger; You who have been my help; do not abandon me nor leave me, O God of my salvation!" (Ps. 27:4, 9 AMP). He knew that in the Father's presence God would put a new song in his heart (Ps. 40:3). I cannot explain it, but God graciously fashioned a new heart within me during those grueling months of illness. The more time I spent in his presence, the more I wanted to be in his presence. My heart changed. Instead of just looking to him because of my circumstances, I looked to him despite my circumstances.

If you find yourself at a place in your life where you don't know what to do, seek his presence. Let him hold you and answer your heart's deepest cry. He made us to do this, and he wants to answer our cries.

Hold On to Hope

In my search to reclaim the joy Jesus promised, God offered several new revelations to me I had never previously understood. Romans 12:12 says, "Rejoice in our confident hope. Be patient in trouble, and keep on praying" (NLT). Rejoice means "to be glad" or "take delight in." I may not be happy about my situation, but I can still experience joy because I can be glad and have hope in God that my circumstances will change or that I'll change despite my circumstances.

We all experience trials. The Bible even prepares us to expect them. Some are harder and last longer than others. No one is immune, not even Jesus. Jesus gave us the perfect model for handling whatever difficulties we encounter and offered his peace in their place. John 16:33 says, "I have told you these things, so that in me you may have peace. In this world you will have trouble. But take heart! I have overcome the world."

I recently went through another challenging season filled with what seemed like a cascade of successive trials. As I sat outside early one quiet morning, I watched the sun play hide-and-seek behind the clouds. It occurred to me that when the sun ducks behind a cloud, we don't question whether it will come out again. The sun waits. Maybe a moment . . . maybe an hour . . . maybe a day. We know that the doom and gloom of the dark clouds will eventually go away, and the sun will shine again. Similarly, no matter what trials we face, they are temporary. The sun will come out again. God will continue to show his compassion. Lamentations 3:22–23 promises, "The faithful love of the LORD never ends! His mercies never cease. Great is his faithfulness; his mercies begin afresh each morning" (NLT). Sometimes I have to remind myself that I have made it through every difficult situation in my life 100 percent of the time. This gives me hope that I'll survive my current difficulties too.

David encouraged us to rejoice as a prerequisite for experiencing joy: "But may the righteous be glad and rejoice before God; may they be happy and joyful" (Ps. 68:3). We first make the choice to be glad and rejoice, then we experience happiness and joy. While we may not initially feel happy or joyful, intentionally choosing to rejoice can put us on the path to a new way of thinking and experiencing life.

During my difficult days, I felt overwhelmed by despair. I observed others smiling and laughing, and I grieved the loss of such an experience for myself. On one particular weekend, my husband and I attended a conference not far from our home. It took every ounce of strength and sheer willpower for me to get up, get dressed, and get out the door. As my husband drove, I continued the silent argument in my mind regarding all the reasons it wasn't worth the effort to attend. Happy and glad thoughts were pretty much absent from my mind-set at that point. Prior to the keynote address, there was a time of praise and worship. During that prelude to the main focus of the conference, I gained insight about this possibility of acting ourselves into a new way of thinking. Without warning or conscious intent, I realized that as I sang I was smiling. Not only was genuine smiling foreign to me during those dark months, but accompanying my smile was also a hint of happiness and joy. In the blink of an eye, I recognized the pleasant emotional experience like the father recognized the return of his prodigal son. I longed for more. I then very consciously willed myself to continue smiling as I sang and was rewarded with satisfying happiness.

Remembering the promise of Romans 8:28, "And we know that in all things God works for the good of those who love him, who have been called according to his purpose," I maintain hope that whatever my circumstances the God who created the universe can cause them to work out well in the end. This world offers few guarantees. Hard times will come, and days will sometimes seem dark, but the Bible promises that no one whose hope is in God will ever be put to shame (see Ps. 25:3). "But as for me, I watch in hope for the LORD, I wait for God my Savior; my God will hear me" (Micah 7:7). That is a guarantee I am willing to trust!

Be Patient

Another key to maintaining joy, as indicated in Romans 12:12, is that we be patient despite our circumstances. Admittedly, "patient" is not how I would describe myself. I've jokingly told people that I no longer pray for patience for myself or others because God will bring circumstances into our lives to let us practice patience! God is never late, and for that matter, he is rarely early. God is always on time. My friend Sharon Hill says, "We serve an on-time God."

I must confess that because of my achiever mentality I like to have a plan from start to finish for everything. Yes, everything from getting laundry washed, dried, folded, and put away to figuring out the who, what, when, where, and how of hiring a new employee. Having a plan allows me the illusion of being in control, minimizing my anxiety about a situation. The problem with this is it takes the control out of God's hands and transfers it back to me—until something doesn't go as planned and I run back to God, give him control again in desperate prayers, and ask him to fix my current mess. I can picture God shaking his head gently as he thinks, "My dear child, if you had just been patient in your situation and let me handle it in my perfect timing, we wouldn't have this mess to remedy." As I practice patience, I remember that the outcome is not dependent on me but on God. He has broad shoulders—he can handle it. Patience in times of adversity is key to experiencing joy.

> *Patience in times of adversity is key to experiencing joy.*

Don't Underestimate Prayer

Prayer is another way to combat the enemy's attempts to steal our joy. Romans 12:12 encourages continual prayer. Ask and keep on asking. Jesus encouraged us to do this very thing when he said, "Until now you have not asked for anything in my name. Ask and you will receive, and your joy will be complete" (John 16:24).

I've struggled to engage in sustained prayer. I pray, but I haven't always been diligent in my prayers—especially for myself. Until I gained a greater appreciation of my identity as a daughter of the Most High God, my prayer life was far from complete. I had faith that God would answer my prayers on behalf of other people. I firmly believed he would answer others' prayers on my behalf.

What I didn't effectively believe was that God would answer my prayers for my own needs. The enemy cunningly whispered to me, "He knows what you've done. Why would he reward the prayers of a sinner like you? If you do more, then maybe he will love you enough to take your requests seriously." These lies kept me silent and made it hard for me to accept, appreciate, and receive God's goodness. But God's Word says his promises are "Yes" and "Amen" (see 2 Cor. 1:20). These promises are as true for us as they were for the people who lived during biblical times. And they are as true for you now as they are for me.

During the days I despaired the most, I could almost hear God imploring, "Go ahead, please ask, keep on asking." I am doing the same to you. Tell him your heart's desires. He is a good God. He came to give you an abundant, full, complete life. Ask him how to receive it. He promises you will receive and your joy will be complete.

Learning to pray fervently was not immediate for me. As I've shared with you, I prayed three specific requests every day for a very long time. I was in a desperate place. I knew I could not rely on myself or my own knowledge to regain a sure footing on solid ground. I also knew I could not trust my emotions because they whipped me around and left me feeling beaten up. God had to be my anchor. I couldn't afford to give up on him; he was the only constant factor in my life.

The enemy wants to discourage us. The enemy wants us to feel defeated. That doesn't mean he gets to make us feel that way! I lived for decades not recognizing the enemy's destruction and deceit in my life. His voice sounded like my own voice. As long as I listened and accepted his lies as being true, he kept me discouraged. For a long time I felt defeated. I finally landed in an overwhelmingly desperate place where I knew that if I gave in, I would self-destruct, but if I kept seeking God, he would save me.

Until then, I hadn't truly embraced the reality of my own choice in the matter. The enemy whispered lies into my ears for years, and I believed them:

"You're always going to feel this way."

"Depression is in your genes—you don't stand a chance."

"You don't deserve to experience joy."

"You're joy-immune."

Maybe you've thought some of those same things. Don't give in to those thoughts, though they may sound convincing. They aren't God's truth!

I had to make the daily choice to believe truth and listen to the Word of God. In the Word, we are encouraged to "pray continually" (1 Thess. 5:17). Hebrews 4:16 urges us to approach God's throne "boldly" so we might receive grace and help in our time of need. Desperation breeds boldness. I boldly prayed, asking God to show me how he viewed me. Truthfully, I wasn't sure I was ready for what I might discover. I also boldly asked God not only to show me what joy was but also to give it to me in abundance. I needed God's grace, and I recognized that if ever I was in a time of need, it was then. I needed to come boldly before God's throne in prayer. Maybe you do too.

Practice Gratitude

In the book of Psalms, David repeatedly reveals the importance of gratitude in the midst of our struggles. "Sacrifice thank offerings to God" (Ps. 50:14). Our gratitude and thankfulness to God are both a sacrifice and an offering. "I will sacrifice a thank offering to you and call on the name of the LORD" (Ps. 116:17). It strikes me that the words *sacrifice* and *offering* were both used in conjunction with David's call to show God gratitude. These two terms suggest an attitude of the heart.

During my bouts of depression, I didn't tend to be very grateful. Depression often diverts our attention inward toward ourselves.

During those painful, despairing weeks and months, I focused on how I felt, how my situation wasn't improving, and what I wanted to change in myself or my circumstances. Even when I considered others, I always came back to how much worse I felt than they did.

Reading the verses from Psalms shook my introspective framework. They made me sit up and acknowledge the change that was necessary in my heart and my subsequent actions. Sacrifice meant I would forego my own needs, wants, habits, and tendencies in favor of another. Offering meant I would not hold back but instead give God the gift of my worship and praise. A sacrifice and offering of thanksgiving meant I would give up my selfish tendency of thinking of myself first and instead give focused attention to the greatness and faithfulness of my heavenly Father as an act of worship. When I felt defeated and prone to self-pity, it truly felt like a sacrifice and an offering to willfully set aside my own aches, needs, and desires while giving God my gratitude for all he had done and would do to provide for me.

When we focus on what we have to be thankful for, a subtle shift takes place in our hearts and our minds. Our focus moves from ourselves and our circumstances to God and his generosity, goodness, and faithfulness.

Theodore Roosevelt said that, "Comparison is the thief of joy." When we compare ourselves to others, we focus on all we do not have. We hear of families taking luxury trips while we are working to make ends meet. We have friends who enjoy the company of family and friends while we have lost loved ones. We hear of the fancy gifts others are giving or receiving during the holidays while we are trying to keep the heat on. When we look at what others have or are doing, we can believe we don't measure up.

Part of the problem with comparison is that we can always find others who have more, do more, and achieve more. But we can also always find others who have less, do less, and achieve less. Honestly, there really is no fair comparison because no two people start off on equal ground. Our backgrounds are not the same, our genetic contributors are different, our prior experiences are varied, and even if we have the same family and are raised in the same home, our gifts, talents, dreams, and aspirations are all different.

The comparison game had defeated me too. One Christmas, my holiday cheer was dampened by severe physical pain from foot surgery that left me in worse shape than I had been in prior to the surgery. My husband and I attended a holiday event. I was still in a surgical boot because it was the only thing that would fit or offer any degree of comfort and protection. I can throw a pretty good pity party, and at that point I did. I was all "woe is me" about having to wear a surgical boot to a holiday party.

A couple of evenings later as I scrolled through posts on social media, a particular post caught my attention and paralyzed me for more than a few moments. Even now I can't tell you what the caption read—that wasn't what captivated my heart or brought me to my knees in repentance. The photo showed the worn shoes on a homeless individual's feet. His feet had worn through the bottom of what were probably the only socks and shoes he had.

I had compared myself to all those I had seen with beautiful feet and even prettier shoes, wishing I had what they had. But now I was the one feeling grateful. A blinged-out surgical boot suddenly looked gorgeous and provided much more warmth and comfort. The photo radically changed my perspective.

Now when I catch myself comparing myself to those who seemingly have more or achieve more, I remember that there are many people who would be grateful to have what I have. I'm reminded to practice gratitude and to count my blessings. Comparison steals our joy when we compare ourselves to others and don't enjoy the blessings we have. I must choose to focus on my blessings.

When we focus on what we don't have or wish we had, life will always feel inadequate and wanting. But gratitude and thankfulness open the door to joy. Gratitude helps us appreciate our blessings and makes them sufficient. Melody Beattie suggested, "Gratitude unlocks the fullness of life. It turns what we have into enough, and more. It turns denial into acceptance, chaos to order, and confusion to clarity. It can turn a meal into a feast, a house into a home, a stranger into a friend. Gratitude makes sense of our past, brings peace for today, and creates a vision for tomorrow."[5]

Do for Others

Karl Menninger was a famous American psychiatrist of the early twentieth century. Once during a lecture on mental health issues, someone in the audience asked him his advice for a person experiencing an impending nervous breakdown.

Comparison steals our joy when we compare ourselves to others and don't enjoy the blessings we have.

Since he was a psychiatrist, you might think he would suggest this person see a psychiatrist who would prescribe medication or inpatient hospitalization. Astonishingly, he responded by suggesting that the afflicted individual leave their home, cross the railroad tracks, seek out someone in need, and meet that need.

What Menninger knew was that depression can be perpetuated by focusing on ourselves. When we focus instead on others and their needs, our own pain is lessened.

Luke shared this principle in the book of Acts: "In everything I did, I showed you that by this kind of hard work we must help the weak, remembering the words the Lord Jesus himself said: 'It is more blessed to give than to receive'" (20:35).

Helping others is not always the easiest thing to do when we are depressed. I know. I remember feeling so down that I wondered if I would ever again have a day without tears. And at the same time, I felt guilty because in my mind I didn't have a valid reason to feel down. I had friends who grieved children who had died from illness, children who had died by suicide, and children who were imprisoned. I had friends whose spouses were ill and friends who had gone through divorce. What reason did I have to feel down?

I often didn't have the energy or the motivation for anything that wasn't an absolute necessity, and even for those things they were tenuous. On one occasion a friend was moving and, in a moment of temporarily renewed energy, I offered my help. When the move date actually came, however, I wondered why I had made the offer. I didn't have the energy I had had on the day I offered my help. But during those few hours of physical labor, putting someone else's needs before my own, my former self reemerged. And in helping someone else, taking the focus off myself, I felt good. For a short while I appreciated a fresh understanding of Nehemiah 8:10: "The joy of the Lord is your strength."

Joy comes through the doorway of thanksgiving and gratitude.

When we are depressed, we have a choice to make. We can let depression define us, or we can desire joy enough to pursue it with prayer, obedience, gratitude, and sacrifice. Jesus offers us the same joy he had: the fullest joy possible. What I've learned is that joy comes through the doorway of thanksgiving and gratitude. As Proverbs 23:7 tells us, we are what we think in our hearts. As we become increasingly grateful, God exchanges our worries and sorrow for his peace, joy, and abundant life. Our circumstances may not change, but our mind-set does.

Your Rx

1. There is no greater priority or any greater protection than being in God's presence. Think about your daily routine. Consider how often you consciously seek God's presence. What is one thing you can do to more frequently or more consistently get alone and be in God's presence?

2. Consider purchasing a new journal or notebook and using it to daily record the things God brings to your mind to be thankful for. Some days you might record only one thing and others you might rattle off a dozen, but aim for three new specific things daily.

3. Look up the following verses: John 16:24; Romans 12:12; 15:13; James 4:8. Write them on index cards and place them where you will see them frequently. Read each of these passages aloud three times daily, committing them to memory.

My Prayer for You

Father, I remember the heartache of those dark days when my daily experience was devoid of joy. I contrast that with the joy you promise us in your Word. You died so that we could experience an abundant life with peace and joy. It is my prayer that you will return the joy of their salvation to this dear one now. Reveal your joy in big and small ways, and use your joy to provide strength for today's battle. As you promised in Job 8:21, I pray that you will fill their mouth with laughter and their lips with shouts of joy! In the mighty name of Jesus, amen.

Recommended Playlist ....

"(Never Gonna) Steal My Joy," Mandisa, © 2007 by Sparrow Records

"Your Presence Is Heaven to Me," Israel Houghton, © 2012 by Integrity/Columbia

"Hope's Anthem," William Matthews, © 2013 by Bethel Music

"There Is None Like You," Darlene Zschech, © 2000 by Word/Epic

"Here Is Our King," David Crowder, © 2013 by sixstepsrecords

"There Is None Like You," Trevor Walker, © 2013 by Trevor Walker

"Find You on My Knees," Kari Jobe, © 2012 by Sparrow Records

"If I Could Just Sit with You Awhile," Dennis Jernigan, © 1998 by Shepherd's Heart Music

"Hope in Front of Me," Danny Gokey, © 2014 by BMG Rights Management

6

Reclaim Your Peace

Now may the Lord of peace himself give you peace at all times and in every way. The Lord be with all of you.

2 Thessalonians 3:16

Peace isn't the absence of the dark. Peace is the assurance of God's presence in the midst of the dark.

Ann Voskamp

As if stealing our joy isn't bad enough, the enemy doesn't stop there. His mission is to defeat us. Remember, he comes to steal, kill, and destroy. We have talked about his vicious attacks to steal our joy, but another reason depression is such a painful experience is because the enemy kills our peace.

While suffering through depression, not only do we not feel "all is well with the world," but in our despair, we also feel "nothing is right with the world." We are no longer able to see the speed bumps of life for the little blips they are in our day. Rather, they often seem like mountains set before us to taunt, tease, and tower over us.

What Is Peace?

You are not alone if you wonder, "What is peace?"

For many years I considered peace a nice word in a Christmas carol. Now I think of peace as an absence of worry, concern, or annoyance—a calm experience in both my mind and my heart. Think of that relaxed sensation that overtakes you as you teeter between wakefulness and sleep.

The enemy's voice sounds just like our own, making it difficult to detect.

Because our enemy, the father of lies, deceives us about ourselves, others, and God, we stray from the truth in our thoughts, beliefs, attitudes, emotions, and behavior. As we veer from the truth, we experience the demolition of our God-given peace, which is the very thing that "transcends all understanding" and guards our hearts and minds in Christ Jesus (Phil. 4:7). The enemy's voice sounds just like our own, speaking to us in the first person, making it difficult to detect. We know faith or believing comes from hearing (Rom. 10:17), and the more we hear the deceptive proclamations of the enemy, the more we believe them and the farther we drift from peace.

What Happened to Peace?

The enemy introduced himself to Eve in the garden. Since his entrance on the stage of our lives, he has sought to separate us from God's truth through deception, cunning, and perversion. After Adam and Eve ate from the enemy's menu, they experienced shame at their newly recognized nakedness and hid from God—the very God who created them and walked with them in the garden. In doing so, they gave up their peace.

Jesus tells us in John 14:27 that he gives us peace as his gift: "Peace. I don't leave you the way you're used to being left—feeling abandoned, bereft. So don't be upset. Don't be distraught" (Message). I suspect that if we could have had peace in our hearts on our own, Jesus would not have left it with us as a gift.

God longs for his children to have peace. God knew we would encounter difficult times, but he came to earth to live as a man and experience suffering so that ultimately he could be our hero, empathize with our suffering, and help us overcome those difficult times with his peace. "I have told you these things, so that in me you may have peace. In this world you will have trouble. But take heart! I have overcome the world" (John 16:33). Interestingly, Jesus combined peace and trouble. The offer of peace does not remove the reality of trouble, and the experience of trouble does not annihilate the promise of peace. He shared a fundamental principle we cannot lose sight of: *in him* we can have peace, not on our own. We can rejoice in the assurance of the outcome! Our victory in this battle has already been guaranteed.

How the Enemy Kills Our Peace

The Enemy Invokes Anxiety

I could give you a fancy definition of anxiety, but if you are like me, I suspect that wouldn't be helpful. Simply put, anxiety is the absence of peace. Anxiety always stems from a feeling of being out of control. If we surrender to God, give up our need for control, and let him be in control, then we can remain in perfect peace. "But as for me, I watch in hope for the LORD, I wait for God my Savior; my God will hear me" (Micah 7:7).

Many who experience the suffering caused by depression also experience anxiety. In fact, for some, anxiety is what they identify with before recognizing depression for what it is. Don Colbert, in his book *The Bible Cure for Depression and Anxiety*, estimates that "about 80 percent of depressed individuals experience physiological anxiety symptoms: unrealistic apprehensions, fears, worry, agitation, irritability, or panic attacks," while "some 60 percent of people with depression experience anxiety-related physical symptoms: headaches, irritable bowel syndrome, chronic fatigue, and chronic pain."[1] An anxious mind is a mind not at peace.

In the popular book series called Don't Sweat the Small Stuff, the front cover or the first couple of pages of each book always mention that "it's all small stuff." I appreciate this perspective, although I rarely remember it when I'm sweating through difficult circumstances. Life certainly throws us challenges, and we will go through times of adversity. The Bible even warns us to expect it. The question is, Will we let the enemy use those times to kill our peace?

Interestingly, I've made it through all those difficult times 100 percent of the time. I've made it through illnesses, surgeries, moves, family members' deaths, my husband's cancer, a miscarriage, and many more, every single time. I didn't enjoy the experiences at the time, and many I wouldn't choose to go through again, but with God's help, I survived them and I grew from many of them.

I still come up against difficult and sometimes very painful circumstances, but my perspective has changed. Previously, I encountered challenges or trials and worried and fretted about what to do and about the outcome. My to-do list grew to great lengths before I stilled my mind long enough to pray. Jesus tells us, however, "Therefore do not worry about tomorrow, for tomorrow will worry about itself. Each day has enough trouble of its own" (Matt. 6:34).

When I worry, I'm believing the enemy's lies: "You can handle this one on your own." Or "If it's going to be done right, you better do it yourself." Or "People always let you down, so it's better not to trust or depend on them and take care of yourself." When I come into agreement with the enemy's lies, I take my eyes off God and focus on myself and my circumstances. I operate in my own knowledge and my own strength. I know my limitations and capabilities and that I have only a limited vision of the very near future, so I worry because I know that in my own efforts I am insufficient. That robs me of peace and joy.

Now I'm learning to live moment by moment, trusting God's care for the situation and being thankful for his provision. My focus then remains on the Solver of my problem rather than on my circumstances. "'Because he loves me,' says the LORD, 'I will rescue him; I will protect him, for he acknowledges my name. He will call on me, and I will answer him; I will be with him in trouble, I will deliver him and honor him. With long life I will satisfy him and show him my salvation'" (Ps. 91:14–16).

Fear is a misappropriation of our attentional resources that robs us of peace. When we worry, we give our attention to our own abilities or lack thereof rather than focusing on God's promises to rescue us, protect us, answer us, be with us in trouble, deliver us, and satisfy us. Faith allows God the privilege of getting the glory for providing for our needs and keeps us in perfect peace despite our circumstances.

> *Fear is a misappropriation of our attentional resources that robs us of peace.*

The Enemy Destroys Our View of Self

In the valley of depression, we tend to focus on, and ultimately compare, our deficiencies to others' strengths, our lack to others' plenty, and our pain to others' joy. In our despair, we often look at the negative rather than the positive because the negative is so pronounced. Imagine trying to watch a movie with a tall person with big hair sitting immediately in front of you. In the same way, the enemy puts negativity in our field of vision to obstruct our view.

Our enemy doesn't play fair. He studies us and knows us better than we know ourselves. He observes our reactions, words, and behaviors and also those of our family members. He knows the generational tendencies that exist and is equally aware of our fear and repulsion concerning them. Depression destroys our opinion of ourselves. The enemy's attacks on our character, our behavior, and our condition devastate our self-esteem and often make us feel worthless. This is in direct opposition to what God's truth tells us in 1 John 4:4: "You, dear children, are from God and have overcome them, because the one who is in you is greater than the one who is in the world."

You may not feel treasured, or even acceptable, but you are. In Ephesians 1:6, Paul says that all who believe in Christ have been "accepted in the beloved" (KJV). That means God doesn't look at us and shake his head disapprovingly because of all our faults and imperfections. No! He accepts us just as he accepts Jesus. To him, our areas of imperfection are opportunities for him to bless us as he helps us to begin living in our new identity as children of a king.

It amazes me how much our attitude affects our success and how people view us. Henry Ford said, "Whether you think that you can, or that you can't, you are usually right."[2] This statement exudes truth. In the same way, I've been making a more deliberate effort to surround myself with positive people and to avoid those who lean toward negativity because I can get wrapped up in their mind-set and slip down the negative slope myself. Hence the saying "Misery loves company."

We must deliberately choose a right attitude. We can't change the past, frequently we can't change our circumstances, and we can't change how other people behave. But we can choose our attitude.

This morning in Texas, storms broke loose. Rain has poured for the past twelve hours and will continue for the next twelve. I slipped while loading my car for work. Rain then drenched my lower half as I ran from the car to the office door. I sit here typing while my pant legs drip dry and my trouser socks turn cold. Patients will be late for their appointments, and my son's cross-country meet will be canceled. And so on. It would be so easy for me to react irritably.

Still, I have a choice. I choose to be joyous and grateful for this rain. The crops desperately need it. Our severe drought conditions have dried up many of the lakes, and where there used to be many feet of water, there is now only sand and weeds. And after a couple days of rain, I will appreciate the sunshine all the more when it returns!

In Philippians 4:8, we are admonished to take steps to ensure our attitude is right: "Whatever is true, whatever is noble, whatever is right, whatever is pure, whatever is lovely, whatever is admirable—if anything is excellent or praiseworthy—think about such things." This verse isn't referring to just things or events; God also wants us to think about the positive, admirable, praiseworthy aspects *of ourselves* and quit listening to the enemy's reminders of all the areas in which he says we don't measure up. This verse reminds us to focus our attention on God's truth and disregard the enemy's denigrating whispers.

The Enemy Paralyzes Us with Shame

Have you ever said, "I am so ashamed"? Or have you ever been told, "You should be ashamed of yourself"? Perhaps you can recall times when you felt embarrassed. Embarrassment is another face of shame. Shame can be described as a painful feeling stemming from an awareness of having done or been involved in something disgraceful, inappropriate, unreasonable, or wrong resulting in guilt or remorse. In essence, shame says, "I am a mistake" rather than the truth, which says, "I made a mistake."

The enemy uses shame as a tool to keep us from going deeper in our relationships with others and God. For many of us shame causes us to hide behind a mask, hoping others will like the illusion of ourselves rather than reject the reality of our imperfection. Shame causes us to believe we cannot risk being our true selves around others for fear of rejection because of our mistakes.

Consider the child who breaks his mother's decorative vase when the ball he was told not to throw in the house accidentally slips from his hand, turning the treasured glass into shattered pieces on the floor. He attempts to clean it up (as well as a typical child might) and never mentions it to his mother, hoping she won't notice. His mother, however, immediately notices the missing vase but waits patiently to be told of its whereabouts. Feeling guilty, the young boy suffers stomachaches, avoids eye contact with his mother, and does additional chores without being asked. The longer he hides the truth, the worse he feels. When he can keep the secret no longer, he tearfully confesses to his mother, fearful of his fate. She embraces him, assures him of her forgiveness, then chuckles before telling him her little secret. She never liked the vase much anyway but kept it on display because it was a gift from her mother-in-law.

Shame says, "I am a mistake" rather than the truth, which says, "I made a mistake."

Shame carries with it fear and causes us to hide. Clients share their most painful secrets with me—painful because they are hidden as a result of shame. I wish people knew that I am rarely surprised by what I hear, and I don't judge. The pain my patients carry while holding on to their secrets is so much worse than anything they experience by telling me. Secrets only hold their power while they are kept in the dark. In our shame, we believe the enemy's lies that "no one will understand" or "you'll lose all your friends if they find out what you did." Once those shameful situations are brought into the light, the enemy loses his negative hold over us and healing can begin.

We lose our peace when we hide our brokenness. We must choose to believe God's truth, which says, "Therefore, there is now no condemnation for those who are in Christ Jesus" (Rom. 8:1). Because Christ died to pay the price for all our imperfections, God doesn't condemn us or view us as guilty. We are loved and accepted because of what Christ did for us when he wiped our slates clean.

Disappointment overwhelms me when I think of the damage inflicted on our hearts by the perpetuation of the stigma of mental health issues. I get frustrated that shame is hurled at those who suffer from conditions such as depression, as if anyone would consciously choose such suffering. Even worse is the message that there is something wrong with the afflicted, until a celebrity talks about suffering from the same condition. All of a sudden the stigma is lessened and the condition is almost celebrated, as if a celebrity is more worthy or worthwhile than the common person who struggles. We are all worthy, we are all important, and if anyone ever suffers, we should consider it a viable concern.

If we destigmatize a condition like depression only when a celebrity or someone famous talks about their struggles, then perhaps we should consider some of the earliest well-known individuals who made their despair known. In the Bible, David routinely wrote of his despair; Job suffered with symptoms of depression; even Jesus wept. Some of God's greatest men struggled, and their stories were included in the most inspired book in history. I believe that if God included their stories in his Book, then he doesn't attach shame to their experience, and neither should we. Unfortunately, that is where the enemy disagrees.

What we have to remember is that anxiety, shame, and a distorted view of ourselves are all tools utilized by the biggest liar to roam the earth. They are not from God. Nor are they consistent with God's truth. And they steal our peace.

How to Live a Life of Peace

Depend on God

The enemy of our souls strives to kill our peace by keeping us focused on ourselves instead of depending on God, the giver of peace. We so easily set our sights on what we have to accomplish, too often forgetting that God prefers to set the course for our day. As Proverbs 16:9 declares, "We can make our plans, but the LORD determines our steps" (NLT). We have traded in our peace and bought into the mantra (which is based on another lie of the enemy), "If it's going to be, it's up to me."

It wasn't until I was bedridden and unable to do anything for myself that I realized the enemy had convinced me of a lie, but God's truth says, "You will keep in perfect peace those whose minds are steadfast, because they trust in you" (Isa. 26:3). Rather than depending on myself to accomplish everything, I had to trust God and depend on him for everything I needed. Depending on myself means depending on my own limited strength, whereas depending on God grants me the assurance that "I can do all this through him who gives me strength" (Phil. 4:13).

Sometimes the word *dependence* conjures up a negative connotation. We are praised and recognized for our independence. We honor pioneers in various fields for being independent thinkers and daring to believe what others wouldn't. In shifting our dependence from ourselves to God, however, we can experience peace knowing the responsibility for the result rests on his capable shoulders. He promised us in Matthew 5:6 that if any of us hunger and thirst for more of him, he will fill us. If we depend on him, he faithfully provides for our needs, allowing us to rest in the peace of his provision.

It took the suffering of a helpless little one for me to appreciate how much God delights in providing for his children. One day as I sat typing reports at my office desk, I heard an unusual but endearing sound. I glanced down near my feet to see our office mascot, a nine-pound Pomeranian named Maddy, whimpering softly. Most days she accompanied me to the office, sleeping in her little puppy pod while patients remain unaware of her presence. Hearing her whimper, I reflexively asked, "What?" She answered with more whimpering while she looked straight into my eyes. I studied her, then noticed the reason for her anguish. Her fur had become matted around a bur, and her nail had become lodged in the matted knot, ensnaring her paw. She couldn't free herself and whimpered for me to come to her assistance. As I did, she quickly licked my hand, then returned to a peaceful slumber.

I've replayed this scene in my mind. This young creature became trapped in a predicament she was helpless to fix without assistance. She cried out in distress, and I rescued her. In return, I received a quick thanks before she returned to her plans for the day. While her suffering saddened me, it also made me feel needed, then disillusioned by how quickly she went on her way.

I wonder how often God feels that way with me. At times, I'm tentative and apprehensive, while too often I blaze ahead with an independent streak, working myself into a tizzy and waiting to go to him until I have no other option but to ask for help. Then I wave the white flag in distress, pray for his rescue, and offer a quick thanks before going off again to do my own thing. Surely he must think, "I wait here eagerly every day for you to call on my name. I come when you call only to receive a brief acknowledgment before I begin my eager wait all over again. How I wish you would grant a little more time in my presence."

I now realize that just as peace is God's gift to us, peace comes from being in God's presence. "I call to God, and the LORD saves me. Evening, morning and noon I cry out in distress, and he hears my voice. He ransoms me unharmed from the battle waged against me, even though many oppose me" (Ps. 55:16–18). Peace is also found when we ignore the lies of the enemy and share our concerns with God. "Cast your cares on the LORD and he will sustain you; he will never let the righteous be shaken" (Ps. 55:22).

I have never heard God in an audible voice, although I know some people have. I frequently sense God's presence through music and in nature. One evening, nearing the end of a walk, I stood outside and stared at the stars. The song "The More I Seek You" wafted through my earbuds and led me into a prayerful conversation with God about recent events in my life—events for which only he could provide answers and solutions.

I poured out my heart and told him I wanted to see him more and to know him more. I wanted to sit at his feet, hear him speak, know his heart toward me. As tears started to roll down my cheek with the gut-wrenching honesty of my plea, I begged him to let me feel his arms around me, to let me know his love in a deeper and more intimate way. As I felt the cool evening breeze envelop me, it was as if the Lord said, "You just did." With that, I melted in his peace.

Rid Yourself of Bitterness and Resentment with Forgiveness

Bitterness prevents us from having peace. Bitterness begins with unforgiveness. When we hold resentment and unforgiveness in our hearts, they are like a clogged septic tank—they begin to stink.

The Word of God is clear on this issue. There is no way to sugarcoat it. Bitterness in our hearts causes many of our problems. "See to it that no one falls short of the grace of God and that no bitter root grows up to cause trouble and defile many" (Heb. 12:15). It's not merely a suggestion but a command that we forgive others, and then God will forgive us. "For if you forgive other people when they sin against you, your heavenly Father will also forgive you" (Matt. 6:14).

The Word not only tells us to release bitterness and forgive those who have hurt us but also gives us the example of God forgiving us for all our sins and imperfections. "Get rid of all bitterness, rage and anger, brawling and slander, along with every form of malice. Be kind and compassionate to one another, forgiving each other, just as in Christ God forgave you" (Eph. 4:31–32).

If we desire to experience God's peace, then we must live peaceably with others. The only way to do this is to forgive them for any offense they knowingly or unknowingly committed against us. "Finally, brothers and sisters, rejoice! Strive for full restoration, encourage one another, be of one mind, live in peace. And the God of love and peace will be with you" (2 Cor. 13:11).

Check Your Thoughts

I knew from my over two decades of work as a clinical neuropsychologist that our thoughts have a powerful effect on our beliefs and behaviors. Scripture declares, "As he thinks in his heart, so is he" (Prov. 23:7 NKJV). I very much dislike giving my patients diagnoses, because too often I see those labels used as excuses rather than explanations or motivations for change. Tom Ziglar has said, "What you feed your mind determines your appetite."[3]

We often cannot control what happens to us, but we can control our responses. And our responses often directly influence the outcomes. When I was struggling, I responded to someone's question about my thoughts with "I didn't have a choice." As the words effortlessly flowed across my lips, my body reflexively shuddered. It was as if my mind, my mouth, and my heart knew there had been a seismic disconnect in that exchange. Something wasn't sitting right within me.

With my mouth I was repeating the lie I had been offered by the enemy, while my mind knew that we always have some degree of choice. My heart knew this was a lie that needed to be transplanted with God's truth. God's Word tells us, "We demolish arguments and every pretension that sets itself up against the knowledge of God, and we take captive every thought to make it obedient to Christ" (2 Cor. 10:5). If God tells us to take every thought captive, he must give us the ability to choose what we will think and what we will believe.

I had to face myself in the mirror and decide how I was going to respond. Was I going to let depression define me? Was I going to believe I was a depressed person, or was I going to take that thought captive and choose to believe I was more than an overcomer and victorious in Christ Jesus?

Did I truly want peace badly enough to seek it, or was I going to continue to believe the lie that I was a victim of my circumstances? I had worked with enough patients and I had seen enough scenarios play out with various friends and family members to know it was my choice.

To a large extent, I had to take responsibility for the outcome. I had to consciously determine to look at my situation from God's perspective and disregard any other, including my own habitual frame of reference. I had to determine not to keep my eyes on my problems and get lulled into self-pity, which never accomplishes anything but makes depression worse. I had to put my eyes on him. Don't let me fool you. It wasn't easy. Some days were so painful and hard it made me wonder if I was peace-immune.

That was just another lie of the enemy, a lie I had believed far too long. I was finally sick of it. I deserved better than that. My Savior died so I could have better than that! "I have told you these things so that you can have *the same joy I have* and so that your joy will be *the fullest possible joy*!" (John 15:11 NCV, emphasis added). It's possible for me not just to experience joy and peace but to have a peace- and joy-filled life. You can too. God said it. It's true. Do you believe it?

God desires to be our peace. One of his names is Jehovah-Shalom, God of peace. His peace can mitigate all our chaos, all our anxiety. We are promised a reward of peace if we keep our mind on him and willfully take every thought captive, aligning it with God's truth and trusting in him. "You will keep in perfect peace those whose minds are steadfast, because they trust in you" (Isa. 26:3).

Your Rx

1. Think about how the enemy kills your peace. Pray and ask God to show you how and when you've given up your peace. Ask him to reveal his truth.

2. Look up the following verses: Isaiah 26:3; Matthew 5:6; John 14:27; 16:33; 2 Corinthians 13:11. Write them on index cards and place them where you will see them frequently. Read each of these passages aloud three times daily, committing them to memory.

3. Three of the ways to regain our peace are to depend on God, rid ourselves of bitterness and resentment with forgiveness, and be vigilant in checking our thoughts and aligning them with God's truth. Pray and ask God whom you need to forgive (which may include yourself!). Then ask for his help to depend on him, forgive those he brought to mind, and take every thought captive to line up with his truth.

My Prayer for You

Father, my heartfelt cry is that you will bless and keep this dear one who is journeying through the valley of depression.

We often forget where our priorities should lie. We allow ourselves to become deceived by the urgency of this call or that, and before we know it, our day is full, we are tired, and you are still waiting to share it with us. Help us to remember you created us for companionship with you—nothing delights you more—and that in time spent with you our peace is renewed. I pray you will be true to your Word as you make your face to shine upon us and be gracious to us. I pray you will turn your face toward us and give us peace. Because Jesus came to give us peace, amen.

Recommended Playlist

"It Is Well," Bethel, © 2014 by Bethel Music

"Here," Kari Jobe, © 2012 by Sparrow Records

"Speak Life," TobyMac, © 2012 by ForeFront Records

"Bless Us and Keep Us," John Waller, © 2011 by City of Peace Media Inc.

"Letting Go," Bethel, © 2014 by Bethel Music

"I Don't Know How," Jason Gray, © 2014 by Centricity Music

"As I Am," Jason Gray, © 2014 by Centricity Music

"Love Not Done with You," Jason Gray, © 2014 by Centricity Music

"The Remedy," Ayiesha Woods, © 2006 by Gotee Records

7

Reestablish Your Identity

You, dear children, are from God and have overcome them, because the one who is in you is greater than the one who is in the world.

1 John 4:4

Define yourself radically as one beloved by God. Every other identity is illusion.

Brennan Manning

The enemy not only seeks to steal our joy and kill our peace but also desires to destroy our identity. Decades of interviews and observations in private practice suggest that many of the problems, struggles, and conditions we deal with result from a case of mistaken identity. In her book *Clout*, Jenni Catron says, "To know yourself, you have to know your Creator."[1] I have found this to be true.

Throughout our lives, many voices clamor to be heard. If we do not remain vigilant about identifying which voices we listen to and hence believe, we will unconsciously exchange our beliefs about our identity for convincing counterfeits.

God Created Good

Do you ever feel small? Insignificant? Overlooked?

Do you compare yourself to others and feel insecure or like you don't measure up? Maybe you just wonder about your purpose.

I camped there for many years. Born prematurely as a low birth-weight baby, I never did catch up in size to my peers. I did not grow after about sixth grade and have always wished for just another inch or two so I would measure at least five feet tall. But it was not to be.

It doesn't seem to matter whether we are tall or short, heavy or thin, rich or poor. We all have insecurities. We all sometimes wish we could be something or someone different.

Early on, we begin listening to the lying whispers that color our perception of ourselves, others, and God. We are tempted to equate our worth with external factors: our financial situation, our relationship status, or our position or accomplishments.

Yet regardless of anything we do, earn, or have, God delights in us as his masterpiece: "For we are God's masterpiece. He has created us anew in Christ Jesus, so we can do the good things he planned for us long ago" (Eph. 2:10 NLT). God created us in his image. In doing so, he graced us with the ultimate compliment. After a child is born, nothing delights the parent more than when people remark about the baby's resemblance to the parent. The same is true of God—he delights in the fact that we bear his image.

The first instance of God blessing anything was in Genesis 1:22, where we read that "God blessed them" (Adam and Eve) and told them to be fruitful and multiply. God deemed all he made good but after creating man, he deemed it was very good (see Gen. 1:31). Since the beginning of time, God has looked upon us as a masterpiece and declared us good. He is incapable of making anything other than good.

The Enemy's Plot to Destroy Our Identity

But there has been a plot against us since creation. Since the beginning of humanity, the enemy has worked to distract us from God's view of us as good, to convince us otherwise. If we think back to the garden of Eden, Adam and Eve were content and enjoyed the garden naked and unashamed. Things changed when the serpent entered paradise. He tempted Eve and lied to her, causing her to question God. Then, as if that wasn't enough, he began his work as "the accuser of our brethren" (Rev. 12:10 KJV). So often we are unaware of our imperfections and flaws until the enemy uses others to bring them to our awareness. "But I am afraid that just as Eve was deceived by the serpent's cunning, your minds may somehow be led astray from your sincere and pure devotion to Christ" (2 Cor. 11:3).

The enemy has worked to distract us from God's view of us as good, to convince us otherwise.

This was certainly true in my own life. Only three years old when I was stricken with an undiagnosable and life-threatening illness, I was left to deal with the physical and emotional ramifications the rest of my life. What doctors could never diagnose but now hypothesize was similar to polio or Reye's syndrome left me of very petite height and with a physically deformed leg and foot. My feet are two sizes: one a normal woman's size and shape and the other a little girl's size and deformed.

Perhaps peers didn't know any better, or maybe they did. It didn't matter either way—words still wound. Their taunts, jeers, and name-calling served to solidify the lying whispers of the enemy:

"You're ugly."

"People won't like you because you're different."

"You aren't as good as everyone else."

"Since you aren't perfect, you're worthless."

I didn't know I was different from my normally formed and able-bodied peers until they and the enemy of my soul painfully pointed it out. Then I couldn't go back. From then on, all I knew was that I was "less than" everyone else.

I know many whose identity has been shaped by who their parents are or who their parents say they are. Scripture says that the tongue has the power to bring life or death. Parents and other role models in our lives speak either curses or blessings over us, which have the potential to affect our identity. What we must remember is that just as some accept their identity based on who their parents are, we have the privilege of basing our identity on who our heavenly Father is and what he speaks over us, regardless of what our earthly parents say.

Let's return to the scene where our identity first came into question. Upon listening to the enemy's lies, Eve disregarded God's instructions, and desiring to be like God, she ate of the fruit and then gave some to her husband. As a result, their eyes were opened to their nakedness, and in shame they sewed fig leaves together to cover themselves.

No longer free to roam unashamed in the garden, they hid from God among the trees when they heard him. God called to Adam, but he was reluctant to answer. Finally, Adam revealed his whereabouts and explained that they had hid because they were naked. God asked who told them they were naked? The same enemy who told them they were naked gladly points out our faults to us today.

In the same way Adam's identity fell prey to the effects of mingling with the enemy, being "different" affected my identity in many ways. Most notably, I never wanted to be the center of attention, for fear that my flaws would become the focus. I hid behind my own fig leaf. I dressed myself outwardly to hide my deformity and minimize the chance that others would see it and reject me for it.

I also hid behind perfection. As a child, I believed the enemy when he warned, "Others can't and won't love you unless you're perfect, so surely God won't either." Unknowingly, I became driven and very much a perfectionist in an effort to be acceptable and lovable in God's sight.

Who do you believe?

Are you listening to the voices that say you aren't smart enough? Beautiful enough?

Good enough?

If you are listening to those voices, like me, like Adam and Eve, you've been deceived.

Our Identity in God's Eyes

God declared his works wonderful, and that includes us. "I praise you because I am fearfully and wonderfully made; your works are wonderful, I know that full well" (Ps. 139:14).

Most assume the word *fearfully* in this context means we are to fear God. But in the original language, in this context, "fearfully" is not referring to us doing something but to the quality God gave us. Here fearfully means to be honored. This verse is praising God because God made us not only wonderful but also worthy of being honored!

We tend to equate others' identity with what they do and the parts of them we can see. People have judged and found me less worthy because of my petite stature or physical deformity, while others have attributed greater worth or position to me because of my profession. God does not use the same measuring stick. He looks at the condition of the heart. "The LORD does not look at the things people look at. People look at the outward appearance, but the LORD looks at the heart" (1 Sam. 16:7).

Scripture repeatedly validates our identity. "To the praise of the glory of his grace, wherein he hath made us accepted in the beloved" (Eph. 1:6 KJV). In the original language, *accepted* means "to be highly favored," and *beloved* means "love." What hope that offers because God, the Creator of the universe, affirms our identity as being highly favored in his love. Put another way, our identity comes from being his. "I am my beloved's and my beloved is mine" (Song of Sol. 6:3).

The problem comes when we don't know what God says about us, so we are more apt to believe what others say. Before long, we say those same things about ourselves.

As a young child, I loved writing. One of my greatest possessions was a diary—you know the kind, with a lock and key. Everyone I knew had one, and I wanted one more than anything. That diary was the first thing I can remember wanting so badly that it bordered on obsession.

God firmly instilled in me a desire to write. I wrote articles for magazines and submitted them to children's writing competitions, frequently winning my category. I knew I was destined to be a writer. Until . . . I began listening to the voices that said I couldn't and I wouldn't. In graduate school, my dream no longer appeared feasible, as my graduate school professors beat every ounce of self-confidence out of me. They convinced me I couldn't speak or write. While I didn't realize it then, I now know that Satan always attacks the area in which God has called us to minister.

For decades I believed the words I had heard instead of God's truth, which promises, "'For I know the plans I have for you,' declares the Lord, 'plans to prosper you and not to harm you, plans to give you hope and a future'" (Jer. 29:11).

When asked to speak, I turned down the invitations, believing that anyone would do a better job than I. Or I reluctantly accepted but after speaking didn't believe people when they complimented me, thinking they were "just being nice."

Over time I believed that my dream of speaking and writing was futile. I also believed the enemy's lies that because of my height and physical deformity, no one would respect or believe anything I had to say. I became painfully shy and withdrawn. Instead of pursuing the longings in my heart, I put all of my energy into trying to be perfect in my job as a doctor.

When times got difficult, such as during my husband's illness, I did more and worked harder. For several years I worked over one hundred hours a week. I worked at the office until midnight, ran home for a shower and a nap, and then returned to the office by 3:00 or 4:00 a.m. Until I couldn't.

Afflicted by the devastating illness in adulthood that required me to be bedridden and sustained on IV nutrition and hydration, I could no longer be the go-getter I had become. In those devastating days of illness, I could not "do" or "be" and was forced to rest—not something this driven, perfectionist, workaholic knew how to do. I found myself at the end of myself; my identity was stripped away.

He showed me that he never loved me because of what I had done for him. He simply loved me.

As I cried out to God more fervently than ever, a change started taking place. He showed me that he never loved me because of what I had done for him. He simply loved me. Such a profound revelation for this doer who could no longer do.

Sometimes we allow our identity to be shaped by the things we have done or the things we haven't done and later regretted. The enemy loves to swoop in and whisper his lies to shame us into believing we are a disappointment to God. In my bedridden months, I had hour upon hour to reflect on the mistakes I had made:

> "You were too busy working to be a good mother."
>
> "You've let your patients down by not being able to work and treat them."
>
> "You were irresponsible to allow yourself to get so run down that you became ill, and now your family is paying the price."

I felt ashamed, embarrassed, and incapable of fixing the damage I replayed in my mind. God used that experience, however, to give me a revelation of his grace and mercy. He isn't looking for us to be perfect or even productive. Jesus explained that the work God desires us to do is "to believe in the one he has sent" (John 6:29). When we believe in Jesus and accept him as our Savior, God sees us through the perfection of Jesus and calls us both holy and righteous—not because of what we do but because of who Jesus is for us.

Jeremiah 31:3 confirms that God loves us with an everlasting love. He loves us no matter what we do or don't do, what we say or don't say, how good we've been or how badly we've messed up. Everlasting means from the beginning of time through eternity. There is no end to his love for me—or for you.

This is the opposite of what the enemy wants us to believe. Just like he twisted the truth with Eve, he does the same with you and me:

> "Do you *really* think God can love you with your flaws?"
>
> "You really messed up big time. Surely God cannot forgive *that*."
>
> "Why would God love you/bless you/forgive you/use you when everyone else is better than you?"

I later underwent reconstructive foot surgery to fix the deformity from my childhood illness. My hopes were high for a new foot. A beautiful foot. A "normal" foot. When the surgeon allowed me to ditch the surgical boot and return to wearing my regular shoes, I spent hours one Sunday morning prior to church trying on every pair of shoes in my closet only to find that not a single shoe fit my foot. The surgery left me unable to wear even the few shoes I had been able to find in my presurgical mismatched sizes, and served as a reminder of my flaws and inadequacies.

I had never been one to express to God my hurt and anger over my disfigurement. After all, I had read the book of Job. I knew how God responded to Job when Job asked, "Why?" But that day I had a temper tantrum with God. That day I cried years' worth of tears in despair and frustration. That day I finally got honest and unburdened my heart and told God how I really felt.

I eventually chuckled through my tears as I sensed him say, "At least you are talking to me about it now." You see, I had believed the enemy's lies when he had whispered into my ear:

"Don't tell God how you really feel. He'll get angry and leave you."

"Quit being so superficial! How dare you complain about your physical appearance when there are so many people worse off than you."

"It won't do you any good to pray to God for healing. If he really loved you, he would have healed you by now."

As my sobs slowed, an image was seared in my heart of Cinderella losing her shoe as she ran from the palace at midnight. I wondered, "What is that supposed to mean? Is that some kind of cruel joke?" I sensed God saying, "You are not your deformity. What I see is your heart, which is beautiful. I created you in my image. To me you will always be beautiful." In the fairy tale of

Cinderella, the prince searched high and low for her, not despite her lost shoe but because of it. In the same way, God searched for me and loved me perfectly in my imperfection. The enemy had taught me I wasn't beautiful, but that didn't line up with God's truth.

God Began a Good Work and He Will Finish It

God knew you, your personality, and the choices you would make before you took your first breath. Jeremiah 29:11 assures us that God knows the plans he has for each of us, and they are good.

So what about when we feel we have stalled and are not advancing along his road map for our lives? Or we have veered from his plan? Or we have gone our own way and set our own course, as I did for so many years when I took on the false burden of being my own provider?

What if you stopped listening to the father of lies and asked the Father of Light what he thinks about you?

That is when the gifts of God's grace and mercy are so precious. God graciously forgives. His Holy Spirit continuously guides and teaches. In his mercy, he gives us time to learn all these things through his leading and through our experiences.

God promises in Philippians 1:6 that "he who began a good work in you will carry it on to completion until the day of Christ Jesus." He doesn't give up on us. He continues to work with us, in us, and through us until Jesus returns.

One of the most problematic issues I see in terms of embracing our identity in Christ is that we succumb to self-hatred. When the enemy offers up our faults for inspection, we agree with him. We compare ourselves to others and deem ourselves less worthy, less valuable, less useful. What have you decided you are less of when you compare yourself to others?

We cannot agree with two kingdoms at once. When we agree with our enemy's assessment, we disagree with God's truth. The more we say derogatory statements about ourselves, the wider we open the door for self-hatred to walk through and take up residence in our beliefs.

What if you stopped listening to the father of lies and asked the Father of Light what he thinks about you? When tempted to review your faults or beat yourself up, what if instead you stopped and asked God for an honest appraisal? "Father, you know I'm not feeling too good about myself right now. Help me to see myself as you do." That might just change everything.

Friend, that was the prayer of my heart for a couple years straight. I consistently prayed and asked:

- that God would give me an accurate perspective of him (because I knew life experiences had colored my perception of him)
- that God would help me understand how he viewed me
- that God would help me view myself the way he viewed me

Transformation of my mind and revelation in my heart did not happen quickly. I had to surrender my faulty thinking and exchange it for his right thoughts. I had to take every thought captive, which meant determining if my thoughts were coming from God or from the enemy of my soul, who wants to destroy me.

What if we decided to no longer let the enemy destroy our identity and dealt with the issue of self-hatred? What if instead of going down the road of comparing ourselves to others we stopped and said, "Father, I'm about to beat myself up, but before I do, why don't you tell me what you think of me? How do you see me, Father?" Wouldn't that change everything?

For decades I had no idea what God said about me. Church taught me that I was a sinner, and I slunk under that cloak for far too long. But God said that even while we were sinners he sent Jesus to die for us (Rom. 5:8) because he loved us so much that he couldn't bear the possibility of us being separated from him.

Do you know what God says about you? Your identity has to be found in Christ alone. Here are just some of the things he says about you:

- *You are beautiful.* "Let the king be enthralled by your beauty; honor him, for he is your lord" (Ps. 45:11).
- *You are an overcomer.* "No, in all these things we are more than conquerors through him who loved us" (Rom. 8:37).
- *You are a masterpiece and are destined for greatness.* "For we are God's masterpiece. He has created us anew in Christ Jesus, so we can do the good things he planned for us long ago" (Eph. 2:10 NLT).
- *You are forever loved.* "The LORD appeared to us in the past, saying: 'I have loved you with an everlasting love; I have drawn you with unfailing kindness'" (Jer. 31:3).
- *You are wonderful.* "I praise you because I am fearfully and wonderfully made; your works are wonderful, I know that full well" (Ps. 139:14).
- *You are worth it.* "For this is how God loved the world: He gave his one and only Son, so that everyone who believes in him will not perish but have eternal life" (John 3:16 NLT).

What are you dealing with today? We all have things about ourselves that we deem ugly, flawed, or imperfect. What have you been trying to hide from the rest of the world? What lies has the enemy whispered to you that you've believed? What is it about yourself that you think doesn't measure up?

- your marital status?
- your health?
- your financial situation?

Those are just circumstantial facts. But here's what God's truth says about the real you:

- When he created you, it was *good.*
- He has a plan for you, and it is for *good.* It is to prosper you and not to harm you. It is for a future and a hope.
- He who began a *good* work in you will see it through to completion!

Your Rx

1. Think about your life. Where have you allowed the perceptions of others or the lies of the enemy to dictate your identity? Now counter that with the truth of God's Word. What does he say about you?

2. Pray and ask God to help you have a true understanding of what he thinks about you and then to help you adopt his view of you for yourself.

3. To really appreciate that your identity is rooted not in what you do or who you are but rather in whose you are, reflect on these verses: Song of Solomon 6:3; John 1:12; 15:16; Romans 8:14–15, 17; 2 Corinthians 5:17; Galatians 4:6–7; Ephesians 1:5; 1 John 5:18.

4. Look up the following verses: Psalms 45:11; 139:14; Jeremiah 31:3; Romans 8:37; Ephesians 2:10. Write them on index cards

and place them where you will see them frequently. Read each of these passages aloud three times daily, committing them to memory.

My Prayer for You

Father, knowing our identity in you is crucial for us to walk in the authority you've given to us in Jesus. It's my prayer that your Holy Spirit will take the blinders off the eyes and ears of this dear one so that they receive a fresh revelation and hear your voice as you reveal what you think of them. And then, Father, I pray that you will seal them from the lies of the enemy, who seeks to destroy our identity, and replace their own view of themselves with the truth of your perfect and loving perspective. This dear one bears your resemblance, and you delight in that, as any proud father does. Help them to delight in that truth as well. Thank you for the perfect sacrifice of Jesus, through which you see us as righteous and holy. In Jesus's name, amen.

Recommended Playlist

"Don't Give Up on Me," MercyMe, © 2012 by Fair Trade/Columbia

"He Knows My Name," Francesca Battistelli, © 2014 by Word Entertainment LLC

"Listen to the Sound," Building 429, © 2011 by Essential Records

"Free to Be Me," Francesca Battistelli, © 2008 by Word Entertainment LLC

"Any Other Way," Tenth Avenue North, © 2010 by Reunion Records

8

Know Your Worth

But now, this is what the Lord says . . .
"Do not fear, for I have redeemed you;
I have summoned you by name; you are mine."
Isaiah 43:1

What we know matters but who we are matters more.
Brené Brown

Depression doesn't define our worth. An undeniable truth exists: God is 100 percent for us. Satan knows this but, because he is 100 percent against us, he works hard to make us doubt this truth or at the very least distract us from living out of the victory this truth provides. When we don't appreciate our worth in Christ, many of our thoughts, attitudes, and actions run adrift, and depression has an open door to enter.

Today the temptation exists to equate our worth with external factors. We might measure our worth by our financial situation, relationship status, education, or title at work. But regardless of anything external that we have, do, or earn, God delights in us as his masterpiece: "For we are God's masterpiece. He has created us anew in Christ Jesus, so we can do the good things he planned for us long ago" (Eph. 2:10 NLT).

When we don't appreciate our worth in Christ ... depression has an open door to enter.

Tragically, we allow the words, attitudes, or actions of others to influence how we feel about ourselves. This tendency begins in childhood when we come into agreement with parents, teachers, coaches, or other influential adults in our lives who make statements about us that do not agree with what God says about us. Have you ever known a teacher who singled out a child with a comment like, "What are you, stupid?" or "You'll never amount to anything." Or a coach who uses one child as a negative example to motivate the rest of the team by calling the child lazy?

Maybe you were the recipient of such comments. Those statements can not only wound a heart but also potentially open the door to a life of believing the enemy's lies about our worth. God's truth says, "For God made Christ, who never sinned, to be the offering for our sin, so that we could be made right with God through Christ" (2 Cor. 5:21 NLT). Other translations say, so we could "become the righteousness of God."

If we do not have a firm grasp of our God-given worth, life incidents can perpetuate the belief that we have to behave or think a certain way to earn our value or gain acceptance. Sometimes we agree to commitments, fearing that if we don't, we will not be accepted or valued. The difficulty lies in the fact that we can never please all people. The only one who offers complete, unconditional acceptance is God. Too often we place the emphasis on pleasing people while underappreciating God's complete acceptance.

We Are Highly Valued

Would you agree that the price paid for an object establishes its value? If that is true, then you must agree that you have infinite worth because Christ paid the price of his life when he died on the cross to save us. Too often we base our worth on what others say about us, including the father of lies. The only one who has any authority to speak about our worth is Jesus. Since he found us worthy of giving up his life for us when he died on the cross, that tells us just how valuable and worthy he deems us.

John 3:16 is one of the most quoted Scripture passages, yet we so often miss a crucial nugget of truth it contains. "For God so loved the world that he gave his one and only Son, that whoever believes in him shall not perish but have eternal life." God deemed you worthy. He valued you so much that he sent his only Son to die so that when you believed in him you would receive eternal life with him. If you were the only one living, God would have done that just for you because he found you worthy.

The enemy doesn't want us to fully appreciate what transpired when Christ gave up his life for us on the cross because then we would know with every fiber of our being that the enemy has already lost. Our enemy desires for us either to remain unaware of his work in our lives or to fear him. Our fear of him enhances his power. But every fear is based on a lie. God did not give us the spirit of fear—that comes from our enemy. God gave us power, love, and a sound mind (see 2 Tim. 1:7).

Once we grasp the enormity of the exchange that took place on the cross, we have access to freedom. Christ exchanged our sin and shame for his perfection, our death for his life, and our bondage for his freedom. "So if the Son sets you free, you are truly free" (John 8:36 NLT). Too often we continue to live in bondage, like in depression, when our ransom has already been paid by the greatest sacrifice in history. Friend, it's time to accept this sacrificial gift, know you are no longer an imprisoned slave but a freed person, and kick the enemy to the curb.

When we focus on how much God loves us and the cost he endured to redeem us, then we can appreciate how God sees us. Then we can understand our inherent worth as children of the Most High God.

God Calls Us His

Our internal dialogue about our worthlessness is a lie of the enemy. It's also in direct opposition to what the Word of God tells us in 1 John 4:4: "You, dear children, are from God and have overcome them, because the one who is in you is greater than the one who is in the world." Just by virtue of having Christ living inside of us, we are not only worthy but also overcomers who are greater than our enemy, who prowls the earth seeking those whom he can steal, kill, and destroy.

In a depressed state, you may not feel treasured, or even acceptable, but you are. While I'm not asking you to deny your feelings, I'm asking you to choose to believe the truth of God's Word over your feelings. In Ephesians 1:6, Paul says that all of us who believe in Christ have been "accepted in the beloved" (KJV).

In our daily lives, we place high priority on things of importance to us and commit them to memory. We record information that we don't want to forget—phone numbers, grocery lists, appointment times. God did the same thing. You are so valuable to him, of such importance to him, that you are tattooed on his hands: "See, I have engraved you on the palms of my hands" (Isa. 49:16).

That should give you great confidence and affirm your worth. That tattoo isn't going anywhere—he is being constantly reminded of you. Whenever you doubt your worth, remember that you are permanently tattooed on the palms of his hands.

Comparison steals our joy. In the darkness of depression, we are more susceptible to comparing ourselves to others. We judge our worth or our value against what we perceive others' to be. As a result, we often feel less important, less loved, or less worthy than our nondepressed counterparts, which then makes us feel even more depressed.

Our enemy waits for the moment we are most vulnerable and then tries to convince us we are "less than" those we admire. Have you ever had thoughts like "Maybe I wasn't asked to be on the committee because I'm not as smart as he is." Or "I'll never be as pretty as she is." Friend, those are not your thoughts. Those are lies of the enemy meant to weigh you down and distract you from what God's truth says about you.

Depression does not define our worth. God does.

God says, "You will be a crown of splendor in the LORD's hand, a royal diadem in the hand of your God" (Isa. 62:3). He loves you so much. Did you know you have stolen his heart? "You have stolen my heart, my sister, my bride; you have stolen my heart with one glance of your eyes, with one jewel of your necklace" (Song of Sol. 4:9). He loves you and values you so highly that he wants to spend time with you. "My beloved spoke and said to me, 'Arise, my darling, my beautiful one, come with me'" (Song of Sol. 2:10).

The physical effects of depression can deplete both our energy and our motivation. If we equate our worth with our accomplishments, our perception of our worth then plummets. It's crucial to separate our worth from our performance. Remember that we are completely loved, accepted, and valued by God regardless of our job, our income, our church service, or our emotional state. Depression does not define our worth. God does.

Sometimes I have to remind myself of the parent-child relationship. From the moment I knew I was pregnant, I called the baby mine. After his birth, I named him. Why? Because giving someone a name shows they are valued. We even do the same with pets; we name our pets because we love them and value them. Because God values us and finds us worthy, he has done the same for us. He named us and called us his: "Do not be afraid, for I have ransomed you. I have called you by name; you are mine" (Isa. 43:1 NLT).

We Are Sons and Daughters

One of the greatest turning points in my faith journey was when a dear woman began to teach me about my identity in Christ. I was accustomed to praying to God and referring to him in my prayers as God, Lord, or even heavenly Father. It hadn't fully penetrated my understanding that if he was my heavenly father, then by default I was his daughter. We are sons and daughters of the Most High God, heirs with Christ: "Now you are no longer a slave but God's own child. And since you are his child, God has made you his heir" (Gal. 4:7 NLT).

As a little girl, I occasionally accompanied my father to his office on Saturday. An executive for a company, he sometimes visited the office on the weekend to prepare for Monday meetings or travel the following week. I tagged along and busied myself playing secretary at his receptionist's desk. I delighted in typing up memos and sweet notes for his receptionist to find on Monday. I also enjoyed tinkering with her typewriter, messing with her margins, enabling all caps, and the like, giggling at the image of her finding evidence of my weekend visit when she clocked in on Monday morning. I knew she wouldn't get mad at me. Why? I was the boss's daughter, and that validated me. In the same way, God validates our worth as his sons and daughters.

When a baby is born, new parents experience an overwhelming flood of love for their child. After I had my first child, a deep love for my baby overtook me and caught me unaware. I didn't know such a deep, unconditional love was possible. My child did nothing to earn my love. He did nothing but eat, sleep, and dirty diapers. He didn't earn my love; all he had to do was receive it. Yet nothing could diminish my love for him—I gave it freely.

Likewise, God doesn't value us because of what we do but because of whose we are—his children. "But to all who believed him and accepted him, he gave the right to become children of God" (John 1:12 NLT). Merely as a result of being his children, we are recipients of "every spiritual blessing in the heavenly places in Christ" (Eph. 1:3 NASB). There is nothing we can do to be more loved or more valued in God's eyes. When he looks at us, he sees his perfection reflected in us. Our worth is not determined by anything we do or earn; it's given to us by God.

I remember hearing an illustration that so clearly helped me appreciate my worth in God's eyes. A pastor was preaching at a conference when, much to the audience's delight, he pulled out his wallet. From his wallet, he took a $100 bill. He held it high and waved it for the audience to see before asking, "Who would like this $100 bill?" Hands rapidly waved in the air, and shouts of anticipation flew across the auditorium. He then took the bill in his fist and crumpled it tight before asking, "Now who wants it?" Undeterred, audience members vied for his generosity. Curiously, he then took the crumpled bill, placed it on the floor, ground it into the floor with his shoe, and asked, "Does anyone want this wrinkled, dirty bill?" Most were still willing.

As he placed the tattered bill on the podium, he explained his point. Most of us operate from the belief that we are useful to God only when we are perfect and unblemished. But the trials and mistakes of life leave us feeling tattered and unlovely, unsuitable for use by a holy God. Yet our mistakes, quirks, and weaknesses can't diminish our worth any more than crumpling and stepping on a $100 bill can diminish its value.

> *God will allow neither depression nor the enemy of our souls to diminish our worth in his eyes.*

The enemy can attempt to steal our joy, kill our peace, and destroy our identity, but in God's sovereign love for us, he will allow neither depression nor the enemy of our souls to diminish our worth in his eyes. God not only prevents the enemy from affecting our eternal worth but also one-ups our enemy when he uses what the enemy intended for our harm to accomplish good. "You intended to harm me, but God intended it all for good. He brought me to this position so I could save the lives of many people" (Gen. 50:20 NLT).

God did not cause us to experience depression. Nor does he allow depression to define our worth. The enemy of our souls seeks to keep us depressed, lacking in joy and peace and unsure of our identity. But God has promised that he will bring good out of our situation and will turn our ashes into something beautiful.

Your Rx

1. Think about your life. What lies have you believed about your worth? Take them to God in prayer, and ask him to reveal to you the truth about how he values you.

2. Write down the things you value most in your life. Maybe possessions, awards, relationships. Ask yourself, "Would I

be willing to die because I love them so much?" Reflect on how valuable God thinks you are that he was willing for his Son to die just for you to live. Take your gratitude to him in prayer.

3. Look up the following verses: Isaiah 43:1; 49:16; John 8:36; Galatians 4:7. Then write them on index cards and place them where you will see them frequently. Read each of these passages aloud three times daily, committing them to memory.

My Prayer for You

Father, what a privilege it is to pray for this dear one who you highly favor and call by name. Society tells us that our worth goes up and down like a barometer based on what we do or who we are. I pray that you will give this precious child of yours a fresh revelation that their worth comes solely from whose they are. They are your child, ransomed with the great price of the death of your Son Jesus on a cross. Let there never be any more question of this one's worth or value. Just as you have written their name on the palms of your hands, I ask that you engrave their worth in their heart so that they will walk with their head held high, knowing they have been declared worthy by you—the only one whose opinion matters. In Jesus's name, amen.

Recommended Playlist

"The Truth Is Who You Are," Tenth Avenue North, © 2010 by Reunion Records

"Keeper of My Heart," Kari Jobe, © 2014 by Sparrow Records

"Identity," John Waller, © 2007 by Reunion Records

9

Remember Your Secure Destiny

My Father, who has given them to me, is greater than all; no one can snatch them out of my Father's hand.

John 10:29

Your past is not the predictor of your future—God is.

Steve Dulin

Have you ever wondered where God is? Or if he even cares?

I did. I don't like to remember those days. Even admitting that I doubted God was near or cared about me during my times of desperation brings back a shadow of sadness.

In the valley of my depression, the enemy tried to convince me that no one cared, not even God. For a while he had me convinced, and I took my pain and anger out on God. Can I share with you a little something I learned, though? God is big enough to handle my anger and yours.

One evening the pain of the darkness dragged me so low that I wondered aloud where God was in my suffering. Did he even care that I felt like a surfer battered against the rocks within a vast, lonely ocean? In my agony and desperation, my wonderings turned to angry venting. I told God of the pain deep within my soul. I held nothing back as I lost control in an angry outburst like a volcanic eruption.

When I had no more words to say and was physically spent from my vulnerable expression of the depths of my pain, I sensed a quiet, gentle voice whisper within me, "Well, at least now you're talking to me." It wasn't a condemning correction but more a lighthearted reflection to help me see the truth in my ways.

The enemy had worked hard to convince me I was alone, no one cared, and I shouldn't share my pain with God because he might judge me harshly. But when I was ready to return to the Father, much like the prodigal son, I experienced anything but judgment. He was not the harsh judge I feared. He responded like a father whose child was hurt and in need of comfort. He proved David's words to be true: "The LORD is near to those who are discouraged; he saves those who have lost all hope" (Ps. 34:18 GNT).

I had been sold swampland in the enemy's resort.

I know now that part of what contributed to my depression was an unloving spirit operating in my life. The ultimate goal of an unloving spirit is to keep us from receiving the fullness of God's love. It also keeps us from loving ourselves the way God desires us to. That spirit repeatedly tries to convince us we are unworthy of being loved.

As a result of agreeing with such an evil spirit, I became prone to self-pity, self-doubt, self-accusation, decreased confidence, and self-rejection (although I didn't realize it at the time). My conscious and unconscious agreements with the enemy opened the door for behavior that was incredibly unhealthy—physically, spiritually, and emotionally. I suffered from deep fear of failure, fear of others' opinions, fear of rejection and abandonment, drivenness, and perfectionism.

I thought the more I did and the more perfect I tried to be, the more others and God would like me and love me. The problem with that mentality is that we can never be good enough for others, and we can never be perfect. I was literally killing myself trying but didn't know it. I allowed drivenness and perfectionism to become so deeply entrenched that I went for a very long period of time working so many hours a day trying to do more and be better. I had been sold swampland in the enemy's resort. That is how the enemy works. In his deceptiveness, he offers up an appealing counterfeit to the truth that God offers.

Destiny Granted

The enemy wants us to believe that God requires us to be perfect in order to love us and in order for us to secure our reservation in heaven. How often have you heard people say they believe they are going to heaven because they are good people? They have believed a lie. Our good works have nothing to do with it. Salvation has everything to do with what Jesus did for us: "When we were utterly helpless, Christ came at just the right time and died for us sinners" (Rom. 5:6 NLT).

I agree that in order to get into heaven we must be better than "good"; God requires perfection. Yet that is as far as the enemy likes to take that argument. The truth is that there has been only one person who met God's standard of perfection: his only Son, Jesus. Because God requires perfection, he had to create a way for all of us imperfect people to meet his criteria. In his mercy and his grace, God allowed Jesus to die in order for him to take all of our imperfection on himself. When God looks at us, he sees the perfection and righteousness of Jesus. That is what Romans 4:5 means when it says, "But people are counted as righteous, not because of their work, but because of their faith in God who forgives sinners" (NLT). God justified the ungodly by putting our sin on Jesus so that we could be considered righteous in him.

When a person feels that they have to justify themselves before God, and they can't, they feel shame. Do you ever experience shame? Can I encourage you today and tell you those thoughts and feelings don't come from you. Nor do they come from God! They come from our enemy, who inflicts a spirit of accusation upon us, tempting us to accuse others, accuse God, and accuse ourselves. Satan wants us to think God is judging us. But God's desire has never been to judge us and to heap guilt on our shoulders. "For God did not send his Son into the world to condemn the world, but to save the world through him" (John 3:17).

As a result of his grace and our faith in him, our destiny is secure.

God desires to bless us. He took away all our sin when he gave it to Jesus on the cross. In this, our destiny is secure. We are accepted by God. He looks at us as righteous. If we have accepted Christ as our Savior, nothing and no one can alter our destiny. "Don't let your hearts be troubled. Trust in God, and trust also in me. There is more than enough room in my Father's home. If this were not so, would I have told you that I am going to prepare a place for you? When everything is ready, I will come and get you, so that you will always be with me where I am" (John 14:1–3 NLT).

The enemy tries to convince us first that we are unlovable (even by God) and second that our destiny is on shaky ground because we are not good enough to gain access to heaven. When I look back,

I see I wasn't striving to be rich or to be famous. I was striving to be good enough to be lovable—the very thing the enemy wanted me to believe I wasn't. You and I won't ever be good enough to be worthy of God's love and acceptance. God knew that, and so did Jesus. That is why Jesus willingly gave up his life: "For my Father's will is that everyone who looks to the Son and believes in him shall have eternal life, and I will raise them up at the last day" (John 6:40).

Destiny Secured

God won't allow our depression, our resulting frustration and despair, or even our misguided anger to change the security of our destiny as long as we are Christ followers. "Therefore, since we have been justified through faith, we have peace with God through our Lord Jesus Christ, through whom we have gained access by faith into this grace in which we now stand. And we boast in the hope of the glory of God" (Rom. 5:1–2). This is good news! Our faith in Jesus's finished work on the cross justifies us in God's eyes, resulting in peace with God because he now sees us through the same lens with which he views Jesus. As a result of his grace and our faith in him, our destiny is secure and we can exchange our depression for the joy Jesus died to give us.

Depression makes it difficult to remember the assurance of our destiny. In the valley of depression, I couldn't see past my pain to the glorious, joyful future God had for me. I can now see that even in my dark valley not only was I not alone, but God also wasn't leaving me there. And he won't leave you where you are either. Take assurance from his promises: "And I will give you a new heart, and I will put a new spirit in you. I will take out your stony, stubborn heart and give you a tender, responsive heart" (Ezek. 36:26 NLT).

Finding my way out of depression's darkness was a slow, gradual journey, and one I frequently grew weary of traveling. The enemy used that laborious pace to convince me of a counterfeit destiny:

"You will always feel this way."

"You will never be free from depression."

"God heals others but not you."

"Depression is in your genes, so you are destined to suffer."

Desperation made me willing to search for real intimacy with God and to ditch my preconceived notions in favor of his promises. Now, on the other side of depression's dark door, when the enemy returns to flirt with my mind, I return to the truth of God's promises.

God does not want any of us to live in depression and defeat. When we fall prey to depression's destruction, God promises, "He will give a crown of beauty for ashes, a joyous blessing instead of mourning, festive praise instead of despair. In their righteousness, they will be like great oaks that the LORD has planted for his own glory" (Isa. 61:3 NLT). Friend, God promises our destiny includes beauty, joy, blessing, and praise.

When my body resembled a battleground and I became emaciated, I all but lost the will to go on. The enemy desired nothing less. The weaker I became, the stronger he grew. The spirit of doubt prompted questions regarding my purpose, God's plan for my life, and any hope of returning to health. I could hardly stand unassisted, much less actively engage in a battle against the enemy. Was this how my life would end, with the enemy of my soul declaring victory in my defeat? In one of my more lucid moments, the Holy Spirit prompted me to search God's Word for the answers to questions I was too afraid to ask out loud.

I recalled a verse I had heard many times since childhood: "Don't be dejected and sad, for the joy of the LORD is your strength"

(Neh. 8:10 NLT). I grew frustrated. The verse was familiar to me, but I experienced neither his joy nor his strength, to which the enemy whispered, "See, that doesn't apply to you. You'll always be depressed, so you might as well admit defeat." This was not just a battle for my life but also a battle for my mind. According to *Strong's Concordance*, in this verse, *strength* refers to "a place of safety, refuge, protection."[1] Here God encourages us not to be sad or despair because God is our protector. Finally understanding his promise filled me with strength.

Returning to physical, emotional, and spiritual health took time. I had to diligently pay attention to my thoughts and actively question whether they were coming from God or from the enemy. Some days seemed like torture and made me wonder if the fight was worth the effort. During those dark days and nights, tears flowed freely, yet I determined to win the war against the enemy of my soul.

I commiserated with the apostle Paul, who wrote, "I press on to reach the end of the race and receive the heavenly prize for which God, through Christ Jesus, is calling us" (Phil. 3:14 NLT). Friend, God is faithful. He brought Scripture, songs, and other believers across my path when I needed them most. I hope he is using this book in the same way with you. God longs to usher you to the other side of depression's cavern.

When my husband had cancer, I came across one of God's promises that gave me hope during my dark days.

> We are hard pressed on every side, but not crushed; perplexed, but not in despair; persecuted, but not abandoned; struck down, but not destroyed. . . . Therefore we do not lose heart. Though outwardly we are wasting away, yet inwardly we are being renewed day by day. For our light and momentary troubles are achieving for us an eternal glory that far outweighs them all. So we fix our eyes not on what is seen, but on what is unseen, since what is seen is temporary, but what is unseen is eternal. (2 Cor. 4:8–9, 16–18)

Hold on to this truth. Our heavenly destiny assures that despite how we feel—depressed, hard pressed, or struck down—God has greater things waiting for us on the journey.

Trusting God Despite Our Circumstances

Some years ago, I was given a diagnosis that even the doctor had to run three sets of labs to confirm. As she shook her head, she offered little more than, "It just doesn't make sense." Suddenly little seemed to make sense. The next day my right-hand staff member was hospitalized for a terminal condition. Within days, my husband came home from the office, sat down on my side of the bed, which often doubled as my home desk, and with every ounce of his normal joviality absent, relayed, "The doctor's office called. My CT scan wasn't clean. They are scheduling me for surgery."

How did I feel? Shocked. Numb. Lost. Grieved. Overwhelmed. Sad. Devastated. Alone. Confused. Betrayed. Hopeless.

Fortunately, those feelings were fleeting. But only because I had come into a greater awareness and appreciation of who I am and who God is for me than I had known when I faced a similar triple attack twelve years earlier.

I don't want to mislead you. I didn't react perfectly. The triple threat I faced took me down for a little while. That is what the enemy wanted. I knew I had an enemy, but knowing that I had a secure destiny gave me even more strength to fight.

The night my husband told me about his results and impending surgery, I called a friend and sobbed incoherently. I felt overwhelmed and was unable to think clearly enough to even make a game plan—so unlike me. Since talking was clearly ineffective, I texted a couple girlfriends and gave them the most recent news and asked for their prayers.

One responded by asking if she and her husband could come over that evening to pray with us. At that moment, I wasn't even sure what to pray. They came and prayed for both of us and our trio of difficult circumstances. They said they were sorry for all we had to endure in a way that conveyed they were sharing in our pain. Both my husband and I came undone. I don't know about you, but seeing my spouse cry does me in. As he cried, the enemy took advantage of my weakened state and slyly whispered, "If he's crying, you know you really have something to worry about!" Before I started to accept what seemed like a valid argument, I was pulled into their prayers for healing, wisdom, peace, and thanks that God already held every answer we would need on this journey.

Whether it was the tears I had shed, the release of the shock, the medicine the doctor had called in to control my nausea, or God's graciousness, I will never know. But I fell into a deep sleep, waking in the morning to a greater sense of peace and inner calm. I still wondered what would be, but I didn't worry. I didn't allow myself to react and make my own plans out of fear. Despite my feelings and the uncertainty of my circumstances, my destiny remains secure in God. He holds me firmly in his hands.

Faith and fear both carry equal weight, and both demand our focus, but I resolved to choose to respond in faith. When the enemy began to meddle, whispering thoughts like "But what about . . . ?" I responded verbally with, "No! I will not worry because my God will supply all my needs." He came back around using well-intentioned people with comments such as, "Have you thought about . . . ?" I then graciously replied, "No, I haven't. We are taking one moment at a time." I thought, "Lord, I choose to trust you. Your Word says those who trust in you will not be disappointed. Thank you that I will not be disappointed. I choose to lay my worries at the feet of your cross because you told me to, because you care for me."

Idle moments were the worst. During almost imperceptible streams of consciousness, we may unknowingly come into agreement with the pronouncements of the enemy over our lives. When I felt sad, lonely, overwhelmed, and devastated, I had to choose to embrace what God says about me and not succumb to the feelings that, left unchecked, had previously spiraled into devastating depression. I consciously and repeatedly recited God's truth: "By his stripes I am healed! I am more than an overcomer. I am victorious in Christ Jesus. His mercies are new every morning. In my own strength I can do nothing, but I can do all things through him who gives me strength. God has a plan for me—it's a plan to prosper me and not to harm me, a plan for a future and a hope."

Old habits are hard to break. I know that, and God does too. He is merciful to give us the time to learn his ways. Looking through God's frame of reference still doesn't always come naturally to me. Thankfully, I have a couple of good friends who will speak the truth in love and help me to see when I've believed the lies of the enemy.

Acceptance Despite Imperfection

One morning I visited my local exercise facility, not especially interested in exercising that day. My preference would have been to stay in my warm bed and get a few more winks on that cold and dreary morning. Instead, I got up and braved the elements, as I knew there wouldn't be time later in the day. The facility was quiet, probably because others were enjoying the comfort of their warm blankets.

As I worked out, endorphins started flowing through my brain and body, creating a sense of contentedness and well-being, rewarding my decision to get up. At this particular gym, weight training stations are equipped with computer monitors that provide automatic feedback regarding an individual's pace and form throughout each exercise. The monitor mirrored back to me my perfect form until partway through the workout my form dipped below 100 percent. Interestingly, with my shift in form, I noticed a correlating shift in my thinking. I began focusing on the negative aspects of the situation: "Why can't I ever stay at 100 percent? Why does the music have to blare so loud in the morning? How come exercising always seems easier for everyone else?"

I realized what was happening. So I did what I often advise my patients to do. I took a couple of deep breaths, and I course corrected. While I waited for the offensive song to finish, I got a drink of water, stretched, and moved the monitor to a more optimal position. While waiting, I course corrected my thinking as well. I had shifted from being pleased with my performance to suddenly equating my less-than-perfect performance with defeat. That was a lie I needed to reject. So I consciously shifted my thoughts to the positive: "I've got more endurance now than when I first started. I'm going to have more energy this afternoon because I got up and worked out. I did more repetitions that were in perfect form than weren't!"

God does not call us to a life of perfection, although for years I believed the lie that he wouldn't love me if I weren't perfect. He accepts us as we are but loves us too much to leave us that way. So then life becomes about living in this destiny we have in him, and we can move past the fear of isolation, rejection, or not belonging and the motivations of guilt and shame that go with those. My routine that morning wasn't perfect but I was able to recognize the ensuing feelings of defeat and shame for what they were and not agree with them. God doesn't expect perfection; our destiny is secure in him, not in what we do or how well we do it.

Even the biblical greats like Paul weren't perfect. He wrote, "I'm not saying that I have this all together, that I have it made.

But I am well on my way, reaching out for Christ, who has so wondrously reached out for me. Friends, don't get me wrong: By no means do I count myself an expert in all of this, but I've got my eye on the goal, where God is beckoning us onward—to Jesus. I'm off and running, and I'm not turning back" (Phil. 3:12–14 Message).

When you are tempted to give up because you've tried and fallen short of the goal or the expectations, take a moment to take a deep breath. Assess the situation, course correct your thoughts and attitude about the situation, and try again. Remember, it's not about perfection; it's about relationship. Neither the enemy of your soul nor your depression can dictate your destiny. Your destiny is secure in Christ.

Your Rx

1. Are you sure of your eternal destiny? If you've never accepted Christ as your personal Savior but want to, you can right now by praying a prayer such as this: "Dear God, I recognize that I have sinned. I believe that you sent your Son to die to pay the price for my sins. I choose to turn away from my sinful ways and receive you as my personal Lord and Savior. Thank you for taking up residence in my heart, saving me, and securing my destiny with you forever. In Jesus's name I pray, amen."

2. Look up the following verses: Psalm 34:18; John 6:40; 10:29; Romans 5:1–2; 2 Corinthians 4:8–9, 16–18. Write them on index cards and place them where you will see them frequently. Read each of these passages aloud three times daily, committing them to memory.

3. What lies have you believed about your current situation? Your future? Your eternal destiny? If you are unsure what lies you have believed, pray and ask God to show you. Then

ask for his forgiveness for believing such lies, and ask him to show you his truth.

My Prayer for You

Father, I thank you for your mercy and grace. I thank you that the moment we come to know you as Lord and Savior our destiny is secure with you. Father, you know the enemy would have us believe that when we mess up, lose our way, or even vulnerably share with you how we are feeling, we risk losing your love and acceptance. I pray now for the heart of this dear one whom the enemy seeks to attack. I thank you that your Word says you make firm the steps of those who delight in you, and although we might stumble and trip, you don't let us fall because you are always there upholding us with your hand. I pray that you will reveal your steadying hand to this one who seeks to hear and believe your truth above all else, and I ask that you will bring peace and hope to the dark places. Because of your mercy and grace, amen.

Recommended Playlist

"Forever Yours," Gateway Worship, © 2012 by Gateway Create Publishing

"Strong Enough to Save," Tenth Avenue North, © 2010 by Reunion Records

"Where I Belong," Building 429, © 2011 by Essential Records

"Still Calls Me Son," John Waller, © 2007 by Reunion Records

"Because God Is Good," John Waller, © 2011 by City of Peace Media Inc.

"I Belong to You," Jesus Culture, © 2014 by Jesus Culture Music

10

Be Confident That Nothing Separates You from God's Love

And may you have the power to understand, as all God's people should, how wide, how long, how high, and how deep his love is.

Ephesians 3:18 NLT

Whether you accept it or reject it, God's love for you is permanent.

Sri Chinmoy

Have you ever felt alone? Unloved? Do you ever fear that people might not love you if they knew the "real" you—with all your faults, quirks, insecurities, and mistakes?

The enemy thrives off convincing us that God forgets or abandons us during those times when we feel alone. That couldn't be farther from the truth. God's Word assures us he won't leave us. In depression's darkness, however, it's a natural tendency to turn our focus inward to our own thoughts and feelings, focusing less on others and God. Then our defenses weaken and we become more susceptible to the enemy's cunning whispers.

We Can Go It Alone or We Can Go with God

As I neared the end of a particularly difficult and painful season in my life, following my husband's struggle with cancer, my mother's death from cancer, and the miscarriage of our baby, my brother asked me a hard question. "So, through all of this, what did you learn?"

It took me a surprisingly long time to find an answer. While I never vocalized it, I berated myself internally for not having an immediate response—it seemed I should.

I reflected on his question during my prayer time. As I prayed, images appeared as if scenes were playing on a movie screen. First, I pictured a young girl riding piggyback on her father's back as they walked through the sun-dappled woods. Smiles and laughter enhanced the sunshine of the day. Then the girl climbed down off her father's back and ran ahead on the trail, not looking back.

Grief overtook me. I knew deep in that part of my being where only God could see that I had glimpsed a picture of him and me. It was clear he knew the real me—the me I avoided seeing, the me I avoided disclosing to anyone else. The grief that knotted my stomach came with the revelation that answered my brother's question: through all the hard times, God never moved. I did. He never left me, but at times I veered away from him. I felt loneliness because I ran on ahead without looking back, determined to take care of myself.

I related personally to Isaiah 30:20–21: "Though he give you the bread of adversity and water of affliction, yet he will be with you to teach you—with your own eyes you will see your Teacher. And if you leave God's paths and go astray, you will hear a voice behind you say, 'No, this is the way; walk here'" (TLB).

The image disturbed me. In my prayer time, I explored the scene with the Lord. Gentle and loving, he directed me to the answers my heart needed to learn. All my life I had been a type A person. When times got tough, I jumped in and did more. During hard personal trials like my husband's cancer, I took up the slack and did even more. It was necessary and helpful, for a period. But honestly, it served as a defense against the pain. In my busyness, my awareness of the hurt within me lessened. There wasn't time to let myself feel the pain, so I numbed it by staying too busy to acknowledge its existence.

I sacrificed the moments of joy God offered me because I was too busy to recognize them when they were there.

By staying busy, I also tried to shield myself from future hurt. I tried to run ahead, predict what would happen, and anticipate the future so I could plan how to handle it or even prevent it. The pain of those events was so great that in my way of thinking I never wanted to be caught off guard by such great pain again. I began to anticipate it and plan for it, and in doing so, I sacrificed the moments of joy God offered me because I was too busy to recognize them when they were there.

Most troubling in the image I had of getting down from my Father's back and running ahead was that I never turned back. I realized I never turned back because just as I had lost my earthly father to death at a young age, my mother to death from cancer, and our baby to miscarriage, I feared, if I looked back, God wouldn't be there anymore either. Rather than risk that, I chose not to look. The enemy successfully held me in bondage to the lie that just as others had left me, so too would God.

I'm so thankful for the truth in Isaiah 30:21. In his mercy and love, God whispered to me to bring me back to his path. He remained faithful to his Word: "Yet the LORD longs to be gracious to you; therefore he will rise up to show you compassion. For the LORD is a God of justice. Blessed are all who wait for him" (Isa. 30:18). Even when I ran ahead, he was there, and he still loved me. "The LORD is good to all; he has compassion on all he has made" (Ps. 145:9). Just as he stayed faithful to his promises to me never to leave me or stop loving me, he will stay faithful to you too. But as I did, you have the choice whether or not to acknowledge him and walk through this journey with him.

When times get hard and answers don't come quickly, our enemy is quick to take advantage of our natural tendency to long for the good old days when life seemed easier, or our circumstances seemed better, or at the very least we had some answers. When those answers aren't forthcoming or the tides don't turn fast enough, the enemy whispers seeds of doubt:

"If God really loved you, you wouldn't still be hurting."

"Do you think God can love someone as messed up as you?"

"The Bible says that 'God so loves the world,' but surely that means the world in general, because if he really loved you, he would have answered your prayers by now."

Remember, the enemy is the ultimate liar. He can say whatever he wants, but everything he says is a lie. The *truth* is that God's Word repeatedly says that nothing, not even depression, can separate us from God's love. The problem occurs when we believe our feelings or the enemy's lies instead of God's truth.

God Is Always with Us

In her book *Why I Jumped*, Tina Zahn shares her desperate battle with depression, which culminated in her attempt to jump off a bridge two hundred feet above the Fox River. God and a state trooper intercepted her suicide attempt at the precise moment she jumped. The state trooper lunged for Tina and affirmed, "I'm not letting you go." He resolutely hung on until two other officers arrived to pull them both to safety. Tina wrote, "In the same way that the state trooper said, 'I'm not letting you go,' so God also has us in his grip and will never let go of us. Joshua 1:5 says, 'As I was with Moses, so I will be with you; I will never leave you nor forsake you.'"[1]

Darkness was all I could see. I had just flown back from a professional conference and was more than ready to be home. As I walked through baggage claim, my eyes met my husband's as he waited to whisk me home, excited to hear about my trip. My answers to his greeting questions were clipped. After my suitcase was securely loaded in the trunk and my seat belt was fastened, tears cascaded down my face, leaving him speechless. Icily I stared out the window while inside I burned with despair and hatred of the enemy, who had introduced depression into my lineage.

"You can't take me home—I don't want the boys to see me like this."

My husband never could have imagined hearing what he did the next two hours. He sat, mostly silent in prayer, while I wept for two hours in our minivan in a grocery store parking lot. His heart dropped and his face drained of all color as he heard the unthinkable. I couldn't believe it myself.

"I understand why people commit suicide," I whispered, not recognizing my own voice.

He stammered as he spoke. "Are *you* thinking of committing suicide?"

I knew I was in a war, a spiritual battle, and while I didn't feel I was winning, I wasn't ready to give in. The enemy had already stolen enough from me, and I determined not to let him steal from my children. Resolute not to vocalize my thoughts and give the enemy another open door, I declared with all the strength I could gather, "I'm not going to put that out there. The enemy would love nothing more."

My poor husband didn't know where to go from there. "Do I need to take you to a hospital?" The air between us was weighty, like the thick humidity after a Florida afternoon rainstorm, as he continued. "Honey, I don't know what to do or say right now."

"I don't either." I honestly didn't.

"Promise me you won't do anything to harm yourself. Promise me you'll hang on."

I couldn't promise anything. Darkness enveloped me like a wet blanket—uncomforting and unwelcome. I sat frightened. I had never thought such devastating thoughts before, nor did I know where they came from. I was afraid to be alone, but I didn't want to be with people.

For most people, considering suicide isn't about wanting to die; it's about wanting the pain to end.

The situation was surreal. How did I get here? How did this happen? More importantly, how would I survive?

I wept for days afterward, longing for the darkness to lift, the pain to cease, and the joy to come in the morning. For most people, myself included, considering suicide isn't about wanting to die; it's about wanting the pain to end.

I continued to read God's Word. I could relate to the words of the prophet Micah: "But as for me, I watch in hope for the LORD. I wait for God my Savior; my God will hear me" (7:7). I cried to the Lord through my tears. I prayed as earnestly as I knew how, "Lord, I don't know if I can hold on. This pain is too much. Please hold my hand and don't let go."

In my brokenness, in my weakness, he met me. His promise leapt off the page into my heart: "So do not fear, for I am with you; do not be dismayed, for I am your God. I will strengthen you and help you; I will uphold you with my righteous right hand" (Isa. 41:10). I needed to remember the truth that despite my weakened state, God would hold me up. When I could not trust my own strength, I had no choice but to depend on his.

Only then did Psalm 23 transition from head knowledge to a heartfelt truth. I relied on God's promised companionship during my dark journey: "Even when I walk through the darkest valley, I will not be afraid, for you are close beside me. Your rod and your staff protect and comfort me" (Ps. 23:4 NLT).

A few days later in my morning devotional time, I wept before the Lord. As I confessed that I felt like I was in a war for my very life, he strengthened my will to fight by leading me to Joshua 1:9: "Have I not commanded you? Be strong and courageous. Do not be afraid; do not be discouraged, for the LORD your God will be with you wherever you go." Other verses I had memorized as a child jumped to the forefront of my mind. "Surely I am with you always, to the very end of the age" (Matt. 28:20). Scripture passages I had forgotten sprang to consciousness and met my need. "I am with you and will watch over you wherever you go, and I will bring you back to this land. I will not leave you until I have done what I have promised you" (Gen. 28:15).

In my despair, I needed to know I was not alone. At my very core, I felt unlovable and didn't even like myself, much less love myself. I needed to know I was loved regardless of how I felt.

God's Love Doesn't Depend on Us

Since my early childhood years, I had always been the doer, the achiever. I had set my sights high. I took Colossians 3:23–24

("Whatever you do, work at it with all your heart, as working for the Lord, not for human masters, since you know that you will receive an inheritance from the Lord as a reward. It is the Lord Christ you are serving") to the extreme. I didn't allow any room for imperfection.

In my formative years, after a traumatic experience, I unwittingly allowed the enemy to kill my peace when I believed his lies, "You can't rely on others to be there for you" and "You have to be perfect or God won't love you." From then on, I worked as hard as I could to be perfect. Failure was never an option. When times got tough, I got tougher. I coped by jumping in with both feet and doing whatever it took to handle the demands, as perfectly as possible.

It took some very painful life circumstances to bring me to the realization that my coping style was not only unhealthy but also potentially deadly—and not in line with God's truth. A few years ago, pregnant with our second baby, I endured the first of several crises that God ultimately used to bring me back to a right way of thinking. As the doctor was telling me that I was miscarrying our baby and that I needed a higher-level ultrasound to confirm it, I called the hospital where I worked to check my schedule, to fit the ultrasound around my own patients scheduled to see me.

What was wrong with this picture? I remained in my achiever mode, not wanting to let others down, rather than making my own health and that of my unborn baby first priority.

There comes a point when doing, achieving, and performing is no longer productive and is completely contrary to our heart's desire for peace.

I wish I could tell you that I learned that lesson the day I miscarried our baby. But I didn't. I was too stubborn. I was too busy picking up the pieces of our shattered life and trying to make a mosaic out of it to learn one of the most valuable lessons.

That lesson came when I pushed my body to such extremes that it cried for mercy and finally shut down. For almost five months, I could no longer do. I couldn't achieve. I couldn't perform, no matter how badly I wanted to. I couldn't even hold down food and required IV fluid and nutrition to keep me out of the hospital. My body said, "No more."

I've never before nor since felt so weak or so helpless. It was such a foreign experience for this go-getter, can-do woman. I had endless hours to think, pray, reflect, read. It brought me to the very place I had been running from.

Over time, I had begun to equate my worth with my accomplishments. The more I depended on myself, the better I did, the more self-worth I had, or so I thought. Unconsciously I reasoned, the more I did, the better I did, the more God would love me, and by extension, answer my prayers.

Raised in a Christian home, I knew Jesus shed his blood and died on a cross to save me from my sins and provide eternal salvation. I had that assurance. But somehow I missed a fundamental principle: there was nothing I could do to make God love me any more or any less. In depending on myself rather than God, I allowed the enemy to dig my valley of depression even deeper.

It took coming to a place where I was no longer able to do anything for myself, when all I could do for months was "be" me and be in God's presence, for me to gain a revelation of God's truth rather than what I had believed to be true. God helped me realize that he never intended for me to spend my life trying to do more and be better in exchange for his love and approval. He already loved me. It was up to me to believe it. The same is true for you.

The enemy aims to cast doubt in our minds regarding the permanency of God's love. Regardless of what the enemy says or does, he is no match for God's unending, faithful love. "Love never gives up, never loses faith, is always hopeful, and endures through every circumstance" (1 Cor. 13:7 NLT).

Once I started to intentionally search Scripture for truth about God's love for me, only then did I receive the revelation that nothing, not even my depression, could separate me from God's love. Do you know what God's Word says about his love for you?

- You are his and he is yours (Song of Sol. 6:3).
- He delights over you: "For the LORD your God is living among you. He is a mighty savior. He will take delight in you with gladness. With his love, he will calm all your fears. He will rejoice over you with joyful songs" (Zeph. 3:17 NLT).
- You are deeply and completely loved forever. "And I am convinced that nothing can ever separate us from God's love. Neither death nor life, neither angels nor demons, neither our fears for today nor our worries about tomorrow—not even the powers of hell can separate us from God's love. No power in the sky above or in the earth below—indeed, nothing in all creation will ever be able to separate us from the love of God that is revealed in Christ Jesus our Lord" (Rom. 8:38–39 NLT).

A relationship with God is often so much simpler than all our religiosity makes it out to be. He made things simple for us because he wants us to know him.

God Only Requires That We Believe

John 3:16 reveals God's incredible heart toward us: "God loved the world this way: He gave his only Son so that everyone who believes in him will not die but will have eternal life" (GW). Before we were born, before we could even attempt anything to gain his love or favor, God gave his Son simply because he loves us. Period. All he asks in return is that we believe in him. We receive salvation and a lifelong relationship with God not because of anything we do but because of his love for us. "For by grace you have been saved through faith. And this is not your own doing; it is the gift of God" (Eph. 2:8 ESV).

He did not say we have to be at church every time the doors are open, or serve on a certain number of church committees, or give a designated amount in offering in order to receive his love or Jesus's sacrifice on the cross. Jesus did not die so we could spend our lives trying to do

God loves us as we are, not as we think we should be.

more or be more in exchange for more of his love and approval. God loves us as we are, not as we think we should be. It is up to us to believe it.

The next time the enemy tries to whisper to you that you aren't loved or lovable, remember the truth in the words of Corrie ten Boom: "There is no pit so deep, that God's love is not deeper still."[2] Truly we can agree with David, who encouraged, "Give thanks to the LORD, for he is good. His love endures forever" (Ps. 136:1).

Your Rx

1. Think about your relationship with the Lord. What lies have you believed about being unlovable or undeserving of love? If you aren't sure what lies you have believed, pray and ask the Lord to reveal them to you. Make a note of them, but then ask him to reveal to you his truth.

2. Take an index card, one for each day of the next week, and carry the card for the day with you. Jot down your experiences, your thoughts, your recollections, or anything else that reminds you that God loves you. As he reveals his love to you, stop right then and thank him for his never-ending,

perfect love for you. Keep the cards so when you struggle you will have a tangible reminder of God's love for you.

3. Look up the following verses: Genesis 28:15; Joshua 1:5; Psalm 136:1; Romans 8:38–39. Write them on index cards and place them where you will see them frequently. Read each of these passages aloud three times daily, committing them to memory.

My Prayer for You

Father, you love each of your children beyond what we can even imagine. Your love is limitless. Your love is perfect and is the antidote to our fears. I pray that today you would show this dear one a glimpse of the height and width and depth of your love in a new and tangible, undeniable way. Father, I pray that you will silence the whispers of the enemy, which make this precious child of yours question the ability to be loved by you. Your Word says that "in Christ Jesus you who once were far away have been brought near" (Eph. 2:13). Since nothing—not even our enemy, or our depression, or our fears—can separate us from your love, I pray this precious one will sense your closeness and receive shelter under your wing. Thank you, Lord, for not only giving your love but also being love, for we live in a lost and broken world. In Jesus's name, amen.

Recommended Playlist

"Jesus Loves Me," Chris Tomlin, © 2014 by sixstepsrecords/ Sparrow Records

"Nothing Ever (Could Separate Us)," Citizen Way, © 2014 by Fair Trade/Columbia

11

God Uses Your Pain

Forget the former things;
  do not dwell on the past.
See, I am doing a new thing!
  Now it springs up; do you not perceive it?

                                        Isaiah 43:18-19

Great faith comes from great victories and great victories
come from great battles.

                                        Steve Dulin

I love traveling through the northeastern United States during autumn, drinking in the jewel-toned colors we don't see much of in Texas. What always seems to capture my attention is the solitary tree in the midst of changing color but surrounded by those that have not yet begun the process. Different from all those around it, the tree stands out.

In the same way, during certain seasons in our lives, God begins changing us from within, perhaps leading us to forge a new path or to stand apart from all those around us not called to the same journey or from those resisting change. Sometimes they even resist the change in us, comfortable with who we have always been while unsure of who we are becoming. It's not easy to blaze a new path, but the rewards are beautiful if we stick with it. Paul writes:

> So here's what I want you to do, God helping you: Take your everyday, ordinary life—your sleeping, eating, going-to-work, and walking around life—and place it before God as an offering. Embracing what God does for you is the best thing you can do for him. Don't become so well-adjusted to your culture that you fit into it without even thinking. Instead, fix your attention on God. You'll be changed from the inside out. Readily recognize what he wants from you, and quickly respond to it. Unlike the culture around you, always dragging you down to its level of immaturity, God brings the best out of you, develops well-formed maturity in you. (Rom. 12:1–2 Message)

Trials always change us. If we love God and trust him in the dark hours, staying open to lessons he has for us along the way, then our hearts receive the blessing of transformation. When walking in the valley, the only way out is up. He is our only path out of our despair.

God promises to restore what the locusts have eaten—what our enemy has stolen (see Joel 2:25). Isaiah 61 reminds us he offers to give us so much more. If we allow him to work in us, he promises we will be comforted. He will give us beauty for ashes, joy for our despair. We can forfeit these blessings if we run from him and his work in us rather than trusting him to bring us through.

God Doesn't Waste Our Pain

I had despaired deep within for weeks. Day after day I stared at the same four walls. On bed rest, attached to IVs, and in continuous pain, I did not resemble my usual self.

My strength was failing. Sorrow was all I could taste. Hope was fleeting. I didn't know what the next day would bring, but I couldn't stand more of the same.

Days blurred together. My only indication of the time that passed was the sun rising and setting, yet I couldn't tell you any of the detail in between.

Life continued as normal for everyone else. Family and friends maintained their daily rituals, with work and school routines. Meanwhile, I continued listening to and believing the enemy's lies, which told me I was useless while unable to continue my usual productive routine. I thought I had failed . . . myself, my family, my patients, even God.

While I was on bed rest and unable to work, others relayed that they were both thinking of me and praying for me. I listened to the spirit of doubt. Were they really? I didn't feel any better. And shamefully, if I was honest with myself, hadn't I promised to pray for others in the past and then forgotten? I too had told people I was "thinking about them," and I did, but what did that mean exactly? What comfort did that bring? Now I really wondered.

The sorrow I felt did not resemble anything I had ever known before. Weeks and months of intense physical pain led to soul-churning despair. As my physical energy and strength depleted, so did my emotional reserve.

I decided if I was going to fight for my physical and emotional health to return, I didn't want to be left unchanged. I wanted to benefit from the experience and come out of it a different person than I had been going in. I prayed that the torment I endured would not be wasted and that the Lord would use the experience to draw me closer to him and to help someone else.

Now, on the other side of this experience, I am thankful. God never protects us from that which he will use to perfect us. He changed me. That painful experience changed and challenged me in unexpected ways:

- It tested my faith and made me seek truth.
- It led me to confront God on some hard issues I had avoided.
- It helped me put my trust in God and not in people.
- It strengthened my compassion for others.
- It made me more sensitive to the brokenness in the people I meet.
- It reinforced how desperately we need God.
- It gave me a chance to comfort others who are in pain and really pray for them when I promise I will.

Going through depression gave me a fresh revelation of Romans 12:15: "Be happy with those who are happy, and weep with those who weep" (NLT). Today if I promise to pray for someone, I will—not just once or twice but every time the Lord puts them on my heart until they tell me the situation has resolved.

Because of what I went through, I'm able to minister to and speak life into others who are suffering, whether it's through this book, speaking engagements, or praying with someone in need who crosses my path. I can now relate in a way I otherwise couldn't because we have walked through similar valleys.

A couple friends and I recently attended our church's annual women's conference. As we sat in the balcony, a young disheveled woman climbed over us a few minutes into the service and took the vacant seat next to me. As the evening concluded with praise and worship, I noticed the woman softly crying. I sensed the Lord telling me to put an arm around her. I didn't know her and thought I might embarrass her. I also sensed the familiar ping of pain. Wouldn't I want someone to reach out to me in the midst of my pain? As I put my arm around her, her shoulders heaved and her tears broke into sobs.

At the conclusion of the service, as all the women around us gathered their belongings and the friends they came with, she took my hand to thank me. I asked her if she would like me to pray with her. Seemingly shocked that anyone would offer, she nodded her consent. Before we prayed, she shared her painful story—the mistakes she had made; her years of depression, anxiety, and loneliness; her concerns that God didn't care and that she might always be destined to feel that way; and her fear that God didn't see her pain and that no one would understand.

God saw her perfectly at that intersection in her journey. He knew where she would sit after arriving late. He put her right next to someone who could relate to so much of her pain but who could also share hope from the other side. She begged to hear more of my story in part, I think, because she needed to borrow hope. We continued to talk and pray as the thousands of women left the building and the maintenance crew cleaned around us. As I wiped her tears, I sensed a change. She walked in crying tears of desperation, but she was leaving with tears of hope and gratitude.

He doesn't waste our pain. He turns our biggest messes into our greatest messages.

God repeatedly offers me the opportunity to partner with him and share my story to offer encouragement and hope to those who are earlier in their walk but on the same journey I traveled. No greater joy exists than watching God use for good what the enemy intended to harm me. I receive fresh revelation of how he gives us beauty for our ashes and the oil of gladness for our despair (Isa. 61:3). He doesn't waste our pain. He turns our biggest messes into our greatest messages.

God uses my pain to help others. And he will use yours, if you're willing, in ways you can't even imagine.

A New Thing

God's Word declares, "Anyone who belongs to Christ has become a new person. The old life is gone; a new life has begun" (2 Cor. 5:17 NLT). When we agree with the enemy's lies about ourselves and our situation, we in essence tell God we don't believe he changed our lives when Christ paid the ultimate price for us on the cross.

When we deal with the roots of depression and live in the new life he gave us, dramatic change occurs. He gives us a new heart, a new identity, and a new perspective. We don't cower before or fear depression but laugh at the enemy's tactics while standing on God's truth. How would you like to be free not only from depression but also from the fear of depression, the shadow of depression? How would you like to look back and say, "I remember those depressed days—how different I am now"? You can!

For years I lived under the influence of the enemy. Under a spirit of heaviness and oppression, self-pity, bitterness, unforgiveness, and resentment, I was unable to love myself or receive the love of others or God. I didn't realize it at the time, so I wouldn't have admitted to it. Only after I began searching for and then believing God's truth about me did the change occur.

I recently received a message from someone that is a testament to the change within me: "I have never seen a picture of you where you are not beaming with joy! I want that!" I haven't always been this way. Previously, I might have smiled on the outside, but I did not have joy within. He has truly done a "new thing" in my life. "Forget the former things; do not dwell on the past. See, I am doing a new thing! Now it springs up; do you not perceive it?" (Isa. 43:18–19).

God doesn't play favorites. If you want God to do a new thing in your life, he will—but you have to do your part first. You have to stop agreeing with the lies of the enemy and consciously choose to believe God's truth.

Moving from the valley of despair to setting my feet on a higher place began when I made the conscious decision to check my thoughts (2 Cor. 10:5) to see if they agreed with the enemy's lies or God's truth. That required hard work! We have between fifty thousand to seventy thousand thoughts each day. It takes discipline to take our thoughts captive and not unconsciously agree with the enemy one, one hundred, or one thousand times in the course of the day. But the rewards are worth the effort. "No discipline seems pleasant at the time, but painful. Later on, however, it produces a harvest of righteousness and peace for those who have been trained by it" (Heb. 12:11). I want that peace, the peace the enemy tried to kill. Do you?

God provides a perspective based not on our moods or our circumstances but on our identity in Christ.

I longed for God to lift the blanket of depression. He did. He changed my heart. "And I will give you a new heart, and I will put a new spirit in you. I will take out your stony, stubborn heart and give you a tender, responsive heart" (Ezek. 36:26 NLT). In doing so, I became less anxious, less self-focused, less angry, and more loving, joyful, peaceful, and compassionate.

God's new heart erases fear, shame, and guilt. He provides a perspective based not on our moods or our circumstances but on our identity in Christ. With this comes a separation from past sins or shame, a purpose, confidence, joy, and peace. The overwhelming experience of depression can become a little smudge in the rearview mirror as God builds a new heart and a different character. He can take this pressing pain and turn it into a motivation for praise, thanksgiving, worship, and service to others as we have compassion for those who struggle. Once he begins to set our feet on high places, we can, like Paul, comfort others with the comfort we have received (2 Cor. 1:4).

Your Rx

1. Prayerfully think back on your journey through depression. In what ways have you changed? Thank God for the positive changes you notice and thank him in anticipation for those yet to come.

2. Look up the following verses: Isaiah 43:18–19; Ezekiel 36:26; Romans 12:15; 2 Corinthians 5:17; 10:5. Write them on index cards and place them where you will see them frequently. Read each of these passages aloud three times daily, committing them to memory.

3. Take some time to create a "travel journal" of sorts. Write down some of your prayers, encouraging songs, and comforting Scripture passages. Reading the journal will encourage you, should you ever encounter another valley, and it will remind you how far you have come.

My Prayer for You

Father, I know the pain of despair and loneliness. I pray for this dear one who is in need of comfort and assurance that this pain is not for naught. Please provide for their needs today. Will you provide a friend to walk this journey with them? You've sent the ultimate comforter in the form of the Holy Spirit. Go into the depths of the despair with your soothing balm and give your peace that truly passes all understanding. I thank you for your faithfulness and meeting our needs even now. Thank you that you never waste our pain but will use it to change us, perfect us, and help us minister to others. Because of Jesus, I ask these things, amen.

Recommended Playlist

"Nothing Is Wasted," Jason Gray, © 2011 by Centricity Music

"Any Other Way," Tenth Avenue North, © 2010 by Reunion Records

"Live Like That," Sidewalk Prophets, © 2012 by Fervent Records

"Lay Me Down," Chris Tomlin, © 2013 by sixstepsrecords/ Sparrow Records

"Even This Will Be Made Beautiful," Jason Gray, © 2014 by Centricity Music

"Nothing Is Wasted," Elevation Worship, © 2013 by Essential Worship

"Something Beautiful," Steven Curtis Chapman, © 2013 by Reunion/Chapman

12

The Way to Hope

Dear friend, I pray that you may enjoy good health and that all may go well with you, even as your soul is getting along well.

3 John 1:2

You can read many self-help books, a daily diet of how-tos ... but the only way to mend a heart is to memorize God's.

Ann Voskamp

For many years I was puzzled by Jesus's question in John 5:6: "When Jesus saw him and knew he had been ill for a long time, he asked him, 'Would you like to get well?'" (NLT). I wondered why Jesus would ask that. The longer I have been in private practice, the more I understand the intent behind his question.

Many come wanting freedom from their ailment, but few actually heed my recommendations after I have delivered the diagnosis and treatment suggestions. Why? The most common reason: it takes work. Doing what it takes to shed depression requires work. We have become accustomed to rapid information transmission. The desire is equally great for quick fixes for our health.

God desires for us to be physically, emotionally, and spiritually healthy, and we have access to the Great Physician!

Another reason is it's often more comfortable for us to remain in our known discomfort than to risk the discomfort of the unknown. Think of the lame man from John 5. Who would he be if he were no longer "the lame man"? People would respond to him differently if he were healed. He would have to integrate into society and learn how to gainfully support himself. Was he ready to shed his old known life as a lame man for healing and an unknown future?

Are you ready to shed a depressed existence and trust God for what the unknown future holds? I think you are. God knows his plans for us, and they are good. The future is filled with hope. God desires for us to be physically, emotionally, and spiritually healthy, and we have access to the Great Physician! "Dear friend, I pray that you may enjoy good health and that all may go well with you, even as your soul is getting along well" (3 John 1:2). But it requires some work on our part. Let's get started!

Watch Your Thoughts and Words

Do you talk to yourself occasionally? That is pretty common, and it's okay. We all talk to ourselves more than we realize. But the things we think and say to ourselves influence our beliefs and attitudes.

When people ask my advice regarding issues they or their "friend" (wink, wink) struggle with, they seem to expect me to suggest therapy or medication. While both treatment methods can be helpful, they aren't usually my first suggestion. One of the most important things we can do to make a positive change in our lives is to guard our thoughts and watch our words. We discussed this briefly in chapter 6.

It's critical to think more like God and less like the enemy. When we agree with and act on the encouragement in Philippians 4:8 to "fix your thoughts on what is true, and honorable, and right, and pure, and lovely, and admirable. Think about things that are excellent and worthy of praise" (NLT), we train our minds to think more like God and agree with his solution. When we know God's truth, it sets us free (John 8:32). Our thoughts must align with God's truth in order for us to find freedom from whatever holds us prisoner. According to 2 Corinthians 10:5, we must take every thought captive. I have heard Pastor Jimmy Evans say, "Any thought you don't take captive will take you captive."

Marian Wright Edelman said, "So often we dwell on the things that seem impossible rather than on the things that are possible."[1] The enemy wants us to believe his lies, but God's truth is transformational, and with God all things are possible. I love how Sheila Walsh highlights the difference in her book *The Heartache No One Sees*:

> Satan tells us: "You are weak!"
> Jesus tells us: "In Me you are strong!"
> Satan tells us: "You are lost!"
> Jesus tells us: "In Me you are found!"
> Satan tells us: "You are a victim!"
> Jesus tells us: "In Me you are a victor!"

Satan tells us: "You are ugly, inside and out!"

Jesus tells us: "You are beautiful!"

Satan tells us: "You will never be healed!"

Isaiah tells us of Jesus: "He was wounded for our transgressions, He was bruised for our iniquities; The chastisement for our peace was upon Him, And by His stripes we are healed" (Isa. 53:5 NKJV).[2]

Our words hold the power to help us or hurt us. "What goes into someone's mouth does not defile them. . . . But the things that come out of a person's mouth come from the heart, and these defile them" (Matt. 15:11, 18). For years my words about myself were negative, critical, and unloving. They certainly didn't line up with what the Father says about me. And you know what? They didn't help me get out of the valley either. In fact, they bought me season tickets! Once I began focusing on what God says, my words began to change, and then my beliefs came into agreement. I received a fresh revelation of what it means that "you will know the truth, and the truth will set you free" (John 8:32).

I used to believe emotions were neither good nor bad; they just were. Now I know the importance of not being led by my emotions. Our emotions, our feelings, are the outward manifestation of the thoughts and beliefs we have. As we learn to control our thoughts, take them captive, and agree with them when they line up with God's thoughts but reject them when they don't, we will control our emotions. Have your thoughts and words been hurting you or helping you?

Seek Perspective Through Therapy

Therapy is one of the most commonly known treatments for depression. People often turn to therapy when they have tried their own strategies with suboptimal results and remain in pain and suffering. Most people have at least a general idea of what therapy is and why it might help, and there are many resources beyond this book that discuss in-depth the benefits of therapy. To be effective, therapy or counseling should include not just conversation about things, although this most certainly can have a cathartic effect, but also objective goals and a targeted change in behavior.

Counseling involves working with a professional who can offer objective feedback and suggestions with the intention of relieving suffering. Therapy can generate insights into our own perspectives and behaviors that often cannot be gained elsewhere. Working with an objective party gives us the opportunity to break habits and change thought patterns we are often unaware of and that keep us stuck.

Therapy requires some time investment. It isn't as convenient as simply taking medication. It also requires a willingness to trust the therapist. Poor therapist-patient relationships can limit or prevent improvement. Patients who experience difficulty trusting others will

The great news is we all have access to what we need in him.

often also have difficulty making progress in therapy. Patients have to start with a positive expectation for change and a willingness to risk. This can be a hard place to start for a person experiencing depression.

My own experience of therapy during depression was positive. I sought out a therapist who was a believer, and we established a strong rapport. My therapy sessions offered times of encouragement and a safe place to share my struggles. I gained insights about myself and my situation that helped minimize some of the environmental negatives that affected me. I gained a better understanding of the effect of my own self-talk on my mood and perspective and so learned to speak to myself more positively and more gently. I also saw the effect of having positive people around me. I chose to increasingly seek out relationships with those who shared a more positive outlook. These perspectives were relatively external to me, though, and I did not at the time recognize or deal with the spiritual nature of depression and the effect it had on me.

While therapy can prove helpful, it's important to recognize who really does the healing. While I love my field and I believe God has given us doctors to help us with our physical and emotional wellness, I'm most thankful that he is our ultimate guide. Even as a professional, I can offer nothing to my patients that heals unilaterally. My words don't fix, and my suggestions don't heal. God heals. The great news is we all have access to what we need in him. "And he will be called Wonderful Counselor, Mighty God, Everlasting Father, Prince of Peace" (Isa. 9:6).

Consider Medication

Antidepressant medications became part of the psychiatrist's toolbox in the 1950s when scientists proved that there are physiological pathways that mediate the symptoms of depression and that these pathways can be modified. In 2015, Drugs.com, a useful and comprehensive website for information on pharmacological agents of all types, listed thirty-nine distinct antidepressant compounds grouped within seven categories, generally by mechanism of operation. For all their differences and different modes of operation, though, current antidepressants all do essentially the same thing. They provide differing amounts of various neurotransmitters to replace what is deficient in the brains of depressed individuals.

Antidepressants don't cure depression. They only reduce symptoms. A reduction in symptoms is helpful for many depression sufferers, but the fact that antidepressants don't cure depression means that patients must eventually deal with the root causes of their depression. Antidepressants can assist people in getting back on their feet so they can work or socialize while they continue to deal with the external or internal factors of depression. Sometimes antidepressant medication is useful to help a person get to the point where they can express a positive expectation prior to starting therapy.

Antidepressants are not without cost, both monetarily and in terms of side effects. Along with mitigating the negative feelings of depression, antidepressant medications may also blunt positive emotions or leave a person without much emotion. Antidepressants also need to be taken on a fairly long-term basis. They do not become effective until a person has been taking them for several weeks, so changing dosages or agents is a multiweek or month experiment, which often leads to frustration.

I learned the value of antidepressant medication when my mother was prescribed medication for depression. She had been depressed much of her life. After she went through menopause, her physician prescribed an antidepressant. She experienced such a dramatic change in her personality, her attitude, and her countenance that it seemed like a miracle. It had such a dramatic effect that years later when she was hospitalized during the late stages of cancer, a close second concern to managing her cancer was maintaining her antidepressant medication so she did not experience a relapse in her depression. In my practice, I often hear, "I wish I didn't need this medicine" or "I wish I could get off this medicine," yet cardiologists or endocrinologists rarely hear such complaints after prescribing medication for high blood pressure or diabetes. There is no shame in using a pharmacological approach to manage depression's symptoms.

We have to be careful not to limit God in terms of the means he may use to provide relief or healing. In Isaiah 38, we find the story of Hezekiah's miraculous healing from what was evidently a terminal disease. We read that Hezekiah prayed and that God both heard and answered his prayer, granting him fifteen more years of life. But that isn't the entire story. Isaiah relayed God's promise of healing but also instructed Hezekiah's attendants to apply a poultice of figs, a common medicinal treatment of the day. Even though Hezekiah appealed to God and God healed him, Isaiah still instructed Hezekiah's attendants to do what they knew to do.

God gave us scientists, doctors, and medicine for a reason. He uses experts in various fields to guide us where our own knowledge is deficient, and he has provided the means and the knowledge to make medicine to relieve the symptoms of depression. I would no more try to fix my own refrigerator than I would try to make my own shoes. God did not intend for us to go it alone.

Take Care of Your Temple

Taking care of your physical body is essential if you want optimal emotional health. When I give treatment recommendations to patients, I highlight those aspects of treatment that are more or less in their direct control: rest, nutrition, exercise, and social activity.

Rest

While there are spiritual implications of rest, when I suggest rest as a component of the treatment for depression, I mean sleep. Sleep is important for emotional well-being. Without sufficient sleep, our immune system becomes less effective, our energy runs dry, our cognitive functioning works suboptimally, and our mood takes a hit. God designed our bodies so that while we sleep they repair themselves: repair tissue, build muscle, and regenerate neurotransmitters and hormones. Without sufficient sleep, you limit your body's ability to repair itself, which over time can lead to disease.

But rest also represents an attitude of humility and an acceptance of God's ways. Hebrews 3:7–11 teaches us that the Israelites did not enter into God's rest because their hearts were hardened and they did not accept God's ways. Resting signifies an attitude of trusting God rather than worrying. Worry communicates we don't believe God is who he says he is. Rest communicates we trust God and his faithfulness.

When God calls us to rest, we can do so because we know he has taken care of everything. In the Old Testament book of Exodus, we read, "God said to Moses, 'I AM who I AM'" (Exod. 3:14). In that short sentence, God declared his ability to be all that the Israelites needed God to be for them and all that you and I need God to be for us. "I AM" has no beginning and no ending; God is always available to be who and what we need him to be in every situation.

In Psalm 46:10, we are encouraged to "be still, and know that I am God." Sometimes when I experience the most stress and am in need of hearing from God the most, I work against myself by not resting. Only when I become still can I hear the quiet voice of God. Resting in God means we believe he is sufficient for every situation. To rest, we must first put our faith in God. "But without faith it is impossible to please him: for he that cometh to God must believe that he is, and that he is a rewarder of them that diligently seek him" (Heb. 11:6 KJV). Resting allows us to step back and remember that while we cannot control every situation, we can trust the One who does.

> Rest is one of our greatest spiritual weapons against our enemy.

I personally struggled with the concept of rest for decades. I always thought of rest with such disdain, as a purposeless activity for the weak or lazy. But rest is one of our greatest spiritual weapons against our enemy. For over a year the Lord kept raising this issue of rest to me in various ways. I heard sermons about it. Friends shared their concern for my inability to rest. Books about the topic seemed to leap off bookstore shelves into my arms. I suddenly noticed song lyrics about rest that I had sung before but never consciously heard. I even took a sabbatical to work on a writing project but was repeatedly given the advice to not write, just rest. At first, I panicked. If I rested, how would I get anything accomplished? How could I take time off work and be unproductive? The first couple of days felt like sheer torture! One morning I got in my car to run an errand, and it was as if the Lord whispered in my ear, "Are you trying to run away from me and my rest?" Before I dared protest, I softly admitted in my heart the truth in that question.

Slowly, God reframed my mind-set. Obeying God in rest is productive. For me it meant breaking off the chains of "doing." The enemy of my soul didn't want me to get comfortable being still. He wanted me to be a worried ally for his kingdom rather than a rested warrior in God's. When we are still, we are powerful . . . full of the very breath of God because we breathe him in.

Doing things differently will go against everything our minds and bodies are used to. The enemy frequently lied to me and taunted me with my "progress" during this time of sabbatical rest. I worried about how I would answer the questions upon my return. "How much did you get done during your sabbatical?" "What great revelations did God show you?" "What did you accomplish during your time away?" I couldn't give a page count or speak of great revelations written for me in the clouds, but I was at peace because I had learned that resting is an act of obedience to God.

Nutrition

Just as rest is an important component for health, so is adequate nutrition. "Then he lay down under the bush and fell asleep. All at once an angel touched him and said, 'Get up and eat.' . . . He ate and drank and then lay down again" (1 Kings 19:5–6). God's plan was simple: rest and nourishment.

Many individuals who suffer from symptoms of depression also suffer from deficiencies in B6, B12, and folic acid. These vitamins affect the production of serotonin and help us feel calm, relaxed, alert, and happy. Foods high in vitamins and minerals, including seeds, nuts, grains, lean proteins, fish, and eggs, are good considerations when fighting depression.

Vitamin C is also necessary for serotonin production and can be found in a balanced diet including citrus, spinach, and peas. Vitamin D also affects serotonin levels and can be obtained not only through sunlight but also through foods such as eggs, dairy, and fish. Low levels of vitamin E have also been linked to symptoms of depression. Foods such as nuts, seeds, egg yolks, and chickpeas may boost vitamin E levels and thus decrease associated symptoms. Protein-rich foods that are high in tyrosine, such as beans, fish, poultry, lean beef, and dairy, help foster the adequate production of dopamine and norepinephrine, which are key mood-regulating neurotransmitters.

Excessive caffeine and sugar intake leads to decreased vitamin B production and an increase in the stress hormone cortisol. Dehydration can also lead to symptoms of depression.

Exercise

As little as fifteen minutes of exercise a day can impact brain chemistry and improve mood. Many depressed people lack energy and motivation. When we need energy most, we have the least. It takes energy to exercise, but once we begin exercising, we have more energy.

Depression makes it hard to think clearly. Both our brains and our bodies go into a lull because of insufficient neurotransmitter production. Exercise helps counteract this deficiency. When I begin to feel down, I ask myself, "When was the last time I exercised?" because I can tell a difference in my mood when I haven't exercised recently.

When we engage in enjoyable physical activity, we are more likely to continue doing it, so choose an activity that appeals to you.

Social Activity

The night before Jesus died must have been the most heart-wrenching of nights for him. He knew what was to come; he had foretold it. That night he went into the garden to pray, to pour out his heart to God. But he didn't want to go alone; he wanted his friends to go with him. I don't know about you, but for me, sometimes the company of a good friend can help ease my pain, rid me of my feelings of loneliness, and bathe me in love.

Sometimes when we feel down, one of the hardest things to do is to get out and be with other people. But social isolation increases the blues. When we allow ourselves to become isolated, others, by and large, aren't even aware we are in pain or in need.

Another reason social activity is important, especially during the journey through the valley of depression, is because it allows for accountability. Accountability is key for lasting change. This is why groups such as Weight Watchers and Alcoholics Anonymous are so successful. Knowing we are accountable to someone else for our actions is a big motivator, and when we are faced with the blues, sometimes we need external motivation to keep us heading in the right direction.

Take Care of Your Spirit

Am I suggesting that spiritual disciplines will help pull you from the valley of depression? I'll go so far as to tell you they are imperative. Healing begins when we bring the lies we have believed about ourselves, others, and the world out of the darkness of our own personal pain and shame and exchange them for the light of God's grace and perfect truth. Let's examine how we do that.

Spend Time in God's Presence

The Bible repeatedly offers key truths and wisdom. If we follow such advice, it improves our physical and emotional well-being. One key truth is that peace comes when we spend time in God's presence meditating on the goodness of God. "You will keep in perfect peace all who trust in you, all whose thoughts are fixed on you" (Isa. 26:3 NLT).

The woman with the issue of blood provides a perfect example for us to follow. Broken and ill, she needed a miracle. She possessed enough faith to believe that if she just touched Jesus's robe, she would be healed. If she hadn't prioritized being in his presence, she would have missed his healing and a life of freedom.

The Word encourages, "Come near to God and he will come near to you" (James 4:8). According to this verse, God wants to be near to us, but we must do our part first and enter into his presence. Loneliness ensues when we remain too busy to take time to rest in his presence and listen to him. His Word is true. He promises he won't ever leave us, but he won't force us to stay in his presence. Yet peace and joy come when we stay in his presence and focus on him. "Surely you have granted him unending blessings and made him glad with the joy of your presence" (Ps. 21:6).

Stay Anchored in the Word

God does not desire for any of his children to suffer physically or emotionally. He provides a way through his Word for us to be physically, emotionally, and spiritually healthy. "He sent his Word and healed them, and delivered them from their destructions" (Ps. 107:20 NASB). God's Word heals us. Jesus said, "If you abide in My word [continually obeying my teachings and living in accordance with them, then] you are truly My disciples. And you will know the truth [regarding salvation], and the truth will set you free" (John 8:31–32 AMP). We cannot be free until we know the truth. This requires intentionality. Ephesians 6:11–13 implores us to daily put on the whole armor of God to protect ourselves—mind, body, and spirit.

I once listened to a well-known Christian speaker. She knew her Bible backward and forward, and she embodied joy. She captivated me by her love for Jesus and for God's Word. I ached to have what she had. I'm embarrassed to admit it, but I clearly remember thinking to myself, "I want that kind of relationship with God. I want that hunger for his Word. But it takes too much work." Wow! The enemy had fed me that lie, and I had believed it. The enemy knows what Scripture says: "For the word of God is alive and active. Sharper than any double-edged sword" (Heb. 4:12). As a result of believing the enemy's lies, for many years I missed out on the greatest blessing I could have asked for, and I thwarted the opportunity to effectively prepare for the battle that lay ahead.

Fast-forward several years to when illness left me bedridden. A friend shared a verse with me that gave me hope when mine was waning: "Every valley shall be filled in, every mountain and hill made low. The crooked roads shall become straight, the rough ways smooth" (Luke 3:5). I knew I needed to grab hold of that verse to stand on. I wrote the verse on a Post-it note and put the note on my lampstand so I would see it and be encouraged every time I saw it. That one verse turned into ten then twenty then over one hundred different verses before my health returned. Before it was all said and done, I had Post-it notes on my lamps, bedposts, light switches, closet doors, and even my IV pole! But even before my physical health returned, I sensed a shift in my emotional well-being. As I began to recite God's Word, especially his promises, the dark cloud that had settled in my heart began to lift and I began to feel more hopeful.

The Bible explains that from the beginning of time God gave us the power to choose freely. We are free to choose him or not. We are free to believe his Word or not. We are free to trust his promises and agree with him about our situation or not. "Do not conform to the pattern of this world, but be transformed by the renewing of your mind. Then you will be able to test and approve what God's will is—his good, pleasing and perfect will" (Rom. 12:2). When we recite God's promises, a shift takes place in our thinking. Not only do we know his will, but our faith also grows. Faith comes by hearing, and by reciting his promises, we bolster our faith. By reciting his promises, we agree with what God has already said about our situation, and in doing so, we give him the freedom to work.

The enemy tries to keep us focused on the things the world promises will bring happiness: career, financial stability, success. But those things are counterfeits for true comfort, satisfaction, and joy. Answers to life's questions will not come from pop psychology magazines or television talk shows or even well-intentioned friends but from the Word of God: "Get wisdom, get understanding; do not forget my words or turn away from them" (Prov. 4:5).

Pray

We already discussed prayer and practicing gratitude in the chapter on joy, but since prayer is essential for maintaining peace and joy, I wanted to share a few more thoughts. Jesus explained, "Until now you have not asked [the Father] for anything in My name; but now ask and keep on asking and you will receive, so that your joy may be full and complete" (John 16:24 AMP). So often when we are suffering the most, we pray the least. But before God will act on our behalf, often he waits for us to admit our need. Then true to his Word, "As soon as I pray, you answer me; you encourage me by giving me strength" (Ps. 138:3 NLT).

Frequently, the words of Hebrews 4:16 comfort me: "So let us come boldly to the throne of our gracious God. There we will receive his mercy, and we will find grace to help us when we need it most" (NLT). God tells us to come to him as a child comes to a parent. Unlike a co-worker, friend, or stranger, God never tires of us communicating with him. He encourages us to pray without ceasing (1 Thess. 5:17). Then we will have peace. "Don't worry about anything; instead, pray about everything. Tell God what you need, and thank him for all he has done. Then you will experience God's peace, which exceeds anything we can understand. His peace will guard your hearts and minds as you live in Christ Jesus" (Phil. 4:6–7 NLT).

Part of prayer is sharing our needs and desires with God. Yet another crucial aspect of prayer is surrendering our needs, desires, and plans to God's more perfect plan. It isn't always easy to surrender to God's plans for our lives, but it is always worth it.

It isn't always easy to surrender to God's plans for our lives, but it is always worth it.

Communicating with God through prayer ensures we are never alone—God is always waiting for us to draw near to him through prayer. Prayer allows the opportunity for God to comfort us in our sorrow. Prayer also offers the opportunity for God to encourage us and to give us clarity about what we need or need to do.

Obey

We cannot fully live a life of peace and joy unless we also live a life of obedience to God's Word. His Word says it isn't enough to hear the Word. We must also humble ourselves and obey. "If my people, who are called by my name, will humble themselves and pray and seek my face and turn from their wicked ways, then I will hear from heaven, and I will forgive their sin and will heal their land" (2 Chron. 7:14). We must not only listen to the Word but also do what it says. "Do not merely listen to the word, and so deceive yourselves. Do what it says" (James 1:22).

David indicated that joy comes from obedience: "I take joy in doing your will, my God, for your instructions are written on my heart" (Ps. 40:8 NLT). He also said that when we obey God, we will lack for nothing. "Honor the LORD, all his people; those who obey him have all they need. Even lions go hungry for lack of food, but those who obey the LORD lack nothing good" (Ps. 34:9–10 GNT).

God doesn't make life complicated; he tells us everything we need to know for life and godliness in his Word, yet we often choose not to obey. When we go our own way and do our own thing, we get burned. It's no different than in biblical days. "A father to the fatherless, a defender of widows, is God in his holy dwelling. God sets the lonely in families, he leads out the prisoners with singing; but the rebellious live in a sun-scorched land" (Ps. 68:5–6). If Jesus visited us today, he would tell us the same thing he told those he ministered to two thousands years ago: "Repent and seek first the kingdom of God."

Take Time for Praise and Gratitude

David was well acquainted with depression, yet he continued to pray and praise. Even when he was down, he didn't stop praising God. "Why, my soul, are you downcast? Why so disturbed within me? Put your hope in God, for I will yet praise him, my Savior and my God" (Ps. 42:5). I'm certain that David's praise kept his faith and hope in the Lord strong during the hard times.

While depression can feel like imprisonment, I'm sure it doesn't compare to the dire treatment Paul and Silas received during their time in prison. In a situation that could have left them angry, bitter, and resentful, they chose to pray and sing praises, rejoicing despite their circumstances. The prophet Habakkuk also determined to praise God regardless of the dire situation he found himself in, trusting God would provide.

> Though the fig tree does not bud
>   and there are no grapes on the vines,
> though the olive crop fails
>   and the fields produce no food,

> though there are no sheep in the pen
>   and no cattle in the stalls,
> yet I will rejoice in the LORD,
>   I will be joyful in God my Savior.
> The Sovereign LORD is my strength;
>   he makes my feet like the feet of a deer,
>   he enables me to tread on the heights. (Hab. 3:17–19)

Nothing we face is too big for God!

We must also practice intentional gratitude. Being grateful opens our eyes to all we have to be grateful for. It helps us stay focused on the positive and allows us to remember the good things in life while deemphasizing the negative. By expressing gratitude, we delight in the goodness of God. "The LORD makes firm the steps of the one who delights in him; though he may stumble, he will not fall, for the LORD upholds him with his hand" (Ps. 37:23–24).

Nothing we face is too big for God!

David revealed the many benefits that result from a heart full of gratitude and praise. He taught that when we thank the Lord and praise him, he replenishes our joy, frees us from fears, alleviates our disappointments, rescues us from trouble, and keeps us safe.

> I will always thank the LORD;
>   I will never stop praising him.
> I will praise him for what he has done;
>   may all who are oppressed listen and be glad!
> Proclaim with me the LORD's greatness;
>   let us praise his name together!
> I prayed to the LORD, and he answered me;
>   he freed me from all my fears.
> The oppressed look to him and are glad;
>   they will never be disappointed.
> The helpless call to him, and he answers;
>   he saves them from all their troubles.

His angel guards those who honor the LORD
  and rescues them from danger.
Find out for yourself how good the LORD is.
  Happy are those who find safety with him. (Ps. 34:1–8
    GNT)

God's Word indicates that he often waits for our obedience (praise, gratitude, etc.) before he acts. If we pray and praise, then he blesses: "May the nations praise you, O God. Yes, may all the nations praise you. *Then* the earth will yield its harvests, and God, our God, will richly bless us" (Ps. 67:5–6 NLT, emphasis added). If we pray and praise, then we experience peace:

> Rejoice in the Lord always. I will say it again: Rejoice! Let your gentleness be evident to all. The Lord is near. Do not be anxious about anything, but in every situation, by prayer and petition, with thanksgiving, present your requests to God. And the peace of God, which transcends all understanding, will guard your hearts and your minds in Christ Jesus. (Phil. 4:4–7)

Trust God

The key to overcoming depression is trusting God. We do our part and obey, and then we trust God for the rest. God is pleased when we trust because "without faith it is impossible to please God, because anyone who comes to him must believe that he exists and that he rewards those who earnestly seek him" (Heb. 11:6). In the Psalms, David continually came back to "and yet will I trust him!"

During my darkest days, it was hard to trust. I surely couldn't trust my feelings, it was hard to trust others because their words clearly relayed they didn't understand, and it was even hard to trust God. Day after day I prayed that God would help me trust him more. One morning I sensed God saying, "We've been over this before." We had.

"Yes, Lord. I just seem to keep struggling. Please help me trust you more." What I sensed next surprised me (which was a clue to me that it was the Lord and not my own thoughts): "It's your choice. Either you choose to trust me or you don't. Either you believe in me or you don't. Don't make it any more difficult than that." Hmm. Putting it like that certainly simplified things, though it didn't necessarily make things easier.

We have to get past ourselves, past our interactions with others that have weakened our readiness to trust, and decide to reengage. Still, it's a choice. It's a risk. But what do we have to lose? Our depression? Isn't that worth the risk? Scripture repeatedly encourages us that if we trust in the Lord, we will not be disappointed (Ps. 25:3; Isa. 49:23; Rom. 10:11; 1 Pet. 2:6). This is an empowering promise.

My struggle to fully trust God has been much like a game of tug-of-war. At times, I trust him so easily, and at other times, I seem to fight with all my might trying to achieve in my own strength, not his. God is not interested in fighting a battle to persuade us to trust him. The Bible provides all the reasons to trust him. Scripture repeatedly tells us that God will restore our health (Jer. 30:17), protect us and care for us (Isa. 40:11), give us comfort and joy instead of sorrow (Pss. 30:5; 126:5; Jer. 31:13), and heal the brokenhearted (Ps. 147:3). He has told us in his Word what to do. Are you ready to get well?

Your Rx

1. Think about your current sleep, diet, and exercise habits. What one change can you commit to making today in one or more of these areas to improve your health and mood?

2. Consider the spiritual disciplines that are key for living a life of peace and joy: spending time in God's presence, staying anchored in the Word, praying, being obedient, taking time

for praise and gratitude, and trusting God. Prayerfully ask God in which of these disciplines he wants to help you invest yourself a bit deeper. Pray for his guidance to make the changes and improvements he highlights, then commit to yourself and him how you will begin to step forward in faith in this area.

3. Look up the following verses: Psalm 34:8; Isaiah 53:5; John 8:32; Romans 12:2; 1 Corinthians 10:13; 2 Corinthians 12:9; Philippians 4:6–8; Hebrews 4:16; 3 John 1:2. Write them on index cards and place them where you will see them frequently. Read each of these passages aloud three times daily, committing them to memory.

My Prayer for You

Father, your Word says that you will restore our health, protect us and care for us, give us comfort and joy instead of sorrow, heal the brokenhearted, turn our wailing into dancing, clothe us with joy, and anoint us with the oil of joy. You cannot lie. I thank you for this dear one who trusts you to be their Great Physician. I thank you that it is your desire that we would be in health and that you promise to give us victory through our Lord Jesus Christ. I thank you for drawing this dear one closer to you and for the good work you have planned, for the harvest of joy and singing that will be reaped. In Jesus's mighty name we pray and boldly ask all these things, amen.

Recommended Playlist

"I Don't Know How," Jason Gray, © 2014 by Centricity Music
"The Words I Would Say," Sidewalk Prophets, © 2009 by Fervent Records/Word

"Praise You in This Storm," Casting Crowns, © 2005 by Re-union Records

"Don't Stop Praising," John Waller, © 2014 by Label Me Not

"Sovereign," Chris Tomlin, © 2013 by sixstepsrecords/Sparrow Records

"Help Me Find It," Sidewalk Prophets, © 2012 by Fervent Records/Word

"The More I Seek You," Gateway Worship, © 2006 by Gateway Create Publishing

"Freedom Reigns," Jesus Culture, © 2014 by Jesus Culture Music

"Made for Worship," Planetshakers, © 2014 by Integrity/Columbia

"You Satisfy My Soul," Laura Hackett, © 2012 by Forerunner Music

You Have a Gift to Give

Dear One,

I'm thankful for the chance to walk part of this journey with you. It has been a sacred time and space. Could you hear me cheering you on? I've prayed for you since before this book was in print that through its pages you would see how wide and deep God's love is for you (Eph. 3:18).

It's God's heartfelt desire for us to be in health (3 John 1:2) and not entrapped by the enemy's deceit! As you became aware and began to kick out the enemy's lies, you opened up your heart to God's truth. He has begun to breathe new life into you (Eph. 3:16). Oh, how he loves you! He loves you too much to leave you where you were or even where you are.

You and God make a strong team (Rom. 8:31). I'm so proud of you for persevering when you weren't sure you could and the enemy didn't want you to (James 1:12). Even more importantly, your heavenly Father is proud. You have run the race and fought the fight (2 Tim. 4:7–8). The enemy's hold on you will never be the same again.

If you feel yourself begin to slip under again, grab hold of the tools you have learned. They are your weapons for warfare. I recently shared with friends that the enemy wanted me to shake in my boots, and I fell for it for a bit. Thankfully, not as long as I used to. God reminded me to put on the armor (Eph. 6:11) of his Word and fight like a girl . . . a daughter of the Most High God.

Think back to the day when you cracked open this book. Do you remember the depths of that valley? In your darkest days, what did you long for most? I longed to know I wasn't alone, that someone understood, and that it would get better.

As God began bringing me out of that valley, he prodded me to begin offering the same comfort to others that he had offered to me (2 Cor. 1:3–4). He didn't wait until I had crossed the finish line on that trek. When we are obedient to God's call, that is where we find his comfort and strength. When I returned to my practice during my recovery, my attitude changed to one of serving my patients out of a richer compassion for their suffering and the love God wanted to show them through me. He had me sow seeds of encouragement and inspiration in patients who were not as far along as I was, even when I was still broken and wounded.

If you can look in the rearview mirror of your journey and think, "I'm glad those days are behind me," even if you don't feel completely home free, you are farther along in your journey to freedom than others who are experiencing their darkest days. God has given you a gift that you can now pass on to others. You have experience, insight, and empathy that could help someone else. Take hold of that gift and lavish it on those who cross your path. Watch how in doing so you not only help them but are also helped in your own healing journey.

You can do this, friend. You already are. Keep trusting God day by day. Then give the same comfort to others that you've received.

Because of him, hope prevails!
(Dr.) Michelle Bengtson

Appendix

Helping a Depressed Loved One

How to help a depressed loved one could be a separate book of its own. If you have never suffered from depression, it's difficult to relate to the experience of one who is suffering. When we love someone with depression, we engage in a dance of learning how to love them through it while they learn how to cope with it.

In order to help you help a depressed loved one, I've created a resource for you called "How to Help a Depressed Loved One." You can find it on my website, http://DrMichelleBengtson.com /how-to-help-a-depressed-loved-one-chapter. There you can also find related blog posts and other resources. I also have a weekly column, "Ask Dr. B," in which I answer reader questions.

Acknowledgments

No project like this is completed in isolation. The support and prayers of many have helped bring it from a vision to a dream fulfilled.

To my husband, Scott, and both our boys, you have ridden the roller-coaster ride with me, prepared to sit in the front row, holding my hand, cheering me on, shouting for joy, and always ready to go on one more ride. I love you! How I pray I served as a good role model for listening to the Lord and following in wholehearted obedience to his call.

Just as iron sharpens iron, so too did my Glory Writers, Rockwall, and Wordsmiths writing group members sharpen the precision of my pen. Special thanks to John Hannah, Jennifer Odom White, Rebecca LeCompte, Leslie Porter Wilson, Henry McLaughlin, Teri Oates Jones, Mary Lee Morgan, Janie MacAskill, and Kim Bangs for their skillful refining as they spoke truth in love.

God impressed upon my heart the importance of having prayer warriors prayerfully support me throughout this project. To my warring friends and my Journey team, you and I know who you are, as does our heavenly Father. What you've done in secret your Father will reward. I could not be more humbled or grateful that just as Moses had Aaron and Hur, I had you to uphold me with your prayers as you stormed heaven's gates across the miles.

God blessed me with a special circle of friends and encouragers who believed in me and this project from the very beginning: Kristin Paschke, Jo Ann Fore, Emily Curiak, Cindy Miller, Jessie Beebe, Shonda Savage, Laura Patke, and Sue Schwabauer Hoeksema. You faithfully breathed life back into a weary heart as your words of encouragement and faithful prayers reminded me why and for whom I was called to write.

To my readers, I wish we could sit down over coffee and just chat. So often you pour out your hearts to me in social media messages, comments on my blog, and emails. I appreciate both your honesty and your vulnerability in sharing from your broken places. You remind me why I speak and write, and you encourage me with your words to continue putting pen to paper. May anything I say that does not align with God fall to the ground, and may what you hear be a beacon of light wherever you find yourself.

To my agent, Chip MacGregor, I may never be on your basketball team, but I'm thrilled to be on your team of authors. Your timely words often calmed my frenzied mind. To my editor, Vicki Crumpton, I'm so grateful that sitting down next to each other the first night we met, before I had one word written, came full circle to working together to bring *Hope Prevails* to life. To the editing, marketing, and creative team at Revell, I consider myself blessed to have you leading this project into the hands and hearts of many.

To my heavenly Father, how can I ever thank you for resurrecting my heart from the valley, doing a new work in me, and giving me your joy? Thank you for believing in me, loving me with an unfailing love in spite of myself, and breathing two simple words into my heart in my moment of surrender: hope prevails. What I thought was just a message for me you have used to do more than I ever could have hoped or imagined. You are my only reason for being. Truly, it is because of you that hope prevails!

Notes

Chapter 1 This Thing Called Depression

1. M. Valenstein, S. Vijan, J. E. Zeber, K. Boehm, and A. Buttar, "The Cost-Utility of Screening for Depression in Primary Care," *Annals of Internal Medicine* 134 (2001): 345–60.

2. Raymond W. Lam and Hiram Wok, *Depression* (New York: Oxford University Press, 2008), as quoted by http://facts.randomhistory.com/random -facts-about-depression.html.

3. http://www.who.int/mental_health/management/depression/flyer _depression_2012.pdf?ua=1.

4. http://www.cdc.gov/nchs/data/databriefs/db07.pdf.

5. http://www.who.int/mental_health/management/depression/flyer _depression_2012.pdf?ua=1.

6. http://www.healthline.com/health/depression/statistics-infographic.

7. http://www.cdc.gov/nchs/data/databriefs/db07.pdf, http://fact finder2.census.gov/faces/tableservices/jsf/pages/productview.xhtml?src =bkmk.

8. http://www.who.int/mediacentre/factsheets/fs369/en/.

Chapter 3 The Underlying Causes of Depression

1. http://www.healthline.com/health/depression/genetic#Overview1.

Chapter 4 Recognize You Have an Enemy

1. John Lynch, Bruce McNicol, and Bill Thrall, *The Cure: What if God Isn't Who You Think He Is and Neither Are You* (San Clemente, CA: CrossSection, 2011).

Chapter 5 Recover Your Joy

1. Reverend James Wood, *Dictionary of Quotations from Ancient and Modern, English and Foreign Sources: Including Phrases, Mottoes, Maxims, Proverbs, Definitions, Aphorisms, and Sayings of the Wise Men, in Their Bearing on Life, Literature, Speculation, Science, Art, Religion, and Morals, Especially in the Modern Aspects of Them* (New York: Warne, 1893), 143.

2. http://www.goodreads.com/quotes/205318-the-more-you-are-grate ful-for-what-you-have-the.

3. Kay Warren, *Choose Joy: Because Happiness Isn't Enough* (Grand Rapids: Revell, 2012), 31.

4. Ibid., 32.

5. Quoted in Dennis Merritt Jones, *The Art of Being: 101 Ways to Practice Purpose in Your Life* (New York: Penguin, 2008), n.p.

Chapter 6 Reclaim Your Peace

1. Don Colbert, *The Bible Cure for Depression and Anxiety* (Lake Mary, FL: Siloam, 1999), 20.

2. http://quoteinvestigator.com/2015/02/03/you-can/.

3. http://www.entrepreneuronfire.com/podcast/tom-ziglar/.

Chapter 7 Reestablish Your Identity

1. Jenni Catron, *Clout: Discover and Unleash Your God-Given Influence* (Nashville: Thomas Nelson, 2014), 128.

Chapter 9 Remember Your Secure Destiny

1. http://www.blueletterbible.org/lang/lexicon/lexicon.cfm?Strongs =H4581&t=NLT.

Chapter 10 Be Confident That Nothing Separates You from God's Love

1. Tina Zahn and Wanda Dyson, *Why I Jumped: My True Story of Postpartum Depression, Dramatic Rescue, and Return to Hope* (Grand Rapids: Revell, 2006), 190.

2. http://www.goodreads.com/quotes/254564-there-is-no-pit-so-deep
-that-god-s-love-is.

Chapter 12 The Way to Hope

1. Marian Wright Edelman, http://www.quotehd.com/quotes/marian
-wright-edelman-quote-so-often-we-dwell-on-the-things-that-seem.

2. Sheila Walsh, *The Heartache No One Sees* (Nashville: Thomas
Nelson, 2004), 52–53.

Dr. Michelle Bengtson is an author, speaker, and board-certified clinical neuropsychologist with more than twenty years of professional expertise in the diagnosis and treatment of medical and emotional disorders in children, adults, and seniors. She has maintained a private practice for fifteen years and lives in the Dallas/Fort Worth area with her husband, their two sons, and two dogs. Her passion is speaking and writing about the hope that prevails in the midst of life's storms, especially with respect to medical and mental disorders, both for those who suffer and for those who care for them. She offers hope, affirms worth, and encourages faith to unlock joy and relief—even in the middle of the storm.

Dr. Bengtson earned her PhD at Nova Southeastern University and interned at the University of Oklahoma with "the Father of Neuropsychology," Dr. Oscar Parsons, and completed postdoctoral training at both the Henry Ford Hospital and the University of Alabama Health Sciences Center. At her website, www.dr michellebengtson.com, she makes available practical tools, answers reader questions, and publishes her weekly musings. (facebook .com/DrMichelleBengtson/ and twitter.com/drmbengtson)

Praise for Katherine Reay

"A delightful story of love, passion and appetite, filled with Italian vivacity and charm."

—ANTHONY CAPELLA, INTERNATIONAL BESTSELLING AUTHOR
OF *THE FOOD OF LOVE* AND *THE WEDDING OFFICER*

"A Portrait of Emily Price is a portrait of grace and love. Reay expertly weaves a story rich in taste and sight, wrapping it all with sigh-worthy romance. You'll think of Emily and Ben and the hills of Italy long after you've read the last page. Reay is carving her name among the literary greats."

—RACHEL HAUCK, *NEW YORK TIMES* AND *USA TODAY*
BESTSELLING AUTHOR OF *THE WEDDING DRESS*

"Katherine Reay is a remarkable author who has created her own subgenre, wrapping classic fiction around contemporary stories. Her writing is flawless and smooth, her storytelling meaningful and poignant. You're going to love *The Brontë Plot*."

—DEBBIE MACOMBER, #1 *NEW YORK TIMES* BESTSELLING AUTHOR

"Great works of literature and other priceless antiques populate Reay's thoughtful tribute to the Brontë sisters. The moral ambiguity makes the story more modern than its premise would suggest—and proves how well its source material holds up over time."

—*KIRKUS REVIEWS* ON *THE BRONTË PLOT*

"Book lovers will savor the literary references as well as the story's lessons on choices, friendship, and redemption."

—*BOOKLIST* ON *THE BRONTË PLOT*

"Reay's latest is an enjoyable trip to Europe . . . The redemption of the characters is heartfelt and the plot is unpredictable."

—*RT BOOK REVIEWS*, 4 STARS, ON *THE BRONTË PLOT*

"Quotations and allusions flow freely in Reay's third tribute to the female giants of English literature. While some readers may miss the more obscure references, the finely drawn characters, flawed and authentic, dominate and ground the story emotionally . . . Fans m

classic novels after savoring this skill

—*PUBLISHERS WEEKL*

"A delightful story of failure and success, of facing the truth about the past and present. Katherine Reay takes readers on a lyrical journey with sights, sounds, and colors that make her story come to life."

—RACHEL HAUCK, *NEW YORK TIMES* AND *USA TODAY*
BESTSELLING AUTHOR, ON *THE BRONTË PLOT*

"Katherine Reay has done it again! *The Brontë Plot* is a literary delight with characters every bit as layered and captivating as the story itself. A deep, poignant tale that explores the importance of searching for truth in order to find healing and facing the past in order to move forward."

—KATIE GANSHERT, AWARD-WINNING AUTHOR OF *THE ART OF LOSING YOURSELF*

"In *The Brontë Plot*, Katherine Reay weaves a contemporary storyline with the threads of Victorian-era literature. The present and the past intertwine as her characters unravel truth from lies, attempting to undo choices with far-reaching consequences. The novel builds, and Reay layers profound life truth into a powerful and satisfying ending."

—BETH K. VOGT, 2015 RITA FINALIST, AUTHOR
OF *CRAZY LITTLE THING CALLED LOVE*

"It's poignant, it's witty, it's got romance and drama and complex characters and dialogue and it's clever and it makes you think and sigh and, yes, even swoon and the food, oh the food. It's the kind of book that makes you want to start again from the beginning as soon as you've reached the end because it has so many layers, subtleties, and depth, it's impossible to absorb it all in one mere read."

—NOVEL CROSSING ON *LIZZY & JANE*

"Reay treats readers to a banquet of flavors, aromas, and textures that foodies will appreciate, and clever references to literature add nuances sure to delight bibliophiles. The relatable, very real characters, however, are what will keep readers clamoring for more from this talented author."

—*PUBLISHERS WEEKLY*, STARRED REVIEW, ON *LIZZY & JANE*

"Reay's second Jane Austen–inspired tale is a layered and nuanced story of faith and hope, enriched by complex but relatable characters. Recommended for lovers of character-driven women's fiction."

—*LIBRARY JOURNAL* ON *LIZZY & JANE*

"Deeply moving and intensely meaningful, Reay's latest gives readers an intimate look into the lives of sisters. Elizabeth's character is raw and real—her desire to live a meaningful life and her authentic fear of rejection will help everyone identify closely with her journey. Delicious descriptions of food and the closeness that it provides to others gives the novel even more depth."

—*RT Book Reviews*, 4½ stars, on *Lizzy & Jane*

"What a wonderful book! Katherine Reay's *Lizzy & Jane* is a beautifully written, deeply moving novel that is a feast for the senses . . . An homage to a famous moment from Austen's *Persuasion* satisfied one of my dearest Janeite fantasies. And the food! Every description of Lizzy's masterpieces in the kitchen will make your mouth water and have you dying for a taste. It all adds up to a poignant, romantic, culinary delight that will bring tears to your eyes and a smile to your heart."

—Syrie James, bestselling author of *Jane Austen's First Love*

"Filled with food and literary food references, this book will appeal to literature aficionados, foodies, and any lover of a good romance."

—*CBA Retailers + Resources* on *Lizzy & Jane*

"This delightful debut novel about how one young woman learns to become the person she was meant to be will resonate with fans of New Adult fiction and with readers who enjoy Jane Austen spin-offs."

—*Library Journal*, starred review, on *Dear Mr. Knightley*

"Katherine Reay's *Dear Mr. Knightley* kept me up until 2:00 a.m.; I simply couldn't put it down . . . If you've read Jean Webster's charming epistolary novel, *Daddy Long Legs*, you'll know where this is going. Webster wrote her book in 1919; *Dear Mr. Knightley* is a brilliant update. I absolutely loved the story of a rigidly bookish young woman who comes to know herself—not to mention the real Mr. Knightley."

—Eloisa James, *New York Times* bestselling author of *Once Upon a Tower*

"[*Dear Mr. Knightley*] is an intriguing story told through letters the heroine writes to her benefactor. It is enjoyable to watch her learn about life, gain maturity, and, in the end, find love. A lesson readers will learn from this engaging novel is that it's not so much where you come from, but where you're going that matters."

—*RT Book Reviews*, 4½ stars, TOP PICK!

"Book nerds, rejoice! *Dear Mr. Knightley* is a stunning debut—a first-water gem with humor and heart. Using Samantha's painfully forthright, often humorous, and increasingly vulnerable letters to her mysterious benefactor, author Katherine Reay invites readers into each moment of a young woman's discovery that real heroes are fallible, falling in love isn't always better in books, and literature is meant to enhance life—not to serve as a substitute for living. I can hardly wait to get my hands on the next novel by this gifted new author!"

—SERENA CHASE, *USA TODAY*'S HAPPY EVER AFTER BLOG

"A heroine Jane Austen herself would be proud of! *Dear Mr. Knightley* is an emotional, haunting tale of hope and perseverance in the face of adversity. With depth and honesty, Katherine Reay's debut novel will grip your heart in the very first pages and not let go."

—SARAH E. LADD, AWARD-WINNING HISTORICAL NOVELIST OF *THE CURIOSITY KEEPER* AND THE WHISPERS ON THE MOORS SERIES

"Katherine Reay's touching debut novel made me cry in all the right places. For joy."

—LAURIE VIERA RIGLER, AUTHOR OF *RUDE AWAKENINGS OF A JANE AUSTEN ADDICT*, ON *DEAR MR. KNIGHTLEY*

"A lovely debut novel from Katherine Reay! A wonderful story told in letter form, *Dear Mr. Knightley* was easy to read (and love) and a delight the whole way through, with plenty of Austen and Brontë sprinkled throughout. This book is going on my keeper shelf!"

—AUSTENITIS, AUSTENITIS.BLOGSPOT.COM

"Reay's debut novel, *Dear Mr. Knightley*, is a fun story told in a compelling voice that kept me up way too late. Highly recommended!"

—COLLEEN COBLE, *USA TODAY* BESTSELLING AUTHOR OF *THE INN AT OCEAN'S EDGE* AND THE HOPE BEACH SERIES

"Sprinkled with classic literary references and filled with poignant characterizations, Katherine Reay's modern retelling of Jean Webster's *Daddy Long Legs* is both reverently crafted and delightfully surprising."

—LAUREL ANN NATTRESS, AUSTENPROSE.COM, ON *DEAR MR. KNIGHTLEY*

A Portrait of Emily Price

Also by Katherine Reay

Dear Mr. Knightley

Lizzy & Jane

The Brontë Plot

12/16

A Portrait of Emily Price

Katherine Reay

THOMAS NELSON
Since 1798

Published in Nashville, Tennessee, by Thomas Nelson. Thomas Nelson is a
registered trademark of HarperCollins Christian Publishing, Inc.

Thomas Nelson titles may be purchased in bulk for educational, business,
fund-raising, or sales promotional use. For information, please e-mail
SpecialMarkets@ThomasNelson.com.

Library of Congress Cataloging-in-Publication Data

Names: Reay, Katherine, 1970- author.
Title: A portrait of Emily Price / Katherine Reay.
Description: Nashville, Tennessee: Thomas Nelson, [2016]
Identifiers: LCCN 2016011334 | ISBN 9780718077914 (softcover)
Subjects: LCSH: Man-woman relationships--Fiction. |
 Americans--Italy--Fiction. | GSAFD: Christian fiction. | Love stories.
Classification: LCC PS3618.E23 P67 2016 | DDC 813/.6--dc23 LC record
available at https://lccn.loc.gov/2016011334

Printed in the United States of America

16 17 18 19 20 21 RRD 6 5 4 3 2 1

For MMR and the "MMR Club"
True seekers of Joy

All Joy reminds. It is never a possession, always a desire for something longer ago or further away or still "about to be."

—C. S. Lewis, *Surprised by Joy*

Chapter 1

piccolo. The restaurant matched its name—a tiny and delicate white stucco building with a short, neat brick walk leading from its front door to the parking lot. It's wilted green awning and window boxes filled with equally droopy flowers made it look worn and comfortable—completely at odds with the man flashing his eyes between his watch and me.

I pulled a couple inches farther into the parking space, dabbed on lip gloss, and hurried to the restaurant's front door. Joseph had already pulled it open.

"Thank you for letting me follow you," I said. "Chicago is nothing like this; it's built on a grid system. I had no idea Atlanta had so many trees and hills and winding roads . . . But you didn't need to bring me to dinner. Not that I don't appreciate it." I pressed my lips shut. It was time to stop talking.

"It's your first night in town, and my aunt and uncle own this place. If you want to feel welcome in Atlanta, this is where you come."

I smiled. Despite the invitation, nothing about Joseph Vassallo felt welcoming. After knowing him for all of five minutes, I

1

suspected it would take a good hair day, flawless makeup, and four-inch heels to comfortably stand next to this man. But today, after a thirteen-hour drive and only a Dairy Queen Blizzard as sustenance, I was the poker-playing-dog-set-on-velvet next to his Michelangelo, complete with lilting Italian accent.

He escorted me into the restaurant with a hand at the small of my back and imperious nods to the waitstaff. A petite, dark-haired woman darted across the dining room, and Joseph's mask dropped as his first genuine smile broke free.

"You didn't tell me you were coming tonight!"

He laughed, then bent and kissed her cheeks, one then the other in quick succession. "Surprise." He gestured to me. "Zia Maria, meet Emily Price. She's the insurance restorer from Chicago I told you about, renting studio space."

"Alone. So far to come." She clucked and bustled us to a table. "Sit. You need a good meal."

Joseph raised an *I told you so* eyebrow to me.

She soon settled us with water and a plastic carafe of wine, forbade us to order, promised us the chef's best, and left us. I looked around the restaurant, not knowing what to say and too worn to give it much thought. The silence stretched.

"Zia Maria said you had company."

My head spun back. To a man kneeling at the table. *Oh my . . . There are two of them.*

Fully aware I must look like a bobblehead, I couldn't help myself. Back and forth, and again, back and forth . . . There *were* two of them. Both tall. At least the one kneeling beside me looked as though he must be as tall as Joseph. His long fingers gripped the edge of the table. *Yes, tall.* And handsome. Just that same kind. The right kind—the dark, lean kind with a four o'clock shadow because five o'clock would be too de rigueur. The guy you watch

walking down the plane aisle, hoping he'll sit next to you. Yet he never does. He sits right behind you—with his wife.

And what was even better, this guy had no clue how handsome he was. You could tell by his eyes. Eyes never hide and never lie. His danced with laughter and no awareness at all that I was melting right before him. But the other? I glanced over and studied his eyes a moment. Joseph knew.

"You must be brothers?" I asked them both.

Joseph lifted a single brow, but its meaning wasn't so clear this time. It felt almost as if the question required thought. "He's six years younger." His English was so smooth—all the right words and contractions, yet eking out the curves of his native Italian.

Joseph faced his brother. "Ben, meet Emily Price. Her insurance company is renting her a worktable in my studio for the next couple weeks." He glanced back to me. "House fire in Buckhead, yes?"

"Yes." I nodded and turned to Ben myself. "I do insurance restoration. This house has some damaged walls, a mural, and other pieces I'll put back together."

Ben's smile called out an answering one from me, except I could feel mine stretch too far from ear to ear. And his hands . . . One reached out and held mine. "We are both visitors. You at Joseph's and me here. I have the better deal. I get to play in a kitchen." The last part was lobbed to his brother.

"As long as you keep your play to the kitchen." Joseph's murmur killed my grin.

Ben's grip tightened as he shot his brother a look. I did the same.

"No. Not her." Joseph drew back, surprised. He flashed his gaze to me. "Not you. Sorry." He returned to Ben, who sported a *You stepped in that all by yourself* grin.

I was right. There were two of them.

Joseph continued, tilting toward his brother. "You should have said no. You say you know, but you don't. You're meddling in things you don't understand."

I thought of my sister, Amy, who often accused me of the same thing.

Ben's tone brought me back to the conversation. "Beppe, stop. Your Emily does not need to hear this."

Joseph's jaw flexed. What was already square became chiseled and pulsed right below his earlobes. "Joseph." To me he whispered, "*Beppe* is short for Giuseppe. And he won't stop using it."

Ben winked at me. "We start again. *Ciao*, I am Benito. Joseph is my brother." He emphasized the name, flattening out the vowels like an American.

"And I'm Emily." I smiled all over again.

Still holding my hand, he addressed Joseph. *"Hai una bella ospite stasera."*

"It's not a date. I just told you. She's a restorer renting space. She arrived this afternoon and doesn't know anyone in town." Joseph thrust out his palm as if tempted to push his brother over. "Stop baiting me."

"I am sorry." Ben bounced up, withdrawing his hand from mine in the process, and leaned on the table. He flexed his fingers across the checked tablecloth as if he had something important to stay. "Let me recommend something special tonight for your non-date." He addressed me. *"Ho convinto zia Maria per pemettermi di fare zuppa di spinaci e ricotta."*

I worked the words through my head, knowing I was changing them, altering them, but praying I understood them.

Joseph waved his hand as if ridding us of a pest. "Fine. Two."

Ben's eyes stayed focused on mine, one brow reaching into his hairline.

"Yes, I'll have that too," I said, without fully grasping what we'd ordered. "Thanks."

He nodded and walked away.

The silence turned oppressive.

I looked around again, searching for a comment, and landed on, "Your aunt and uncle's restaurant is lovely."

Outside, the white stucco and faded awning had given a rumpled cottage look, almost as if it belonged in a small English village, but the inside was quintessential Italian—at least my impression of it. Dark green walls, red-and-white-checked cloths, red plastic votive holders with matching breadbaskets, and small bottles of vinegar and olive oil. Wine served in clear plastic carafes. It felt like family had to sit close, share dishes with their stories, and the garlic would linger on your clothes and in your hair as you carried home your leftovers.

"Hmm . . ." Joseph's eyes followed the trail mine had just completed. "Ben comes for a visit and they pounce on him, thinking because he works at our family's restaurant back in Italy he can help, he can make all this better." He rattled on, each word overlapping the next. "And Ben agreed. He didn't even know them before he arrived, and he agreed. He made all these plans to change everything, from the menu to the decor. It will end in disaster." He stopped and stared at me and, I suspected, remembered that we'd only just met.

"Why?"

"Why did they ask or why did he agree?" Joseph sighed. "Piccolo is slowing down. Look around—even your first time here you must sense it. Vito and Maria are older now, tired. There is no *vita*, life, here anymore, and if they want to sell, it won't bring

enough. It could, though. It's good space and in a good neighborhood. As for Ben . . . He's not the guy to do this kind of work. He's a chef, a dreamer. At least as a kid that's who he was. Always eager to help and jump aboard any sinking ship. But righting the ship takes another personality."

"But—" I clamped off my protest. Who was I to have an opinion at all? Just because a guy has a gorgeous smile and dancing eyes . . .

After a few moments the silence lay too heavy again, and I wondered why Joseph had invited me to dinner at all. He had no obligation. Covington Insurance had merely rented me a workstation at his studio for two weeks, nothing more. I had a job to do, a Residence Inn suite to sleep in, my books, my paintings, and a Netflix account to keep me occupied in the evenings . . . I had no need for awkward dinners with a surly Italian in the midst of a family feud.

I asked, "What did you order for us?"

Joseph's eyes took on a flash of alarm. "I'm sorry, he set me off and I assumed you understood. Soup with spinach and ricotta. He'll bring it with a salad and bread; it will be enough."

"Oddly, I'm not that hungry. You would think I would be, with only a Blizzard today."

"A blizzard?" His arch tone killed my enthusiasm and my explanation. I nodded, as if he had questioned my choice rather than my meaning.

The food soon arrived and *not the guy* pulled up a chair. I wasn't sure what kind of guy Ben was that precluded his ability to help his aunt and uncle, but he was a demonstrative guy, hands waving like a cyclone. He was a happy guy, eyes lit with laughter even when Joseph's tone—I couldn't catch many of the words—conveyed a reprimand. He was a kind guy, hands slowing and

voice softening as he tried to draw me into the conversation while easing his brother's clear annoyance.

He was exactly what I had always envisioned my ideal *that guy* to be. Actually, the whole list, fully formed at age eight, started and ended with *Italian*—all the rest was icing.

I sat quietly and watched Ben's hands move. They were strong, with long fingers, not tapered, but blunt at the nails. And they flew, moving at the rate of his words. I tried to catch the gist of them, but his Italian eclipsed his English and I missed much of it. Something about pizza, the restaurant closing to paint, not closing to paint, and Papa.

I heard *irresponsabile* and *lavoro*, meaning "work," but was certain I'd missed the mark as *leprechaun* and *swirl* made no sense. Clearly checking out Rosetta Stone a few times from the library had not made me fluent.

The conversation drew to a quiet close as Ben's hands dropped to his lap. *"So che posso . . ."*

I know I can, I translated in my head . . . then, *"Aiuto,"* we whispered together. *Help. He knows he can help.*

I clamped my hand over my mouth; I hadn't meant to say it aloud.

Ben seized my hand. "You understand."

I could only nod. Yes, I understood. I got it—not all he'd said, but what he was trying to do. He wanted to give his aunt and uncle something more. A chance. A better life. Joy. I wasn't sure any of it was possible, but I appreciated that he believed it. It was so clear, so beautifully clear, that he believed it.

Ben nodded at me as if an entire conversation was passing between us and we sat in perfect agreement. He then turned back to his brother, perhaps not realizing he still held my hand captive beneath his. "I can help, Joseph. Let me do what I know."

Joseph looked between us as if stumbling upon something unexpected. He didn't reply.

Ben looked down at our hands. His eyes widened with embarrassment and he pulled his away so fast I felt an instant chill. *"Mi scusi."* He sat back, crossed his arms, and smiled slow and broad. "You speak Italian?"

"Un po." I tapped my fingers together. The whole moment flustered me, so I stood—and knocked back my chair. Ben lunged to catch it. I added, *"Ho bisogno di usare il buco."*

"You do speak *un po*." Ben compressed a smile. "You mean *il bagno*. Bathroom."

"What did I say?"

"Hole."

I felt my face flame as I strode to the front of the restaurant. "Zia Maria" intercepted me with nods and a guiding hand on my arm, pointing to the ladies' room.

"Grazie."

"You are welcome, my dear."

Moments later I pushed back through the door and into the small lobby to find Joseph waiting by the hostess stand.

"We can go now." He held open the front door. "We shouldn't have gotten into it with you here."

"It's all right. I didn't understand most of it."

"You caught enough, and I apologize." He stepped into the warm night, then away from me. "Welcome to Atlanta, Emily, and I'll see you at the studio tomorrow morning." He crossed to his car, and I stood next to my station wagon.

"Thank you for dinner," I called after him.

I stood by my car a few minutes, tempted to go back inside. There was something about *that guy*—not only what he wanted to do, but who he was and how he listened to his brother's rantings

and insults with patience, with those bottomless brown eyes that didn't carry resentment or indignation, but instead, gold flecks, barely contained laughter, and even joy.

And although he seemed playful—sending a few winks my direction when Joseph got really heated—I somehow knew he wasn't flighty. He meant what he said. He wanted to help his aunt and uncle, and he would. It was that, that *drive* to fix what was broken, that resonated with me.

I finally dropped into my car with another ear-to-ear grin. *Welcome to Atlanta.*

Chapter 2

*M*y eyes ate up the empty studio. I hadn't stepped inside the day before, as Joseph had met me on the sidewalk and immediately invited me to dinner. But what a space . . .

Atlanta Conservation, Inc., was a dust-free conservator's Nirvana—the likes of which I'd never seen. Cement floor, thirty-foot ceilings, metal ducts, polished pipes—nothing soft, nothing that allowed a speck of dust to float, much less land. And each workstation outfitted with LED, ultraviolet, and infrared lighting capabilities, freestanding Leica F12 I microscopes, Decon FS500 vents on retractable arms, state-of-the-art carbon-handled tools, a heated suction table in the center, and some unknown and intimidating-looking machine poised against the far wall. And the solvents—vials of raw elements that required a chemistry background to pronounce, let alone mix in the tall glass beakers.

It was everything I dreamed restoration could be when we first met at age eight. My father took me to the Art Institute of Chicago's Caravaggio exhibit, and rather than look at the paintings, I spent the entire afternoon trailing a tour of grown-ups on a tour called "Maintaining the Masters." The leader, not a docent,

but a graduate student with a passionate, melodic—and Italian—accent, mesmerized me. He didn't talk about the subjects of the paintings. Instead, he told the story behind them—the processes of preserving them, identifying everything that attacked them over time—moisture, age, microbes—and all he and his kind did to keep art safe. I hung on his every word, certain he held the secrets and the tools needed to fix things, make them whole, and keep them healthy.

It was the last outing I remembered with my dad before he moved out of our house. And no coincidence that I believed that man's dictums about paintings would serve as well as a manual for life. We could keep things together by putting all the pieces in place and gluing them there. If you worked hard enough and were diligent, anything could be fixed.

I began scouring garage sales in my neighborhood for trinkets. In high school, I read every book the library held on art criticism, restoration, and design. I even checked out the Rosetta Stone's Italian courses over and over—somehow knowing Caravaggio's Italy was the Asgard of art and if I knew its secrets all would be well. And I was good at it. My mind could see how the pieces fit, my fingers were nimble enough to get the minutest shard of porcelain back in a broken figurine, and I was creative enough to use anything that came my way to make the process more efficient, clean, and stable. In college I found it a great way to make extra money. Any other ideas I held or embellished about that man's looks and accent over the years were probably fed around this time by a steady diet of romantic comedies and art documentaries.

But this morning, when finally gaining entrance to my own Asgard, I made a less than stellar impression. I was so over-whelmed when Joseph ushered me inside that, looking across the room now, I couldn't remember who he said worked at each

station. I did recall that his three conservators held degrees from the country's best postgraduate programs; one was on site in San Francisco working on a Rembrandt, another was on sabbatical at the Vatican, and the third must be nearby. At one workstation there was a Cassatt propped on an easel and some wooden loveliness behind a Leica magnifying scope.

"Move any equipment you don't need out of your way," Joseph said. "Don't you use superglue and acrylics and call it done?"

His accent threw me. It made the question sound sincere, and it took a second for me to find it insulting.

I offered a slightly less than bright smile and pretended the question was real. "You'd be surprised how useful superglue truly is. But you're right, I don't use most of this. And I bring my own tools since I usually work on the small stuff on site or at my hotel. Having Covington rent me studio space is rare."

After a few more moments of Joseph pointing out what I probably *would not need* and *need not touch*, he walked away. And I had to come to terms with the truth of all of it. While I might do a first-class professional job on Aunt Edna's wedding portrait damaged by a water leak, or the Lladró figurine shattered when Bobby pretended the umbrella was a light saber, there was no use pretending I knew anything about restoring a Cassatt—even a copy of one.

With a deep breath, I opened my toolbox and fingered the tools inside as if meeting old friends. I was reluctant to unpack them into ACI's shiny glass mason jars. My baby toothbrush for fine metal cleaning was going to look ridiculous next to the studio's bamboo brush with its fine horsehair bristles. I couldn't even imagine what Joseph might say about my purple plastic tongue scraper or my bright red gum depressor. Cheap and odd, dental tools did the job when it came to distressing wood and applying adhesives to tight spaces.

I dropped each into a jar, reminding myself with every *plink* that I did first-class work—the grown-up equivalent of *I think I can.*

My phone startled me with a loud rendition of Cyndi Lauper's "Girls Just Want to Have Fun," and I fumbled to answer it. I did not want Joseph to emerge from his office—especially on this note.

"I think I need a new song for your ringtone," I whispered.

"Oh, don't change Cyndi. I love that song."

I brushed aside my sister's protest. "What's up?"

"Are you there yet?"

"I got here yesterday. You knew that."

Amy sighed with great drama. "You must be exhausted."

I could hear chatter and laughter in the background. More noise than the accounting office at Covington Insurance generated in a year.

"Where are you?" I barked before I remembered the reason I'd been whispering.

The background sound lessened, and she ignored my question. "I was kinda hoping I'd get your voice mail."

Our twenty-two-month age difference instantly stretched to years as I took a deep breath. I released it slowly in an effort to keep calm. I knew what was coming next—what always came next with Amy.

She huffed a small sigh. "I wanted you to hear it from me . . ."

"You lost your job."

Silence.

"Amy, I asked the accounting department to hire you—as a favor. I helped you move to Chicago for it."

"I only missed one meeting . . . *one*. But that wasn't it, honest. They're making cuts. Three others got let go last week."

"I haven't heard about any cuts." I closed my eyes, sure she was lying. "Can you go back in and beg? I can't ask for any more favors."

"Forget it, Em." Amy's voice became strong and clear. "It wasn't right for me from the start. I hate filing, and I kept messing up the phone messages."

I closed my eyes and saw images of blond, bubbly Amy sliding little pink pieces of paper across the department's central desk. *Here, y'all. Come grab your messages. I'm not sure who's who yet, so y'all just sift through them.*

She'd flip her blond hair, bat her unnaturally long lashes—made more annoying by actually being natural—and draw upon those six short months we'd lived in Alabama. She was only seven years old at the time, but she'd quickly learned the power of a pretty face and a deep drawl.

I opened my eyes. "It was good money . . . and benefits. We have great health insurance."

"True, but it's also gone." She paused. "Look, you're in Atlanta and you don't need to deal with this. I'll handle it. Half our high school lives here; I've got tons of friends with leads."

"No, I'll start looking tonight. I saw some solid listings on Monster and ZipRecruiter last week."

"What were you doing on—"

"I'm always on those sites, Amy. How do you think I always know about these jobs? How do you think *you* get the good interviews? It's why—"

"Slow down."

"If you'd keep a job, I could slow down." I pressed my lips tight. After a thirteen-hour drive, an awkward "work dinner," and a hotel pillow made of Styrofoam, I was too tired for this conversation. "Did you tell Mom?"

"Why would I do that? It's as bad as telling you. She'll shed a few fake tears and send me money. It's like a pat on the head, only worse, and you go off—"

"Don't bite the hand that finds you the jobs, sis."

"Yeah . . . I know." Her voice dipped low. "I just didn't want someone from Covington contacting you before I did."

ACI's front door swung open.

"I gotta go. I'll send you ideas later." I tapped off my phone and switched it to silent as a woman stepped into the studio and stared at me.

"Company!" She threw her arm out as she crossed the studio. "You're the insurance restorer!" Her low heels made a staccato click across the floor. She looked about my age, but taller, darker, her black hair cut into a sleek bob that swung with every step.

I stood and met her in the studio's center, hand outstretched. "I'm Emily Price."

"Lily Crider."

I gestured to the empty worktables. "I think Mr. Vassallo said we three are the only ones here right now."

"Ugh . . . Don't call him that." She grinned and dropped her bag at her station. "Besides, you won't see much of Joseph out here. He has a workroom behind his office."

I touched her microscope with a light finger. "Your equipment is extraordinary."

"Isn't it? He spared no expense when setting up this place." She tapped the Decon's bright yellow hood. "You can stick $(E)2$-butene-1-thiol and 3-methyl-1-butanethiol under your nose with this on and not smell a thing. Cameron tried. He was fortunate it worked. Joseph would've fired him before he could've recapped the vial."

"Butan—?"

"The stinky elements in skunk."

I felt my fingers pinch my nose and dropped them. "Oh . . ."

"Yeah . . . It was a risk." Lily propped herself on her stool and

rolled to her scope. "Come see this." She reached over and flipped the Leica's switch. A bright focused beam lit a one-inch circle on the triptych—a patch of deliciously green grass.

"Oh my . . ."

"I feel that way every day. This baby is part of the Rijksmuseum's collection. Fifteenth century. Oil on wood. It'll be here in the High Museum for a year once I'm finished. A full cleaning and restoration was part of the loan contract. I've got about a month of work left."

I leaned closer and fully absorbed the difference in our worlds. Lily was working inch by inch through a masterpiece. I focused on boxes full of stuff and wall space measured in feet, and kept my time commensurate with the insurance company's valuation of damages. But still . . . I loved it.

Lily gestured for me to peek through her scope. The inch expanded, and I could see the microscopic crackling as if I were kneeling in a mud puddle after the water evaporated. Each crack was huge and the edges clear and precise.

She'd restored about half of the area captured within the scope's field of vision, and her work was excellent. She hadn't erased or filled in the painting's natural evolution or signs of decay; she'd inpainted subtly through them with exquisite delicacy, allowing the piece to be its full and best self. The changes were now part of its story, but stabilized so as not to end the story.

I straightened up. "How do you get the paint in? It's so fine."

"I've developed an incredibly lean paint for this. Very low fat content."

"And the brush?"

She reached over to a cloth on which lay a dozen brushes. She raised one. Its head was as fine as a needle.

"It's so tiny."

She held it close. "I expect there aren't more than five hairs in there. Horse. Each tipped on the bias. I'd spread them and count, but that'd ruin the brush."

"No. Don't do that." I stepped back.

She twisted on her stool to face me. "So what brings you here?"

I liked Lily's expression, open without condescension. I liked *her*. "I'm the company's go-to girl for midlevel on-site restorations, but I only got the call for this one last week. An emergency." I made air quotes with my fingers.

"There can be emergencies."

I flicked a finger at her triptych. "For you, maybe. In my world, getting the fire out, clearing the water, bringing art, wood—anything organic—to a level of stasis, constitutes the emergency. And all that happens long before I get on site. I'm the girl who glues Auntie May's Precious Moments figurine back together."

"Okay, you win. But Auntie May might disagree."

"True . . . and this might be one of those times. It usually takes weeks, if not months, to schedule restoration work, but my boss got me down here within forty-eight hours of the claim's approval, and he sweetened the deal by renting me a spot here."

"Well, I'm happy to have you." She pointed across the room. "Cameron's in San Francisco, Will's at the Vatican, and it's too quiet. Do you like Pink Martini?"

"Is that a drink?"

"A band. They've been keeping me company lately, but feel free to stream your own playlist. Joseph's got the place wired on Sonos."

With that she rolled in front of her Leica scope and I returned to my table to finish sorting my dental tools.

Chapter 3

That afternoon, after forty-five minutes and countless missed turns, I pulled into the driveway of a lovely white wood colonial in Buckhead and let my eyes trail over the house: clean black shutters, crisp white paint, plantings fresh and watered. Its perfection let me know I had the right house. In my six years of insurance work, I found no one keeps up on home repairs and maintenance until forced—usually by loss.

The insurance files reported that they'd caught the fire early and most of the interior damage came from smoke and water. I suspected the inside was entirely brand-new—insulation, dry-wall, fixtures, and even appliances—as fire travels fast and hot along electrical lines. And, covered or not, clearly the outside had gotten a significant lift as well.

I walked through the open front door and wandered the first floor, saying hello to workmen as I passed. It smelled new—plaster, woodwork, adhesives, and paint—with a fine coating of white construction dust everywhere. That was always my greatest challenge—keeping the ever-present dust out of drying varnish.

The contractor's quick use of several desiccant dryers had

saved the dining room. Painted in the 1930s, the walls' delicate brushwork and burnished blue glaze gave the room depth and the illusion of light and movement running over the walls. There was distinct water damage near the baseboards and smoke discoloration, but nothing that a thorough cleaning, a little inpainting, and some fresh varnish couldn't fix. It'd be a good project, a soothing project.

"Are you Covington's restorationist?"

I turned and found a middle-aged woman, several inches above my five foot five, assessing me, arms crossed. In art and life, that gesture ran two ways: aggression or protection.

"Restorer. But yes, I'm Emily Price."

She dropped her arms. *Protection.* "Restorer, restorationist, restorationer, restorist . . . I wasn't sure what to call you."

"No one ever is." I took a quick catalog of what I saw. Rachel Peterson looked like a soccer mom who lunched, highlighted her blond hair, and changed her lipstick and nail color with trends and seasons. On the whole, good clients, efficient, knew what they wanted and recognized a job well done.

But she didn't quite fit the mold at present. Her eyes were lined and tired, skin dry; roots dark and threaded with gray; and her chapped lower lip slightly swollen on one side as she dragged it through her teeth. There was a wariness about her, as if she'd learned something new and didn't know what to do with the information.

I ran my hand over the wall's stippled surface. "These are dry and sound. They look great."

"Can you save them?" Her voice wavered at the end of the question.

My hand stilled. Listening, not looking, I recognized that too. She wasn't talking about the walls.

After Dad left, Mom's clock kept breaking and Amy's toys needed constant gluing or mending. *Emily, can you fix this?* Money was tight, so if I couldn't fix it, we lost it. Over and over . . . Suddenly I had a purpose, a job, and everything else made sense. Objects carried weight, and in fixing those, I found one could mend so much more.

"Yes, I can. It'll take a couple weeks, but they'll be gorgeous."

Rachel shifted her weight and gestured to the stairs. "Have you seen my daughter's room? It's bad, but . . . more important."

I followed her, recalling my notes. Originally the upstairs mural was to be cut out with the rest of the damaged drywall. But after the claim was filed, it was added to the list with a note. *No expense spared. Cost covered by client.*

We turned into an upstairs room void of furniture and painted a bleached cotton white. The bathroom was equally bright with new white tile and curving chrome fixtures set on a white marble countertop.

"All this in two months?"

"The contractor has been wonderful. He flooded the house with his team. They say we can move back in a few weeks."

"That's remarkable. I've seen situations in which it took a year to get this far." I offered encouragement, but Rachel's face fell.

"I don't know how people survive that," she whispered, then started, as if she hadn't meant to say the words aloud. "The mural's over here."

We walked deeper into the L-shaped room and faced a square mural, pink and dingy, starkly dirty against the white walls. Deep grooves around it made it look more like a scab than a treasure.

"We were going to take it out with the drywall. You can see the cut into the picture here." She ran her finger along a jagged line in the picture severing the young girl's shoe as she reached high into

the sky on a swing. "But my daughter, Brooke, lost it. The contractor said it's safe to keep."

I pressed my palm against the wall and dragged it between the new and old drywall. "It is."

"You can tell by touching?"

"After a while you can feel it. There's no change in temperature, humidity, or strength. No sponginess or disintegration. Listen." I drummed my fingers over the two surfaces. "The same."

"It's worse than downstairs."

"It took on a lot more water." I stepped back to take in the full scene. A little blond girl, about three years old, swinging up, her face looking up in wonder as if she could touch the sky. Brown shoes, brown swing, brown bark on the tree behind her. Water had discolored many of the colors—the browns were tinged to orange in some places, the sky's blue was pocked, the pinks of the girl's dress and face carried slight puce tones.

"I can make it lovely. I promise."

Rachel released a breath that sounded like it'd been held for months. She touched her fingers to her lips and hurried from the room as she called back, "I'll leave you to it."

I was standing in the room where the fire started. A curling iron left on and a tissue too close. What a burden for a fourteen-year-old.

I'd seen pictures of the room in the insurance file. The girl who lived here had felt popular and carefree—I could tell by examining the details: posters pinned across the walls, pictures of friends on a huge bulletin board, clothes and makeup scattered, food wrappers crumpled under the desk. Her mother had taken the photographs in an effort to convince her daughter to clean her room. Instead, they proved invaluable for the insurance claim.

They also revealed how the mural had survived at all. It had been hidden behind a huge framed One Direction poster.

I got out my notebook and studied the picture, determining what to do. I wanted to give that girl a little of her childhood back, but mature it somehow, redeem it. I decided to employ a faux framing technique to give the picture distinction and a little sophistication. There was also a sallowness about the drawing, beyond the damage, that I could massage away. *Blame it on smoke.* There was a look in her eyes that was clouded. It could be cleared. *Blame it on water.* A restorer's job was never to enhance, simply reveal. And yet . . . I felt confident no one would call me out on it.

I shoved my notebook back in my bag and propped myself on the window ledge to check e-mails on my phone.

Human Resources? I tapped the e-mail.

To: Emily Price
Fr: Covington Insurance, Human Resources
Re: Employment Termination

Dear Ms. Price,

As you've been informed, Covington Insurance will dissolve its restoration department as of May 19th. Please be advised that this e-mail constitutes a formal release agreement and employment will be terminated on that date. All details or ancillary terms will be outlined within your department.

Thank you.
J. Cummings

I slid down the wall and tapped my boss's number.

"I'm fired?"

Henry groaned. "You weren't supposed to get that e-mail until next week."

"But I was supposed to get it?" I pressed my fingers against my forehead. It felt ready to explode.

"It's why I sent you to Atlanta. I was buying you time."

"But I'm still fired? Then I need to be in Chicago. How can I find a job stuck down here?"

"I'm sorry, but by sending you down there I got another couple weeks' pay for you. Randy and Bonnie have already transitioned to customer service. Yesterday. I was trying—"

"Yesterday? How long have you known about this, Henry?"

"A month . . ." He paused, as if expecting me to explode, then rushed on when I didn't. "I can get you a job in customer service."

"No . . ." The warmth of panic washed over me. "I like what I do. I'm good at it." Joseph's dig came to mind, and my defense shot out before I could stop it. "It's more than acrylics and glue!"

"I know that."

I heard a soft chuckle, which only bothered me more. "Don't, please. Don't laugh about this."

"I'm not. That's why I classified this one as an emergency. It'll buy you another week or two and give you time to look for a job. That studio I found? The owner, Vassallo, had an online query for a conservator a few months back. He pulled the posting but never filled it. I thought perhaps . . ." Henry let his words drift.

"I wondered why you found me such swanky digs, but I'm not in their class. It's a conservation studio. Master's degrees and masterpieces."

"A gifted restorer like you fits anywhere she wants."

I didn't want a pep talk. "Are you going to customer service too?"

Henry gave a soft snort. "They offered me a severance package and a watch. No one keeps workers my age, not if they can help it."

"I'm sorry."

"Me too. I've been here forty-five years, and it's been good. It'll never love you back, though. Remember that."

"Yeah . . ." The warmth left in exchange for a sudden chill. I crossed my arms.

Henry continued. "Look, I know it's not Chicago, but I couldn't find anything here. They've already outsourced all the work. But out-of-town gives you that great expense account—at least for now."

"Thanks. You've always looked out for me."

"Call if you need anything, okay? Now that HR has reached out, you'll get a flurry of e-mails. Let me know if something doesn't make sense."

"I will." A noise drew my eyes to the door and I quickly said good-bye.

A young boy with tousled brown hair stood above me.

"Are you the mural lady?"

I smiled, loving the title and hoping to remain one, and not cry on this small child. "I am. I'm Emily. Who are you?"

"Parker." He held out a plastic horse with two legs. "This is Patches."

I touched the horse's nose. "Nice to meet you, Patches. I think you must have trouble running."

Parker pulled the horse back. "He lost his legs." He reached into his pocket and drew out a small plastic leg about the size of my pinky and handed it to me.

I fingered its sharp edges. "The fire didn't do this."

"Brooke stomped on him. She was mad."

I tapped the leg against the body, then handed it back to him. "I may be able to fix that. Think he could run with three legs?"

"Maybe stand too."

"Standing's good." I waited for Parker to hand me the horse. I wanted him to know he had a choice. He stretched both parts to me.

"You're sure it's okay if I borrow him?"

"Can you fix him?"

"I believe so." I pushed up against the wall to stand. "Can you take me to the garage? I understand there's a box out there with more stuff I need to fix." I slid the horse and his leg into my bag and followed Parker out the door, wondering how I was going to fix everything else that was crashing around me.

I drove out of Buckhead in a daze, trying to make sense of Henry's phone call and wondering how I could possibly find jobs for Amy and myself and stay focused on the task before me. Did I take a wrong turn, or did some part of my brain deliberately guide me onto this street and past a strip mall I'd seen before? That white stucco building. That short brick walk to the restaurant's door. Twenty-eight years old and I felt like a teenager driving by a crush's house or waiting outside the school's front doors to watch him emerge when the bell rang.

With a sharp right turn, I landed in a parking spot directly in front of Piccolo. I sat there for five minutes, telling myself to throw the car into reverse and get back to ACI. Part of me knew this was crazy. I didn't know this guy or his family. And yet I couldn't help myself. My sister . . . Henry's call . . . I felt

adrift, and somehow Piccolo, Ben, all his plans for the restaurant, and those crinkly brown-gold eyes felt like a gift . . . They felt like joy.

I vacillated for several more minutes before I forced my knuckles to the glass door.

A young man answered. "We're not—"

"I know you're not open, but is Ben Vassallo in?"

"Wait here."

He left me by the hostess stand and strode through the dining room and into the kitchen. Not even a beat later, dressed in a white jacket and looking . . . perfect . . . Ben emerged.

His stride hit a snag when he recognized me. "Emily?"

"Yes, I . . ." *What? I want to help? You make me smile? I think I . . .* I tried again. "Last night . . . Your plans to help here, fix it up . . . I've run teams for restoration projects, I know paints, scheduling, fixing all sorts of stuff . . . I'm kind of a compulsive planner . . ." I stopped in a confused mixture of embarrassment, humiliation, and unexpected longing. I turned to leave.

"You want to help me?" His tone spun me around. It held an eager anticipation that matched my own.

"Yes!"

"Bene." He laughed. "I need you. Beppe—Joseph—is afraid I misled Maria and Vito. That I will hurt them by trying to slay their dragon."

I looked around. "He might be right about the dragon part. There's a lot of work to be done if what Joseph mentioned at dinner is true. What are your plans?"

"Come. We talk." He waved his hand back to the kitchen and I followed.

I dropped my bag inside a gray-toned kitchen with stainless steel counters and the biggest stove I'd ever seen. Ben walked

straight to it and started stirring something with a large wooden spoon—a tangy mix of tomatoes, garlic, anchovies, and something I couldn't name wafted on the steam rising from the pot.

He pointed to a stool.

I grabbed my notebook and a pen and sat down. "Tell me all you're thinking."

He smiled, then began to talk . . . He'd wanted to find his brother again, after many years, wanted to leave home to develop a pizza recipe he couldn't perfect at his family's restaurant due to family ties, tensions, and expectations. Although his words were halting, stumbling over unfamiliar English translations, I understood them, understood what was behind them.

About twenty minutes in, his tone changed. It softened as he told about meeting his aunt and uncle for the first time. He'd not known they lived in Atlanta, or that they even existed, until Joseph introduced them. They were wonderful and already he loved them. They'd welcomed him and needed his help—and he wanted to give it to them, leave them happier and more whole for having been with him, having trusted him.

His monologue left me with more questions than answers, but I didn't interrupt. He wasn't sharing a list or a plan, as I often did; he was sharing himself. And it was . . . mesmerizing.

Somewhere along the way his "I" morphed to "we," and my hearted melted a little more.

Forty-five minutes and three pages later, Ben stepped behind me to read my notes. His hand rested on my shoulder. "You picked all that out? Is it too much?"

"It's a lot, but it sounds beautiful too." I looked up and found my face inches from his.

"You have green eyes," he whispered.

"You don't."

Ben's eyes crinkled in reply. "I do not," he agreed and brushed a strand of hair behind my ear.

He grazed my cheek with a quick kiss before he straightened and stepped away.

I was thankful he turned back to his sauce, as a blush warmed my face. I took a deep, silent breath.

"Joseph is angry. He feels protective of them and I understand, but they asked me," he continued, "and if they are to retire, they need more from this place."

"I only have a little over two weeks here, so if you want my help, we should start soon."

"That is all I have left too. Can you come to the supply store with me tomorrow?"

I quickly assessed my next two weeks of work. The Peterson house was going to take significant time . . . Finding Amy a job . . . Finding me a job . . . "Four o'clock?"

"Three thirty?" he countered with a smile.

"Three thirty." *Note to self: Cut out all sleep.*

He twisted fully from the stove and watched me, a smile settling on his lips, as if I were something fine and delicious—not merely ready help in a time of need.

"Come." He crooked a finger at me, then reached across me for a small spoon. "Taste." He dipped it into the bubbling sauce, dark and thick, and held it out to me.

I touched it to my lips, surprised by the intensity.

"*Bistecca alla Pizzaiola.* You might say *la bistecca della moglie del pizzaiolo* to be precise."

"The beef of the pizza mole?"

He chuckled. "The steak of the pizza maker's wife. It is a nationally favorite recipe from Napoli, with sauce so thick it stands—a winter dish, warm and intimate. Not for summer, but it

was on my mind today." He glanced back at me. "I cannot tell you how glad I am that you are here, that you came today."

"Because you need so much help?"

"Because, I think, I need you."

Chapter 4

True to my word, I cut out sleep. After a night of futile Internet searches and, at best, minutes of sketchy sleep, I tried to let the job hunts go. Maybe Amy could find her own job. *Not likely.* Maybe Joseph would hire me at ACI. *Not likely.*

As I lay in the dark, a line from a book read long ago ran on repeat through my mind: *An ever increasing craving for an ever diminishing pleasure . . .* The author had been striving to understand vice, sin, and addiction. I lay there grasping for peace and yearning for something more.

I threw the sheets off before dawn, made mediocre coffee in the hotel suite's mini machine, and headed to ACI. Too early to arrive at the Petersons', it was time to attack their box of knick-knacks and see what could be done about Patches.

Lily had already arrived and was poised over the Leica scope.

"Hey," I called softly.

She bounced up. "Hello. How was your first day?"

I gave the standard answer. "Very good. How are you?"

"Okay so far. Moving inch by inch." She drifted back to her scope as if her mind hadn't left it.

I set down the box from the Petersons' garage and cataloged it—five porcelain figurines broken in the chaos, three picture frames stained and warped, and some random odds and ends that meant too much to throw away—including one plastic horse. Small fun projects to fill early mornings and a few evenings. I smiled because I now had Piccolo to do that too.

Rather than dig in, however, I drew out the small bundle of wood supports I lugged to each job and tapped finishing nails into the corners to create frames. I then pulled out five rolled canvases from a box I'd shoved under the table the day before. These were where my heart and dreams lay, and despite their inadequacies I carried them everywhere I went.

I glanced around—Lily was absorbed at her desk and the rest of the studio was empty—then unrolled the first canvas. This was private stuff. Paintings even Amy had never seen. I usually worked on them in my apartment or in hotel rooms on the road. But the lighting and equipment here were too tempting. Maybe what was missing wasn't something I lacked, but some external element I could find here and now.

I pulled smooth the painting of a couple boys on a slide and fastened it into the supports. Next came the poppies, then the churning waves at Chicago's Oak Street Beach, the old man watching his dog, and, my favorite, the young girl peeking through the leaves at a park in Evanston. After framing the last one, I propped it on the easel and stared at it.

I'd come across her last fall as I was snapping pictures of the changing leaves along the lakefront. She was a surprise—her young face open and expressive—and I didn't even see her looking out through the gold and red until I clicked the shutter. Brown eyes, big and almost perfectly round, a pointed chin within a heart-shaped face and curling dark hair.

She hadn't seen me either. She was in a fairy world, her eyes gazing through the branches unfocused and dreamlike. That was the challenge—I was desperate to capture that moment in my painting, that soft, innocent, wondering look.

But I had failed. Over and over again.

I lowered myself on my stool and held the photograph up to the painting. My girl's eyes were too *aware*, and the resulting image was dull and calculated, not innocent and young. On my last attempt they'd become two-dimensional black dots.

"Your problem lies in layering."

I snatched the painting from the easel and spun around. Joseph stood next to me staring down at the picture now hanging by my side.

"Put it back. It was good."

"It's . . . only a hobby."

"Please." He gestured to the easel.

I obeyed, and Joseph stepped toward the painting. I rolled away.

The silence grew oppressive.

"It's a mess," I blurted. "Humans need eyes. I've tried to paint people without them, turning the faces, but it comes off staged and creepy. So there she is, a five-year-old with black Modigliani dots for eyes in a face that needs . . . I don't even know what."

He smiled. "You know your Italians. Very good."

I shrugged.

"You're right, they don't work." He nodded in agreement. "But your technique is outstanding. Your brushwork. Exquisite detail." He offered another crooked smile. "Your style is more classic. Luini. That's why you need eyes. They are the windows to the soul."

Luini. I was stunned. Comparison to an Italian master—false and exaggerated as it was—was still lovely. I could tell by

his expression that Joseph knew it too—he'd gone over the top deliberately.

But I didn't care. It was offered in understanding, jest, or camaraderie, one artist to another, and I accepted it.

He propped himself on the worktable. "If eyes are such a problem, paint landscapes or stills."

"I have, but they're no better. Here." Joseph's attempt at a compliment had given me courage. Or I was simply desperate enough to ask for help.

I pulled out the field of flowers. Bright colors, a mix of poppies with daffodils sprinkled into the edges. I'd seen it along the highway during an assignment in Iowa the previous summer.

Again, it revealed good brushwork and even a sense of movement. You could almost catch the wind working to bend the stems. *Almost* because the stems didn't yield, wouldn't yield, no matter how strong the wind. Rather, they strained against snapping.

Joseph's eyes flashed from the flowers to the little girl and back again. I knew he caught it too. So much of the girl radiated warmth. There was a dewy softness in her cheek, an animated rose to her mouth, and a suppleness in the curve of her hand grabbing the branch above her head. She was alive and warm, and yet . . . There was an excitement or an anticipation that was missing from my hand and therefore from her—an animation that should play out in my soul and translate to her eyes. *Windows to the soul.*

"These are all yours?" He flipped through the other three unfinished canvases.

"All mine."

He scrubbed at his chin, then nodded. "Stick to portraiture."

I snickered. It was meant to sound light and lively, but disappointment and self-derision twisted it.

Joseph's eyes softened. "Your people are alive, *piena di vita*,

and powerful. I can see that your heart is in them, not in the flowers. That's why I say portraiture. Chase life."

I liked that and quickly committed it to memory. *Chase life.*

He pushed off the table. "Ben told me you stopped by Piccolo yesterday afternoon."

My breath caught. *Brothers.* Of course they talked. Ben was probably staying with him. Joseph wasn't my boss, and yet I felt as if I'd stepped into something sticky.

"At dinner I got the impression he was going to go ahead with his plans, so when I found myself driving by Piccolo yesterday, I stopped by to see if I could help." I heard my voice trail up with each word. I hoped I had stopped before he caught those final pleading notes.

"Why would you do that? You have your job."

I gestured to my paintings. "This isn't enough to keep me busy between drying times at the Petersons'. And I like projects. I'm very organized. And if this can help your family . . ."

Joseph tilted his head. "That's the problem. Ben is under the same misapprehension. You can dress up Piccolo, make it ready to sell, but that won't help the family. Not the way he thinks."

Not the way he thinks . . .

Joseph's comment struck me. It felt like he was saying that helping Maria and Vito retire was not Ben's primary goal. Then what was? And why couldn't he achieve it?

As Joseph walked away, I put away the paintings and picked up Patches. His leg required fast-drying adhesive and a dab of joining compound to soften the break lines. I then moved on to a Bing & Grøndahl figurine, a nineteen-inch-high shepherdess—the porcelain so thick it had broken only into a few dozen pieces rather than shattering into thousands. A couple coffees and a few hours later, I was satisfied with both.

It was time to head to the Peterson house to wash Brooke's mural. Cleaning a painting or a mural brought out its true colors—like a rainbow after a storm—and made it feel new and bright. It made *me* feel new and bright. It was my favorite part of my job.

Two more coffees and I was moving apace across the top third, relishing the colors revealed, when a high-pitched scream stopped me.

"What are you doing? You're ruining it!"

I spun around and found myself two feet from and eye-to-eye with a very angry girl—blond hair, close to the tone of my own, pale skin, and the most anguish-filled blue eyes I'd ever seen. Brooke.

I held up my hands. "No, no. I'm cleaning it, to fix it. Look."

She dropped her backpack with a massive *thud*.

"See?" I pointed to the top of the mural. "I've already cleaned this section. It's a slow process, but I can get all the smoke damage, dirt, everything that's corrupted it for the past decade off without damaging the paint underneath. See how much brighter the sky looks. Then I'll fix any damage I find . . ." I shot her a quick glance. "Then reseal and varnish it."

"She's not even pretty."

She. The tone. The pronoun. Both made me sad.

"It's a beautiful mural, and I think the girl is lovely." I resumed working.

"Can I help?" She spoke so quietly I barely caught her question.

"Of course. Take this and dab only within a couple inches. When you see a lift in color—a brightness—stop and blot, don't rub, with this damp rag." I modeled the procedure for her, then handed her a clean linen rag.

We stood like that for over an hour, silently dabbing, blotting, dabbing again until two-thirds of the mural was clean.

"What will you do about this?" She ran her finger along the fissure through the little girl's brown shoe.

"I'll fill it in, then touch it up with paint. You'll soon forget it was ever there."

"I doubt that."

"I had another idea."

She looked at me, her eyes no longer pinched and tight, but round with curiosity.

"What do you think about taking this whole area and framing it? I could apply a wood frame if you'd like, to give it dimensionality—like a painting you hang on the wall. Or I could paint you a frame, which would give you the option of covering it with another poster."

She studied the mural. "I don't want to cover it."

I waited.

"Can you put a real frame on it?"

"Of course. I was thinking because your room is so white now, we could frame it in a color that either matches the room, like if you have a dark color you're putting on your bed, or we can pull one from the picture itself. What about polished wood, a deep brown, maybe a mahogany that matches the brown of the swing?"

"I like that." She looked around the empty room. "It was all ruined. All my pillows. Everything."

"Soft things never give up the smoke, no matter how much you wash them. I'm sorry about that. Have you decided how you want to decorate?"

She shook her head.

"It'll all come together. Everything can be fixed—it just takes time."

My words stopped me. I said them to myself, to my sister, to friends. I said them to clients. I'd said them to Ben and Joseph

during dinner—like I was some midcentury peddler selling a cure-all elixir—and again to Ben yesterday. They suddenly sounded empty, floating between me and this hurt girl.

Usually by the time I arrived on the scene, the major devastation had been cleared away and reparation was in full swing. The words didn't feel useless and trite, especially when said to adults who were ready to move on and get the workers out of their offices or homes.

But this time I'd been wrong to fling my words so quickly, so carelessly. Brooke didn't love the mural for the mural's sake—she loved what it represented: a happy time, a happy childhood, a happy home. And standing in this empty house, every surface new but tenaciously holding a lingering whiff of smoke and that tang of burning tar paper that takes months to fade, who was I to offer such assurances?

Chapter 5

$\mathcal{A}$re you sure you have time?" Ben leaned into my car window. I'd pulled up to Piccolo a few minutes before four o'clock and found him sitting on the small bench outside the restaurant's front door.

"I do and I'm sorry I'm late. I needed to finish washing a mural."

"Joseph called to remind me this was my mess. He said I am imposing on you." Ben hopped into the car.

"You aren't. I came to you. Remember?" I looked over at him as I pulled onto the road.

"Tell me about your mural."

"Really?"

"*Sì*. Tell me what you do."

As I talked, I put my finger on something that had intrigued me about him—not everything, but one thing. His stillness.

During dinner that first night he was fire and action, squeezing himself into our small table and quarreling with Joseph. But yesterday he'd been slow and thoughtful, his wrist, stirring the sauce, providing the only movement. Then he turned and looked

at me and not a muscle moved. I liked that. It felt as if he understood the proper speed of things, the proper weight of life, and it didn't intimidate him. He didn't need to fill it up with clutter.

After describing Brooke and the mural, I trailed on, hardly thinking where I was going until "I was fired yesterday" popped out. I glanced over to catch his eyes widen, but he didn't speak. "My company is closing its restoration department and outsourcing the work, so this is a good distraction. Keeps thinking about the inevitable at bay."

"I am sorry."

"I'll be okay." I shrugged off his concern.

"Work is important. It is an extension of who we are."

His words settled between us.

"I came here as a last effort to get my head around work too." He said it as if sharing a piece of his soul with me.

"You did?"

"Back home in Montevello, my family owns a restaurant, Coccocino. Four generations have worked there. I will be the fifth. My papa was chef for years, then Mama took over—he's much older—and now she has quit to be with him. I have worked as sous chef for years, but she controlled the kitchen. And change is hard. She . . ." Ben searched for a word. "She barks . . . balks . . . at my changes, so Papa suggested I go and work on them. Master them. Away from Coccocino."

He nodded at me as if it all made sense between us. And it did.

"So here I am, to see my brother after so many years, and to get to the place where I take over Coccocino, without becoming lost."

I turned into the supply shop's parking lot.

"You have the list?" Ben hopped out.

"I do." I grabbed my bag and chased after him.

By the time I reached the door, I knew that stillness was gone.

Ben was ready to roll and had secured a cart. The restaurant supply store was a warehouse the size of a Costco, overflowing with every item a restaurateur could need—from light fixtures to appliances, from lemon peelers and napkin rings to the tiny umbrellas bartenders fling into drinks. I grabbed a second broad, flat cart and rolled after him.

We stacked boxes of antiqued wire breadbaskets, cut-glass votive holders, inexpensive picture frames that I could enhance with a little mottled silver appliqué, and slim glass carafes onto one of the carts before I figured out what was niggling at me. The glimpse in the car wasn't enough. Everything about him fascinated me.

"Joseph said you didn't know about your aunt and uncle? That you'd never met them? Aren't you all close? Living together? Big families and all?"

Ben's lips quirked up on one side.

"That didn't sound right. I didn't think it was like some *Godfather* movie, I just meant . . ." I took a breath and started over. "You hadn't met your aunt and uncle before?"

Ben reached for a stack of menu holders and laid them on the cart. "Mama never talks about her family. I knew nothing before Joseph introduced me to Maria. She is Mama's older sister. And there is a brother, too, Antonio, back in Italy. He is in Rubano, near Venice. Two hours away and I never knew him either. Joseph said he chose Atlanta at first because he knew they were here." He lifted a package of dark table linens. "Yes?"

"I wouldn't. White will stay fresher longer with a little Oxy Clean, bleach, and a vinegar rinse every now and then. Besides, lighter will give that linen feel you're going for with your wall color. Remember, Piccolo is a small space."

"White." He grabbed three wrapped stacks of white linens.

"How long has Joseph lived here?"

"Ten years."

"Ten years and he never told you he lived near family? That you had an aunt and uncle?"

Ben smiled. "I do not blame him. Mama does not talk to him either. And she could have told me thirty years ago, yes? That is family, how it works."

I pushed ahead, thinking that when it came to family dysfunction, our experiences weren't so far apart after all.

We moved on to pans, and he selected a couple forty-gallon stockpots and a stack of pizza stones.

I tapped one. "Pizza isn't on Piccolo's menu. Are you adding it?"

"Against Maria's wishes." Ben grinned. "She may not talk to Mama, but they are very alike. Mama dislikes pizza too. But Piccolo *and* Coccocino need it. I almost have the dough perfect."

"You don't know how to make a pizza?"

His laugh held the same disappointment and self-derision mine had held that morning when discussing my paintings with Joseph.

"I was kidding."

"I was not." Ben stopped. "Coccocino is a beautiful place, three times the size of Piccolo, and it swells in the summer with tourists. It has an impeccable reputation, and I wanted to give it something special. Mine. Tourists expect pizza, and Italy offers the world's best. I want to offer the best, so I brought a suitcase of flour to my brother's to work on it away from prying eyes and tongues." He tilted his head. "I sound like a fool. Perfection is not possible."

"You don't sound like a fool, except for the suitcase of flour." I looked down and regretted my last words. I had tried to offer a joke, but he gripped the handle of the cart so tight his nail bases

had blued. I reached out, then just as quickly withdrew my hand. "I'm sorry. I was trying to make you smile."

He shrugged off my concern. "Flour is unique. The grains are different, textures different, and what you learn with one does not pass . . . translate? . . . and the yeast is an always changing variable. I needed the flour to be a constant so I brought my own." He dropped his head and continued to himself, as if working out a problem, before he looked up at me. "Bread is life in Italy. Papa makes it. All kinds. And Mama makes pasta so light it rises to your mouth. Pizza is the form of bread left for me—a way to make the restaurant different, mine, and prove my hands are good." He shook his head. "No, that sounds wrong. I—"

"You mean that it's in good hands." I reached again and laid my hand on top of his.

He stared at it and continued. "Yes. They can trust me. I am close, but . . . I will go home soon. Maybe with nothing to show." He brought his gaze up and traced a finger from his free hand along my cheek.

"Let's at least give something to Maria and Vito."

We finished our shopping and packed my station wagon so tight Ben was buried in the passenger seat.

"Thank you, Emily," he called.

I smiled at the disembodied voice and the way he pronounced my name, as if the first and last syllables rolled with an extra *e* or two, or three.

"You're welcome," I called back.

"Will you come to Piccolo tonight? I will not be out of the kitchen until about ten, but could you come?"

The voice sounded more vulnerable this time. It quickened my heartbeat. I looked over and was confronted with a wall of cardboard.

"Are you there?" it called again.

"Of course I am. It's just strange talking to a box."

"It is worse than squishing by one." He waited. "So?"

"Yes. I'll be there."

"*Bene*. I will have a surprise for you. Something special."

We pulled around back to the service entrance of Piccolo, and a couple guys emerged from the kitchen to help us unload the car. We stacked everything into a back closet with great efficiency and few words—until Maria found us.

"Look. Look what you've done!" She oohed and aahed over everything in a lovely Italian Southern drawl. "It's going to be *bellissimo*." She grabbed us one after the other into hugs and kisses between loads from the car.

After the last trip, I left Maria digging through the storage closet and found my hand captured within Ben's as I passed him, heading toward my car. He made tiny circles in my palm with his thumb. "Tonight?"

Without thinking I stepped closer. Thinking, and glancing Maria's way, I stepped back. "I'll be here."

I walked into the restaurant around nine o'clock and stalled three steps inside the door. Joseph sat at the bar directly in front of me, his back to the door. I wavered and stepped back, but he spun, most likely catching my reflection in the mirror facing him. He smiled and tapped the next stool.

"Hello, Emily. I should have known you'd be here tonight."

"Ben asked me to come."

"Yes . . . I heard you had an exciting afternoon."

I slid onto the stool. "I know you're against it, and I hardly

know either of you, but it's a good plan, Joseph. It can work. And Ben—"

"My brother is very compelling." Joseph turned back to his plate. "I also know you underpromise and overdeliver, not the other way around. I called your boss."

"You did?"

"You're a good worker. Good at your job. Creative. Organized. On time. And your results always exceed expectations. You are more than you appear."

Again . . . *Insult or compliment?* I waffled. "And?"

"And I'm out." He held up his hands. "I don't see my brother much. In fact, I haven't seen him more than a handful of times in eighteen years. But I know he was a good kid and now he's a good man, and Maria and Vito asked for his help. I learned today that any skills he may lack, you have in spades." Joseph twisted his stool toward me. "So I guess I'm asking you to take his plans seriously now too."

"I . . . Of course." My head spun.

He laughed, lighter than I expected, and raised his glass to me. "I expect you'll have fun too."

That settled, Joseph's manner quickly warmed. We sat and chatted about art—paintings he'd seen in person and I'd studied in books. We talked about new restoration techniques; again, he was employing them and I was only reading about them. We were on equal ground, however, with the discovery that we both loved mystery novels.

"You should try Iain Pears. His Jonathan Argyll mysteries always feature good art."

He reached around the bar to grab another glass and share his wine. "And you, Donna Leon."

"Of course I've read her. She's Italian. I have a weakness for . . ." I stalled, warming.

"American, actually, living in Venice. After twenty-five years, we've begun to claim her." Joseph smiled with a seventy-thirty mix of delight and condescension.

"Fine. I'll recommend Daniel Silva. American writer, who lives in America, with a former Israeli secret agent turned art restorer protagonist. And they're excellent."

After about an hour, Joseph stretched and looked around. "It's almost empty. Whatever Ben wants with us, he'd better get to it quick. I've got an early appointment tomorrow."

As if cued, Ben pushed through the kitchen door. I caught his eye as he wove through the tables and received an electric grin. I tapped Joseph, who turned around.

He then looked back to me with too many questions in his eyes.

"Bella! Beppe! It is time."

Ben stepped behind the bar and immediately picked up Joseph's wine bottle and topped off our glasses. He then reached his hand behind my head and pulled me forward, laying a quick but firm kiss on my mouth.

I sat back, eyes wide. Only Joseph noted my surprise with a wry smile. Ben had already gestured to the waiter who stood next to him. "Please." He spread his arm to the bar.

The waiter laid four broad white plates before us. Each was topped with a different pizza. The bit of crust I could see on the edges was light and airy, and the toppings stunning: one with arugula and prosciutto; another, figs and mascarpone; a third, sausage, duck eggs, and pecorino? And the last, all green with who knows what. And the smell? We were enveloped in Italy.

"You inspired me this afternoon. After you left . . . it was

time. No more fear." He darted a glance to his brother, who stared at him.

Emotions flew across Joseph's face—wonder, jealousy and its slight variant, envy, pride, and . . . respect.

The artist in me wanted to capture each. The human in me wanted to ask a lot of questions.

"Congratulations." Joseph said the word softly. Sincerely.

"Finalmente." Ben nodded to him.

Joseph turned to me. "Ben's been chasing this forever, so he tells me. The perfect crust, found metaphorically somewhere between Rome and Naples." He slid a teasing glance to his brother. "It's a heavy burden, perfection." He paused. "Our father believes bread is as close to the divine as we get on earth. An element of life, made holy by its relation to God. And Mama . . . She may not agree, but she runs the show. Rigid lines, never to be crossed. She makes the pasta. So with a family restaurant, we sons must find our place. In or out." He picked up a knife and fork and took a good-sized bite.

Ben released his breath and came around to our side of the bar. He dropped onto the vacant stool on my right, sandwiching me between the brothers. I shifted back a little so they could see each other, but that didn't stop Ben from resting his arm on the back of my stool and leaning across me. Somehow, I didn't mind.

"Well done, little brother. It's everything you've wanted."

Ben's eyes rounded in surprise at Joseph's blessing. In spite of his strong jaw and chin, his deep-set, dark eyes—the defined, cut face of a man—I saw a boy. A boy young enough to need his older brother.

We sampled the pizzas in silence for several minutes, then Joseph put down his fork and stood. "I'll see you at home, Ben. This was outstanding." He tapped my shoulder. "Tomorrow, Emily."

Ben jumped up and crossed behind me to pull Joseph into a hug. Then, as his brother walked out the door, he dropped down and let out a deep breath.

"Are you okay?"

"Were they good?" Ben leaned close.

"Completely delicious, and more importantly, Joseph thought so. He knows you, he knows what you're after, and . . ." I scrunched my nose. "I don't get the impression your brother doles out compliments carelessly."

Ben chuckled. "He never did."

As the tables cleared, we moved to the restaurant's one booth. And curled into the back corner, we talked—about everything and nothing. We talked through the last customer's departure and through the staff's cleanup and Uncle Vito's mischievous good-bye: "Be sure to turn the ovens on at four for the bread."

Without breaking his story, Ben waved off his uncle and continued to tell about his family, the names rolling off his tongue, and his life back home. Among all the richness of his tale, I noted he didn't answer my many unasked questions. Why hadn't Joseph seen him in eighteen years? How had he not known about his aunt and uncle? The intimacy of a back booth in the dark almost gave me the courage to pepper him, but I held back. After all, I suspected, there'd be time.

Soon we moved on to food, art, books, more about my work, and our plans for Piccolo . . . and his delight that both our countries drive on the right side of the road.

Finally I stretched and looked beyond our entwined hands, resting on the table. "I thought your uncle was joking."

"What?"

"Look." I pointed to the front windows. The light outside was changing. I could see gray creeping into the black.

"I need to let you sleep." Ben trailed a finger up my wrist.

"You too. But first, I suspect we need to turn on his ovens." I leaned back and glanced around the empty dining room. "Do you start the bread too? You won't get any sleep."

"I will steal a few hours, then come in early this afternoon to prep. Vito makes his own bread." Ben sat back as well. "Thank you for coming with me today, yesterday, to the store. For this too." He pulled my hand to help me scoot from the booth.

We walked outside, dawn creeping fast from gray to hints of pink. I stopped by my car to dig around for my keys—secretly pleased that older cars don't open automatically when you approach. My fumbling gave me time to figure out how to handle the moment.

I pulled the keys from my bag before I found a solution. "Got 'em."

Ben wrapped his hand around them, lowering both my keys and my hand to my side.

"I am going to kiss you now. Again."

"Oh . . ."

He moved in so slowly that I reached up to close the last few inches. Clearly he understood stillness better than I did.

He drew me closer, enfolding me in his arms as I dipped in response to his touch. Some time later, but still too soon, he pulled away. "I think you like Italian art?"

"Yes."

"Do you know Francesco Hayez? *Il bacio?*"

I shook my head, trying to think coherently.

"Look it up." He touched his lips to mine again. "This was that moment."

Chapter 6

The next day began a three-day rinse, wash, and repeat cycle: early morning at the studio working my way through the Petersons' box, late morning to early afternoon washing the Petersons' dining room walls, afternoon to evening moving upstairs to work beside Brooke on her mural.

And then came the evenings . . . Three delicious evenings sitting at Piccolo's long wooden bar catching glimpses of Ben and snacking on anything yummy he sent from the kitchen. And when the kitchen closed, he would collect me from the front of the restaurant and settle beside me in the back booth. Time stopped at night—time spent in the booth talking and kissing, and in the kitchen cooking, baking, and . . . as nonsensical as it sounded, falling for him, fast.

"I looked up that picture. *Il bacio?*"

"And?" Ben leaned forward. No blinking.

"Quite a picture. Quite a kiss. I have one for you now . . . by Gustav Klimt."

"Another beautiful kiss."

"You know it?" I deflated.

"Bella, it's one of the most famous paintings ever."

"Maybe, but ninety-nine out of a hundred Americans wouldn't be able to identify it."

"Not all had Joseph for a brother. Besides—"

"Don't give me that. It's not because you're Italian. It's not in your water. You all don't absorb art by osmosis." I laughed.

He'd spent the last two nights regaling me with his country's superiority: *migliore* cheese, *migliore* wine, *migliore* art, *migliore* sports. Better, better, better . . . Actually, we called a tie on sports because he refused to discuss "soccer" at all.

"Okay, leaving that behind, here, I found a picture of what I want to do with those frames we bought." I handed him my phone. "See, I'll put a silver wash on them and it'll lighten up the whole aesthetic, then we'll hang them in the hall on the way to the restroom."

"Perfect." He looked at me like he wasn't talking about the frames at all. He tapped my phone and started to hand it to me, then pulled it back.

I grabbed for it. "No."

He grinned. "Bella." He said the word softly while staring at the phone rather than me. *Il bacio*, Hayez's, not Klimt's, was my home screen.

❧

The weekend arrived—with little sleep, delicious food, and a grin I couldn't pull down if I tried.

I packed up the Petersons' now completed box of treasures and examined my work on Patches' leg.

"Are you going to make him a new one?" Lily called from her worktable.

"I'm about to paint over the filler on this one. It's dry." I held him high. "How could I make a new one?"

She flicked her finger the opposite direction. "Program the 3D printer. That's what it's there for."

"You've got a 3D printer?" I jumped off my stool. "I've never seen one. I wondered what that thing was."

"I'll help you program it. I need a break anyway." Lily rolled her stool away from her triptych to a computer. "Joseph upgraded our CAD program a few months ago. He used to it create molds for detail work on a Fabergé egg. You should ask to see the pictures; it was the best work I've ever seen."

I grabbed my stool and rolled next to her, and we measured, designed, and programmed the fourth leg.

"I could learn this."

She looked at me, puzzled. "Of course you could."

"No, I mean . . ." I paused. It felt like begging, but I loved my field, my small field in which jobs were competitive and scarce, and I wanted to stay in it. "Covington is shutting down their restoration department. Come next month, I'm out of a job." I rolled a few inches away. "Do you think learning something like this could help me land another? . . . Maybe here, helping you all?"

"There's plenty to do here." She glanced over to my workstation. "I hope you don't mind, I examined your work on the porcelain figurines yesterday. It's really good. Exceptional, really. And the frame . . . I wouldn't have thought of taking wood from the inner edge to build the supports, but it makes perfect sense. It's already tempered to structure and will conform in perfect harmony."

"Exactly." I grinned.

"You should talk to Joseph. He took on an estate being prepped for auction last month, and we could use the help."

"I will." I looked to Joseph's office door. *As soon as I finish a stellar job at Piccolo.*

The leg was soon programmed, and Lily showed me how to thread the gray filament into the printer. It sprang to life and started pulling the filament into itself with a high-pitched whirl.

"Done." She wiped her hands together. "It'll take about four hours to crank that baby out, but Patches will have a new leg soon."

"Thank you."

She returned to her current inch of green loveliness, and I tapped on Joseph's door.

"Other than a little work on the walls, I've finished the repairs for this Covington job and I have some spare time. Do you have anything I can help with?"

"Piccolo." Joseph's tone was sharp.

I pulled back from the door.

"Emily, wait," he called.

I put my head back in.

"Here." He grabbed a box off a side table and carried it out to my worktable. "I could use your help with these. I saw the figurines you repaired. You did an excellent job. These I want to paint myself, but could you handle the reconstruction?"

"Let me look."

While he went back to his office to grab the second box, I peeked inside. It was a late Ming Dynasty bell jar broken into several large pieces—clean breaks, as if it had fallen onto a carpeted floor rather than wood or stone. The edges held little shearing. With careful layering, tucking pieces behind each other, I was certain they'd fit perfectly with almost invisible crack lines. There were a few chips, but filler and paint would deal with those.

Joseph stood beside me as I moved piece after piece into place, working out the puzzle.

"I suggest a non-yellowing clear epoxy, one with no less than a five-minute drying time as there's some layering to do in the porcelain."

"I agree." He unpacked the final pieces on the table's corner. "Can you finish them by early next week? I'd like to start the painting midweek."

I nodded.

"Thank you, and I'm sorry about what I said before. It was unfair. I said I was staying out of it." He flicked me a glance as he walked away. "And get some sleep. Ben's wandering around like the living dead, and you look no better."

There was no use replying; he was gone. I noted Lily hadn't moved a muscle. She was either too focused on her work to hear us or too polite to comment.

I laid out each piece of the blue-and-white vase into a grid system on the table for later, then headed for the Petersons' for a couple hours on Brooke's mural.

Painting was one of my favorite aspects of my work. Second to washing. Unlike my own attempts at painting or portraiture, restoration work was like a sophisticated paint-by-numbers exercise. Great skill meant you stayed in the lines and matched your colors, textures, and viscosity to perfection.

And the melding of rote action to creative expression allowed my mind to roam, dream, and solve problems. Usually I worked out how to fix some mess, work or otherwise. But for the last few days, every dream circled around and through Ben—every dip of his voice, touch, quirk of a brow, or the fact that he could make one side of his mouth move independently of the other when annoyed or amused. And his kisses—

"It looks really good." Brooke crashed into the dream.

I didn't turn around. I'd learned something else in the last

four days. If I didn't pay attention to her, she relaxed more. So I simply continued to apply dabs of color with my homemade Q-tip. The texture it produced matched the wall perfectly. "Just you wait."

She stepped beside me. "Can I help again today?"

I'd hoped for that, prepared for it. Brooke had joined me each afternoon, and yesterday she'd begun talking. But even before that point, I had listened. I had been still. I had waited. That was new for me—another thing I attributed to Ben. I pushed my thoughts back onto Brooke.

Her body language told me all I needed to know about her. Stiff and jarring at first, it had softened with each day and each cotton ball. It almost made me wonder if I'd gotten it all wrong. Perhaps fixing things wasn't about the end product—it was, oftentimes, about the process.

I waved my Q-tip toward the brushes standing in a small mason jar, borrowed from ACI. "If you'd grab the pink solvent in the box and wipe those brushes with a little of it, I'd really appreciate it. Wipe only *with* the bristle, not against." There were a few of ACI's gorgeous brushes in the jar with mine, and I did not want to ruin them.

I heard her drop to the floor and the brushes tinkle about in the jar as she removed one. She soon began to talk about her room. What she liked before, what she'd chosen to replace it, and how she might, maybe, like the new choices better.

She also talked about the hotel they were staying at, how it was far from school and her friends, and how she hated sleeping in the same room as Parker, who apparently snored. She even admitted to purposely stomping Patches.

"He said you're fixing him."

"As best I can. I can glue the leg on, but the jury's out about

more." I didn't want to reveal the possible new leg until it was adhered and painted.

"I shouldn't have done that."

A hitch in her voice made me turn. "We all do things we regret. Living in a hotel . . . and all this . . . It's stressful."

She reached for another brush, and I rolled another cotton swab. I then used it to mix a dollop of umber within three greens. Time to start on the tree.

"Mom says it's all fine, but that only makes it worse."

"Worse?"

"Like admitting it's awful would only make me feel guilty, so she doesn't. But pretending that it's no big deal, that everything's fine, that just makes it worse. Like really it's so bad we can't even talk about it."

"Have you told her that?"

Brooke snorted. "That *would* make it worse."

"You do realize that made no sense."

She shrugged and rubbed the soap against the bristles.

Since it was my brush, I stifled my cringe and returned to the wall. "What's your dad say?"

No answer.

I painted on.

"He's gone."

I closed my eyes briefly. Her voice carried a weight I knew. I flicked her a quick glance. If she'd been me, she would have continued cleaning the brushes and never stopped. There was always a new brush. I was surprised and oddly relieved to find her sitting perfectly still, legs crossed, staring at me.

Insurance files include everything—I mean everything. So I knew her parents weren't divorced. Same address. Joint policy. I also knew this was sacred ground and I needed to tread carefully.

"Gone gone? Trip gone? Work gone?" There are many types of gone.

"Work gone?" She said it like a question.

"Done." I nodded to the tree. Then I dropped next to her to pull out a new plastic palette to mix two browns, one for the swing, one for the shoes. It was also time to attack that fissure across the bottom, which I'd sealed the day before.

I sat facing her. "People deal with stress in a lot of ways. This is stress." I dabbled the brush in the air as if coloring over said stress. "I think you should probably tell your mom how you feel. She may not know you need to talk about it, so you can't blame her for wanting to protect you." I squeezed a dime-size dollop of raw sienna onto my pearl drop of Venetian brown.

Brooke shrugged. "I told her what you said, about everything getting fixed."

"And?"

"She says some things can't be fixed. We just have to endure them."

Chapter 7

I left the Petersons' house at noon. After all, it was the weekend. And Ben had invited me on an adventure. Only seven hours apart and I already missed him . . . It amazed me how, sitting in that back booth or standing side by side in the kitchen, we hadn't run out of things to say, stories to tell, or dreams to share.

"Why don't you ever wait inside?" I pulled up to find him, once again, waiting on Piccolo's front bench. "It's cooler."

"I get to see you sooner." He stepped to the driver's door and kissed me through the open window before circling the car, dropping into the passenger seat, and kissing me all over again. "We have a lot to do today."

It was the first time I'd heard nerves, even fear, in his voice.

"Not really. Piccolo's still open for business tonight. Once we close tomorrow, it'll get crazy and stay that way for several days. Think of this as the calm before the storm."

"Joseph was right. I poked a dragon."

I twisted in my seat. "Do you want to pull back? Nothing is set in stone, and Maria and Vito will be pleased with anything we do. New linens alone will be a good lift."

"I trust you. All your lists. You have this planned." Ben reached for my hand. "I trust us. The menu changes over the past month are making a difference already. We can do this, and I want it for them." He kissed my palm. "I am only getting nervous. *Terrified* is the best word, I think."

"It'll be work, but it's doable. Very doable."

He directed me first to a coffee shop. Dripworks. It was a small place with metal counters, industrial stools, and a hipster vibe that would thrive in Seattle or Chicago's Old Town. We sat up front and I pulled out my notebook, which Ben gently grabbed and shoved back into my bag, laying a light kiss on my lips. "You said we were fine. Today is about fun."

"I . . ."

"Fun."

I smiled and took a bite of my croissant, promptly forgetting about my notebook. "This is amazing."

"Just you wait."

He then led me to a farmers market in the small neighborhood behind the shop.

"How do you know about all these places? You've been here, what, a month? It's like you live here."

"Joseph thinks I do nothing with my mornings, but this is research and, yes, this is life. Piccolo needs fresh produce, and the way you get the best is changing. They can order direct and get fresher goods at better prices. Farmers like it, too, because they have a committed buyer. So now I know these farmers, share with them, and now I will set up orders. Come on, I will introduce you."

Ben did just that. I met a couple farmers who came to the markets on the weekends but were thrilled to make scheduled deliveries at Piccolo. The butcher even remarked that after meeting Ben he'd approached a few other restaurants directly and

had increased his "secured" weekly revenue by over 50 percent. That comment erupted into a moment of firm hand pumping and backslapping. Ben was as delighted as the butcher.

After a second market, we passed down a side street and found ourselves in a small block of artisan shops and galleries.

"The coffee shop is around the corner." Ben slid his hand down my arm and captured my own.

"Another?" I wasn't sure how much more caffeine I could take.

He pushed open a worn green wood door and we found ourselves in a small workroom-cum-shop.

"A coffee*maker* shop?"

"What did I say?"

"A coffee shop. Which I guess is right. I just expected another cappuccino and tasty treat."

"This is better. Come see." He walked across the small room to a large stainless-steel La Marzocco machine sitting on a high wood countertop. "It has digital display, dual boilers, and pulls three shots at once. Maybe one more than Piccolo needs, but it will set the tone at the bar and make beautiful espresso."

He was right. It was gorgeous and would definitely make a statement. I lifted the tag. There were two prices. One extraordinary. One astronomical. "Do you get to pick your price?"

"*Sì.*" Ben smiled as if about to share a secret. "One if I want them to refurbish it; the other if I do the work. Costly, but this is the best and coffee is popular. Piccolo cannot skimp."

"Can you refurbish it?"

The smile dropped. "No. Piccolo must pay the higher price."

I studied the machine. "I'd have to open it up to look inside, but after years of restoring lamps, clocks, radios, even a model steam engine, I bet, with the schematics, I could do it."

Ben raised a brow.

"Fixing can't mean too much more than valve work and getting this electrical panel functional."

"Are you sure?" At my nod, he grinned and pulled me into a hug. He pushed me back, holding me by the shoulders. "You don't need to do this. Are you very sure?"

"I hope so." My matching grin faltered; I wanted so much to be all he saw in me. I ducked my head before he could see any doubt.

"Bene." He squeezed me again, then called for the salesman. The two of them soon carried the La Marzocco to my wagon. Ben's second trip brought all its extra parts and another machine.

"What's that?"

"A La Pavoni with a matching knock box. He gave them to me."

The machine was rusted, the glass on the gauge broken. "I can see why."

"It is for you."

My head bounced up.

"I tasted your coffee yesterday when you came to Piccolo, remember? Cold drip is not coffee, Bella." His last word rolled off in an anguished breath.

"It's not that bad."

"It is."

Machines safely ensconced in the car, we walked on, hand in hand, in and out of the shops and galleries. We found an antique plate rack. Ben envisioned replacing the plastic flowers on Piccolo's long interior wall with Italian plates. We found cut crystal bulb holders to be used alongside the votives at the larger tables. We even found a couple old prints in pristine condition for the small front lobby area. I could build the frames easily.

Then we found lunch—an amazing place with rough-hewn tables flanking a long communal table that seated at least fifty and stretched the length of the restaurant. The ceiling was high,

with antique brass pipes and vent work, clean and shiny, adding a touch of industrial class.

"Ammazza." I picked up the menu.

"*Ammazza*," Ben corrected me, and the word sounded completely different and infinitely lovelier.

"Didn't I say that?"

"Not close." He smiled and scanned the menu. "Do you mind if we order pizza? I brought you on purpose. They serve Neapolitan style, first rate and all the flavors I choose. They know pizza."

"Are we checking out the competition?"

"Much can be learned from the competition." Ben's face softened. "Did I not tell you that I did not learn to cook at Coccocino?" He looked around. "And this is not competition for Piccolo. This is the heart of the city's young; they make their own mozzarella, cure their meats on site. Maria and Vito cannot do this, and I would not ask them to try. They feed families. But this has good excitement, I think."

"So this is what we're trying to create. *Vita*. Life." I looked around. "Then we have our work cut out for us. I may need to pull out my little notebook."

"Come here instead." He wagged a finger, and I leaned over the small table. He laid a light kiss on me and smiled. "Thank you for believing in this—in me."

As I rocked back on the bench, a new and disconcerting thought threaded through me. When I returned to Piccolo that first day, I never imagined that it was for anyone but me. It never occurred to me that someone could find a sense of wonder, a sense of wholeness or delight in me—that I could be someone's great surprise. But if it was true and I was or could be—what did that mean?

Chapter 8

Sunday started too early.

I met Ben at Piccolo at five thirty and we spread tarps over the equipment in the kitchen, stacked the tables to the center of the dining room, and began to tarp them as well before the painters arrived.

By noon we had finished prep, eaten Maria and Vito's amazing lunch, and begun painting. With a small army of painters busy at work, Piccolo transformed before my eyes. What was a dark, kitschy, small space opened and widened as the walls were coated in starched white primer, then, by late evening, in a linen white.

Joseph's studio and Ammazza had inspired me to make a last-minute change to our plans. I changed the trim color from white to a deep brown and spent the early-morning hours mixing an inert cleaning solution to brighten the exposed copper piping and brass metalwork. The resulting gold and red tones added a splash of warmth and light against the white. I also suggested we paint the ceiling a complementary deep brown to further the effect. Ben agreed, and by late afternoon the first swipe of brown stretched across the ceiling above our booth.

Maria loved the changes as well and, despite my protests, climbed a tall ladder and led the charge to clean the pipes.

I reached up to tap her knee. "Please let me do that."

"You may grab another ladder beside me." She looked down and smiled. "And you should. Wiping this across the pipes is like discovering a sunrise."

"Thank you." I grinned, warmed by her praise. "I will."

Hours later, we both climbed down. Ben was instantly at my side.

"It is beautiful." He swung an arm around my shoulders and tucked me close. "We did so much. Maybe I was wrong to ask they close for the week."

"Don't say it." I laughed, circling my arms around his waist. "There's still a ton to do. Next Friday will be here before you know it."

"We must stop or we will tire out. It's already much too late." Maria waved her hands at the painters and waitstaff scattered around the dining room.

As she circled the room with thanks and good-byes, shooing everyone out the door, Ben drew me to the kitchen.

As soon as the door shut behind us, he pulled me close and kissed me. "It is more than I thought. We did this."

"We did." I smiled. *We.* My work was usually so solitary. This was new, and the joy of it bubbled within me. "You might want to include Maria and Vito."

"Not at this moment." Ben kissed me again. "They can lock up. Let us go too."

I grabbed my bag from a kitchen cubby and, while he returned to the dining room to say our good-byes, checked my phone. Three missed calls and a voice mail from Amy.

Ems, it's me. Surprise! Where are you? I'm at your hotel, but they won't let me into your rooms. Call me back.

Ben swung the door to the kitchen back open. "Where shall we go? I know a couple more places I think you will love."

I shook my head. "First things first; I need a shower."

"Good idea." He smiled.

I held up my hand. "You're going to Joseph's, me to my hotel. Call me in an hour?"

Ben tilted his head. I knew my tone caught him; it was strident, angry, but I couldn't explain. Maybe I'd misunderstood the message. "Do you want a ride to Joseph's?"

"He lives only a few blocks away. The walk will feel good. Are you sure you are well?"

I rushed out the back door. "I'm fine. Call me soon?"

Ben followed and I drove away with him standing still, watching me. My heart folded in; I had hurt him. But what if I had heard correctly? *Amy? Here?*

I walked into the lobby of the Residence Inn and stalled. I felt her. She was here . . . somewhere.

"Ems!"

I heard her before I saw her. I hadn't noticed her waiting by the door, and now she bounced into my arms. In so many ways it was like seeing myself fly at me—we were about the same height, though highlighting gave her more varied and blonder tones; we had the same eyes, though hers were a deeper green; and we . . . I took in her short skirt and tight tank top . . . we did not dress alike.

People often mistook us for twins. But looking at her, I instantly felt stretched thin and dried out.

I stepped back and tucked a chunk of hair behind my ear. Ben had flicked paint on me, but the moment, and the fun, was gone, and only embarrassing and sticky white paint remained. "How'd you get here? And why? You've got interviews this week."

"It's good to see you too."

"It is good to see you, but . . ." I closed my eyes. This was not the time or the place to get into it. "Come on up." I headed to the elevators.

She picked up her bag and followed me. "Before you freak out, I called both those companies and neither minded pushing the interviews back."

"That doesn't mean they won't fill the positions before you get there." I jabbed at the elevator button.

"Then they weren't the jobs for me." She grinned and reached for something on my head. "What did you do to your hair?"

I groaned and pulled the clump of paint from her fingers. "That's not how it works. *You* want the job, not them. *You* work on *their* schedule." I pushed my way into the suite, the door sticking in the humidity.

Amy spun around. "This is great. You have a little living room, even a kitchen."

"They do a good job here." I pointed to the couch. "That's a pullout. You can sleep there."

"Thanks." Amy dropped her small suitcase and plopped down on it. "What do you want to do?"

Go out with Ben. "I kinda had plans."

"You did? Tell me." Amy's face brightened.

"Let me start with a shower first." I didn't want to talk about Ben. I didn't want to share him. Every sweater, every coat, every guy. They met me, then their eyes followed her.

"Great. You do that and—" She opened the kitchen's small refrigerator. "What have you been living on?"

"Italian food," I called on my way to the bedroom.

"Pricey," she yelled back.

"Free, actually. Those are my plans tonight. Dinner with the chef of an Italian restaurant." *There. That's all I'm going to share.*

"Ooohh . . . You shower, and I'm going to grab something at the little grocery across the street. I'm starving, but I want to hear the whole story. Can I take a key?"

"Grab one off the counter."

I heard the door slam right before I turned on the water.

I had finally combed out the last of the paint when a firm knock on the door rattled the entire suite. *She forgot the key!* I crossed the living room with a groan and yanked the doorknob, forgetting how thin and light hollow doors are. It careened into me and sent me stumbling backward, wet hair whipping me in the eyes.

Ben caught my arm.

"What are you doing here?"

His face was inches from mine. "You were tired and something was wrong . . . I brought dinner. Besides, I was at a lost myself."

"At a *loss*."

He smiled down and released me. "That too."

Righting myself, I stepped aside. "Come in. My sister showed up today."

"That is what that was about?"

"I'm sorry I didn't tell you. I got the message as we left Piccolo."

"You know my brother. Can I meet your sister?" Ben smiled as if this was a "meeting the family" moment.

No. Yes. No. While I mentally cycled through a variety of answers, he shoved a green cloth bag into my hands. It was heavy.

"I borrowed Joseph's car and bought us dinner. Take this to your kitchen."

"What is this?" I looked in and found produce, pasta, oil—groceries. "Are you cooking for us? Me? Us?"

"No." He cut off my words with a solid kiss. "*We* are cooking for *us*. Sister, too, now."

"Speaking of . . . Where is she?" I balanced the bag to reach for my phone. Amy had texted while I was in the shower. "It may be only us. She's met some guy in the lobby . . ." I laid down the phone, unwilling to read the rest of her message.

Ben pulled the teetering bag from my arms and set it on the counter.

"You don't have to do this." I stepped into the tiny kitchen behind him. "But what are we making?"

He smiled back at me. "I want to try something new. With you." He passed me a bottle of olive oil and a large sauté pan. "You be in charge of the shrimp."

I poured in the oil and twisted the burner knob to medium, then unwrapped the brown paper package.

"You said you never cook." He raised a brow. "You knew to heat it first."

I winked, that feeling from the morning returning—the light and free feeling that ended in sticky white hair and a swipe of paint across his cheek. "You never get a reaction without a little heat."

"Ah . . ." He stole another kiss, and we spent the next few minutes with me sautéing the shrimp and him washing, dicing, and splicing a variety of vegetables. Over the past several nights, we'd perfected this dance—moving around a kitchen together, talking, tasting, and me cleaning rather than cooking. This was my first cooking assignment. I snuck a glance at Ben, oddly delighted to be trusted with shrimp.

He didn't notice and continued to chop his vegetables. I didn't comment and continued to sauté the shrimp. We didn't speak, and I savored the silence. It lay softly with Ben, light, warm, and beautiful. Until I thought of Amy . . .

He nudged my shoulder. "You make a terrible face when you

concentrate. Those?" He ran his thumb across the space between my eyebrows. "They come right together. In here."

"Never tell a girl she looks terrible."

"Not you." He pinched his face tight. "That expression."

I narrowed my eyes, working not to laugh. "Still . . ."

"I should flatter you?" Ben pulled my shoulder until I faced him. "We are past that."

"We are? When did that happen? We've known each other about a week."

He closed the tiny distance between us as if prepared to stare me down. I had to tilt my head back to keep eye contact. "The moment we met."

"Really?" I whispered. "I like that."

The click of the key card broke the moment.

I heard Amy push open the door. "I got us . . . Hello?" She froze, staring at Ben.

I trailed her gaze to absorb what she must see—tall, lithe, short dark hair, stubble from having started the day so early, and flecks of paint here and there that the shower hadn't washed away but only made him more adorable. I couldn't blame Amy for the unabashed interest that flashed through her eyes.

Wait until he speaks.

I flapped my arm between the two. "Amy, Ben. Ben, my sister, Amy. Ben's brother is Joseph, who owns the studio I'm at. He's a chef and . . ." *Get it over with.* "He's Italian." I clamped my mouth shut.

Ben sent me an amused glance.

"Hi." Amy didn't stumble like I might have. Instead, she floated the three steps as her single word became a monosyllabic greeting with a decisively Southern drawl.

I rolled my eyes.

Ben was no better. His accent thickened with every word as he welcomed her and told her that we had dinner under control.

"Wonderful. I'll just perch here and let you two cook." She poured herself a glass of wine and climbed onto one of the high stools at the counter.

Ben and I continued cooking. Me, silent. Him, keeping up a charming prattle, laced with way too much flattery.

Soon he tossed his vegetables, my shrimp, and the pasta together and carried the three dishes to the small dining table. I still hadn't spoken a word since the introductions.

After a few bites I relented and tapped his bowl with my fork. We'd made a shell pasta dish full of fresh vegetables and sautéed shrimp and bound it all in a creamed basil pesto with smoked chilies. "Not bad."

"How can you say that? It's delicious." Amy raised her glass. "To the chef. Cheers."

Ben mimicked her motion and laid his other hand on my shoulder. "Chefs." He smiled at me as I, too, raised my glass. "It is not delicious enough." He leaned back, still watching me. "Think on it. What are we missing?"

I almost laughed. Amy and I grew up on Kraft Mac and Cheese or Annie's, if we had enough to splurge. I shot her a glance and knew she was in the same predicament. Neither of us had a clue as to what might be missing.

I poked my fork around what was left and found an opinion. "Smoke the shrimp? Can you grill them or sear them to get that flavor?"

"Yes . . ." He nodded for me to continue.

"It needs depth, but without any spice that might overpower all your vegetables and the basil. You've already got chilies in the sauce, so you need something else, not more of the same."

"Hmm . . ." He stabbed a shrimp and chewed it slowly, considering my suggestion. "Again, you said you never cook."

"This feels like a good painting. It's layering, flavors rather than color, and tasting rather than seeing."

"I feel that way. This is my art."

"You two," Amy cut in. "No wonder you're friends." Her last word lifted in question, and I knew what she was asking.

I ignored her.

She tried a different tack. "Have you been here before, Ben?" She poked her fork around the room.

I worked hard not to narrow my eyes at her or show any emotion at all.

"No. I am staying with—"

Something caught his eye and he reached to the sofa's side table, only feet away in the tiny place.

"Vasari?" He lifted the heavy book. "You know Vasari?"

"Of course. He's basically the founder of art history and criticism, and his writings form the basis for restoration . . . He's Italian too. But of course you knew that. He was no big fan of Caravaggio, who is kind of my favorite painter, but I've forgiven him for that."

Ben's eyes warmed, and I forgot every uncharitable thought I'd been sending Amy's way.

"You should see some of Caravaggio's work."

"I have, years ago at the Art Institute in Chicago."

Ben laid his hand on the book. "No. In the churches. In the original places. In Rome, you walk into Santa Maria del Popolo or San Luigi dei Francesi and he's there. His works are all around you."

I sighed. "I wish." I was no longer talking, or thinking, about Caravaggio. And from the look in his eyes, Ben wasn't either.

"I think you could also add more parsley." Amy tapped her fork on her bowl. "To the pasta."

Ben's eyes widened as if he'd forgotten Amy sat across from him. He swallowed and said, "I can tell you a story about parsley . . ."

The next hour was filled with Ben's story of his Nonna, her garden, and the year her parsley overran all the other vegetables. And by the end, I couldn't blame Amy for any crush she might have on him.

As Ben had drifted back into his childhood, his face softened, his hands moved more fluidly, his accent tripped across octaves, and Italian sprinkled his English like jimmies on a sundae—each utterly delicious.

The spell broke only when I stood to clear the table.

"Do you mind if I go hop in the shower?"

I smiled at Amy's timing—just as the dishes needed to be washed. "Not at all. There's only one shower, through my room."

Amy grabbed her bag and disappeared while Ben picked up the glasses and followed me the few steps to the kitchen.

"And you said you don't flatter," I gently teased.

Ben glanced toward my closed bedroom door. "Is that not what she expects? One always says lovely things to a *girasole*."

"A what?"

"You call them sunflowers. They turn all through the day, following the sun. They cover the fields this time of year at home."

"Oh."

He touched my chin, lifting my face to his. "It is nothing to say lovely things to someone who expects them, needs them. The beauty is when one who does *not* expect them comes to believe them—that only happens when the compliments and the love behind them are sincere."

Love?

Before the question could hit my eyes, I tamped it down with a "Harrumph . . ."

Only Ben could make *not* giving compliments sound like a compliment.

"My own *girasole*." He laughed. "Please, Bella, only turn toward me."

The comment was so suggestive and enticing it startled me. It was also alluring—that sense that the warmth and electricity between us weren't fleeting, but could last and spread through my bones, warming me for life. I wasn't sure if we were having a language issue, an amazing flirtation . . . Or what would happen next week.

He waited a beat more before continuing, a teasing light in his eyes. "Were you jealous?"

"Not at—"

He closed the distance between us. All words stopped. All thought stopped.

"I am here for you." He tugged my hips closer and kissed me.

It took me a few moments to catch my breath and whisper, "What will you do when Piccolo's ready? You've done what you came to do, right? The pizza. The restaurant."

Ben leaned back against the counter, pulling me with him. "*Sì*. But you complicate things."

I bit my lip.

"I need to go home, Bella. For you, I would stay if I could. Already I know that. But Papa is not well, and I stole all the time I can. Saturday, I go."

"We have less than a week."

"Every moment of a week." He captured my lips and kissed me again and again.

After a few moments I heard the bathroom door open. "Amy," I whispered.

"Her timing is good."

"It is?"

"As you said, you never get a reaction without a little heat. That is plenty of heat for now. Besides—"

He stopped as Amy opened the bedroom door, straight across the small living room.

"Hey." Her voice dipped to a purr. "Hey . . ." She glanced between us, confusion skittering through her eyes. "Am I interrupting something?"

"Dishes." Ben winked at me and grabbed a rag to wipe the counters.

Chapter 9

$\mathcal{M}$onday started too early as well—or maybe Sunday had ended too late. It was dark. I was sore from wiping the copper pipes above my head. And upon entering my tiny living room, I stumbled into the couch. *Amy.*

"Ouch!"

"What time is it?" she mumbled into the dark.

"Five a.m. I'm turning on a light."

"Are you kidding me? What are you doing up?"

I heard her punch the pillows and moan as I flipped the switch in the kitchen. "I've got a lot of work today and I want to get to Piccolo by midafternoon."

"He's adorable," she sighed into her pillow.

Rather than comment, I scooped the coffee into the machine, remembering his comment about my bad coffee and remembering the two machines on my worktable. I wanted to finish those as well. A surprise.

"Make me a cup. I'm coming with you." Amy appeared beside me.

"You can't come with me."

"Then drop me off at Piccolo. I'll keep Ben company."

Oh no . . . My heart constricted. All those guys in high school . . . Guys who dated me, then met my sister. Guys who dated me to meet my sister. Guys who didn't look at me, but only at my sister. We looked alike, but she had that something more—*vita*. If I was Piccolo before Ben and I started to transform it, then she was Piccolo after. She shone brighter, laughed with lovely intonation, questioned with rapt expression and wide eyes, and drew people to her. It was Amy's great gift—she galvanized everyone around her into a happy band of devotees.

And yet the reality was—she was here and wasn't going to sit in my tiny hotel suite all day. So, knowing at least Maria would be at the restaurant so early, I dropped her off at Piccolo on my way to the studio.

Lily was already there, coffee on her worktable, eye in her scope. "Good morning." She glanced up as I slammed through the door.

"We'll see . . ." Something caught my eye. A painting was propped on my easel. I'd seen the style. I paused for a moment to form my own impressions. Russian realism. Mid-nineteenth century. "What's this?"

"Joseph left you a note." She waved at my worktable and returned to her scope.

It was a letter really, written in a neat up-down script.

Emily,

    I'd like to see what you'd do with this. Nikolai Yaroshenko. Girl Student. 1883. It's a commission from the Van Geld estate and needs to be completed quickly, as the estate goes to auction at the end of the month. Assess the damage, make a report, and

estimate the cost for restoration—based on your own metrics. Then, if all is well, I want you to handle the work.

Joseph

A Yaroshenko? That meant the painting valued near thirty thousand dollars. "He wants me to restore it."

"Don't you want to?" Lily looked up.

"Yes. But—" Doubt crept in—on all fronts.

"This is what you wanted. Start. If you get in a jam anywhere, give a shout."

I laid the note down and started deconstructing and polishing the La Marzocco, giving my hands something to do as I studied the painting. I jotted a few notes, then put it under the Leica. There was so much to see. The damage was minimal—dryness about the eyes, some scaling within the woman's shawl. I laid it on the worktable and carefully removed the framing to examine the stretcher. Oxidation had left a yellow tinge only visible when taken in contrast to the clear borders. In the end, it required nothing more than a cleaning, minimal inpainting, and a new coat of varnish.

Joseph knew all this.

By midmorning I'd finished cleaning both coffee machines and left them readied for their new parts, e-mailed Joseph my report on the Yaroshenko, and headed to the Petersons'. As I drove by Piccolo, it took all my willpower not to turn off the street and into its parking lot.

After applying the varnish to Brooke's mural, I stood back and studied it, making sure I'd done all it needed. Set within the applied faux frame, it was certainly a more sophisticated treatment—if not a little sad. The formality of its framing reinforced that the little girl, and perhaps her joy, was gone.

But that was reality. The girl in the picture *was* gone. I pulled the photos out of my folder and compared them to the mural as it appeared now. There was no doubt I'd enhanced it. But what was I to do? With Brooke sitting right beside me, was I to squeeze out fawn and ochre colors and say, "Isn't this nice?"

They weren't. They were dull and sallow colors. And if adding a little life and liveliness to her mural made it better in some way . . . it was worth it.

"Jeremy hired a painter to create that from a photo I took the day we moved in. There was a swing out back. It felt like the most romantic thing ever."

I capped the bottle of varnish. "It was. And it's beautiful. Good as new."

"Better than, I think . . ." Rachel's voice drifted away. She leaned against Brooke's windowsill. "You've been a good friend to the kids this past week. And that? It's definitely better than the original." Rachel struggled with a smile.

"Please don't say that. Don't even think it." I laughed. "I'm supposed to restore, never enhance."

"I won't blow your cover, but you . . . you made her face happier. I always thought the picture made her look sallow, and she thought she looked like a brat. Now she loves it."

"She's fourteen. She'll change her mind tomorrow."

"Wouldn't that be nice? If we could all go back . . ." Rachel looked away. I noticed her grip on the windowsill. Nail tips white, bases purple. "Brooke was sitting with you the other day."

"She did that all last week. She did a good job cleaning the mural, then I moved her onto brush duty."

"Did she . . . She doesn't talk to me, but I noticed . . ." She let her unasked questions drift between us.

Rachel and I hadn't talked the previous week beyond logistics.

Anything I'd picked up, beyond Brooke, had sifted onto me like dust.

"I think doing things with your hands, like painting or cleaning brushes, helps. The physical activity allows the mind to wander. It doesn't feel so scary to talk." I shrugged, knowing I'd probably revealed a deep truth about myself and how I coped with things rather than anything she didn't already know about her daughter.

"Should I buy a bunch of brushes?"

I laughed. "If Parker plans to paint, yes, but I offered to let Brooke paint and she only wanted to clean. It might be weird if they start showing up after I've gone."

"We're all fine—alive and well—and the house, it's standing better than ever. We've got freshly painted rooms, a new roof, a new kitchen, and two new bathrooms. And yet it tore us apart. How strong I thought we were. How naive I was." Rachel let go of the windowsill and crossed her arms. "Did she tell you how it started?"

"I read the insurance report." I shrugged. "It helps me to know what's happened to the pieces I restore."

"Ah . . . She blames herself."

"I can understand that." I didn't know what else to say. "How's Parker?"

Rachel quirked a small smile. "He's okay. He misses that silly horse. Jeremy gave it to him."

I reached into my bag. "Look."

Rachel's eyes filled. "You found another?"

"This is Patches. Parker had saved the one leg, and I made another." I handed it to her. "It was a nice clean break, so I filed the edges after gluing it back and then filled any gaps with a light caulking compound. And then I learned how to use a 3D printer. Have you ever seen one?"

Rachel looked up at me.

"I'm babbling. You couldn't care less about the process."

"Not really." She burst out a sobby laugh. "But I'm so thankful. It's such a stupid horse."

"You should give it to him."

Rachel shoved Patches back to me. "You did all the work."

I bent and threw all my equipment into my small crate. "If you don't mind, I have to get going." I lifted the box, arms now full. "Tomorrow?"

"Tomorrow." She jiggled the horse in her hand. "Thank you."

Piccolo. Part of me wanted to be there more than anything, and the other part wanted to hop on I-75 and head home to Chicago. Ben had been a dream that lasted one week. And for that one week, I was the Amy—the light and shining one. Side by side, I could never compete. It wasn't even that I wanted to compete; it was that I couldn't be "that girl" in front of her. She knew me, and I wasn't me right now. I was brighter with Ben—like those copper pipes that turned to sunrise with a simple swipe of solvent. And I loved it. Would she notice a change and ask? *Why are you trying to be someone you aren't?* Would I have the courage to ask back? *What if I'm trying to be someone I can be?*

I pulled into Piccolo's parking lot completely shaken—until I saw Ben through the window. He was helping a painter remount the small lobby's lighting fixture. He noticed me and jumped from the ladder, pushed through the door, and reached the car in a few strides.

"You are here."

"I am here." I climbed out to be pulled into a hug.

"Come see."

He led me inside, and the place was unrecognizable. They'd finished the painting and were cleaning and mopping, careful to stay clear of the walls. My solution had worked, and the copper pipes glowed warm from the ceiling. Amy was leaning over the bar rubbing a paste wax I'd bought, a beeswax and carnauba mixture, into the wood. Half the bar glowed so bright you could see an accurate reflection of the lightbulbs from the ceiling above.

"You did this on purpose," she threw out with a huff and a smile. "What ever happened to a simple furniture spray?"

"It doesn't work. Bad for the wood too. Think how shapely your upper arms will be."

"They already are." She lowered her head and kept buffing.

A few hours later found the last survivors slumped at a table over food Joseph brought from his apartment.

Amy wiggled in her seat and looked around the room. Her large blue eyes widened in wonder. Not real wonder, just the image of it. It was a look I knew well and suspected she practiced in the mirror. Doe-eyed, glowing, innocent. "This is adorable. It's going to be such a hit."

Joseph leaned forward, mesmerized. Their eyes met and held, and I almost rolled mine. But as Amy looked away to further absorb Piccolo's "adorableness," Joseph shifted his gaze to mine and winked.

You snake! I held back my laugh. I was quickly learning that despite many icy features, Joseph was a warm guy. He simply forgot how to melt most days.

He schooled his expression and addressed Amy. "Ben's always been a busy one. As a kid, he was into everything, wanted to share in every experience. Aunt Maria fell in love with him the moment he arrived and threw all this at him."

"But you had to help. Ems says you're the artist."

"Conservator," I interjected.

Joseph's eyes clouded, then cleared. "Ben doesn't need my help. Your sister helped quite a bit, though. You should ask her about it."

Amy continued as if she hadn't heard, popping a sage leaf–wrapped anchovy into her mouth. A quick "yummy" distracted her before she put her hand over her mouth and kept talking. "You two sound extraordinary."

"You don't know us yet," Joseph challenged.

"That'll be my top priority this week." She dabbed her napkin at the corners of her mouth and smiled.

This time I did roll my eyes.

"Sounds delightful." Joseph locked eyes on me and smirked.

"I think we should head home, Ames. It's late."

Amy preempted my move and jumped from her seat. "I need the ladies' room. You stay here." She dragged her eyes across the table. "Don't let her leave, y'all."

As she sashayed away, Ben reached for my hand. "She *is* good."

I slid him a look. "You noticed."

"Everyone did. She had every worker today falling over himself to help her." He smiled and kissed my temple.

I held still, enjoying being near him for just that moment. The sense of relief, or understanding, or acceptance—I honestly couldn't name it—flooded over me.

"Thank you," I whispered.

"No grazie necessari."

Joseph stood and narrowed his eyes at me. "I'm going to do you two a favor."

"You are?" I sat straight.

"I'm taking your sister back to your hotel. It'll cost me twenty minutes, but if it'll get you two to stop looking like you're missing out on dessert, it'll be worth it."

"Beppe!" Ben grinned.

"Save your thanks, little brother, and stop calling me that." He softened the command with a crooked half smile. He turned on Amy as she emerged from the ladies' room. "These two have work to do, so you're coming with me. I'll take you back to Emily's hotel." His tone left no room for discussion.

Amy glanced to me in momentary confusion, then followed.

"I think my brother . . ." Ben paused, searching for a word. "He outmaneuvered your sister."

I grinned. "Isn't it wonderful?"

Chapter 10

Joseph's shoes squealed across the cement floor. "You've begun?"

I paused, leaned back from the scope, and held the brush away from the Yaroshenko. "I got here early this morning."

He'd kept leaving me notes and tasks. Between these and the Petersons' work, I found myself stretched to reach Piccolo by midafternoon each day. But I didn't begrudge him any of it—each night he drove Amy home.

He stepped closer. "The cleaning looks good. You've eradicated the ill effects of that poor restoration job. I suspect it occurred sometime in the sixties."

"I wondered how long it'd been." I rolled away. "You did your own analysis first, didn't you?"

He smiled. "Of course."

"And the eyes?" I gestured to the scope.

As he pressed his eye to the viewfinder, I took in the whole painting. It was a portrait of a young woman, dressed for the rain and walking toward the artist, eyes locked. She was luminescent in the morning light—her skin translucent and her wool shawl so soft you could roll it between your fingers.

"I've never known anyone as hungry as you." Joseph backed away. "Or as naturally talented. That work's exceptional." Before I could respond, he continued. "How can you achieve it in this, but not in your own work? Every emotion is in those eyes."

"Down at its core, this is a sophisticated paint-by-number," I managed. "Yaroshenko did all the hard work; mine's not a creative decision. I simply stay true to what's there—and the closer I get, the better." I tapped the Leica scope. "This is unbelievable. Maybe that's where my talent lies; I'm a master imposter."

"Ben says you have the soul of an artist. One can't fake that. You've captured what Yaroshenko expressed. Don't diminish it." He tilted his head to the crate under my worktable. "You should try that girl's eyes now. You've gained something new."

Gained something new? Hope bubbled up within me. Part of me wanted to call after him, *What have I gained?* I rolled back to the scope. Joseph was right; I had stayed true to the artist's intent. The woman's focus and hesitant innocence endured. She was on the cusp of something new. Perhaps I was too . . .

Joseph was also right about seeing something new within my work; there was a lightness to my touch that I'd never felt before. And it felt visible. It wasn't a paint-by-number. I had entered into Yaroshenko's vision and emotion to convey it, and not cover or diminish it.

"She's almost finished."

I looked up hours later to find Lily studying my *Girl Student* as well. "A few more hours today, a day or two to set, and I'll varnish her."

Lily glanced back to Joseph's office. "Has he offered you a job yet?"

"No, but he's sending a lot of work my way. If he doesn't, I may have to start charging him."

"He will. You're becoming valuable around here." She patted my shoulder and crossed to her station.

Aloud "*Buongiorno*, Emily. *Ciao*, Lily" boomed across the room. I rolled clear of the painting. "What are you doing here?"

Ben crossed over and kissed me. "I came to see my coffee-makers." He tugged at my hair.

"What?"

He leaned down and whispered, "You've got paint in your hair."

My hand shot up and found a clump underneath in the back. My hair had been pulled into a ponytail last night. Or was it early this morning when Ben had flicked his paintbrush in my direction and I'd retaliated?

"How did I miss that?"

Ben gently tugged it again. "I will always love that shade of linen."

I giggled, then turned it into a cough and cleared my throat. "Coffeemakers." I pointed to the far end of the worktable. "They're almost done. I'm waiting on the parts you ordered."

"I had them sent to Joseph. Let me go check."

Ben loped across the studio, and I cleaned up my scattered tubes of paint. When both men emerged, Ben carried a small box. "I have the gasket and the valves."

He handed me the box as Joseph examined the machines. "I hardly recognize them. You did this?"

I nodded.

"Then I have a question for you. Olivia Barton asked me to

make supports for a client's mixed media piece. She's trying to suspend it from fishing lines. Wait." He walked back to his office.

I looked at Ben and mouthed, *Olivia Barton*, but he only raised his brows in reply.

Joseph returned with a sketch and photograph. "Here. What do you think?"

The piece looked several feet long, a mix of wires, paper, sheet metal, and . . . rock? "How much does it weigh?"

"Twenty pounds, maybe slightly more."

"I guess I'd say to use aluminum and put two supports in, crossing, from this fold to here and here." I pointed to two spots on the picture where the piece appeared to have the most strength.

"Could you build them?"

I laid down the pictures. "I'd need to see it and make measurements."

"I'll text her you're on your way. Her gallery is near Piccolo." Joseph walked away, the matter decided.

"Is he always like that?" I flicked my finger at his retreating figure.

"He likes you. He knows you want to prove yourself."

"I do?"

Ben raised an eyebrow.

"Stop that. Fine. I do." Without waiting for a reply, I continued. "Do you know who Olivia Barton is?"

"No."

"She's this gallery owner, been featured in *Art Papers* constantly, but that's Atlanta-based so that's no surprise. But she's in practically every other art publication too. She's edgy, critical, has a perfect eye, and owns a small gallery with an impeccable reputation for launching new artists—maybe not the blockbusters, but the award winners." I finally drew a breath.

"And?"

"I'm kind of a fan girl."

Ben chuckled. I wasn't sure he knew what a fan girl was, but I couldn't explain. I followed Barton's critiques and essays in *ARTnews*, and secretly her gallery was my dream. I knew exactly where it was; I glanced at it every time I passed and had even walked through it one day. But I hadn't spoken to her. Quite the opposite—when she caught up to me near the back ogling a stunning gold appliquéd woman on Tahitian paper and asked if I had any questions, I had fled. Mumbled a quick "No thanks" and beelined it out the door. I hoped she couldn't recall that moment.

I grabbed my bag and toolbox. "Do you want a ride back to Piccolo?"

"I need one. I brought back Joseph's car." Ben glanced over to my portrait of my girl, not Yaroshenko's. After Joseph's comment, I'd set them side by side. "You've changed her."

"I've been playing with her." I stilled, realizing that although I'd been working on her, I hadn't really stepped back and taken her in. While painting, I had felt something soft and light come through the brush, but I hadn't wanted to analyze it or dwell on it too much. Staying in the moment had been a new experience—almost a laying down of self—and I wasn't ready to look, even now.

Ben raced a few steps to catch up. "You are not going to tell me about it?"

"I can't. If I do, I might lose it. I didn't think about her, I felt her." I shook my head. "I can't explain it any other way."

Ben opened my car door for me. "There is no need to."

In a few minutes we were at the gallery. How did one approach an Olivia Barton? I'd already failed to talk to her once, but now I had a reason to be there. A reason behind an introduction. This was my chance.

I stalled just inside the front door. It was freezing. Next I noticed white. Nothing but white—a polar-bear-sitting-on-an-ice-cap kind of white.

When I'd visited just days before, I'd been intrigued by her use of grays. The color had played against the gold within the pieces perfectly. Now the floor, ceiling, every wall and hanging space between them, was flat white. The effect was to make the structure completely disappear. There was nothing to compete with the bold chaos of the art, as she'd also removed all tables, benches, and chairs. You had to leave the gallery to find any seating. Crossing the room to look out the side windows, I saw she'd set up several high tables, stools, and a bar on her bricked patio.

"Startling, isn't it? I lowered the temperature to clear the paint fumes, then felt it complemented the show's aesthetic."

I spun around to find Olivia Barton walking toward me, hand outstretched. Her wrist dropped down as if it was too much effort to hold it out straight. She looked exactly as she had the other day, tall with raven hair, tightly coiffed and glinting red-toned under the lights. She wore a white cotton A-line dress. "Olivia Barton."

"Emily Price. Joseph Vassallo sent me."

Without a beat of recognition she faced Ben and narrowed her eyes. "Have we met?"

"I am Ben Vassallo. Joseph's brother."

She held his hand loosely within her own. "I had no idea. Where's he been hiding you?"

Ben smiled. "I am visiting for a couple months. I return home next week."

"To Montevello?"

Ben nodded.

"Lovely. I visited there, years ago." She dragged her eyes from him back to me. "Joseph says you can fix my little problem."

"I have some ideas."

Without more words, she led us through a maze-like series of faux walls to the back. On the floor rested the mixed media piece, and as I expected, it was about six feet by eighteen inches.

"He said you want to use fishing lines?"

"If possible. Vaughn sent it with bars for hanging. Can you imagine? It would look like a beached whale or a dead animal, legs straight up. It needs to float."

I knelt to measure it and test its strength. "We can make it float."

"I'll leave you to it then." She strode away on her four-inch heels, and I got to work.

Ben crouched next to me. "What can I do?"

"Write down these numbers for me." I handed him my notebook and measured each dimension, lifted it to feel for bend and flex, then marked the piece for soldering points. "All done. I'll make these at the studio, then fuse them here. I'm sure she has a back room." I looked up at the ceiling. "I'll also paint them white rather than the gray of this metalwork. That way the supports will disappear into the ceiling rather than become part of the piece."

Ben whispered, "Go talk to her. Tell her."

"About what?" *How does he know?*

"Your work."

"I can't." I felt like a kid whispering behind the teacher's back.

"Go." He reached for my tools and shooed me away.

I wove my way through the maze and found Olivia in a small alcove.

"Ms. Barton? I've got all the measurements and can have the supports here to solder tomorrow. I don't think you'll need more than three thirty-pound braided lines to hang them."

"Perfect. Joseph said you had talent." She dragged her gaze from my head to my toes. "As an artist too."

"He did?"

"Send me pictures of your work. I never promise, but I am intrigued by anything Joseph finds interesting."

"Thank you." Stunned, I made my way back to Ben. "Your brother made the entire introduction for me."

"I told you. He likes you."

"Who knew?"

As we made our way out, Olivia nowhere in sight, a painting caught my eye. It was bold, a cross between Picasso and Pollock, but like neither too. It had fine brushstrokes at the very center, reminiscent of seventeenth-century classical work, but the geometric designs surrounding it and washing over it at the corners made it feel jarring and random, beyond postmodern. Then the edges—pure chaos.

Exactly how I felt.

Chapter 11

I spent the entire day applying the final coat of varnish to the Petersons' dining room walls, pondering the painting I'd seen at the gallery. All my life I'd studied art criticism, restoration, the rules and the procedures, and I worked to master the technique. I didn't stretch boundaries; I worked within them. A master imposter. I shook my head. Not an imposter. An imitator.

And in restoration it worked. It was a field based on the finite nature of any work—a work already in existence. But that painting? It was as if it and I were bursting out of that central focal point together. It was something new. A surprise. If I let myself go, forgot the boundaries, forgot the rules I myself fashioned and imposed, what could happen?

"You've worked hard today."

Rachel's voice startled me, and I accidentally dropped the brush I was wiping back into the jar of soap.

"Sorry. I was somewhere else. That's the beauty of laying down varnish and even cleaning up. You get to escape."

"I knit."

"I've never tried that." I waved my hand to encompass the

three walls before us. "These weren't bad at all. Tiny water damage and a light layer of smoke soot. Once this dries, forty-eight hours, you can hang art and move back in here."

I stepped back to stand next to her. The blue walls glistened like lapis lazuli with threads of gold catching in the sun.

"I find this room peaceful."

"It feels like water. Working on it, I felt like I was on the tip of something wonderful. That it was going to rise up on a wave and crash into me." I glanced at her. "In a good way."

Her eyes took on a gleam I hadn't seen before. "I don't think you needed these waves for that." Before I could form a reply, she stepped toward the kitchen. "Would you like a cup of coffee?"

"You have coffee?" The last time I noted the kitchen, yesterday, it'd been empty.

"I do. Thanks to Jeremy."

She hadn't mentioned her husband much. I knelt by my crate and grabbed another rag to re-wipe the soapy brush. "Let me box this up and I'll be right in."

I walked into the kitchen a moment later to find Rachel next to a La Pavoni coffeemaker exactly like the one Ben acquired for me.

"You have one of these? I just refurbished one."

"Jeremy and I bought this years ago—actually, we bought two, one for home and one for his office. He's a total coffee snob." She looked around the kitchen. "He brought this one from his office. Now it's beginning to feel like home again."

"Can you show me how to use it? I tested mine out this morning, and the results were horrid." The idea of surprising Ben pleased me.

"Sure." Rachel ground the beans, weighed the coffee, tamped it down, pulled the shot, steamed the milk . . . all the while explaining each step.

"I'll never remember all this. My . . ." I stalled. *What do I call him?* "My boyfriend. He's visiting here, like me really, and we're fixing up a machine . . . a whole restaurant, really, and—"

"Oh my gosh, you're blushing." Rachel squeezed my arm. "You're adorable. I mean . . . That sounds so condescending, but you are. You're adorable. Now you have to tell me. Please."

I felt heat flood my face. I hadn't told anyone. I only knew Lily and Joseph, and there was no way I could talk to them. I didn't want to call friends at home. They didn't know Ben, hadn't seen him, wouldn't understand. And, although Amy asked countless questions each morning when I woke her and each early dawn when I tried to sneak back into the hotel room, I didn't want to share—not a single moment, not with her. But I knew I was about to spill everything and there was no way to stop myself.

"I just met him. He's here from Italy, some tiny town I guess, visiting his brother, but his aunt and uncle live here too. They're the ones who own the restaurant. His brother owns the studio I'm working in and that's how we met . . . but I'm helping him refurbish his aunt's place and that's how we really met. I go each night, and we talk and we work on stuff and he's been teaching me to cook and . . . We've only got a couple days left and I've got paint in my hair all the time. I can't get it out and I can't imagine not being with him, not getting to share every thought. At first I just wanted to help because I love projects, but now I love—" I stopped, fully aware of where I was headed.

Rachel caught it too. "Was that a surprise?"

I flapped my hand, trying to cycle through the days. "I've hardly slept. I'm sure it's because . . . It's been seven days? Eight? I probably just need sleep. But . . . do you think? No, I've known him a week."

"I'm sure it's just lack of sleep." Her eyes danced.

"Of course, but . . ." A horrid giggle burst out. I bit my lip to stop it. "What if it's not? What if he goes home and I go home and I never see him again? I mean, it could be more, right? He's different. He sees things completely the opposite of me. Not completely, but creatively. He shares, like he wants to be a part of your world and you his. That's what helping his aunt and uncle was about. And he speaks perfect English with this beautiful accent, but no contractions. He can't figure them out, or doesn't want to. Do you have any idea how adorable no contractions are?"

"No." Rachel shook her head, eyes still dancing. "I have no idea how adorable no contractions are."

"Sorry. That was pretty bad." I wrapped my hands around the cappuccino she handed me. "I'm going to stop now. That was so much more than you needed to know."

"I asked. And I think it's nice. When you get to be my age . . ." She threw me a glance, a challenge, as if daring me to protest our twentyish-year age difference. "You sometimes forget. But marriage should be like that too. Sure, you might get more sleep, but you can feel just that alive every day—as long as you don't forget. After all, you get to be with that one guy—for you, the adorable no-contractions guy—who lights up your world and shares it with you. For me, he makes good coffee and sings to me. At least he used to . . ." She took a sip of her coffee, too, remembering. "Enjoy it. Hang on to it."

I settled back on firm ground. "Mine's just a blip. He's going home and . . . Chicago's a long way from Italy."

"Ah . . . 'Summer lovin', had me a blast; summer lovin', happened so fast . . .'" Her voice rose and dipped in song. "No? You don't know *Grease*?"

"Oh . . . I've seen that."

"*Phew.* For a minute there I was going to worry about your generation."

I studied the brightly painted mug in my hands. "This really is delicious."

"Then don't be so eager to let it go." Rachel winked and started singing again.

Chapter 12

I pulled open Piccolo's front door. The tables were still grouped in the center of the room, but everything around them was unrecognizable now that the ladders and drop cloths were gone. The space felt huge. It was light and bright, with the white linen playing against the dark wood accents.

They had already hung the plate rack we'd found and it was filled with hand-painted Italian plates, bringing character and color to the space. Ben had also laid out the templates I'd given him, and Amy was perched high on a ladder stenciling a delicate design within the center panels of the back wall.

"You're doing a beautiful job," I called up to her.

"Hey." She leaned back.

"Careful." I reached up my arms.

"I'm fine. It is looking good, isn't it? Your design is super cool."

"Thank you." Her compliment surprised me. "Where is everybody?"

"Ben cleared everyone out a few minutes ago. He said they had all worked hard and deserved a break." She stepped down the ladder. "Can we talk a minute?"

As she took the last steps down, I realized that although

we'd shared the same space for several days, we'd barely had a conversation. I knew I'd set it up that way, by arriving home long after she'd crashed on the sleeper sofa and only waking her each morning in time to head out the door, but now it felt like a small way to treat my sister.

"Sure." I dropped my bag and pulled over a chair. She leaned against the ladder.

"I wanted to talk to you about those interviews you set up."

"You didn't cancel, right? They're still next week?" I reached into my bag. "I was checking this morning, and there are a few more postings at—"

"Stop." She laid her palm over my notebook. "I don't want to take them. I want to find this next job on my own."

"That's fine to say, but who gets called when you get fired? Me. You call me. Mom calls me. You even asked, 'What's next?' last time, so I called Covington."

"I know, but when I told you and Mom what I wanted to do from the first, neither of you would let me. You forced me into that accounting firm. I hated it, and then it was just easier to quit arguing."

"That's a little dramatic."

"Not really. You wouldn't know; you do what you love." She held up her hands. "Look, I know what I want to do. That's what I came here to tell you, if you'd only talk to me. I've got a lead on a party planner job right in Lincoln Park, so I can stay in Chicago."

"You know nothing about party planning. It's not like being a professional guest; you don't actually *go* to the parties."

"That's so patronizing, Emily. And mean."

I slumped in the chair. "I'm not trying to be mean, but—"

"Thanks for the vote of confidence." She climbed back up the ladder. "I've got work to do."

"Amy," I called up to her. "That was nasty of me. I'm sorry."

She narrowed her eyes. "Seriously?"

"Seriously. I'm sorry." I didn't want to say any more. I didn't know what *to* say. I gave a last nod and headed to the kitchen.

I found Ben cleaning away dust.

"It looks wonderful out there."

"Thank Amy. She is a hard worker." Ben grabbed a white bag and handed it to me. "I bought you a gift. There is a bookstore across the parking lot." He couldn't wait for me to open it. "It is a book. *Acqua Alta*. That is a true phenomenon in Venice—the tide can rise and flood the city—but this is a mystery novel by an Italian writer. You said you love mysteries. Her detective, Guido Brunetti, solves mysteries in Italy. This one is about art."

"Art *and* a puzzle." I smiled.

"You like it?"

"I love it."

"Good. I also cleared everyone out for another surprise. As soon as Joseph gets back, we will begin. He will bring us food and bread too. Lots of bread."

"What are we doing?"

"We must rebuild the wine list. I will keep all they have, but they need to add younger bottles. Americans like tighter, younger reds." Ben crossed the kitchen and lifted a box. He proceeded to pull the corks on six bottles.

"All of them?"

"These are the ones I question. Good price points, but I wonder if too young, which is why the good price points."

"I don't know that much about wine."

"I do," Joseph called from the doorway.

Amy pushed through behind him. "Ems, can I take your car? I'm tired and think I'll head back to the hotel." She turned to

Joseph and asked in an arch tone, "Can you give *her* a ride home tonight?"

Joseph chuckled. "Of course."

I passed him and followed Amy back into the dining room. "We're having a serious wine tasting. Don't you want to stay?"

"Not tonight. I'll grab something at the grocery across the street and . . . I need to talk to my contact, find out more about that job."

"Amy . . ."

"I'm okay. Please."

"I feel like you think I've been squishing you."

"Not squishing. But somewhere along the way you didn't notice that I grew up too. I don't need you to fix everything. I don't want you to anymore."

"Ouch."

"Sorry." She shrugged and flung her arms around me in a tight hug. "I still love you, though."

"Thanks." I eked a laugh out of compressed lungs, then handed her my keys.

Joseph and Ben made up plates, and soon the three of us were seated at a table in the center of the dining room surrounded by glasses, bottles, and bags of takeout.

"Grab your notebook, Bella."

I took a sip and poised pen over page. "This one has mellow aspects of cranberry and cinnamon in a bed of fine, mossy dirt."

"You're making that up and it sounds ridiculous," Joseph said.

"Of course I am. It tastes like wine."

Joseph swirled his glass. "No. It tastes like gravel underlying chocolate. It hails from a Piedmont property and the ground gives up the elements reluctantly, making the Nebbiolo grapes work for those deep notes."

"Well then . . ." I scribbled down each word. We ate and sipped, and I listened and recorded everything the brothers said about each wine—mostly Joseph, I observed.

"You're really good at this," I said.

Joseph smiled and said, "It was my job, long ago."

Ben sat back. "You cannot just leave it at that."

I looked between the brothers. "What?"

"When Joseph was a teenager, it *was* his job. He chose Coccocino's wine and wrote the menu. He did such a good job Michel put him in charge of Osteria Acquacheta's too. He has a gift."

"You all really do believe in helping the competition." I laughed.

"In fact, one time I brought us food from Osteria while we tasted. Michel was teaching me sauces that summer, and we . . ." Ben's voice trailed away.

Confusion skittered through his eyes, and Joseph's face darkened. We fell silent as if something chilly had come upon us.

Joseph looked up. "I remember that night."

Ben was silent, and I could see in his eyes that he was returning in time, figuring out a puzzle of his own.

"I had not realized," he said. "That was the night—"

"Not now, Benito."

"When?"

"Never?"

For a moment I saw the same expression Ben had worn when asking Joseph about the pizza—except it was Joseph now who looked young, who needed something from his brother.

The eyes are the windows to the soul. Joseph had pegged that one. They convey every emotion, cloud to hide you behind an impenetrable wall, or strip you bare and leave you fully exposed.

Joseph blinked, and the vulnerability was gone.

Ben accepted it with a nod and reached for another bottle, pulling himself back to the present. "Try this one. No cranberry, no cinnamon, but see if you can taste plum notes."

I smiled and went with the change in conversation.

After a few more sips, Joseph pushed his chair away. "I need to go. I've got an early day tomorrow. I'll walk so you can drive Emily home later." He wagged his finger to the wine bottles. "Will you be okay? Forget it, I know you two; you won't be taking her back for hours."

Ben stood and gripped his brother's shoulder before Joseph ducked away and walked out the front door.

Ben and I cleared the containers, moved to our favorite booth, and sat with a last sip of wine.

"I'm about to pry." I leaned back and let him absorb my warning.

"I would too." He shrugged. "But I have no answers. We were all at Coccocino that night. I was fourteen, and it was my first year to share in selecting the wines. It was a good time. But that night something happened. Joseph left Coccocino and went on what you would call a bout of . . ." He sat thinking. "Vandalism. It is near the same word for us too. Don Pietro, our priest, is the one who kept Joseph from jail. He took responsibility for him and gave Joseph a whole summer's worth of jobs in reparation. But Papa sent me away to my cousin Anne's family, and when I got back, Joseph was off to university in Naples. Gone."

"How far was Naples?"

"Distance is not only physical."

"True." When I graduated high school, I, too, left home. College was only a few miles away, but it might as well have been around the world for all the care, attention, or time I gave Mom

and Amy. I never went back, not really. Not in the ways that mattered.

Hours later, the sky was graying with morning as we stepped outside and locked the door. Ben walked me to Joseph's fancy car.

I rested my hand on his chest. "Joseph's place is just around the corner. If you trust me with this beauty, I'll drive myself home. You can be asleep in five minutes and I'll bring this back here later in the morning. Amy can follow in my car."

"Are you sure?"

"Yes. It makes the most sense." I reached up and kissed him. "Sleep well."

Ben pulled me close and with a much better and lingering kiss, he left me with a *"Buona notte, cara mia"* pressed against my cheek.

As I pulled out of the parking lot, I watched him walk across the lot and around the corner—his long legs eating up the pavement and his shoulders rounded with exhaustion.

Everyone talked about Piccolo's transformation and all our hard work. Each day things changed faster than I could absorb them, and it was all good and right. You could see the obvious delight, relief, and joy in Maria and Vito's faces.

And the nights . . . I knew Ben savored them as much as I did. But tonight revealed something new. Something I hadn't known. Ben hadn't come to Atlanta to visit his brother—he came to chase him.

Chapter 13

my was awake before me and banging around with my new coffee machine.

"What are you doing?"

"Trying to make coffee with this thing. Where'd it come from?"

"Ben and I found it last week, and I restored it. Here, let me show you . . . It makes the best coffee you'll ever taste."

I poured water into the La Pavoni's reservoir, measured the beans Ben had ground for me at Piccolo, and went through every step Rachel showed me, counting down the time and tamping the beans with what I hoped was the right pressure.

I pulled Amy a shot, steamed the milk, and handed her the small porcelain cup we'd also found that Saturday. "Here."

She held the delicate cup high, her face full of questions. I nodded and twisted free the portafilter, slamming it against the knock box to release the grounds and make myself a cup.

In my periphery I saw her lower it and touch the rim to her lips. "Umm . . ."

"Delicious, right?"

She stretched the cup to me, offering me a sip.

"It's horrid!"

"I wondered . . ."

I wiggled the machine. "I don't understand."

"Maybe it takes practice."

"It wasn't supposed to be hard. It's coffee—a morning basic. You should've seen Rachel, Mrs. Peterson; she flew through it. Why is nothing fun and easy? You think one moment, maybe, and then . . ." I flopped on the couch. "Hey, you made your bed."

"It wasn't hard."

I looked at her. "Why do I feel like you're handling all this better than I am?"

She smiled, small and without humor. It was odd to see myself in her. "Hey . . . What happened? This isn't like you."

"What?"

She dropped next to me with a smile. "I mean, not like you this week."

I tilted my head back, looking for answers on the ceiling. "I think I remembered last night that life is hard. No one gets off easy." There was a water spot on the ceiling. "Ben's leaving soon, and he didn't get what he wanted from Joseph. I'm leaving soon, and I didn't get Ben or a job. Not that I was going to get to keep Ben—life's not that good . . . I just thought Joseph would give me a job, and though I know Ben will move on with some gorgeous Italian girl, it'd be like being close to him too."

"In a very weird way . . ."

"I hadn't thought that one through. Basically, I need to get a job and let all this go."

"Would you move here?" She nudged me, and I stopped studying the water spot.

"Yes. No. If Joseph gave me a job, I'd be a fool not to take it. Restoration isn't a huge field."

"Office jobs are much more secure." Her voice mimicked mine to perfection.

"Yes. Good benefits too. And health care," I droned in my *big sister knows best* voice, cringing as I found it uncomfortably close to my normal one.

"Always a must." She tipped into me.

"We make quite a pair, don't we?" I looped my arm around her shoulder.

Amy twisted out from under my arm and looked at me straight on.

"What?" I said.

"That's the nicest thing you've said to me in years."

I pulled into my now usual spot at Piccolo. Amy opened her door.

"Aren't you coming in?"

"I have a surprise at the studio I need to pick up. Will you tell Ben I'll be here soon?"

She dropped back into her seat. "He talks about you, you know. While we work. He talks about you constantly. His eyes light up."

"It's a fun flirtation. Amazing one, really, but he'll go back to Italy, and I, hopefully, will stay here."

Amy got out of the car, then leaned in and looked at me. "I've never seen anyone like Ben with you. If a guy looked at me that way, I'd . . . well, I'd do anything."

"You mean if a guy simply looked that way."

Amy laughed. "That too." She shut the door and waved behind her back as she headed into the restaurant.

I drove back to ACI to fetch the surprise I had for Maria and Vito, and for Ben. I'd taken a few family photos out of the storage

closet, restored them digitally, then reprinted and reframed them in a larger format so they'd fill the space in the short hallway to the restrooms and tell their story of family and food.

As I was stacking them in a crate, a shadow fell over me. I looked up at Joseph. "How do you do that?"

He leaned against my stool and lifted a soft leather driving loafer. "Partly good shoes. Partly skill. While growing up, you did not want Nonna to catch you sneaking past the kitchen. If she did, you cooked for hours."

I laid down the picture. Joseph never talked of family or home. Anything I'd learned came from Ben. *He* talked of family all the time, and they sounded pretty ideal—boisterous, but ideal. Ben used warm words like *laughter*, *love*, *teasing*, and *hugs*. Words that tasted sweet and coated you. Joseph, if he did have anything to say, used words from my lexicon: *obligation*, *work*, *duty*, *challenge*. Hard words I could tap with my small finishing hammer. I suspected Joseph and I had both spent years tapping at those words.

"Ben makes me miss home." Joseph reached forward and fingered some tubes of color on my tray. "Is it hard having your sister here?"

"In some ways. It was a complete surprise, but it's not turning out quite like I imagined."

"Do things ever?" Joseph took a deep breath and held it.

Silence fell, and I didn't know where to go next. *Family*. That was how he'd started.

"Ben said your father isn't well?"

"Papa's older. Twenty years older than Mama. He's . . . over eighty now." Joseph rubbed his chin as if the math surprised him. "In my mind, he's still what he was when I left. Ben was, too, until he showed up." He shook his head. "I can't imagine now. My father came a few years ago, but I don't even remember how he looked.

My mother has called me three times this month. That's enough to worry me."

"Can you go visit?" I asked softly, suspecting after last night that this was dangerous ground.

"Once the High opens the Muniz exhibit, I could. I've got three pieces for it, and I want to be at the opening." He looked around the room, then fixed his gaze on me. "Lily told me about Covington's downsizing."

"I figured she did, and all your 'favors' were tests."

Joseph had the grace to chuckle. "And you passed each with colors flying, as Ben would say." I smiled at the twisted colloquialism. "The supports for the Vaughn piece worked perfectly. Three thirty-pound braided lines, as you said. It soared. Olivia thanks you."

"I sent her pictures of my paintings, by the way. Thank you for that."

Joseph squirmed. He seemed as uncomfortable with thanks as I did. He continued. "And you were spot on with the Harnett."

The Harnett, a small landscape, was another of Joseph's tests.

"The Connor job too," he added.

"I liked that one. It feels like the integrity of the piece is maintained, doesn't it?" I propped myself on the worktable, enjoying this discussion. Enjoying my work. "Not that adding new supports would be bad."

"It wouldn't be bad . . . but you were right. The canvas was so delicate . . . And your placement, Mrs. Connor will appreciate that. She was nervous that the supports would be intrusive. She likes to display it freestanding on a table." He was back to fiddling with my paint tubes. "I hope you'll consider staying. Here are terms." He handed me a cream linen envelope.

I tapped the envelope against my hand. It looked so formal,

elegant linen paper, sealed. Like something in a movie. "Am I to open it now?"

"Look through it later and let me know. If you accept, I know you'll need to find a place here and get settled. I've included allowances for that."

"Thank you, Joseph." I knew there was more to say, but like him, I wasn't good at that stuff either.

He saved me from it as he pushed himself off the stool, nodded to me, and turned back toward his office.

I tore open the envelope. It was detailed—expectations, salary, hours, vacation time. He even gave me two weeks up front, paid, to get settled. Lily was right when she'd said they needed a "fix-it girl among their gilded lilies." I'd laughed at her, but this outlined that exact role—a support role, a prep role, an organizational role—all meant to facilitate the conservators' work.

Part of me wanted to be offended. I'd worked years and in many ways knew more about the nuts and bolts of fixing basic things than they did. But it was also perfect, for I could do those things and still learn more, be a part of more. The Yaroshenko had been a thrill. Building the supports for the Vaughn, exciting. Figuring out the Connor drawing, a stretch and a success. And my own art was changing daily. I was changing daily.

Chapter 14

I backed my way through Piccolo's front door, clutching my box of photographs.

Aunt Maria was at the hostess stand putting all the details back in place. Vito was dusting the bar. Amy was laying out the linens and positioning the votives. Ben was nowhere in sight.

I smiled and greeted them all as I headed to the kitchen.

"*Ciao*. Ben?"

"Bella!" he called from behind the freezer door. "We start to prep. Tomorrow night!"

"I can't believe it." I waved him over. "Come see what I brought." I set down the box and pulled out the pictures, laying them across the stainless-steel counter to unwrap them one by one.

"You did this?" he exclaimed, then froze. "That is Mama." He pointed to a striking teenager with jet-black hair and wide, expressive eyes.

"That's your mom? She's gorgeous." I pointed to the girl next to her. "Is that Maria?"

"*Sì.*"

"Who's this one?"

Ben shook his head. "I do not know. I told you, Mama never mentions her family. I do not know of any of them, but I suspect that is older brother Antonio."

"Have you ever asked why they don't talk?"

"*Sì.* I have asked all my life. When I met Maria and Vito, I asked. I asked Joseph. No one will say," Ben said quietly. "Let us hang these tonight after they leave. They will love the surprise." He pulled me into a hug. "This is a beautiful gift, Emily. Thank you. Maria . . . She still loves Mama. They will appreciate this." He pushed me back to arm's length. "I love how you are such a romantic." With that he placed his palms on both my cheeks and pulled me in for another kiss.

I hadn't thought of restoring the pictures as "romantic," but I guess it was. Planning a surprise for no reason other than to bring another person delight was, in fact, romantic.

Ben and I spent the rest of the afternoon prepping for Friday's reopening. Rather, he prepped and I got in his way. He'd given me small tasks over the evenings, but unsupervised—as he now had to move more quickly—I was more hindrance than help. Cutting an onion into rings rather than chopping them for a Bolognese sauce was the last straw. I moved on to odd jobs around the kitchen—a loose pot handle, a wiggly light switch, a door not closing fully.

We also learned that I excelled at hanging pictures. That night we hung most of the photographs in the hallway, salon style, and the one of Maria and her sister by the hostess stand. All finished, we poured a glass of wine and relished our work from the corner booth. The tables were set with the new cut-glass votives and vases; the hand-painted plates set the right tone; and the AC was turned low to reduce the humidity and clear the paint smell.

"Joseph offered me a job today."

"Bella." He said it softly, and I couldn't tell if it was pleasure or

regret that danced within the notes. "I told you he liked you." He sat silent for a moment. "Will you take it?"

"I need it, and I've liked it here. I've been . . . brighter." I took a sip of wine. "Of course that might be all you and disappear when you go home."

Ben didn't look at me. "It will be nice to know where you are, to be able to see you in my mind. You will not feel so far away."

"Will you be sad to go? To leave all this?" I gestured to the restaurant, but I meant me.

"It was never mine to keep." Ben shifted in his seat and caught my eyes. "But you? You I want to keep. Imagining where you are is not enough. Could never be enough."

When I didn't move, Ben leaned closer still. "I need to be clear, Bella. I do not mean a visit; I mean a life. I know you have one here. But I love you. Please. Come. With. Me." He articulated each word clearly, as if they alone could create a bridge across the Atlantic.

He reached for my hands and held them between us, elbows resting on his knees. "I have loved you since the moment we met. Right here." He pointed to the back table, and I remembered that first night. Trying to understand him and missing almost every word, but understanding his heart. *Aiuto.* The word we'd spoken together. Had we been apart in any sense since? I doubted it, but then again, I'd worked hard not to analyze it. I'd worked hard, as weird as that sounded, to simply enjoy it.

He tucked a strand of hair behind my ear as if the action would heighten my hearing, my presence. "Please. Marry me?"

Marry you? The question caught me as the biggest surprise, then again as the most logical step. The very idea tasted rich and delicious on my tongue, and I waited for logic to sour it.

It didn't. Nothing did. Instead, it was there—that excitement

or anticipation that what had been missing from my head and my heart was right before me, and that to reach out, while scary, was also right because such a possibility didn't come often, if ever again, and to let it go would be devastating.

If Ben thought my silence was odd, I had to give him credit. He said nothing. He merely held my hands and watched my eyes go through . . . who knows what. I'm certain every hope, dream—dashed or not—fear, and uncertainty flittered through. Finally I felt my vision and my heart still. Everything stilled—into perfect clarity.

"Yes."

Chapter 15

Amy was still asleep when I snuck through the room, careful to keep my shin from knocking on her sofa.

I left her a note and gently shut the door behind me. I didn't want to share, not yet. And I didn't want to defend my decision.

Ben was already at Piccolo—again waiting on the front bench.

He was at my car, opening the door, before I'd turned off the engine. "Bella." He pulled me to him as I stepped out, and with a quick, firm kiss he asked, "Are you ready?"

"Absolutely."

"First coffee." He reopened my car door and we headed to Dripworks, the coffee shop he'd taken me to the week before. We sat at the high counter and I pulled out my phone.

"Have you looked any of this up? I mean, we can't actually get married today, you know. We'd have to go to Vegas for that. Most states have waiting periods." I searched for the rules and regulations in Georgia.

"Italy. Illinois. In my home and yours, you must wait, but not in Georgia. Today is the day."

My head shot up. "You looked it up?"

"Of course. Last week."

"Last week?"

He grinned. "This is not a spur in the moment."

I hiked a brow at him, knowing I couldn't create the same arch look he and Joseph achieved.

"Maybe *un po*," he conceded with a soft smile. "But I had hoped."

I stared at him, again waiting for that voice of reason to step in, and found myself shaking my head back and forth. "You're the romantic."

"Come on. Oh . . ." He twisted one hand within mine to hold it and used the other to reach for my chocolate croissant. "You cannot leave this behind."

"Where are we going?"

"Fulton County Probate Office at 136 Pryor Street," he recited, looking at his phone.

Within a half hour we'd found chairs in a large lobby area surrounded by booths, much like Chicago's Department of Motor Vehicles, and Ben filled out his section of the form.

"We meet all the requirements. In person. Over eighteen. And my passport has a certified English translation."

"How do you have that?" I leaned over his shoulder.

"I needed it to work at Piccolo, even as an unpaid nephew, in case the health board visited."

He handed me the clipboard to begin my section and settled back into his plastic chair. "It is what I hoped for them. It will sell better now, when they are ready."

I sat back too. "It's beautiful, but it makes me sad too. All our hard work, and a new owner will probably rip it out and put in a frozen yogurt shop or a Build A Bear."

"A what?"

"You know, you build a stuffed bear and put in a little heart . . . Oh, never mind."

Ben tapped the clipboard, drawing my attention back to the blanks. "I love that you defend me, us. But it was a gift for them. That is what you do for family. They have no family here."

"There's Joseph." I wasn't sure why I needed to offer him up. Ben didn't need reminding, but in some way I felt as if Joseph was getting left behind. In the months to come, he'd be left driving by that Build A Bear alone.

I dropped the clipboard into my lap. "Well, I'm going to miss how the bar gleams, and the woodwork and those pipes. It's some of my best work."

"You can redo Coccocino if you like."

"It's probably already perfect." I filled in another blank. "Even Joseph thinks that."

"He does?"

"You know he does." Despite Joseph's imposed isolation, he thought about family as often as Ben did. It wasn't hard to figure that out.

Ben peered over my shoulder and tapped a line at the bottom of the page. "If we had decided this earlier, we could save money with 'premarital education.' Forty dollars."

"And how much earlier could we have decided this?" I smiled as a booming "Number 47" filled the room.

"The moment we met." He winked and reached for my hand. "Our number."

He wrapped his arm around me as I laid the clipboard on the counter. A broad woman pulled it to her and, without looking up, ticked off a series of boxes while examining Ben's passport and my driver's license. She finally glanced up and droned the same words she'd probably said a million times before.

"If you're marryin' here in Fulton County, that'll be fifty-six dollars."

Three minutes later we held a marriage license and a sheet of paper with the names and phone numbers of area judges.

I tapped the third down the list. "Call that one."

"Why?"

"His name's Ben."

Ben dialed the number and listened. "Voice mail."

I picked another. After a short conversation, ending with a series of "Yes . . . Yes . . . We can find it . . . Yes . . . Thank you," he hung up and grinned. "Judge Briggs and his wife are near Capital Gateway Park. We are to meet them there in fifteen minutes."

"Fifteen minutes?" I looked down at my white T-shirt and floral print skirt. "This isn't exactly what every girl dreams of for her wedding dress. I should've at least worn heels, maybe a blouse."

"You look beautiful."

I spent the drive fidgeting with my hair. Up. Down. Low ponytail. High bun. I finally settled on leaving it down, as I was the only woman *ever* who liked what humidity did to her hair—a little wave was a good thing.

We found parking and walked down a broad sidewalk to a central fountain. People milled about, but no one looked like they were preparing for a wedding.

"Doesn't it feel strange? Like there should be flowers or something? Gaudy dresses, boutonnieres, drunk relatives?"

Ben stopped. "We should plan something."

"I think we did, and it starts in about five minutes." I nodded toward an approaching elderly couple.

The man fit my mental idea of a judge. He and his wife were almost the same height, about mine, and she had her hand in the crook of his elbow. He had little hair; she was a perfectly coiffed

and frosted blonde. He wore glasses and squinted in the morning sun. She wore large sunglasses and had smooth pale skin. Southern skin—only found on women who have long understood the power of shade and sun hats.

Ben pulled my hand back as if logic had kicked in for him. "We should wait."

"You aren't sure?"

"You should have a dress, anything you want. I only want you."

"And this is the most romantic thing in the world. Better than I could ever imagine."

He pulled me close, and his eyes trailed over every inch of my face. "*Ti amo.* I love you."

I felt my lips part. "I caught that one."

"Mr. Vassallo?"

I smiled. The judge pronounced Ben's last name "Vass-aloe" like a variant of Vaseline ointment.

Ben spun. "*Sì* . . . that is, yes."

The man thrust out his hand and seized Ben's between his own. "No need to be nervous, son. This is an excitin' day. We don't need witnesses here'n Georgia, but I'm with my wife, so do y'all mind if she stays?" His voice was slow and gentle.

"Not at all." I stepped forward. I'd had too much coffee for this pace and my nerves were ramping up. "I'm Emily Price . . . The bride, I guess."

"You don't know?" Judge Briggs now folded my hand within both of his. They were soft and cool.

"I do." I nodded with determination. "I'm the bride."

"Well now, that's settled. Come on over here. I love this grove of trees for a city settin' on a day like this." He looked up at the sky while he walked. "In another couple hours this would'a been too hot and I'd ask y'all to go to another favorite spot. But that's

about an hour away and I don't have that kinda time right now. You would'na believe how busy you can get once ya retire."

Ben and I smiled at each other over the rambling and followed the judge and his wife into a small courtyard surrounded by cherry trees. Mrs. Briggs laid her handbag on a nearby bench, then came to stand next to her husband.

"All righty then." Judge Briggs looked around with satisfaction. "This is just right. Now, I charge $250 for the ceremony, and y'all can pay me with a check or cash."

I looked to Ben and widened my eyes. I hadn't thought about money.

"I have cash."

"You do?" I blurted.

Ben unfolded two hundred-dollar bills, a fifty, and the marriage license.

"You *are* prepared," I whispered to him. He held a finger to his lips.

Judge Briggs had not heard me. "Thank you. I'll sign this and mail it in."

Ben nodded. I followed suit.

"All righty then," the judge repeated as he stood straight and held the marriage license in front of him. "Let's begin." He looked each of us in the eyes, then nodded. "We are gathered here to join Benito Vassallo and Emily Price in a civil union as allowed by law and United States Supreme Court decisions. This is not a religious ceremony and I have no religious authority. You have presented a marriage license issued by the Probate Court of Fulton County on the nineteenth day of May, 2016." He then folded the license and passed it to his wife.

"Now let's be clear," he continued, "that each of you affirms to me that you have not gotten counsel about these matters from

me, and you have thought about these matters on your own or y'all have gotten counsel on the issues related to a civil union from competent professionals and/or personal acquaintances. Is that correct?" He paused, then added, "You say yes or no."

"Yes," I whispered.

Ben said his yes more clearly and calmly.

The judge glanced to his wife with a *Here we go* look and continued. "Do you understand that you are givin' up considerable rights and freedoms in exchange for the benefits, liabilities, and duties imposed and granted under Georgia and United States laws and regulations?"

Giving up? I had felt as if I were chasing something good and right. His words cracked open doubt, and I missed the next part.

". . . understand and agree to the exchange? This answer is an 'I do.'"

Ben spoke immediately. "I do."

I paused, trying to track this thought to its end. "I do."

"The US Supreme Court recently identified a number of benefits. These aspects include taxation, inheritance and property rights, rule of intestate succession, spouse privilege in the law of evidence, hospital access, mediate decision-makin' authority, adoption rights, the rights and benefits of survivors, birth and death certificates, professional ethics rules, campaign finance restrictions, workers' compensation benefits, health insurance, and child custody, support, and visitation rules." Judge Briggs's eyes danced as if this were his favorite stuff to discuss. "And there are some important nonlegal duties and benefits as well: attentiveness to each other, tolerance, care, love, and affection. Do y'all understand these matters and freely and voluntarily commit to them?"

Before he could tell us the proper answer, Ben declared, "I do."

The judge smiled at me.

"I do too."

"Do each of you commit to the other your life, your property, your loyalty, and your faithfulness in wealth and poverty, in sickness and health, and in sorrow and joy?"

This time we spoke together. Two "I do's" sounding as one.

"I don't expect you have rings." Judge Briggs waited.

"I do. Right here." Ben dug into his pocket.

"You do?" the judge and I called out together. He was surprised. I was impressed.

The judge beamed. "That's so nice, son. They're optional, and so many couples don't bring 'em anymore. Now I can say a good bit about the outward and visible sign of your promise. These rings . . ." He fingered the small gold bands. "They are powerful symbols of deep, abidin', and eternal love. And now, with these rings, I pronounce you to be, as of this moment, a couple united under civil law. And I present to you, dear"—he flapped his hand at his wife—"since you're the only one present today, Benito Vasallo and Emily Price as a married couple. You may kiss . . ."

A married couple? I looked to Ben and felt that first flicker of doubt swell. What if I'm not *that girl*? What if I hadn't realized, hadn't known that I was trying to be someone I couldn't be, but was only pretending . . . What if he saw through me . . .

His voice tunneled and I couldn't find him.

One . . . Two . . .

The world morphed to blue.

Chapter 16

*E*verything was cloudy and heavy, without form. Shadow. Then light.

My hand hit something solid. My head flew back. My eyes stung and my nose throbbed.

"No . . . Oh . . . Bella," Ben called gently through the haze. His hand, warm and solid, folded around the back of my neck.

My vision cleared. Judge Briggs's wife was no longer wearing sunglasses. She had cold blue eyes and a red cheek. She held a small vial in one hand as she lifted the other to her face.

Ben knelt beside me. "Are you okay? You dropped hard."

"I didn't faint."

"Is that not the word?" He looked up at Mrs. Briggs.

"Oh no, darlin', you fainted." She shook her head. "And you have a mean left hook, young lady," she added dryly.

I struggled to sit up. "I hit you? I'm so sorry. That's horrible." A wave of blue threatened to break, and I leaned back into Ben's arm. "Was I out long?"

"A few seconds." Mrs. Briggs capped her vial. The judge stood silently next to her. They shared a quick wordless exchange before she tapped Ben's shoulder. "Take her to the hospital, young man.

In her condition, you can't be too safe." Her voice oozed with Southern gentility and blatant condescension.

"Her condition?" Ben looked down at me, his dark eyes wide with concern.

"She thinks I'm pregnant." I struggled to stand.

He lifted me to my feet. "Why would she think that?"

"You're kidding, right? Everyone will think that. Why else would someone get a license and marry within a moment? This is standard shotgun wedding procedure." I faced Mrs. Briggs and continued. "But ours isn't one, actually. No pregnancy. No shotgun. Just a croissant and too much coffee." I swayed.

"I'm glad to hear that." Mrs. Briggs looked to her husband. "We'll leave you in privacy then."

A weak "Okay" was all I could muster.

The judge stepped forward and shook Ben's only available hand. "You'll receive your certificate from the probate court's office within three weeks."

"Thank you." Ben nodded as Judge Briggs and his wife headed to the gravel path. He lifted a hand to the back of my head. "You have a large bump."

I stretched my back and felt around his fingers. "I whacked it, didn't I?"

"I almost caught you. Almost. I think she is right. We need a hospital."

"I'm clearly not pregnant, Ben."

"But you might have a . . . *sbattimento*. Brain bruise."

"A concussion." I couldn't deny the possibility, so after a little debate, recognizing it as our first marital skirmish, we settled on a MinuteClinic at the corner Walgreens.

Twenty minutes, a pack of Skittles, a Diet Coke, and no concussion later, we exited the double doors.

"Now what, husband dear?" I looped my arm through Ben's and looked around the parking lot, scattered with cars, and wondered what came next.

Ben followed my gaze. "Lunch?"

"Yes. Lunch."

He tucked me safely into the passenger seat and, after another twenty minutes, I dropped into a booth at Farm Burger Buckhead and sighed. "This feels good. That park was warm. That Walgreens was warm. On the whole, Atlanta is warm. Is Montevello?"

"At this time of year, yes. And no air-conditioning."

"You couldn't have told me this before?"

Ben reached over and touched my hand. "Are you sure you are okay?"

"I'd had little to eat, stood in the heat, probably locked my knees, and got married. I'm surprised I only fainted." I took a bite of my burger to end further questions. One more query and I'd probably start blabbing all that was spinning through my brain.

But Ben didn't notice—he was focused on sending and receiving a flurry of texts. I asked about them repeatedly, but only got cryptic answers.

"Prep questions at Piccolo. The ovens . . . The menu . . . Do you mind if we drop by this afternoon?"

"It's reopening tonight. We can't miss it."

Ben laid down his phone. "We can if you want to; this is your night."

"True . . ." I leaned back and thought through the implications of that sentence.

Ben smiled. "Do not think too much. Your eyes are getting big again. Like the painting of the girl you called 'freaky.'"

I smiled at the way his accent made the word sound like a compliment. "That's for the eyes I paint, not mine."

"It is for your eyes too." He smiled. "Eat your burger. Enjoy the day."

So we did. We sat in that booth and chatted for several hours. After finishing the burgers, he bought us shakes. Slurping down a thick chocolate shake, infused with spicy honey, I learned more about his family—my family now. Francesca, his little sister, was going to be thrilled with his news. Lucio, his father, he wasn't sure about. Donata, his mother, he was sure about—she'd be furious.

"What about your family?"

I shrugged. "We'll tell Amy today, but no one else is going to care that much. Mom's been married a few times and kinda checked out on us awhile ago . . . I'm not sure about my dad."

Dad was my wild card. He either wouldn't care at all or would read me the riot act. As long as I kept adding to my 401K, paid my taxes on time, locked my doors, and carried pepper spray, I wasn't lectured often.

"Joseph?"

Ben mirrored my shrug. "He is like Mama. He likes things very controlled, in order and on time, but I think he will be happy. Though he loses an employee." Ben shifted in his seat. "This time has been good with him. It felt like old times here and there."

"Old times before that night? His last at Coccocino?"

Ben's eyes clouded. "His last as my brother."

"What happened, Ben?"

"I wish I knew. You ask and I ask and no one talks. Maybe, in Italy, you ask Mama." Ben grinned with his challenge.

"Sure . . ." I nodded with an exaggerated motion, noting the pain at the back of my head. "I think that'd be a great way to start our relationship."

We talked on until the restaurant reached that quiet moment

between lunch and dinner, and Ben scooted out of the booth. "Let us go check on Piccolo."

I scooted out, too, dropped my hand in his, and he pulled me through the door and toward the car. "Will you be sad to leave Joseph?"

"It is time to go home, and I am taking you with me. How can I be sad?"

"Flattery will get you everything."

He raised an eyebrow and pulled me close, and my jaw dropped as I recognized the emotion in his eyes.

Ben kissed me lightly once, twice, then lingered . . . He leaned away and smiled. "Get in the car before you faint again."

Ben pulled into the restaurant's parking lot, and I was surprised by the number of cars. "Piccolo doesn't open until six. What's going on?"

"Come on."

Amy stood just inside the door and pounced on me as I crossed the threshold. "Ben texted me to get here. He said you have a surprise. Is it for me?"

"No, I . . ."

Ben pulled up behind me and grabbed me around the waist. I looked up at him, then trailed his gaze deeper into the restaurant. The entire waitstaff stood there . . . waiting.

A shout of "Surprise" mixed with "Congratulations" hit us as we stepped from the lobby into the dining room.

"We married!" Ben announced.

Joseph strode forward. "You mean you're *getting* married."

Ben shook his head and lifted our hands. The gold bands glowed. "We *are* married."

The room fell silent.

Chaos broke out—as much as can be created by about fourteen people—as everyone moved forward en masse for hugs and handshakes.

Amy yanked me aside. "This is a joke, right?"

"No."

"You planned this? You and Ben?"

"No. Yes." I glanced back to Ben. "He asked me last night."

"And you him married today? Without telling me?" She dropped my arm.

I expected her eyes to be fighting and hard. We were often in that place. But they weren't. They were sad, hurt, and they struck me. They reminded me of our childhood—each time we packed to move to a new apartment, each time she leaned on me to sort out the details and make our new room feel like home. They reminded me of myself just yesterday when I leaned against her on the couch and asked why everything had to be so hard.

"Oh, Amy. I'm sorry."

"As long as you're happy . . ." She turned away, then spun back. "No, forget that. This is supposed to mean something. Despite Mom. Despite Dad. We always said it was supposed to be for life. That when we married, it'd be forever."

"I still believe that." My head felt fuzzy again. "What makes you think this won't be forever?"

"You barely know this guy. Two weeks and you're married? That's not for life, that's for lust."

"Hey—"

"Also, if it was for real, you would've told me. I'm your sister; I was supposed to stand beside you." Her voice cracked.

"Amy." I drew her back into a hug, but she didn't lift her arms. "It is real and I should've told you this morning when I left. I guess I didn't want to lose courage. I wanted to be *that girl*. That girl who could do something like this, knowing it was right, and not fear the jump. You're like that. You would've done it."

"I would've told you."

"You're right, but you always did have more courage." As she stepped away, I tugged her back. "You should have been there. You would've gotten a kick out of the judge. He talked like Willie Nelson and had a whole bunch of legalese and thought it was the most interesting stuff in the whole world. And I punched his wife when she shoved smelling salts under my nose. She thought I was pregnant. She said that after I fainted and—"

"You fainted?" Amy pushed out of my arms.

"Fell like a rock. Feel." I placed her fingers on the back of my head.

"Oh, Ems. I'm so sorry . . . Not really. I hope your head really hurts." She shoved her lower lip out in an exaggerated and well-practiced pout.

I could only laugh. "It does. And again, I'm sorry."

After a few bites of cake and a few sips of Prosecco, the staff resumed their preparations for the big night.

"We do not need to stay. We did what they wanted," Ben whispered.

I looked over at Maria and Vito. Maria had hugged me and cried happy tears over the family photos. Vito swelled with pride as he laid the new menus on the hostess stand and lit the candles within each glass votive. Ben was right. As they hurried their staff back to work, they'd clearly taken control of their restaurant again and were fidgety to open the doors—fidgety to move forward.

Ben slipped his hand into mine and pulled me to him. "We

are not needed here, Bella. So where to? Your place? Joseph's? I did some more research . . . We can have a room at the Ritz."

I twisted toward him and considered his question. Amy would be on my sofa bed. But there was no way I could wake up to share morning coffee with Joseph. Yet neither of us had a ton of money. And I was unemployed . . . and not going to accept Joseph's offer . . . and . . . "My place, probably."

Ben smiled as if he'd followed my spiraling thoughts. "That is sweet, but it is the wrong answer. We are headed to the Ritz . . . It is our wedding night, Mrs. Vassallo, and that only comes once in our lifetime."

Chapter 17

The next morning I awoke with Ben's arm draped around my waist. It lay heavy, solid, and infinitely comfortable. I snuggled deeper, savoring it, and marveling at this feeling of completion and wholeness—knowing it came from nothing I did or could control. It was simply us—and I couldn't see or feel a separation between his heart and mine. I finally rolled out from the covers to order us coffee.

I curled into the armchair across the room and watched him sleep. He now had one arm thrown above his head. I could only see his chin and the shadow created right beneath his lower lip—and the fact that his typical three-to-five o'clock shadow approached roguish status at seven in the morning.

I watched him a few seconds more, then reached to check my phone. I hadn't checked messages or e-mails in a couple days. One from Gallery Barton had arrived late in the night.

Dear Emily,

Again, I thank you for your work with Vaughn's *Pegasus 16*. It positively floated, and it sold within fifteen minutes of

opening the doors. His show is proving to be a remarkable success and a profitable introduction for Vaughn to Atlanta and to American contemporary arts. That isn't always the case. While small galleries thrive on discovering and introducing new talent, it puts us in a vulnerable position when our gambles don't pay.

This leads me to the pictures you sent. Your work is intriguing. Your perspective is fresh, colors vibrant, and even from the photographs, I can discern a touch that is both precise and innovative. You play on the past, yet push to the future.

I've only seen a few artists employ both brush and palette work within a single piece. Your skill in this area reminds me of Jaline Pol.

Nevertheless, I can't offer a show at this time. I sense a restraint and confinement within your work. That said, consider me very interested if and when you cut loose.

All the best and I hope to see you at our opening for Stratton in August.

Olivia Barton

"What is it?"

I looked up to find Ben sitting in bed watching me, a smile curving his lips. It was intimate and for me. He tapped the space between his brows, indicating that I was not returning his lovely smile.

I scrunched all my facial muscles to release the tension as I crawled back onto the bed beside him and handed him the phone.

"Olivia Barton. She didn't like my work."

Ben read the e-mail. "She does not say that. She is saying the same as we thought. There is more changing in them now."

I tipped over sideways into his lap. "The fact that we already knew it doesn't make it better."

Ben laughed. "Yes it does." He trailed his fingers through my hair. "What if she found something you did not think? Or rejected it all?"

I pushed myself up. "It'd be great if she'd found something else. I might be able to fix that. This is the one thing I can't work on. I have to *not* work to make it happen. Says so right there, *cut loose*. That is not one of my strengths." I looked at him, all those fears from our wedding flooding in. "You already know that, right? I'm not very much fun."

"I disagree." Ben's voice lifted.

I tipped over again, this time from embarrassment. "I'm not talking about that."

"I am. You are not a bunch of people. You are one whole and beautiful person." He chuckled and pulled me close. "Do not get discouraged. This does not require something new, just more you." He rested his lips on the top of my head. "Every day brings something new."

"True." I wrapped my arms around his waist. "Who'd have dreamt this?"

"Me." I felt his lips spread into a smile. "I have something to cheer you."

"What?"

"We need to buy you a ticket."

I was slow to catch on. "A ticket?" I pushed myself up.

Ben tucked my hair behind each ear. "It is Saturday, Bella." He shook his head. "I did not think this part through. I did not cancel my ticket. I fly home at six o'clock."

"You what? Tonight?"

He nodded. "I can try to change it." He reached for his phone.

I laid my hand over it. "Why? We've finished Piccolo and, with your dad sick, you don't have time right now to visit Chicago. Let's just go. It'll make for a busy day, but what else do we have to do?"

❧

"Are you out of your mind?" Amy stood, hands on her hips, in my hotel bedroom. "Where's Ben?"

"I told you. He's packing, too, then going to say good-bye to Joseph . . . Of course I'm going, Amy. He's my husband. I love him. So help me pack, but no yelling. Not today." I pulled my neck back. She looked different somehow. "My goodness, you look and sound like me."

She rolled her eyes.

"Besides, I don't have much to pack, clothes-wise. Most of it will fit in a single suitcase, and you can drive the rest back to Chicago."

"All your books? All these little projects you've got lying around?" She palmed a miniature mantel clock and an eighteenth-century snuffbox in each fist.

"Awww . . . I haven't fixed that hinge yet." I stopped myself from reaching for it. "Doesn't matter. We'll box them all up."

"Your blankie?" She then picked up my copy of *The Way Things Work*—the binding barely holding together, the front cover disconnected at the top.

"Be careful with that." I reached for it and sat down on the bed to thumb through the pages. "I love this book."

She dropped next to me. "It's falling apart."

"It's twenty years old."

She scanned the room. "You carry around a lot of stuff, Ems. We'll never get through all this."

"There are several boxes in the living room closet. We'll pack it all, and you can take them to my apartment."

She gently pulled the book from my hands and carried it to the living room. "What about the magazines?" she called. "You've got like twenty copies of *Architectural Digest* here."

"Pack those. There's stuff in all of them I like. I get ideas for restoration and color from those. And don't even ask about the mystery novels. Pack them all."

She moaned but didn't complain further.

The two rooms were soon cleared of any sign of either of us.

"You sure you don't mind driving my car back alone?" I shoved the last box onto the kitchen counter.

"Not at all. I'll figure out where to park it. How long until the lease on your apartment is up?"

"Two months."

"Then I'll park it at your place and figure it out from there." Amy narrowed her eyes as if committing a checklist to memory.

"Take over my lease, if you want. It's a good building."

"I'll need a job first. That's been the great thing about living with four girls—low rent." She blinked as if a lightbulb turned on. "And if I don't take your apartment? What happens to your stuff?"

"Storage?"

"And I'm to handle that?"

"Please?" I bit my lip. "You can move it all to that facility on Dempster."

Amy crossed her arms and stared at me. "So this is what it feels like to be you." She shook her head. "And being you, I have to ask. Have you called Mom?"

I unscrewed the faucet cap, cleaned it, and replaced it.

She swatted my arm. "Stop fixing stuff. Did you call Mom?"

"I left a voice mail. She hasn't called back."

"Dad?" She perched herself between me and the kitchen faucet. The hot water handle was loose, and I hadn't gotten to it yet either.

"He laughed at me, then grew livid when he realized I was serious. I guess I can't blame him. You said it yourself, two weeks, then marriage must be for lust, not love."

"I'm sorry I ever said that. It's not true." Amy stepped away and let me get to the handle. "Besides, when do you listen to me?"

I shrugged. "But what do I know?" I slanted her a small smile. "He *is* Italian."

Amy burst out laughing. "Nice try. And with any other Italian I might give it to you, but I've never ever seen anything like you two. Why don't you accept the reality that love, true love, can and does exist? And that you are *that girl*."

I felt my breath catch.

"The way he looks at you? It's pure magic." Amy crossed the room and rolled our suitcases to the door. "Hurry up and fix that handle so we can load the car. Your husband and Italy await, and I've got to get on the road."

Chapter 18

*I*taly. I pressed my forehead against the window as the plane descended. Morning was breaking over the countryside and spilling gold onto the fields and villages. Rome approached, low and broad. It was gold, too, and the ground seemed to reach up and both absorb and reflect the light at once. It was everywhere and it was everything I had imagined and I hadn't even touched down yet.

It wasn't plotted in a grid like the Midwest; the lines curved and swept. I was already too close to discern the whole. I strained to see farther.

I jabbed Ben. "Aren't you excited?"

He leaned past me. "For you to see my home and meet my family, yes. But I enjoyed Atlanta too. It is good to get away at times."

"I've moved so much; I like the idea of roots and a home."

The plane touched down, and the passengers erupted in cheers.

"Why's everyone clapping?"

"Why don't you?" Ben laughed. "No one in America does."

I had no answer for that one, so I returned to the window.

Rome's airport felt like an extension of the city, low and spread wide. Large sections were hidden behind scaffolding and bright yellow canopies. In the morning light, it, too, looked washed in a patina of gold.

"It's beautiful."

He poked his head past me. "It is yellow tarping." He grinned. "If you think the airport is beautiful, wait until you see the Sistine Chapel or St. Peter's Basilica or the light hitting the *duomo* in Florence. Or Montevello on a summer evening when the sun warms the stone walls or when the *girasoli* turn and stretch . . ."

"I didn't mean the airport . . . I meant everything."

When the plane was parked, Ben grabbed our bags from the overhead bin and I was ready to launch. But the exit line moved incredibly slowly, as if everyone was saying personal good-byes to the flight attendant. Even Ben paused. From a few people behind, I couldn't see or understand the holdup until I reached her myself. She handed me a large red foil heart.

"For me?"

"Thank you for flying with us and welcome to Rome." She smiled, poised and perfect, with a precise German accent.

"Thank you." I followed Ben, balancing my handbag and assorted junk that hadn't made it into my duffel, as I shoved the chocolate into my mouth. I looked up from chewing to find him pointing across the room to a sign, *Non EU Passports*.

"Someday we will not have to separate. You will be Italian."

Italian? Everything stopped. People pushed around me, as if in slow motion, and the whirlwind of the past two weeks crystallized into a single moment. I looked across the terminal. Nothing was familiar. Even the English spoken rolled in a different cadence and tone. *This is home.*

"Emily?" Ben rested his hand on the back of my neck.

I looked up at him. "I think it's all hitting me."

He squeezed my neck. "Take deep breaths. Planes go both ways. You have not dropped off the end of the earth."

"I know that." I shook myself awake.

He pointed to the line. "Then go get in line so we can go to Anne's."

Passport stamped, I caught up with him at baggage claim. "Where is this castle exactly?"

"It is fifteen kilometers away on the outskirts of the city. Vincenzo has oil and wine we need to get . . . And you can meet Anne."

"Got it. And she's what again?" I rolled my bag behind him, taking two steps to each of his.

"Papa's second cousin's daughter. She was my closest ally growing up."

"What does she do again? Is she the teacher?"

"That is my sister, Francesca. Anne's parents made their home into a small hotel, part of Relais & Châteaux, when she was young, and now she runs it. We will stay there tonight and then tomorrow, rested, we go to Montevello." He reached up and touched my hair.

"Are you trying to tell me something?"

Ben only smiled as I ran my fingers through my ponytail and cringed. It was tangled, I was rumpled, my teeth felt fuzzy, and my eyelids scraped like sandpaper. Not to mention that one broad smile would crack my dry face. But I didn't feel any paint.

I glanced up to assess him. Clearly I loved this man because, to me, he still looked perfect.

With a *harrumph* I dragged my bag alongside him to the car park, where we piled into an impossibly tiny car, smaller than a smart car, if any American could imagine that. Ben then dashed like a lunatic onto the Roman roads. Cars were everywhere,

careening between lanes, zipping at high speeds down frightfully narrow streets, dodging trucks and pedestrians, and climbing hills in switchback turns.

Twenty harrowing minutes later he pulled onto a gravel road and, not decelerating at all, dusted up a cloud behind us as pebbles pinged the car's underbelly, shooting to the end of a long drive. He stopped with a flourish and a skid at the front door of the most beautiful castle, the only castle, I'd ever seen. It was three stories, a mix of stone and brick, with a tower stretching two stories higher. All topped with terra-cotta tiles.

I unfolded myself from the car and stood staring. But only for a moment, as a woman launched herself from the front door, a cacophony of flowing color, light brown hair, and bright sandals, into Ben's arms.

"You rotter! How dare you marry without me!"

My mouth dropped.

She pushed him away and yanked me into a hug. "I'm Anne." She then whacked Ben in the chest. "You didn't tell her about me, did you? She was expecting Francesca. Lovely and demure—and Italian?"

Ben grinned.

I shook my head. "I just assumed."

"This family's like a good puzzle. Takes time, but the pieces all fit." She looked back to Ben. "Have you told her about Donata?"

"It is best to simply meet Mama." Ben cast me a glance before continuing. "We head home tomorrow."

"Oh . . . I'd love to be a fly on that wall." Anne looped her arm through mine. "Don't be scared. You're going to love Ben's mum." A distinct note of sarcasm danced between us as she waved a hand back to Ben. "I reserved the Castelluccia Suite. And you're lucky it was available, considering you gave me one

day's notice. Actually, it wasn't, so you'd better not tell Daddy I moved a Dutch couple."

"Is your dad Australian or your mom?"

Anne gripped my arm tighter. "Mum. She's a hoot, but she's out of town right now. My sister just had a baby in Paris, so she's doing the doting grandmama thing. But I'm sure she'll pop up to see you soon." She laughed. "And you really *will* love her. Everybody does."

We passed the lobby with an "I've got you all checked in" as she led us up a winding staircase. It wasn't broad and grand, but tight and narrow and only led to the second floor. It opened onto a series of hallways leading in four directions.

She walked toward the right and pointed out the window. "This'll be your view." She then called back to Ben. "It's the room your parents always stay in. Remember, we used to watch movies in it?"

"That one's too grand for us," Ben replied.

"Not for your honeymoon." Her voice arched with innuendo.

"*Grazie*, Anne."

She unlocked the door and led us in. "I'm not going through the spiel. You know where everything is. Sleep and come find me for dinner, or lunch in a couple hours if you want. Up to you. *Ciao, piccioncini!*"

The room was spectacular. Red tiled floor, cream plaster walls with a gold glaze, and gold brocade quilts with rich blue velvet pillows. The same deep fabric draped from the windows and covered the chairs and a small couch. Above the bed was a huge circular fresco, a lion's head painted in gold on a lapis-blue background.

"How old is this?" I climbed on the bed and reached toward it, touching it lightly with a finger. I noted a few points of restoration—excellent work. A section of the lion's mane had crumbled, but

someone had filled it and then sealed it with a clear glaze. "It's amazing. He looks alive."

"I expect it is original—mid-twelfth century."

He flopped on the bed, shaking it. I lost my balance and landed on him.

"And you are right, it is very beautiful," he whispered, brushing my cheek with his thumb. "You tired?"

"No . . ."

"*Bene.* Me neither."

I slept. Really truly slept, probably for the first time in two weeks. And when I woke, the room, the fresco, everything was more beautiful than I remembered. I reached to the side of the bed to find it empty.

A quick shower, a linen skirt and T-shirt, and I was in the corridor, completely lost. I trailed down one hall, then another, and soon found myself following voices, hoping they'd lead me out and to Ben.

Eventually I landed in the lobby.

"Breakfast is in the dining room, miss."

"Thank you." I walked into a large room with three long tables. One was covered in cheeses, another in breads and salamis, and the third overflowed with beautiful fruits, a large bowl of hard-boiled eggs, and a variety of tarts and pastries. I stalled, tempted and hungry.

A young man was clearing a white linen-draped table under a matching sunshade beyond the dining room's doors. I stopped in front of him. "Could you . . . I'm sorry, I don't speak Italian."

"I speak English."

"Excellent. I'm looking for Ben Vassallo. He's Anne's cousin. Are they here?"

"Ah . . . They went to the cave." At my lost look, he continued. "Down the steps. They're loading wine into your car."

The side of the patio seemed to end into nothing, like one of those infinity pools you see in *Architectural Digest*. I crossed it and found steps leading from the terrace. Down. Down. Five flights of steps, cut from stone and worn by time and feet.

I hadn't realized the previous morning that the castle was built into a hill. The back went down more stories than the front went up. Four flights later and one long flight from the bottom, I reached a grassy ledge with black openings into the hill. *Caves.*

I stepped into the shadow. It was instantly dank, dark, chilly, and quiet. It was an old, deep quiet, a listening quiet that seemed to promise something profound and powerful. Somehow it reminded me of the lion above our bed. He'd lurk in an old place such as this.

I stood at the edge absorbing it. I felt this way sometimes when working on a painting, when I became lost in the work and realized I didn't have control over it—that something large and powerful, intrinsically good, lay out there, out of reach and out of sight, and that only by stillness and surrender could I reach it. But as much as I relished those moments, I was also quick to retreat from them. I'd flip on the radio, take a break, or move on to another project.

True to form, I tapped my phone's flashlight on and the moment ended. I stepped forward, listening to the pebbles crunch under my feet and the sound echo off the walls around me. Soon I heard a noise and dashed beyond the stretch of my flashlight, sure it was Ben, Anne, and another way out.

When I slowed, I realized it was only water dripping over stone. I kept on a few minutes more, one passage leading to

another, then spun around to find my way back and was confronted with three dark holes in the earth. I had no idea which one I'd come through.

"Hello!" I called. My voice didn't bounce back, as expected. It was absorbed into the wet darkness. "Brilliant, Emily. You'll die here." I picked one tunnel and followed it. There were shallow stairs leading down that I knew I hadn't walked up. I retreated.

"Ugh!" I wandered down another tunnel, but it didn't feel right so I again retraced my steps to the widening. *How is it possible they're all wrong?*

"Emily?" A voice thin and too far away called.

"Hey! I'm here. Where are you?"

I heard Ben's faint laugh. "Where are *you*?"

"If I knew, I wouldn't be here."

"Stay where you are. I will find you."

I pressed my back against the wall. It was damp and I imagined thousands of little creatures crawling down it. I jumped to the center of the widening and called again. "Are you still coming?"

"*Sì.*" His answer came back a little stronger, a little closer.

After what seemed an interminably long wait, a flashlight wavered through the second tunnel.

"Ah . . . You found the caves, Sleeping Beauty."

"I was told you were in here."

"Not these. Vincenzo cut into the hill beyond the pool and built a cellar. These haven't been used since . . . I do not know when." He waved his light around the cavern. "Anne and I found bones here when we were kids. Aunt Nell said they were pig bones, but I did not believe her." He clasped my hand and led me out. "I was sure they were human. Then there was treasure. But that was plastic and Aunt Nell planted it." He stopped. "You are shaking."

"It's cold and . . . I got a little nervous."

He stopped at the dim light of the entrance and pulled my hands together against his chest. "Those were good summers. I was too young to be scared. But when I was about twelve, I went missing too." He tilted his head back into the cave. "Papa found me; he followed the sound of sobbing. I was farther back than you were—it goes deeper to the south. When Papa found me he knelt down and said, 'I will always come for you.' I have never forgotten that."

"I can imagine."

Ben raised my fists and kissed the back of one hand, then the other, keeping his eyes trained on mine. "I will always come for you."

He drew me close and kissed me, moving his hands from mine to frame my face, as if sealing a promise, a covenant. We stood like that until we heard a throat clear nearby.

My vision felt fuzzy as I glanced out of the cave. It landed on Anne, her arms crossed, one hip jutting out. "Enough, you two."

Without another word, she headed up the stairs. Chuckling, Ben pulled me along in her wake, up to the dining room where he piled my plate with cured meats, cheeses, and fruit, and Anne regaled us with childhood stories of a boisterous Ben I had yet to meet.

And all was fun and right until Ben said, "I called home and told them we are finally coming today."

"Wasn't that always the plan?" I popped a melon ball into my mouth.

"Yesterday was the plan. You slept through it."

"You let me sleep through an entire day! How? Who does that?"

Ben merged onto the highway. "You were tired."

"What must your family think of me?"

"That you were tired," he offered again.

"This is bad. I wanted to make a good impression, and now . . ."

"I love you and you will be fine." Ben shot me a quick glance.

"Tell me who's who again. I need to at least get that right."

He shook his head, as I'd asked that question a few times on the plane, trying to solidify all the details within his many stories. But rather than clearing everything up, he started in with new details, new stories.

"Aunt Sophia is Romanian, which is funny because she can be nasty to outsiders. She has completely forgotten she is one. She and Mama do not mix well some days. Francesca, you will like. I have told you all about her, but not that she is like Amy, bright and eager, but in a dark and quieter way. As you know, she is the teacher, and we have seven, no eight, young cousins in her school and . . ."

I kept my eyes trained out the window, listening to his words, but soon all the names jumbled and I found myself absorbed by the scenery.

It was filled with light and color and a texture completely foreign to me. The landscape rose and fell in gentle hills. And every now and then the highway cut through a mountain, rather than rising over it as they do in the US, and we emerged from the tunnel into sunlight on the edge of a valley dipping below us, bathed in green—often with a beautiful medieval walled village perched above. Cypress trees, pine trees, olive trees, vineyards, and pastures sloped all around us.

I noted the same rises and dips in Ben's voice as he trailed through his long list of relatives. I had thought he spoke English like an American fairly well—minus contractions, colloquialisms, and some intonation. But here his voice took on a new undulating tone, different syllables lengthening and catching.

"How many languages do you speak?" I interrupted him.

"Four. Italian, English, German, and French."

"I only speak one."

"American." He patted my knee as one does a small child.

"Hey . . . English."

"That is debatable. You use odd contractions and wrong pronunciations. You will love Francesca. She went to an American school in Florence. You will think her accent is flawless."

"Why didn't you go? Where'd you learn your English?"

"Joseph and I had a standard Italian curriculum, first in Montevello, then in Florence. But my father only spoke in English or German at home. He taught us first. Papa is like that; he was a good chef, but would have enjoyed teaching more, I think." Ben tapped his finger on his window. *"Girasoli."*

I lifted up to see past him. "Sunflowers! They're amazing. I've never seen so many." A huge field of sunflowers stretched up a hillside. Thousands upon thousands of happy yellow petals with bold green stalks. "They're all facing away from us."

"As I told you, they follow the sun. This afternoon they will grace the road with their smiles, and you will never find a rebel. I know. I ran through a neighbor's field once and searched. I twisted a few and they snapped. They must turn on their own."

Chapter 19

Ben pulled onto a single-track gravel road. Soon it became lined with trees and I realized it was a driveway ending right at the front door of a two-story stone-and-brick house. It was tall and symmetrical and fit into the countryside perfectly. The upstairs windows were swung wide as if letting the world in or as if there were no inside versus outside at all—it was all one.

But the massive front door, situated directly center and made of dark polished wood, at least eight feet tall and five feet wide, stood firmly shut.

"This is home?"

"Home." Ben climbed out of the car and stared at it with a warm smile. "It has been in Papa's family, on his mother's side, for at least eight generations. You must ask him. He loves to tell the story—monks in the sixteenth century sold it to his family." He lifted the door's huge iron knocker and let it drop.

"You're knocking?"

"Wait and see."

We heard an *"Un momento"* from inside just before the door swung open, yanked by a petite woman with black hair threaded

with gray. Her eyes, so dark I couldn't find the irises, were harried and tight until she focused on the sight before her. In an instant her face and body became animated and years dropped away. The girl from the photo stood before me. Donata.

"Benito!" She pulled him by the shoulders until she'd engulfed as much as she could seize of his taller frame within her arms.

"Mama. Non è così stretto." He then switched to English, whispering to me, "She hugs too tight." He untangled himself from her arms. "I have someone for you to meet." He pulled me forward, directly in front of his mother, and her eyes narrowed again. "Mama, this is Emily Price, now Vassallo. My wife."

"You were to come yesterday. It is only a few hours' drive." Her English was slow, hard, and precise.

I threw Ben a quick look. He watched her.

"Mama, we were tired. It is okay now. Meet Emily."

Another second passed before she pulled me into a small hug. "Welcome to *la famiglia*, Emily." She articulated my name slowly, pulling each syllable long, paying special attention to the center *mal.* It stretched forever. In Italian, I knew it meant "ache" or "evil," and I figured her emphasis was no coincidence.

I missed Ben's beautiful trail of *e*'s and instinctively stepped back—bumping into his chest. There was no retreat.

Ben's mother continued in the same clipped tone. "I am Donata. Benito's mama. It is a shame we meet after the marriage, rather than before."

"Mama," Ben gently warned. "I told you on the phone. We married at the right time and in the right way."

"Says who?"

"Mama." The sharpness softened to pleading.

"Va bene. You work to make it reasonable." She flapped her hands at him. "And Papa says I am to be quiet."

"That will be new," Ben teased and hugged her again.

"Do not start or I will forget this promise and give you that earful grandchildren will remember."

Their banter surprised me, and I stood tense, waiting for the "earful." It didn't come.

"Come inside. Come." She pulled us both through the door.

Ben headed to the back of the house, but I paused in the hallway. On the right, thick wood steps led to the second floor, supported by a wrought-iron railing sunk in stone. The floor was flagged stone, of a matching tone, but it turned to tile where Ben had entered what was clearly a kitchen. I caught sight of a huge basket filled with fruits.

To the left, a short hallway led to a room bursting with light. The door was wide open and I could see books on a far shelf and yellow, a sense of bright, happy, sunflower yellow. I took a step in that direction before I caught myself and followed Ben to the kitchen. It stretched the entire back of the house with its double ovens, stainless counters, two sinks, multiple refrigerators, and three sets of double doors opening onto a stone patio. A huge butcher block formed an island in the center.

I stalled. "Wow . . ."

"Do not get used to this. No one in the history of kitchens has one so grand. Mama went crazy a couple years ago."

"Noi cuciniamo—" She stopped, hands midair, and pursed her lips as if tasting something sour. "We cook. The whole village comes here. Why not be comfortable?"

Ah . . . The English tastes sour.

Once the words were out, she followed Ben across the kitchen, pulling food out of the refrigerator and from the baskets. Her face smoothed. She clearly loved her son and her kitchen—and was preparing *him* a late lunch.

Ben kissed her cheek again. "Is Papa at the restaurant?"

Donata's expression fell. "He was not honest with you. He rests upstairs."

Her tone set off alarm bells. My eyes flew to Ben. He had said his father was ill, aging. But this felt different; it felt urgent.

"What?" Ben's stiff posture confirmed it.

"Wait!" Donata pulled at his arm. "Do not be angry. He wanted you to have your time, and I respected that wish."

"You have had to keep quiet a lot, I think." Ben touched her cheek and strode from the kitchen. He immediately ducked back in, arm outstretched. "Come. You will love my papa."

"Don't you want to see him alone first?" I stepped backward.

"I want him to see you first." With that, Ben overtook me in two steps and folded my hand within his.

At the top of the stairs, the house split. He pointed to a room. "That one is mine. Ours now." He was still talking, but all my thoughts had stopped at one word. *Ours.* Here? We were going to live here? How had I not known this?

Ben continued. "Papa was born in that room, too, but do not let him tell you that story."

"Do you mean we live . . ." My question stalled as he pulled me around to the front of the house and tapped on the doorjamb of the bedroom overlooking the drive.

Its windows were the ones I'd seen from below, open to the sunlight that spilled in and turned the wood floor to a golden blond. A huge wood bed stood in the corner, but my eyes quickly trailed to the seating area in front of the windows. There I found his father.

He was reading and didn't look up until we stood before him. When he did, his rheumy brown eyes brightened and he struggled to stand. "My pizza maker . . ." He beamed. Then he looked around Ben and pointed to me with a soft, joyful laugh. "And his wife!"

Ben dropped onto the ottoman in front of him and pulled him into a hug. "Don't get up."

I stood there as pieces clicked into place. A puzzle, as Anne had called it. *La bistecca della moglie del pizzaiolo.* Ben's favorite dish. An old recipe from Napoli. He had been making it when I'd arrived at Piccolo the day after we met. *The steak of the pizza maker's wife.* He said it was a winter dish but that he hadn't been able to get it off his mind. *Me.* He hadn't been able to get *me* off his mind. The thought made me smile anew, and I suspected he hadn't been exaggerating when he said he'd looked up Georgia marriage rules right after we'd met.

Ben's voice drew me back to the moment. "Why did you let me go? And six weeks? You could have told me. That was not honest, Papa." I could see the muscles in his arms tense, hugging his father tighter.

"You needed to be there and see Joseph." He held his hand to Ben's cheek. "You are here so much, and yet, you are like me. We need the outside world. You brought some home." He looked over Ben's shoulder and caught my eye. "Move so I may welcome my new daughter."

Ben pulled away and leaned back so his father and I were face-to-face.

I leaned down and offered my hand. "I'm Emily. It's nice to meet you."

He swatted a thin hand at Ben. "Get up, son. I want to hug her."

Ben slipped away, and his father gathered me close. "Call me Lucio. Someday Papa, but Lucio will do for now. Ben says you are an artist and you like mysteries and can fix anything and you worked with Joseph."

"I . . . Yes, that's all true." I glanced at Ben, wondering what else he'd told his father.

"He is like you." Ben chuckled. "He asks lots of questions."

Ben's expression caught me. My Ben was deep, funny, creative, and even light—but before me stood a more boyish, exuberant, and free Ben. Lines I'd seen around his mouth and eyes seemed softened and lifted, despite his lack of sleep. Ben was most definitely home.

"I want to hear about the ceremony, short as it was." Lucio tapped my knee.

I glanced to Ben.

"You stepped into that one." Ben shook his head slightly. "I did not tell him."

"Tell me what?" Lucio glanced between us.

"I fainted. I said 'I do' and hit the ground like a stone."

Lucio laughed. "Oh . . . I hope he caught you!"

"I tried," Ben said.

Lucio chuckled again. "That is a story for the grandchildren."

"Within five minutes, you and Mama have both mentioned them." Ben dropped onto the ottoman next to me. "No more for now."

"Done," Lucio lied with a wink. He then moved his eyes out the window. "Since we must talk of something new, look out that window, Emily."

I smiled. He said my name the way Ben did, with all those lovely and welcoming *e*'s. I stepped to the window.

"All the land to that hill has been in my family for over eight generations, through my mother's side. My father came from the north; he was accepted for her sake. That's how family works, and you are part of that now too. You are family. Close to the house, you see the olive trees. They are for oil, not eating. Make Ben tell you how he cracked a tooth, then was up all night vomiting after a dare to eat a tree full."

"Not a tree—"

"Hush, Benito, you're ruining my story. Then, Emily, look to the right, up the rise, and you see grapevines. Beyond that, Montevello. Has Ben taken you?"

"We came here first," Ben offered. "But there is wine and oil from Vincenzo in the car. We will go unload that, and I can show her Coccocino. Then we need to sleep." Ben cast me a wry smile. "I do. Emily is better rested."

"Mama has your room prepared. She worked hard on it."

"That was kind. I got the impression she is not pleased with me."

"She missed a wedding. Her first child to marry and she played no part. You cannot blame her." There was a light reprimand in Lucio's tone. "And be gentle. This is hard." Lucio tapped his fingers to his chest.

"Papa." Ben shook his head as if trying to erase his father's last comment.

"My life has been long and good. No sadness now."

Chapter 20

As Ben led me downstairs, I felt his hand stiffen against the small of my back, pushing me to go faster and faster on the stone steps. At the bottom I twisted to ask, but he strode past me and was in the kitchen before I crossed the hall. Tense Italian whispers reached me long before I reached them.

I stood there a few moments before Donata looked past Ben and locked eyes on me. She turned back to her son and continued. She must have told him I was there, because he fluidly switched to English.

"It was not right."

"*La mia fedeltà è quello di tuo padre.*"

Ben glanced my way. "English, Mama. Emily won't understand."

"My English is not strong," she challenged.

"It will do," he replied flatly.

"As I said . . ." She drew the words long with exasperation. "My loyalty is to him. He asked me not to tell."

Ben pulled his hands through his hair as if yanking out the strands might relieve pressure. "When has that ever stopped you?

Who is at the restaurant now, anyway? You should have called me home."

"Francesca." Something tangible filled the air. Donata thrust out her palms. "She can help."

"She can, but she never wants to. She hates it, and you know it."

"We need her." Donata waved her hands, tears in her eyes. "I did what I think right."

Ben folded her into a hug. "I know, Mama. I know."

Donata slumped, as if holding Lucio's secret had kept her upright. "Dario came and thinks Papa had a stroke in the night. His hands shake. He is tired and not eating. We knew we were there; our time borrowed. But he is going and . . ." As she talked the words drifted into a soft, rapid Italian.

Ben rubbed her back and kept up a whispered litany of "I know, Mama, I know. I am sorry."

I tiptoed from the room to hover in the hallway.

Minutes later, Ben found me. "Shall we go? I need to get that wine to Coccocino."

We climbed back into the car. It felt as if a vacuum sealed us in—and we were safe there. Just the two of us. Ben stared ahead, no words, no movement.

After a moment, I ventured an "Are you okay?" When he didn't reply, I continued. "You're very much like your father, which is odd because I would've said you looked like Joseph, but he doesn't look like your dad, if that makes sense. He's lovely . . . not that Joseph isn't . . . And your mother, I *think* I like her, but I suspect the feeling's not mutual. Not yet." I let my voice lilt up, trying to get a reaction—a grin, a sigh, a bark, something.

Nothing.

"When will I meet your sister?"

"He's worse than I expected—in six weeks. What is next?" Ben's voice was flat.

The car grew hot as we sat. I tried to offer something light and lovely for him. "You have a gift for him, though. The pizza. Did you see how his eyes lit up?"

Ben finally faced me.

"Now I know . . . He wanted me to go, learn, because he knew I needed it. Something of my own. Something I could never do here. He believes that is the gift, the bread." Ben's eyes drifted back to the solid front door. "Ask him about it. If you want to know Papa, that is where you start. It is his love story." Ben quirked a smile, and there was that little boy again. He then shook his head as if chasing away a memory and twisted the key in the ignition. "It grows warm in here—not good for the wine."

Driving back down the road, pebbles a-flying, silence lay between us. I broke it as Ben accelerated our tiny rental around a hilltop corner and a quintessential medieval walled village appeared before us.

"Ohh . . . Why didn't you say you lived near one when I was droning on?"

"It was so cute. You pointed to each one as if it were a little present and you would not ever see another. I wanted to surprise you."

He darted through an impossibly narrow archway and drove up a bricked street, hemmed in by tall walls on either side. He ducked down another, even tighter street and pulled into a small courtyard.

"Come on." He popped the car's trunk and grabbed a box.

I grabbed one, too, and followed him through a gate and another smaller archway—this one for people. No car, no matter how small, could fit. We entered a tiny courtyard lined with benches and a large placard set into the wall. *Coccocino.*

We stepped up broad stone steps and entered the restaurant. The dining space was bright, with huge windows on the far wall looking into another tiny courtyard. The rest of the natural light came from skylights. There was an open fireplace with a waist-high hearth built into the side wall.

"That is where we grill the meats." He pointed to it as he led me through the empty dining room to the kitchen door. "Here we go," he said softly before calling out, *"Buongiorno!"*

Wait? What? People are here? My mind raced with all I needed for a good introduction—composure, less wrinkled clothing, a warning. There was a lot required to make a good first impression, and I'd already failed once today.

The conversation, which had been moving fast like *vivacissimo* music, stopped. There was a beat of silence before a chorus of *"Benito!"* pounded our ears.

Ben was folded into the kitchen, and I stood by the door with my box. Silence returned as eyes found me.

"Everyone meet Emily, my wife."

I shrugged beneath the box. "Hello."

Ben lunged for it. "I am sorry. Let me take that." He pointed to the group. "Noemi, Giada, Alberto, and Nicolo. And over there is Luigi, who just walked through the door."

"La moglie di Benito!" came out of the blurred chaos before Ben asked, "Where's Francesca?"

"She's at the market in Greve-in-Chianti today. Don't tell me you've forgotten?" Noemi's English was smooth and, to my ear, almost accentless.

"I forgot it is Tuesday. I have forgotten my days." He reached for my hand and squeezed as if conveying something important. "I am not here today for prep, but I will be in tomorrow to see how we are doing, and everything returns to normal Thursday."

"Normal might take some time," Noemi commented.

"Not now." Ben shook his head. "I cannot deal with any mess."

"And Francesca?" Noemi asked.

"She can stay if she wants."

"If she hears you're back, she may not return from the market at all," Noemi said with a wry smile.

"Keep it a secret then. We need the produce." Ben waved and pulled me through the door.

"They all speak English too?" I trailed him through the tables and back out to the car.

"Noemi and Luigi do. They will translate for the rest." Ben opened the car door for me. "You will find most people do here. Europe is a small place."

"Still . . . it's impressive. After two weeks, I was only beginning to speak Atlantan."

"Atlantan?"

"You know, when someone says, 'Y'all come back now,' and it really means 'Don't bother us again.' That took me a few days. And don't even get me started on 'Bless her heart.'"

Ben laughed as he backed the car out of the restaurant's small lot and drove it up the steep single-lane brick road to an open plaza.

"This is Montevello—almost all of it, really. The town was founded as a walled fortress in . . . I forget, but the village started in 1249 when the fortress got sacked by Frederick II." He pointed around the square. "We have the hotel that used to be a private home until about sixty years ago; the theater where the guild holds summer plays; the town hall, which will be renovated next year; and tourism shops. You will meet everyone soon. It is a small town. And Andre . . ." He pointed to the last shop on the right. "He owns that grocery and the *enoteca*, the wine store, next door. You will like him."

Ben pushed the accelerator, circled the plaza, and headed us down another tight street, our side mirrors almost scraping the house walls on either side. Right before he reached an arch, distinctly too small for the car, he zipped to the left into a parking lot.

"Let us go now."

"Go where now?"

"It is lunchtime. Many will be at Tartaruga, and you can meet them."

"All your friends? Now?" My voice squeaked.

"Come on. It is not every day someone brings back a wife from holiday. You are not a typical souvenir."

"How many people are we talking here?"

"Everyone." Ben nodded as if that answered the question.

I grabbed for his hand and pulled. "Slow down one sec. I'm going to need a moment." I smoothed my ponytail and ran my tongue over my teeth.

"You look beautiful."

"You lie, but thank you." I stopped fidgeting and looked around. "This is beautiful."

Ben followed my gaze to the high stone walls, the brick paths sloping up and down the hills. "It is. It is home."

Home. That word again. In my life, it had always been transient, replaceable with each stepfather or with Mom's next job. But there was nothing transient about this place. Lucio had said eight generations. This was the dream—stones warmed from above and roots that gripped deep below.

As we crossed the small road out of the parking lot and walked up the hill, it narrowed to a mere bricked walking path. It was lined with blond stone leading seamlessly up into the walls of the surrounding houses. It felt old and stable, as if you could feel centuries of walkers before you treading these same paths.

Flowers grew in some of the mortar work. I ran my other hand along the mortar lines; some thick and straight, but every now and then my hand caught a patch where the bricks had been replaced with different sizes and shapes and the lines ran curved and irregular. These were the scars, cracks, crevices, and patchwork that told their story, their history.

"Drainage?" I pointed to two deep grooves in the stone at each edge of the walk.

"We quit using them a couple years ago." Ben winked and pulled me up the hill and into a narrow opening. It was cooler in the shade, but twenty steps and we emerged again into the bright sunshine on the next walk over.

"This will not be confusing soon. There are only three streets wide enough for cars. Each goes through the piazza like spokes on a wheel. One drive and you will understand."

"I'm not driving here."

He stopped. "As soon as we get a cappuccino, we must return the rental. Otherwise it will be another whole day before we get it back."

I opened my mouth, but no words emerged.

"Do you drive standard transmission?"

"I do, but you can't be serious."

Ben kissed me as if that solved everything. "You will be fine. Chianti-in-Greve is only twenty minutes away, and there is a place there for a real lunch, a butcher shop and restaurant in one, Macelleria Falorni." He kissed me again.

"Is that your idea of bribery?"

"Is it working?" Ben grinned as we stepped up to a small café with two distinct outside patios. One consisted of four open tables side by side along the walkway, while the other was made of a tight collection of about six tables on a raised wood platform. The upper

patio was packed with people and covered with an awning that magnified their noise.

I pulled out a chair at the only empty table on the ground-level patio, but Ben tugged at my waist before I could sit.

"Not here. Come." He led me to the counter and wagged his pointer finger and thumb at a tall woman with short blond hair. She had time only to nod acknowledgment before her attention was pulled back to a monstrous silver machine behind her.

It took only a second before she processed Ben's presence. Her head spun back around and she gave me a quick once-over. Ben caught it too. "Told you. They are curious. That is Sandra. She moved here a few years ago from Rome."

Sandra reached over and gripped Ben's shoulder with affection as she used her other hand to push two china cups on saucers across the counter. *"Non lasciare."*

"We will not leave." He tilted his head at me. "You need to meet Emily, in English."

Sandra smiled, small and flat. "Anything for you, Ben." Her English was thick and jarring. "Welcome, Emily. I wish you the luck." She nodded to the raised patio.

She turned back to her work as Ben ushered me toward the upper patio.

"If you order sitting at this lower patio, you are a tourist and Sandra charges you four euro for a cappuccino. At the counter, she charges you only one euro, but you cannot sit. You must pay to sit. Up here, she quit charging us to sit when Andre set up a coffee stand outside his grocery in protest. It took three weeks for her to give in. Now we pay one euro and we sit with friends."

As soon as his foot hit the top step, a chorus of *"Benito!"* again rose into the air, and we were met with a flurry of Italian, hand waving, kisses, backslaps, and hugs. Everything then grew

still, as if, just as at Coccocino, they collectively figured out my significance.

Ben pulled out a chair for me and dropped into one beside it as a man in a green shirt stepped forward.

"I'm Andre. Ben texted me about his pizza and you, in that order . . . Don't feel bad, though—he's known the pizza longer."

"She did not come second," Ben weakly protested.

"You did." Andre nodded to me and pulled an empty chair next to mine, on the other side. He reached across me and thumped Ben on the shoulder. "Don't deny it." He then surveyed the group and bellowed across the noise, *"Solo inglese* . . . Baptiste, you're off the hook. You shoulda learned English long ago." He nudged me. "You don't speak French, do you?"

I shook my head.

"No talking to Baptiste then . . . You're not missing much." He looked around the group again. "Same with Monica. She owns the china shop right there. Both of them only speak French and Italian. The rest of the lot speak English; don't let them fool you." He leaned toward me. "How long will it take for you to learn Italian?"

"I have no idea. I catch some words, but . . . Forget it. I get most of those wrong too."

"English then," he announced, "until further notice."

"Thank you."

Ben smiled at me and squeezed my knee under the table. "I told you; you will like Andre."

Two cappuccinos and I was flying. I tried to follow the conversation as it switched back to Italian, but it felt like swatting at flies.

I whacked down a few words, but most buzzed past. I knew when Ben said good-bye, as the whole group moaned. I caught all the *arrivedercis* and *ciaos* and repeated them back as we made our way through the tables and off the patio. But rather than return to the narrow passage between the buildings, Ben took my hand and led me up to the town square.

"I don't think two was a good idea." The flying sensation held the distinct possibility of tipping toward a crash landing.

"I will feed you soon. That will help."

We walked up the hill and out of shadow into the bright sunlit square.

I tugged at him. "Explain *tartaruga* to me. It's an odd name for a café."

"Sandra says she came out of her shell and fully alive when she married Paulo. He owned the café and was against the name switch, but I think he feels the same about her, so we quit poking him about it."

"Turtle Café . . . I like that image."

"Here, I want you to see this."

We walked up a few stairs and Ben pulled open the massive front door of a church. Inside was dark and, as my eyes adjusted, I breathed in. You could almost taste the age, incense, and heaviness of paper, wood, and stone. The only light streamed through the stained glass windows in shots of red and blue.

"It's so quiet. Peaceful."

"You will hear the bells even at the house for this evening's Mass, then again tomorrow morning. I come here sometimes if I am at Coccocino and cannot make it to church with my family on Sundays. They go to Santa Maria in the valley to the south, but this . . ." He stepped deeper into the nave. "This is where Joseph worked that summer I told you about."

"Here?" I stepped forward, my soft ballet flats barely making noise on the stones. The pews were ash wood, worn and warm, and the altar hewn from some kind of stone. I couldn't tell from the distance, but by the way it reflected the light, I suspected marble.

A flicker of gold drew my attention to a side wall. There was a series of paintings along the nave, seven on the wall near me, and an equal number on the other side. "The Stations of the Cross," I whispered.

"*Via Cruces*. You know these?"

"Lily showed me pictures of a set she worked on for a Catholic church in Memphis." I stepped closer. "These are oil on wood. Early nineteenth century?" I caught Ben's shrug in my periphery as I moved to the next one. "These could use a little love, but some of this . . ." I noted places of repair that were expertly executed. "I bet Joseph did this."

"He may have."

"There's still more that can be done." I touched the curled edge of a frame. "This moisture damage is fairly new. It should be scraped out and sealed."

Ben chuckled softly. "Are you looking for a project?"

I smiled. "I think I am."

"When we come for services, you can corner Don Matteo and tell him."

"That seems rude, but . . ." I moved to the next and the next, my excitement growing with each warped frame, surface crack, and nick. "Do you think he'd let me help?"

"His predecessor let Joseph." Ben turned and strolled back out, but I lingered, already determining which glues to use and which pigments might work best.

He ducked back inside the door and called, "Are you coming?"

As we walked out of the church's shadow and hit the sun-

drenched center of the town square, I slowly spun in a circle, taking in the small grocery, the wine shop—trying to remember the word *enoteca*—the church, the single hotel, the tourist shop, the town concert hall—solidifying each in my memory.

Home.

Chapter 21

Boom.

I shot up and shook Ben. "What is that?"

"I forgot to warn you." His eyes remained closed as he waved his hand in the general direction of the window. "See the top of that tower? Over the hill?"

I rolled over, taking the covers with me, and looked out into the golden morning. The side of the house sat at the base of a hill. Over the rise I could see the tip of a broad bell tower.

"Church bells?"

"Santa Maria. Every morning at six. First Mass of the day. In a few days you won't notice them."

I hauled the pillow over my head and dug deeper into the covers.

Moments later someone or something poked me. I swatted at it.

"Easy. You will spill it." Ben's voice came from . . . above me.

"What time is it?" I crawled out of my cocoon into a brightly lit room and looked out the window again. Blue sky. Quiet.

Ben held out a small white china cup. "Your cappuccino, Sleeping Beauty."

"Oh . . . I could get used to this." I scooted up against the head-board. "I didn't miss a whole day again, did I?"

"No. Drink that and I'll take you to the village. I need to check in at Coccocino, and you can corner Don Matteo."

"Your mother mentioned going to morning Mass yesterday. Is that soon?"

"You did sleep through that."

"You can wake me, you know." I sipped my coffee, suspecting that ruining Donata's plans, again, was not a good thing.

"Enjoy that and come to breakfast. I'm going to the garden to see if Mama's herbs are ready yet."

I dressed and found my way back to the kitchen. Donata was wiping down the counters.

"You missed breakfast and Mass." Her censure came out thick. She then looked around, as if she couldn't help herself, and pointed to a plate on the table. "There is what is left."

I glanced over. A platter was piled with fresh peach slices, melon, prosciutto, another meat I couldn't name, and a couple cheeses.

"Thank you, and again, I'm sorry I missed dinner last night too. A mixture of little sleep and jet lag is still swamping me . . . I couldn't keep my eyes open."

Her *hmmm* bordered on a *harrumph*.

I walked over to the table. "Am I the only one eating, or should I wait?"

"It is for you alone." She busied herself at the stove, tightening the knob on her stockpot's lid.

"I can set that for you so the screw will never come loose."

She looked at me, softening for a moment, almost as if I were a memory rather than a person. She then shook her head.

"It wouldn't be—" I stopped. There was no use continuing. She'd left the room.

Ben joined me about halfway through my platter of food. "When I left, small shoots; now many are ready."

I tried to hand him a peach slice but it kept sliding through my fingers. "You've got to try this."

"I had one; that is yours." Ben laughed as another attempt slipped back onto the plate.

"They never taste like this at home."

"You do not tree-ripen most of your fruit. It ripens in transit. That took some getting used to at Piccolo. Have you tried the pecorino?"

At my nod, he continued. "A friend of mine, Alessandro, makes that. You will meet him soon too. He lives a little ways away and does not like Tartaruga."

"He doesn't?"

"He does not like Andre." He tapped my now-empty plate. "Are you ready?"

"Let me brush my teeth, then I am." I dashed up the stairs and halted right before slamming into Lucio.

"Good morning. Will I see more of you today?" He gave me a formal, yet playful, bow.

"I'm sorry I fell asleep and missed dinner."

His face lit with an ear-to-ear grin, much like his son's. "Do not apologize. I did the same and missed it too."

By the time we returned from the village, minus finding Don Matteo and any discussion of possible work, the house was full of

family for a celebration. Donata said it was because Ben was home. Lucio said it was to welcome me. Regardless, family had arrived.

The kitchen was packed with women, the patio with men, and kids ran through the vineyards and in and out of open doors. After a seemingly endless round of introductions, cheek kissing, hugging, nodding, and smiling, and a failed attempt to be useful in the kitchen, I snuck off to find a small dark corner to myself. Ben had long since disappeared among the men.

The room I'd spied when we first entered the house was in fact a library and was, at this time, blessedly empty. I dropped into a large armchair covered in a soft floral-patterned fabric.

"Here you are."

I startled and jumped up.

"Don't get up." A young woman with long black hair waved me back down. "We'll hide together."

She curled up in the chair across from me. Raven hair and dark eyes. And if I was right, she was three years younger than me, spoke "American" like a native, and had trailed her older brothers relentlessly as a child.

"You're Francesca," I said. "Ben talks about you a lot. I'm so glad to meet you."

Her face split into that same contagious smile. "And you're Emily, my new sister." She looked around the room. "We'll hug and kiss later." She laughed as if she knew how uncomfortable I might find that. "It's nice and quiet here. Did they all scare you?"

"Maybe a little, but it wasn't that. After meeting everyone, I couldn't understand anything that was being said and I was bothering your mom." I held my hand out. "Justifiably so . . . They've got a lot going on and I've never made pasta, don't speak Italian, dropped my wineglass, was standing everywhere I shouldn't have been . . . It was better I retreated."

"Aunt Sophia said Mama barked at you."

"Nobody could blame her. I really was in the way—I couldn't understand what she wanted me to do." I tried to smile.

"Often Mama doesn't require translation."

I smiled. Ben was right. Francesca sported a perfect American accent—one that stretched flawlessly from Chicago to Seattle, dipping down through Colorado rather than passing up near the Canadian border.

"You were a big hit with Aunt Sophia, though."

"How so? I think she's the one who stepped away when I tried to hug her."

Francesca burst out laughing. "Don't take that personally. She's not Italian. She hates hugs and despises the double cheek kissing. She loves that you don't fit in, 'cause she says she still doesn't and no one lets her forget it." Francesca waved her hand again. "It's not true, of course, but she plays it up."

"She'll love me forever then . . . I don't make pasta, cook, sing arias, speak ten languages, or anything else you all do around here."

"That's how we look?" Her eyes narrowed. "Let me assure you that's not the case. I, for one, can't carry a tune, hate to cook, speak only three languages, and . . . pasta is a sticking point."

She twisted deeper into her chair and tucked a leg under her. "It's the greatest sin for an only daughter not to cook—and especially, not to make pasta. In my mom's family, it's the responsibility of the youngest daughter. Very old-school traditional. Mama was the youngest of four girls and has made pasta every day for the past fifty years." Francesca cast me a sideways smile. "According to her, I should've taken over long ago. But I didn't—so she's kept on, annoyed with me on a daily basis. She doesn't like it when things, or people, step out of line."

"Be fair, *Passerotta*." A soft voice drifted to us.

"Papa calls me his sparrow," Francesca whispered before I saw him entering through a paneled door I hadn't noted. Ben followed him.

Lucio continued as they came toward us. "She wanted to share it with you and has fully respected that you don't wish to continue the tradition."

"Fully, Papa?"

"Perhaps not completely and perfectly fully." His voice tripped into laughter.

Francesca smiled at this qualification as I stood to offer Lucio my seat. He greeted me with a quick kiss on each cheek and motioned for me to sit back in the chair.

"I'll be fine here, if you don't mind us joining you. I'm tired tonight and, although family is wonderful, it can be overwhelming too." He lowered himself onto a small love seat.

Ben perched beside me on the chair's arm and ran his fingers through my hair. "You two look comfortable."

"We are. Please don't make us move," Francesca whined.

Lucio held up both hands. "We plan to hide too." He then settled back into the corner of the love seat. "It was the pasta that made Donata fall in love with me."

I could almost hear Ben relax as his father continued.

"She walked into Coccocino one day looking for a job. It was not yet five in the morning and there she was, so young and beautiful. I don't know if you can tell"—he winked at me—"but I am older than she is. I hired her that first moment, and every morning she was there. In the quiet, magic time between night and dawn, I wooed her as I made the bread and she the pasta." He raised his finger. "All by hand, with care, each and every day. It's work, it's life, a sensual pleasure, and I won her."

"You are such a romantic, Papa."

He smiled at Francesca. "As I always say, my girls make it easy."

I, too, folded one leg beneath me and tucked into the chair as they shared family stories. Ben left my armrest and sat next to his father. His tall frame looked strong and sturdy next to his father's thinner one. The contrast made me sad, as if I were seeing the beginning and the end of a beautiful story.

Gradually Ben and Francesca grew quiet, content to let Lucio wend through time and share his best moments with me. It was the most comfortable, the most welcome I'd felt since walking into the house—far better than all the hugs and double, even triple, cheek kissing Aunt Sophia so despised.

Suddenly Lucio stopped midsentence and pointed out the double doors with a smile. "Watch," he whispered.

I threw a glance to Ben. He nodded confirmation, then focused his gaze out the window. Francesca twisted in her seat as well, and the four of us looked over the fields as the last sunbeams touched the hills. They ignited in a golden orange, fire against the darkening shadows. None of us moved or drew a breath until the blaze disappeared.

The instant it did, the front door banged shut.

Lucio stood and stretched. "And that, my children, was our last moment of peace. Shall we join the others? I suspect dinner is about to begin."

Chapter 22

The next morning I made sure I was awake to accompany Ben downstairs to breakfast. One, I didn't want to be rude again. Two, I didn't want to face Donata alone. I even wondered whether I could accompany Ben to work, each and every day.

"You are up and dressed early." Lucio was already seated at the huge farm table with a book and an espresso. "You just missed Mama. She is out in the garden."

"That may be best." Ben pulled out a chair for me. "I need to go to Coccocino. I did not like the mess I found yesterday."

Lucio laid down his book. "That is my fault."

"I should not have left. Six weeks was too much."

"You thought I was there and I didn't tell you otherwise. And Francesca? She's never worked in the restaurant before. It was unfair to put her in that position." Lucio held up a hand. "But time is racing fast now; you needed that trip."

"Papa." Ben reached across the table and squeezed his father's hand.

"Not unusual at eighty-three, Benito, but I didn't want to believe. It is what it is." Lucio scrunched his eyes shut as if putting

a stopper in his emotions. "I am sorry about last night too. I can't believe I slipped. I never told Mama that Joseph lives near Maria and Vito or about Piccolo. That was my fault too."

I sat back, remembering the evening. The family, so large we were spread across the dining room, kitchen, and patio to eat, was loud, boisterous, and fun—until I heard Lucio call across the table.

"Joseph said Piccolo is twice as busy since your work, Benito. You have the magic touch, you and Emily."

"What's Piccolo?" someone asked in English.

I was so delighted to understand the question; I jumped in without thinking. "Ben's Aunt Maria and Uncle Vito own a wonderful restaurant in Atlanta. Joseph took me there my first night and already Ben had revamped the menu, but together, we—" I stopped, finally noting the absence of all noise and movement across the three rooms.

My eyes shot around the dining room. Every face stone-still. I glanced at Ben. He watched Donata. I glanced at Lucio. He watched his plate.

After a few seconds Lucio looked up and whispered, "Donata . . ."

She raised a hand to him and looked to Ben. "I thought you worked on your pizza at Joseph's home. You went to see your brother. That is what you told me. Maria lives there? She owns a restaurant and knows Joseph? She knows my son? How?" She turned to Lucio. "And this does not shock you?"

"No. Joseph contacted Maria years ago. From Naples. I didn't know he went to Atlanta because she was there until . . . until I visited."

"Egli fa questo a male di me." Donata spoke quietly.

Lucio reached for her hand. "I don't think he's trying to hurt you. I choose to believe he is finding his way back. To family."

"And now you?" She faced Ben.

Ben's lips parted, but no sound came out. His eyes flashed confusion, and I realized he didn't know what to say.

"Please. We'll discuss this later." Lucio squeezed her hand, lifting it within his. "Francesca, please bring me a napkin. I spilled some wine on the table."

It started slowly, but the cacophony soon resumed, though I noted that Donata did not engage again.

Now Ben's voice drew me back to the present. "Are we ever going to talk about that?"

Lucio shook his head, checked the motion for a second as he caught my eye, then resumed, and I wondered if I'd imagined the hesitation. Then he straightened his back and looked at me. "What are you doing today?"

"I-I'm not sure. I . . ." I glanced at Ben, hoping he might have some great insight or invitation.

"You can paint my portrait."

I scooted my chair back. "I'm not that good. And besides, I don't have my paints with me."

"Oh, but you do," Ben announced. "I got them from Joseph when I went to say good-bye. He said you would want them."

"He did? I told Amy to grab them on her way out of town." I envisioned Joseph's tall figure, so like Ben's, but less open, less thoughtful—arms usually crossed. "That was kind of him, of both of you."

Lucio nodded as if all were settled. "You will fix Coccocino," he said to Ben, "and we will be together." He stretched across the table to pat my hand with each word.

He then gave his attention to Ben. "Last night was all wrong, and it meant you did not tell about your pizza. Tell me before you go."

Ben leaned across the table. "It seems silly now, packing flour, traveling across the world to cook. I should have been here."

"It wasn't." Lucio matched his posture. "You needed to see Joseph. He needed to see you. We are family and we've been fractured too long. I always thought it was the bread—that if I fed you, made something so elemental and basic, like the air we breathe, I could keep us whole. I have been the silly one, hiding my head in Coccocino, books, my own imagination." The hand covering mine now slid to Ben's. "And you could not have done that here. Pizza? I might have stopped you. I resist change, and Mama hates it." He offered a small smile. "You wanted to make something new. Coccocino needs new. You needed new."

"I made a crust I am proud of, Papa. I want to add it to Coccocino's menu. And I want to keep in touch with Maria and Vito, more with Joseph too. I loved my time there and may even visit them again someday. The States is Emily's home."

"I know. All that is right." Lucio sent me a warm smile before facing Ben again. "Make your pizza. Keep Joseph close, and Maria and Vito. I'll figure this out. I promise." He reached up and laid his palm on Ben's cheek, and I noticed how thin his hand truly was. The veins lifted out of the almost translucent skin. The nails were tinged yellow, purple at the bases. He wasn't well, and it was far more than being tired.

Lucio continued. "You will make some for me. I can taste it now."

"Tomorrow. No, give me a few days. I want to play with the water and yeast here; it needs to be perfect."

"Nothing is perfect, son."

"It needs to be my best effort."

"I will wait then." Lucio pursed his lips, his eyes alight with laughter. "Don't tell your mother yet."

"Not after last night. She did not look at me or speak to me again." Ben pushed up from the table and kissed his father's cheek. "I need to go." He squeezed my shoulder. "You will be okay?" he asked softly, as if he'd known all along that I feared being left behind.

I smiled and glanced to Lucio. "I'll be just fine."

"Bene. Ti amo." Ben bent down and kissed me before leaving the room.

"Espresso?" Lucio pointed to the hand-pull machine on the counter.

"Ah . . . of course." The La Pavoni matched my own. "Don't get up. Ben and I refurbished one of these in Atlanta and I know how to use it. I think your son was preparing me for just this moment. May I make you another too?"

Coffees made and cups in hand, I followed Lucio out of the kitchen.

"Look up." He stepped into the small hallway outside the library door. "This house was purchased from a monastery in 1693, and those are the family crests and the shields of the bishops. Then here . . ." He pointed to each corner in turn. "These are depictions of the known continents at the time—no Antarctica. See the grains and green of that one—that's your home, North America.

"But that corner? Ben flooded the hall bathroom as a boy and we fixed the water damage, but the paint, the red changed, and that flaking has bothered me for years. And here . . ." He trailed his finger above my head. "That crack has grown." He looked straight at me. "Could you help?"

I squinted to see the mural more clearly. "I see the flaking,

and maybe some discoloration. The varnish is most likely animal based. But until I get up there I won't know." It was my turn to drop my head and look him in the eyes. "You should ask Joseph. He's the true conservator, and this is his home."

Lucio blinked several times before replying. "He is not here, and it's now your home too."

I nodded. "If you have a ladder, I can examine it."

"Wonderful. Let us go to the shed and get one. It's at the edge of the orchard." He headed through the hall and back to the kitchen at a much faster pace. I set the coffee cups down on a table in the library and hurried to catch up.

I spent the morning in the library with Lucio. While I sketched him, we chatted about books, Ben, and life. Ben had been right about his father. While he may have been an excellent chef, he certainly was a natural-born teacher.

As we'd entered the library, he had asked, "Where do you want me to sit?"

"Right there is fine." I then settled across from him and nodded at the book pile next to his chair. "You can read if you want. I'm only going to sketch you now, to get a feel for the lines of your face."

He picked up the top book and flashed me the cover.

"*Don Quixote*. I remember that one," I said.

"I like him. He reminds me of myself lately, tilting at windmills as if I could change things too."

Lucio paused and looked out the doors through which we'd watched the sun set the evening before. "Sometimes, before I fall asleep or when I catch a piece of music that lifts my soul, I envision another way to live, like that moment last night when the setting

sun hit the top of that rise and the leaves glowed. They were alight with life, and it lasted only a moment. That's when I suspect I've gotten it wrong and I've wasted my time, tilting at windmills—not anticipating the unexpected or being present enough to recognize it." He waved his hand again. "Musings of an old man . . ."

I noticed something about the cover. "Do you read it in Spanish?"

Lucio twisted the book as if he'd forgotten he held it in his hands. "This? Yes. If I can, I like to read books in their original languages. I can read five languages. Portuguese, I can only speak."

"Ah . . . only." I settled my sketch pad on my lap and selected a charcoal pencil from my toolbox.

"I feel you gain the author's original intent in his or her own language. I only switch if I need a different perspective."

At my befuddlement, he continued. "Words don't always translate, and I'm a different man in different languages. I interpret things differently, I think differently. A story changes for me like something alive and growing."

He laid down the book, warming to his subject. He needed his hands. "In general, I read, watch television, do math, and make plans in English. In Italian I sing, cook, work in the garden, and make love to my wife. In German, at least in my head, I form debates and arguments . . . I often reprimanded my children in German." He grinned. "I also used to clean Coccocino's kitchen in German. It sparkled."

"It astounds me how many languages you all know."

"They're all around you here. German and Spanish I solidified working in Berlin and Barcelona for years before I took over Coccocino. The restaurant was my mother's place, passed down from her father. She was chef for many years before me. I had only taken over the year before Donata arrived."

It wasn't long after that he'd drifted away in memory, then into sleep.

∽

Shortly after Lucio drifted off, I crept out of the library and climbed the ladder in the entry way to have a look at the fresco.

Donata's voice startled me.

"Emily, what are you doing?"

The ladder shook, and it rattled worse as I flew down its few rungs.

"Lucio asked me to examine the ceiling. There are some things I can do to help it."

"It is not your concern."

"I . . ."

She pushed past me and entered the library.

I crouched down on the ladder to peek through a crack in the door. Lucio wasn't asleep anymore.

Donata started in a quiet voice, but soon the words flew up, both in speed and in volume—in Italian. But I didn't need to be fluent to understand that something was wrong. Me.

Lucio's calm voice interjected at first, then died away in the torrent.

I climbed off the ladder and stepped away from the door, but within two steps I realized I had nowhere to go. Ben and I lived here. *Do I go to my room?*

The library door flew open.

"Fine. Lucio wants you to do the work." Donata ground out the words as she stalked past me.

Lucio smiled from his armchair and waved me inside. "As I told you, she does not like change. She fears what is to come."

I dropped into the seat across from him. "I don't have to do this."

"Don't you want to?"

I couldn't help nodding. I needed something to do, something to fix. Forty-eight hours and I was already feeling lost. I had secured Donata's pot handle the day before. I couldn't help it.

"That was not about the painting. She knows it needs to be fixed. It is about my timing. Have you ever noticed how much that matters?" He continued without waiting for a reply. "She would have been pleased if I'd asked you to do that years ago, but now she feels I'm 'putting my affairs in order,' as the English say. That she does not like."

"Is she right?"

Lucio studied me so long I thought he wasn't going to answer. He hadn't been forthcoming with Ben; what made me think he'd tell me the truth? What business had I to ask?

He nodded, once. He could not have been more clear, more decisive.

"I'm sorry."

"I have lived a good and long life, full of love." He shifted. "Now, will you continue to draw my picture?"

I looked out the library door, feeling again like an intruder and wondering if Donata should be sitting with her husband, not me.

Lucio followed my gaze. "She has gone to her garden. Again, it is about timing. She needs to get out."

I lifted my toolbox off the floor, grabbed a few pencils, and reopened my sketch pad.

"Tell me what you've seen since you arrived. Have you been to the church? San Biagio?"

"The church in the square? Yes, Ben took me there on Tuesday."

"You need to go back. I will take you." Lucio's eyes drifted shut, then popped open. "You need my eyes open, don't you?" He glanced to my lap. There was no hiding the five deep brown pencils.

"I'm working on your nose," I lied. "Actually, I'm not drawing anything. I make a bunch of little lines on the sides of the charcoal drawings to capture color; I don't actually color my drawings."

He wrinkled his nose. "May I see it?"

"Soon." I smiled and went back to our conversation. "I thought you and Donata went to Santa Maria."

"We do, but I want you to talk to Don Matteo. There is work at San Biagio we must discuss."

I laid down the pencil. "Did Ben tell you that?"

Lucio's eyes flashed something I couldn't name. "How does Ben know?"

"How do you know? That's the first thing I noticed. The paintings. He thought Joseph worked on them when he was there his last summer, but there's more to be done. There is definitely moisture in the framing, if not the artwork. I thought I'd ask."

"I was talking about the mural."

"I didn't see any mural." I mentally retraced my steps through the church.

"It's there. Covered. On the south side of the transept, across from the small altar . . . It's a job for someone who fixes broken things."

Chapter 23

The bells woke me again. Despite Ben's assurances, they were not fading away.

I lay awake and revisited the previous day. After lunch, I'd climbed the ladder again to examine the ceiling paintings. At first it was uncomfortable as Donata huffed and puffed her way around me, going to and from the library. But she finally calmed down, sat and chatted with Lucio, and I was able to focus. I could catch notes of their conversation and bits of laughter. Donata's voice surprised me. It was soft and coaxing, like a lullaby.

But I was certain that wasn't the Donata I would encounter today. Every time she looked at me the music stopped.

I whispered into the lightening room, "Are you awake?"

Ben grabbed me around the waist and pulled me close. "No. Are you awake?"

"Can I go with you this morning? To Coccocino?"

"Why would you want to do that?"

"To be with you." That sounded much better than *To get out of here*. And it was true. I loved watching Ben work and come alive as he made his pizza dough or his bread starters or even as he peeled

vegetables. He often forgot others were around and sang. It was enough to be near him.

"Of course you can. It is time I got up, though." He leaned over and kissed me. "Things are a mess."

I sat up. "What's a mess?"

He shook his head as he pulled on jeans and stepped into the bathroom. "It is our busiest time. We make 75 percent of the year's income in the summer, and our farmers have not been delivering, the books have been left unmanaged, the kitchen is in shambles. We do not have enough produce, and the meat and fish orders are wrong."

"How did all that happen?"

"Francesca." He smiled, small and flat.

We headed downstairs, and once again there was a beautiful platter of fruits and meats on the table.

"*Sei in anticipo*," Donata called from across the kitchen.

"I need to be at the restaurant early. We are behind on prep and . . ." Ben stopped as if he decided it was news best not shared. "There is much to do."

He crossed to the espresso machine and began to pull us both shots. "Mama?" He gestured to a small cup.

"*Sì.*" She nodded with a smile—which completely disappeared as she glanced my direction. "You are up too. To paint?"

"I thought I'd go to Coccocino with Ben. See if I can help him."

Donata merely raised an eyebrow. I had to give her credit; not one word spoken, and she said plenty.

I dropped into a chair, accepted my espresso with a tolerably fluid "*Grazie*," and ate a little breakfast. Ben joined me, but Donata kissed him on the top of the head and carried her coffee out of the room.

I caught his eye.

"She just wants to see Papa."

"I'm sure that's it." I smiled.

Within minutes, we, too, were out the door. Ben tossed me the keys.

"You're kidding?"

"You cannot spend all day and night in Montevello. You will have to get back somehow. You have already driven it."

I dropped into the driver's seat, remembering our trip to return the rental car. I had lurched along behind him in this very car, stripping its gears and stalling at every intersection.

Ben sat very still as I ground around within the gears and finally got his car going the right direction. At the first intersection he sat silent.

"You aren't going to tell me where to go?"

"You have driven this way before. You will remember better if you figure it out."

"Don't blame me if you're late." I turned the car left. He flinched. "Ha!" I drove to a roundabout a few meters away, circled it, then doubled back the way I'd come and straight up the hill beyond.

Ben grinned. "Told you."

Once I got out of the valley and could see Montevello perched above me, it was easy to find my way. I wove carefully through the narrow archway, up to the town square, then back down the one artery I knew—the one to the car park near Coccocino.

"Are there other parking lots?"

"This is the best. There is one more on the other side, but getting through the arch there is tough, even for me, and the spots are smaller."

"This is the one for me then. I can't imagine any parking spaces smaller than these."

We hopped out and wove our way through the narrow walking passages to Tartaruga Café.

"Have you ever thought about living here, in the town?"

Ben looked around and shrugged. "When Francesca moved here, she asked that too. I never thought about it."

"Francesca lives here?" I hadn't thought about where Francesca lived. "We should . . ."

Ben waggled his thumb and finger at Sandra in greeting. "We should what?"

Something told me now was not the time . . . "Nothing. Nothing at all."

We carried our cups to Coccocino. No one else had arrived.

"I have the *soffritto* to make. Do you want to help?"

"What is it?"

"The cut vegetables, the dressings, that form the base of sauces, risotto, much of what we make." While he spoke, he laid down bunches of carrots and celery and a bowlful of onions. Soon his knife was flying.

I started in beside him, cutting more slowly, and in larger pieces.

He glanced over. I could see his brows furrow and could barely resist touching between my own as he'd done to me many times.

"It's not my forte, is it?"

"You can help in other ways."

I wiped off my hands and looked around. "I'll find something." I walked over to a side counter. There were about twenty knives resting next to the sharpening stone. Those I knew how to handle.

About an hour later Ben came over. "You are so quiet."

"I enjoy this work. Do you want a new knife?"

"Yes. Mine felt dull. That is another thing; no one sharpened knives the entire time I was gone."

I handed him one and followed him back to collect his. The next moment brought a scream and a flash of red across his white coat as Ben held his hand tight.

"What did you do?" he demanded.

"I sharpened it. What?"

He crossed to the sink and rinsed his hand. "It is not bad." He spoke more to himself than to me. He then walked to a side cabinet and pulled down ointment and gauze.

"Let me help." I reached for his hand. The cut wasn't deep, a tiny thin slice across the pads of all four fingers. "What happened?"

"I . . ." Ben's voice lifted in question as he pulled away and walked back to the knife. He lifted it to the light. "These are only beveled on one edge of this side of the blade. You never sharpen both. I sometimes use this flat edge for leverage."

"I didn't know." As he laid it down, I reached for his hand and quickly cleaned it before wrapping it in the gauze.

"It is not your fault, but—"

"I should've asked. I thought I could . . ." My voice drifted away as Ben closed his eyes. I knew that look, not because I'd seen it on him before, but because I'd felt it on my own face—usually when dealing with Amy.

"I am worried, Emily." His voice was low and tight. "There is too much going on. This is too important."

"I know. I'm sorry."

"Come here." He opened his eyes and waved me over with his good hand. The other was clenched in a fist at his side. He draped

his arm around my shoulders and pulled me close. "I do want you here. Is there something else you can do?"

"As much as I'd like to say yes, we both know you don't need me here right now. Let me head back home and work on your dad's ceiling. He would like that, and it is something I know how to do."

Ben's face cleared, then clouded. "I am not trying—"

I laid a hand on his chest. "I know you're not, but you're busy and now you're hurt." I pushed back and pulled the strings of my apron loose. "I will go, you get stuff done here and I'll see you back at home tonight." I reached up and kissed him.

"This is not how I wanted your first days to be." He shook his head.

"There's a lot going on, and none of it is your fault . . . I'll see you tonight. Okay?"

"Bene." Ben returned to his vegetables, and I slipped out Coccocino's back door.

I wandered up the walk, not ready to return home quite yet.

"Good morning."

"Lucio? What are you doing here?"

"Donata had some errands, and I came along. I have had a robust coffee at Tartaruga and visited with Sandra. I like her."

"Me too." I fell into step beside him.

"Are you going to help Ben?"

I looked back toward Coccocino. "I've already done enough there. I was in the way. I was actually heading home to your ceiling."

Lucio linked his arm through mine and stopped. "Then you have a moment."

"I do."

"Let me catch my breath. I'm so tired."

"Do you want me to get Ben's car?" I looked down the narrow

road. This was not one on which the car could fit. "Tell me what to do."

"I'll be fine. Just move slowly . . . Come with me." Leaning heavily on my arm, he led us to the church.

I pulled open the heavy door. Two steps and we were engulfed in a cool quiet—the only sound the tapping of Lucio's cane in between our brief moments of rest.

He turned at the altar and headed into one of the transepts. There was a small altar on one wall and a few pews facing it. He walked to the plain back wall and spread his hand flat against it, much the way I did when trying to feel moisture within a wall.

"It's here, the mural I told you about."

"It's covered? I can't just start stripping the paint." I stopped talking as the sound of a door shutting echoed through the church.

A man, a priest by his black clothes and white collar, rounded the corner.

"Lucio?" He paused. *"È bello vederti."*

Lucio stepped forward, kissed him on both cheeks, and ended it all with a hug. "Good to see you too," he said in English. "Emily, let me introduce Don Matteo. Don, please welcome Ben's wife, Emily."

"Ah . . ." Don Matteo smiled and spread his arms wide. After a double kiss, ending with another hug, he, too, continued in English. "I had heard Ben married. It is so nice to meet you."

"It's nice to meet you too." I nodded, wondering how quickly I could ask about the Stations of the Cross paintings.

But Lucio had another job in mind.

"I need to talk to you, Don Matteo." Lucio stepped back to the wall. "Joseph painted a mural here many years ago, while working for Don Pietro. He spent an entire summer on it. I would consider it a great favor to allow Emily to uncover it. It is her work, restoration."

"A mural? I have never heard of this."

"It was long before your time. He worked for Don Pietro in the summer of 2000, doing repairs, restoration, and odd jobs in the church. Then he started the painting, and it . . . it consumed him for three months."

"Where is it?" Don Matteo looked at the blank wall.

"Under here." Lucio tapped the wall. "I need to see it again . . ."

Before I die finished his sentence even if he didn't say the words.

Don Matteo pulled his neck back in surprise, then nodded in understanding. He'd heard the unspoken ending as well.

"I will look through our records and see if I can find any notes. Will you come back in a few days? We can discuss it then."

"*Bene.* I thank you." Lucio clasped the priest's hand within both of his own as if it were a done deal.

Chapter 24

The next day I stayed home. And after another fairly silent lunch, I climbed back up the ladder to finish washing the second half of the mural. Ben had spent almost an hour the previous night rubbing out the neck crick the first half gave me—with his one good hand. I'd spent that hour apologizing that he had only one.

Donata and Lucio again sat in the library. I liked seeing them like this. He was the same no matter where he was or with whom he was chatting, but she was transformed. Around me she was lines and angles, stiff words and clenched fists. Peeking through the door, I saw the fluid movements of a dancer, a curving neck and hands rising and dipping as if telling a slow and beautiful story. I heard soft laughter fill the room.

They were talking of books. I caught titles here and there and words I knew connected to stories.

Lucio was telling her what he'd read, how it felt, and what it meant to him. She didn't answer back, as if her stories didn't come from books, but she kept asking questions. *"Dimmi di più."*

Tell me more.

Soon I noticed the lack of all sound, and moments later the door opened fully.

"He is asleep," Donata noted as she passed by my ladder. I peeked in the open doorway to find Lucio, head to chest in his favorite armchair.

I worked on, dropping my saturated cotton balls into a bucket with a soft *plink* every few minutes.

Much later I heard another voice somewhere below me.

"Anybody home?"

I looked down and had to grab the back of my neck with the motion. The 180-degree shift sent shooting pain down my spine. I stepped down to ease the angle.

"Your father is sleeping in the library, and your mom . . ." I had no idea how much time had passed. "I think she left the house. I heard the front door shut a while ago."

"Her car isn't here. I came in the back." Francesca stepped toward the kitchen. "Come meet a friend." I followed, trying to fix my hair and straighten my T-shirt as I went.

Anne had been right that first day. Francesca was a beauty, delicate and quiet. She had the raven hair of her mother, but a more delicate jawline and nose. It made her feel like a whisper, while Donata, to me, personified a scream.

A small yelp stopped my attempts at grooming and dropped me to the floor. "Who is this?"

The dog immediately climbed on me as if trying to dig into my lap, its tongue darting up to capture my face. "Oh . . . okay . . . We're going to tip . . . We're tipping now."

"Natale, get off her. *Via.*"

"I like it." I righted myself as the dog settled into my lap and offered up her belly. "Natale?"

"It means Christmas. Ben gave her to me last Christmas. Silly, huh?"

"Not at all." I rubbed Natale's silky ears. She was white with light brown spots. "You are so cute." I rubbed her all over. "Is she a spaniel?"

"Probably a mix of several spaniels . . . She's never going to leave you alone now."

"That's a good thing. I might keep you," I said in the singsong voice globally reserved for dogs and babies. I dropped my voice and looked up to Francesca. "What are you up to today?"

"I was finishing up end-of-year cleaning at school. Tomorrow I start setting up for summer camp." She gestured to the dog, still wrapped within my arms. "Do you want to see her work?"

"What does she do?"

"She's a truffle dog." At my expression, she continued. "You know . . . truffles. You serve them in restaurants, shave them over pasta."

"I know what they are, but I thought they used pigs for that."

"In France. Here we use dogs, and she's the best. Aren't you, girl?"

My doting dog immediately left my lap and leapt to Francesca. "Traitor," I called after her.

"She knows who feeds her." Francesca rubbed Natale behind her ears, and the dog's left hind leg started an *allegro* tap on the floor. "Come with me tomorrow. It'll be the last time I can go until camp ends. Alessandro and I will head out around nine."

"Alessandro? Ben mentioned him."

"You haven't met him yet? He's one of Ben's best friends. You'll like him."

"That's what everyone says about all Ben's friends."

"And?"

"I do."

~

Ben climbed into bed beside me. "What are you reading?"

"Your father gave me this."

Ben tilted the cover toward himself. "*The Taming of the Shrew*?"

"He and your mom were talking all morning, and when they came out for lunch he reached up and laid this on the ladder. Not a word. Just a wink. What's up with that?"

"You'd have to ask. He loves his books." Ben tapped my nose. "Almost as much as you love yours."

"Not exactly the same books." I laid the book in my lap. "I met Natale today."

"Was Mama here?"

Speaking of shrews. I bit my tongue and simply shook my head.

"That is a good thing. She hates dogs. Francesca sometimes brings Natale to annoy her. Now is not the time for that."

I began to get a fuller picture of why Francesca didn't live at home. "She invited us truffle hunting."

"Ah . . ." Ben leaned back. "I forgot to mention that. She texted me today, too, and I accepted. Is that okay?"

"Sure. When she asked me, I did the same."

Ben closed his eyes.

It gave me a chance to study him unobserved. The lines around his eyes dug a little deeper tonight. "Good night?"

"Busy. Too many bumps."

"Would it be easier if we lived closer? In the village? Maybe near Francesca?"

Ben cracked open one eye and stared at me. "I . . . Are you okay

here? I caught that before, but . . . now is not the time for that. Are you unhappy?"

I reached over and clicked off the light.

Hiding my emotions, my expressions, was easier in the dark. "Of course not. Forget I said anything."

After a deep exhale, he pulled me close. "This cannot be easy. I know that. But I need . . . I need your patience. I wanted to bring you home and I envisioned how it would be, how it would feel. This is nothing like my vision."

My heart dropped as every fear rose before me. "Is it me?" He had discovered the truth. He saw the real me. I was not *that girl*. I was . . . me . . . And that wasn't enough.

He squeezed me tight. "Never you. Other than the knives." I could hear a smile on his lips. "But Mama and Papa . . . Life will never be the same again, and I should be here. But instead, I am there even more than usual because it is a mess. Coccocino was his life's work, Papa's family legacy, and I cannot let that slip. Not now."

I curled into him because, while I might not know much about his family, I understood pressure, fear, the need to fix things, and the black hole that opened within you when you realized nothing could fix all that was broken.

Chapter 25

"What are we doing again?" I pulled on a pair of jeans and a long-sleeved T-shirt. "Won't we be hot?"

"You dig through brambles up there. You will want to be covered, and we will be home before it gets too hot. I need to be at Coccocino by noon." Ben tapped my back, urging me to go faster down the stairs. "Alessandro, if we are lucky, will feed us."

At the bottom I turned to the kitchen. He opened the front door. "No breakfast?"

"No time. We are late. Francesca promised me all Natale's truffles. I do not want them to leave without us."

I followed, but not without a sense of dread. Somehow not showing up at breakfast was going to be my fault, and somehow Donata was going to make it very clear.

Ben circled the house rather than hop in his car. "It is a rough ride up the mountain. We will drive the truck."

I caught up as he hopped into an old pickup truck, like 1950s old. "Why'd Joseph tease me about my station wagon? This is much older."

"Joseph hated this truck, but it runs well. Papa would never sell it."

Soon I understood the truck's necessity as we bounced along a rugged country road, climbing higher and higher up the side of a mountain. Ben's tiny tin-can car was much too delicate for such an adventure.

"Explain to me dogs versus pigs. Francesca said Italy is dogs; France, pigs."

"And therein lies our national superiority." Ben winked. "Dogs are as effective in sniffing the truffles, but they do not eat them. A pig you have to pull off quickly or no truffle. A dog will dig it up and bring it back."

The switchback turns grew tighter and tighter as we reached the top.

"Aren't those olive trees? . . . They're different," I commented.

"They are, but the leaves are smaller and sparser up here. These are the last until we dip back below six hundred meters. They will not grow above that altitude." Ben looked out the window. "And those only produce about five kilos of olives per tree. My parents' trees will give twenty to twenty-five kilos. More oil, but more subtle flavors than what those trees give. I use both at Coccocino."

He leaned forward and pointed out my window as we crested the top and began a rapid descent. "All this land, from that hill"—he swept his hand across the full expanse of the horizon—"has been in my family since the thirteenth century."

"All this land is yours?"

"With seven other families. It is private land the church sold to us in the mid-1600s. All direct descendants can hunt on it—no one else. For us, it is through Nonna. But the land around it is all fair game, even though it, too, is private. Different designations.

We can hunt that land, but it is best not to get caught. A standing agreement about no daytime hunting on someone else's land exists. It is impolite. Night is another story."

"And I'm betting you took full advantage of that." I shook my head at Ben's mischievous smile.

"After we stripped the truffles from close by, we took Alessandro's dog to a few select farms. She was so quiet, no one knew. We earned our spending money. Here truffles do not bring much, but back then was the beginning of shipping them to the States. We were paid a few hundred euros from a couple restaurant buyers, and they then sold them abroad, probably earning thousands."

"That hardly seems fair."

"That is the way of the world. And we would not turn down a few hundred euros."

Without slowing, Ben pulled a sharp right and drove us into a narrow lane. "Alessandro caught on, though. He has expanded his family's farm to host truffle hunts, lunches, and full-day experiences for tourists. *Agriturismo* at its finest. Today will only be us, though."

The truck lurched into a compound—more accurately, a random collection of farmhouses built around a central courtyard. There didn't seem to be any sense of planning, as though another structure was simply built when and wherever there was need.

Francesca waved from a side yard filled with dogs. "You're late." She bounded toward the car and hugged Ben.

"Stop whining." He laughed. He then bent and picked up Natale, who covered him with kisses.

"Don't try to steal her. You can have the truffles, but she hunts for me today."

"She knows who loves her. Yes you do, *cucciola*. I knew you had

the nose. Yes you do, yes you do." He lowered Natale to the ground, but she kept trying to jump back into his arms.

"Benvenuto!"

A short, broad man strode from between the buildings and hugged Ben tight, slapping him on the back.

When they separated, Ben gestured to me. "Alessandro. Emily."

"Ah . . ." Alessandro nodded. *"La moglie del pizzaiolo."*

The pizza maker's wife. Andre had started calling me that too. It was new, being called not by name, but in relation to someone else. At first it scraped up my spine. Now . . . I was beginning to enjoy it. It gave me a sense of place, in a place where everyone else already belonged.

Ben glanced at me before correcting Alessandro. "Emily."

I shifted my eyes away, a little embarrassed at what he may have seen in them during Andre's first teasing.

Alessandro pounded Ben's back. "Come grab an espresso and we'll be off."

Ben followed Alessandro back to the squat house. Francesca watched them both and kept patting Natale. I watched Francesca.

Ben emerged minutes later holding two small china espresso cups. He handed one to me, then threw his back like a shot. I tried to do the same and ended up coughing. Alessandro laughed. Ben winked. Francesca said nothing.

"Let's go." Alessandro waved his arm in the air and barked out a quick command that all the dogs understood. We set our cups on the stone wall and followed. Ben caught up with him quickly, while I hung back with Francesca. Within five steps, Alessandro and Ben veered to the right and headed up a steep footpath. The dogs raced after them, passed them, dove through the brush, and were gone.

"Here we go." Francesca spread her arm out, inviting me to climb the path first. "I love these mornings. When we were kids they never let me come, especially on their night raids. I was probably too young, but I hated being left behind."

"Is this why he gave you the dog? To truffle hunt?"

Francesca's eyes followed her brother. "He simply said I needed one. He even had Natale trained for me."

Within minutes the dogs started pawing at the ground, tails wagging. Some squealed and danced. Others remained quiet and focused. They would dig a small hole, nip at it, then scurry to either Francesca or Alessandro and drop a small black rock into their hands, then nose their pockets.

"They're only interested in the treats." Francesca held her palm out with a small kibble in it for Natale.

"That's it?" I laughed.

"She's very easy to please." When Natale dashed away again, Francesca held the truffle out to me. "Want to see one?"

"Sure." I expected my hand to drop with the weight when she tossed it into my palm, but it didn't. The truffle was hard, wrinkly, and brown, but light. "I thought truffles were white. And it's so hard." I scraped at it with my nail.

We walked on.

"These are summer black. You're thinking of winter white." Francesca gestured to a string bag hanging from Alessandro's waist. "What we've collected so far today will bring in about a thousand euros. If they were winter white, it'd be twenty thousand. But you'd never find so many white at one time. Very rare. And they're all hard. Haven't you seen them shaved in restaurants?"

I handed it back to her. "Not the restaurants I frequent."

"You'll get to taste these. They're wonderful." Francesca carefully put the truffle in a bag hanging from her waist. "A gentler

taste than the whites. Probably gauche to say, but I like them better."

We followed the dogs around a path with which they were clearly familiar, pushing in and through brambles. Ben had been right, long clothing was needed, as every exposed inch was soon covered in small scratches. Within about an hour we arrived at the farmhouse.

"We're back? Was it a circle?" I looked back up the path.

Ben joined us. "It was. We have four routes, as truffles tend to be in certain places and return again and again. We walk the same paths many times a season." He thumped Alessandro's shoulder. "Are you feeding us today?"

"*Certamente.* Come on." Alessandro led us into the small building from which Ben had emerged with the coffees. It was a beautiful kitchen, almost rivaling Donata's, with countertops a mixture of stainless steel, marble, and wood. "We cook the lunches in here when we lead the tours." He glanced back to Ben. "Eggs?"

"Whatever you want to serve. You are the chef."

Alessandro grumbled and pulled over a basket of eggs. He flipped on the gas burner under an iron pan and started cracking the eggs into it.

My jaw dropped slightly. This man knew his way around a kitchen. One hand to crack eggs. Knife flying over a variety of herbs. He whisked a fork faster than my hand mixer. And minutes later he scooped eggs out onto plates, drizzled them with olive oil, and shaved a good portion of one of our truffles over them. He pushed the plates across the counter.

The first bite melted in my mouth. "I splurged on a tiny bottle of truffle oil last year for salads, but this is so much better."

"Bella! You did not." Ben slapped his forehead. "You were swindled."

"How?"

Francesca smiled. "Because there's no such thing. It's only olive oil and synthetic flavoring. Truffles have no oil."

"I paid thirty bucks for that bottle."

Alessandro scooped another helping onto my plate. "Happens to us all. I got swindled once too."

Ben and I left a few minutes later, happily full and carrying a good-sized bag of truffles for Coccocino. Francesca stayed to help Alessandro clean the kitchen.

As we bumped along home, I turned to Ben. "Does Francesca like Alessandro?"

"Yes." Ben offered nothing more.

"And?"

"There is nothing more to say. I know she does."

"Have you mentioned it to him?"

This caught Ben's attention. "Why would I?"

"Eyes over there." I flapped my hand back toward the road. "Because maybe he hasn't noticed. He seems really shy."

"He is, and we need to leave him be."

"Why?" I saw a project emerging.

"My sister and my best friend do not need me digging into their lives, especially their love lives. Got it?"

"Got it." I laughed at his tone. It veered toward repulsion. "No brother and best friend digging into their love lives."

Ben chuckled softly. "That includes my wife."

He drifted away in thought, which was fine with me. I had a plan to develop.

"You are too quiet. It worries me."

I glanced over at him and thought up a quick distraction. "Do you want to get a dog?"

"Hmm . . . You are making me think, Bella, that you are not happy here. Are you?"

Something in his tone made the hair on the back of my neck prickle. "Why would you ask that?"

"First an apartment. Now a dog."

My mind instantly recalled Ben's statement. *Mama hates dogs.* Another statement of his smacked me simultaneously. *Now is not the time for that.*

I looked out the window and wondered how long I'd get things wrong. A month ago, life made sense. Now I was sitting in a pickup truck, in Italy, next to my husband, who had a bandaged hand, living with his parents. And I'd just insulted everything he held dear . . . again.

I felt a tap on the back of my head.

Ben was watching me; his eyes held a simultaneously sad and loving look. "This is different from your world. It is different even from mine. I hope you understand."

I shrugged—to answer would bring tears. I took a deep breath and thought of something I could do.

"Do you think Francesca would let me help her set up for camp?"

"She certainly would." Ben reached over and rubbed the back of my neck. I leaned into his hand; my neck still hurt from working on the ceiling.

Ben took the final sloping left off the mountain and headed to his parents' house. He glanced at me. "It is not so bad, is it?"

The hitch in his voice caught me. I twisted fully to him. "Not at all. I love your dad. And the ceiling is looking wonderful, isn't it? Even your mom has stopped grumbling about it."

"Bene."

I reached over and laid both my hands on his arm. Sometimes you need to feel someone to know they're with you, completely with you. "I am fine, Ben. Please don't worry about me."

"I do worry. I love you. I worry about Francesca too. And Mama. It will not be easy. What is to come."

Lucio.

He continued. "Thank you for going to Francesca's camp. She will need a sister right now."

"I'll go tomorrow. I might also offer to help out at camp when the kids arrive. Bring my paints in or something."

"She will like that too."

Chapter 26

I walked up the short path to the school. It was a low building and I entered at ground level, but I could see the hill drop away behind it. I suspected it was built into the hill like Anne's castle and that its floors extended many levels down. It took a few minutes of wandering the bright and fully decorated hallways before I found Francesca's classroom.

"Hey." I knocked on the doorjamb. "Are you busy?"

"Just finishing up. What are you doing here?" She was sitting on a tiny chair filling white plastic bins with crayons, scissors, and other supplies.

"I came to see if I could help and show you something I thought the kids might enjoy." I propped a white canvas against her desk and dug through my toolbox for a bottle of my gentlest solvent. I didn't need to be too careful, so I soaked a cotton ball and dabbed it against the white. Red burst through at my first touch.

"You painted over a painting?"

"I thought they might think it fun to discover a painting rather than make one."

"They will." Francesca leaned against her desk and smiled.

"You remind me of Joseph. He used to get excited by stuff like that too. Even as a kid, I remember him repairing things, uncovering things. He used to help out at the church a lot and even worked at a small gallery here in Greve, touching up damaged pieces."

"He doesn't come home much, does he?"

"It's been several years now. Papa went to Atlanta a few years ago to visit, probably five now. As you gathered, Mama didn't go." She shook her head. "Papa didn't invite me, but I don't know that I would've gone if he had. I'm tired of chasing my brother."

"I got the impression something happened." I heard my line hit the water before I could stop it. I shook my head. "It's none of my business."

"It kind of is now, isn't it?" Francesca quirked a smile, lifting one side of her mouth. "And if you can find out what it was, you're a better detective than I am, because I've asked. Papa says Joseph chose to leave, but prays he'll find his way home. Mama won't discuss it at all. And if Ben knows, he's never said. He and Joseph were close once, but that's gone too."

"I'm sorry." I understood fractured families and the glue we dabbed on to try to repair them. It never stuck, never held fast. "Families are complicated. My dad was furious that I got married."

"Why?" Francesca barked.

I wanted to hug her. Loyalty spread through every aspect of her being. She clearly couldn't understand why anyone would be upset about his daughter marrying her brother.

I laughed. "It had nothing to do with Ben. I don't think it even bothered him that he hadn't met Ben. It had to do with me being impulsive and rash and dropping the ball with my sister, shirking responsibility. As I said, families are complicated."

Francesca nodded but didn't ask any more questions.

I gestured to the white canvas. "The solvent is a specialized

soap, completely safe. The kids can use it themselves if you think they'd like to do this. I could bring several small canvases."

"They'll love it. Do you want to come present it to them?" At my eager nod, she walked to her desk and flipped open a calendar. "I keep the mornings fairly free for self-directed activities. You can come any day you like."

"Perfect. I don't even have a calendar to check. I'm wide open." I picked up the painting and propped it beside the table.

"Ben's busy right now, isn't he?" She laid down the calendar and returned to the small table. "I messed up at Coccocino. Noemi should have been in charge, but Mama forced me and, it being my family's place, no one had the guts to tell me what I didn't know. And I knew nothing."

"He's busy, but I can't help either. Actually, I'm doing the opposite. The bandage on Ben's hand? I did that by sharpening all his knives. I had no idea that some knives have blades with only one beveled edge."

"They do?"

"See? Who knew?" Whether she knew about the knives or not, she got my humor, played along, and with a single question made me feel at home. I almost hugged her for it.

My biggest struggle with Italy was not the language. Ben was right, most people spoke English, and I understood enough Italian to misinterpret almost every conversation. But nuance, humor, sarcasm, and reversals—all that was lost. Everything was heavy and literal and lonely. And Ben couldn't help me. I was alone. I'd even called Amy a couple times, just to spar.

We sat quietly for a few minutes, filling the plastic boxes, and I finally felt at ease.

Francesca broke the silence. "What'd you think of the hunt?"

"I loved it. Something about it made me feel a part of this land

and your family like I hadn't before." I quirked a small smile. "Sitting here comes a close second."

"I'm glad . . . I won't be able to go for a few weeks because camps run on the weekends, too, but Ben can take you back up to hunt. Or wait, and I promise, you, me, and Natale will go once camp ends."

"Deal." I moved on to another box. "Alessandro's a handsome guy." I was back to fishing.

Francesca slid me a glance. "What did Ben say?"

"Nothing, I promise. In fact, when I asked him about you two, he very clearly told me to keep away."

Francesca blushed a beautiful rose color. It was warm against the black of her hair. A blush on me was more of a blotchy oil-mixed-with-water affair, a discordant clash of color. I envied the whole cream-and-roses look.

"You can report back that there's nothing to tell." Francesca dropped her voice.

"I'm not reporting anything to Ben. I've already treaded on dangerous ground asking. But . . . I'm not so sure. I saw the way Alessandro looked at you. He watches you, and guys don't do that with friends or sisters of friends."

Even yesterday morning when he'd been annoyed, Ben had looked at me like nothing could or would change his love. Never consciously noting it before, I recognized it now. There was a look. It was special and it needed to be savored, protected, cherished.

I rested there a minute, and the giddiness of discovery passed as a flutter of guilt wafted in. I was not protecting it now—Ben had asked me not to interfere.

But I didn't retreat. "I think if Alessandro thought one day that he couldn't look at you like that—he'd miss it."

"What do you mean?" Francesca's hands stilled.

"You can't miss what's always in front of you."

She lifted both brows. "You remind me of Emma."

"Who?"

"A character in a book. A matchmaker." Francesca sat back in the tiny chair, tipping it onto its back legs. "Mama isn't demonstrative, instructive, I guess, and Papa . . . You know him. He's a storyteller. If he can't put a lesson into a story, he'll give you a book and hope you learn it from there. He's not very direct."

I thought back to all the books Lucio was stacking next to my chair. I'd been sure there was a plan.

Francesca continued. "Anyway, Emma's a matchmaker. Papa made me read her story when I was about ten to teach me humility; at least that's what I think I was to learn. Then before I could go on a date, at sixteen by the way, he made me read *Vanity Fair*. That was supposed to teach me about the hypocrisy of humans, the games we play and the ways we use each other. Open my eyes and all that. But I haven't dated anyone . . . I've been in love with Alessandro since I was eleven, fifteen long years. Talk about a humbling experience."

"Maybe you need a plan."

"It isn't that I haven't been trying to come up with one, you know. Do you think it's fun waiting on the sidelines hoping you'll get noticed?"

"I know it isn't."

"Did Ben keep you waiting?"

I barked out a quick laugh. "Two weeks from meet to marry? No. Ben was the dream that swept me off the sidelines. He sees something in me I still don't see, and I pray every day he won't realize he imagined it all along."

"What do you see in him?"

"In Ben . . ." I, too, leaned back in my chair. "He's bright and true and cares about all the right things. The world is better with

him near, and the idea of his leaving was like the thought of losing an arm or a leg, or some part of me I'm not sure I could live without."

"I've never heard love described that way, but it makes sense. That's how I feel, even about Alessandro's friendship. To risk that feels foolish."

"I get that." I dropped a pair of scissors into the last box. "But you're still on the sidelines."

Chapter 27

ees buzzed. Something heavy held me down. I tried to wriggle away, certain I'd be stung and that I'd done something wrong. *Did I swat the nest?*

Garbled words met my ears. I opened one eye to find Ben reaching across me to grab his phone. He shifted himself upright as he listened.

"What's wrong?" I whispered.

He held up one finger, asking me to wait. *"Bene, bene, Mama."* He said the phrase over and over until he hung up.

"What's up?"

"Francesca didn't show up at camp this morning, and the director got worried and called Mama."

"It's only eight in the morning. She probably overslept." I sat up. "Why's your mom calling? Isn't she downstairs?"

"She took Papa to Assisi today."

Lucio had talked about it during dinner. Donata was against it. Ben was against it. Francesca was against it. I was silent. And Lucio was determined to go.

"I need to see the Basilica again. Assisi is very special to me.

Or you could take me to Roma? To see San Pietro . . ." He'd even laid his hand on his heart.

"Papa. You can't go to Rome. It's a long drive. You're not up for that." Francesca rested her hand on his arm.

"Good. Assisi is only an hour away. We will leave in the morning. I am best then."

Donata had been silent the rest of the meal.

Ben climbed out of bed and pulled on a pair of pants and a gray T-shirt. "I told Mama I will check Francesca's apartment. Do you want to come?"

"Sure." I scampered off the other side.

We left the car outside the outer wall of Montevello this time and walked through a pedestrian arch. We followed the wall across two "spokes" to what appeared to be an old aqueduct collection area. Ben knocked on a door built into the wall.

"This is the coolest place ever."

"Her roommate, Caterina, inherited it from her aunt. And it is literally the coolest place also. Her top floor looks out over the wall; otherwise all her windows are on this side, and because of the few windows and the thick walls, it stays very cool. I store overflow wine here."

"Only you would think of that."

"I'm not the only one. Osteria Acquacheta does it too."

"Michel's place? She shouldn't help him; he's the competition," I teased.

"Bah . . . What helps one helps all. Besides, he taught me most of what I know. Coccocino's kitchen was too intimidating at times."

"Ah . . . Mama." I nodded with meaning.

Ben bobbed his head in time with mine. "Yes, Mama." He banged on the door. After several good thwacks, he lifted a flowerpot and grabbed a key.

"You can't do that. What about the roommate?"

"Caterina should be at work, too, and if not . . ." He opened the door and called inside. "*Ciao*, Caterina!"

There was no answer.

The door opened into a small dark kitchen, as wooden shutters blocked the window. I placed my hand against an interior wall. Ben was right. The stones were cool. While I stood looking around, Ben flipped a light switch, then walked straight to a small glass table and picked up a piece of paper.

I peered over his shoulder, but I couldn't read the cramped script. Cramped Italian script. I craned closer and saw Francesca's name at the top. "So?"

No reply.

"What's it say?"

"It says Caterina would like to know where my sister slept last night, that she has not seen her since yesterday afternoon, and that she is angry she cannot reach her." He put the note down and pulled out his phone. He tapped it for a call. No answer. He tapped out a text.

"Could she have slept at Alessandro's?"

Ben spun around. "Why would you ask that?"

"Because she's in love with him. He's in love with her, too, you know."

He narrowed his eyes, thinking. He whispered to himself in Italian, but *stupid* translates.

"Wait a minute. What's so—"

He held up the same finger he had in our room, asking me to

wait. But it was not a gentle request this time. His stiff posture made it a demand. He tapped his phone again.

I stood there as a torrent of fast-flowing Italian spewed into the phone and back out. Standing three feet from Ben, I could hear Alessandro's tense raised voice as clearly as if he stood beside us.

Ben tapped off the phone and sank into one of the kitchen chairs.

I pulled out another, scraping the legs across the stone floor, and sat across from him. "So? What's up?"

"Francesca went up there last night and told him she would not be around this summer. Some nonsense about time, space, moving on or maybe forward. It made no sense." Ben lifted a brow, annoyed. "He was yelling."

"I heard . . . So he got angry and convinced her to stay?"

Ben sat perfectly still, his eyes on the tabletop.

I snapped my fingers in front of his nose. "Why was he angry?"

"He was angry because he felt she was manipulating him. He told her to be gone already."

"I don't—"

Ben raked his hands through his hair, pulling at the short ends, his nails white with tension. "Alessandro was married for a couple months about six years ago. No one talks about it, because it was annulled and we spread the rumor that it was no big deal. He had met her in Rome and she wanted to go home; she was young and regretted it. End of story."

"And . . ."

"The truth, which only I know, is that his wife 'moved on' with a wine buyer from Germany. And he was destroyed. Alessandro never trusts easily, but when he does it is firm and he is a solid

friend. It takes long to get that trust. Francesca had it, and now . . . it is finished."

"You said you didn't even know if they were interested in each other, and you knew all this?"

"I am not blind. Why do you think I gave her Natale? It gave her a reason to be up there."

"You gave her the dog as a matchmaking tool?" *And she called* me *Emma?*

"Francesca needed to grow up, and Alessandro needed time. It felt right."

"Could you have clued me in?"

Ben looked sharply at me. "Why? It was not our business. I told you it was not." He leaned back in the chair, all sharpness draining away. "He is a good man, Emily. But this is not good."

I reached out and touched Ben's hand, then withdrew mine. This was going to be easier with no contact. "I need to tell you something, but you can't get mad."

"Why not?" he asked with curious sincerity.

I stifled a groan. It wasn't literal!

I took a deep breath and tried again. "I mean I'd rather you didn't. Because I think this will make you mad and . . . I pushed Francesca to talk to Alessandro. No, that's not true. No pushing, but seed planting. I definitely planted a seed about talking to him. Not a big seed. Very small. Mustard-seed size. Tiny. Tiny seed." I rushed out the final words.

"Those can be powerful seeds." Ben's jaw flexed.

"Are you mad?"

"Disappointed. I thought we understood each other. This . . . this is my family, Emily."

I cringed. There were no extra *e*'s in my name. There was no soft look. In fact, he avoided my eyes as he stood and walked to

the door. He gestured for me to go through it first before silently locking it and returning the key under the flowerpot.

"What are you going to do?"

"If Alessandro said half the things he said he did, Francesca is devastated, and I need to find her. It is my job."

"Why—"

"I am her brother, Emily. Papa cannot do it, and Mama is the wrong person. So it lands on me, as it should. That is what brothers do." He headed down the walk. "I need to take you home. If my parents get back before I do, tell them I have gone to Florence, to Martine's apartment."

"Why not call?"

"If Francesca will not answer, Martine will not. Loyalty. This will require more door banging."

"I'll come with you."

"I . . . I need to handle this alone."

I trudged along beside him, fully convinced *mad* would've been better.

❧

Ben pulled up to the house but didn't get out with me. I dropped back into the car. "I want to help. What can I do?"

"Niente."

Niente. The very word hollowed out my chest. *Nothing.* And not said in English. Ben was so faithful, so careful to use English around me, to include me in every conversation, to make sure, even when I wasn't part of the discussion, that I could understand, follow along, feel connected. *Niente.*

I tried again. "What about the restaurant? It's so busy. I . . . I could go there to help."

He held up his hand to stop the *worst idea ever*. "This will take only a few hours. I texted Noemi. She will start prep early. I need to go, Emily. Please."

I reached up and kissed his cheek. "I'm sorry."

I unlatched the door and walked into the silent house as he drove away. At home and at work, I'd often walked into unoccupied, silent spaces. Houses that weren't ready for their families yet; work spaces not approved through final inspections; my own apartment, where I'd set up a workshop in the dining room area for small items. Silence had never bothered me.

Until now.

It didn't belong here. This house was meant for warmth, hugs, kisses, crowds of family, and yelling. Its thick stone walls were meant to keep the family close and force the impact of their passion and love to spill out the windows and doorways into the countryside.

Not today.

Today it was silent. I walked the few steps to the short hallway into the library and looked up at the ceiling mural, knowing I should work on it. I should climb the ladder and work on the only thing I had permission to touch and the skills to fix.

Instead, I headed into the library and plopped into my favorite armchair. I plucked at a loose thread, considering the irony that it was Donata's favorite chair too. I knew that much from peeking into the room from the ladder. I should find a new favorite spot—I certainly didn't need to give her any more ammunition for disliking me. But I couldn't bring myself to move. Since I'd dropped into it on my first day, it had felt like my only safe place in the house—if I didn't want to spend all day hiding in my room.

I reached for the sketch pad I'd propped against the chair's skirt and pulled a few colored pencils from my toolbox resting

under the side table. I could see him so clearly. Lucio, off to his beloved Assisi this morning. I closed my eyes to picture the tones of his face, then chose soft beiges and browns for his cheeks, sun-worn and time-weathered, grays and whites for his hair and brows.

I then dug out darker tones to capture the stubble across his chin and cheek, turning again to gray down his neck. Ben looked so like his father. Would he, too, be this soft and gentle past eighty? He had such energy, but I could see it mellowing, deepening with wisdom and even more gentleness with time.

I missed him. *How extraordinary!* Ben was only driving a half hour away, but I missed him. I'd created a wall between us, and though it might be small, it existed. Little betrayals mattered, and I ached to make things right.

I grabbed another shade of brown to capture the shadow within Lucio's right cheek, which sank a little more than his left. That was the more interesting side of his face, as though it was the side that had made all the tough choices in his life. That would be the focal point of my next painting. I would capture that side more fully—for one picture couldn't capture even a fraction of Lucio's essence.

When I'd recorded all the shades within his hair and face, I dropped the pencils back into the box and studied the picture. It was time to begin painting. It was my own ritual, to start fully in charcoal—it drew me deeper into the art before I set it in oil. I ran a finger over my interpretation of his eyes, smudging, softening them a touch, and then I stopped. Ben was in them too. There was an expression in those eyes that captivated me; it held regret, memory, love, and loss, even a touch of wistful defiance, but mostly a soft acceptance. They were beautiful. And I'd captured them.

Chapter 28

By midafternoon the stillness drove me crazy, and I escaped to the paths at the back of the house. They led me past Donata's garden, through an orchard of apple trees, and up through the vineyard, as the hill climbed to the north. At the top I found a field of sunflowers on the downward slope. Every single one faced away from me.

I wandered back, and as I approached the house's back patio, I noticed that the huge doors were now open. Someone was home.

Donata leaned over dough on the wood island.

"Ciao." I stood in the doorway.

She looked up, watched me a moment, then resumed her work. She punched the big ball of dough and worked it back and forth, her full weight and shoulders rocking with the effort.

"Ben's gone to Martine's in Florence. He thinks he may find Francesca there." I mentally calculated time and distance—Ben should be back by now. I pulled my phone from my pocket. Nothing.

Donata didn't lift her eyes from her dough.

"Are you making bread?" As soon as the words came out, I knew they were wrong. Donata made pasta. At first, it seemed a silly

distinction to me, but I'd quickly learned identity was wrapped up in bread. For Lucio and Donata, even Ben, it was self-defining.

She confirmed it with one word. "Pasta."

And although the word is the same in English and Italian, her vowels and eyes screamed in Italian. Very distressed Italian.

I leaned against the doorjamb trying to fix what was or wasn't between us. "I do that, too, work with my hands when I'm upset. Fix a clock, put together a shattered china plate, make all the pieces fit back into the puzzle if I can."

"You work on that platter." She pointed to a charger resting on a side table.

"I found that last night, after everyone had gone to bed. I couldn't sleep . . . I should've asked."

She shrugged. "It is good work."

I couldn't help but smile. It was the first concession, warmth, I'd received. "Thank you."

Her eyes shifted to the farm table across the kitchen. Mine followed. I'd left my sketch pad there on my way out the door.

She stretched a flour-dusted finger to it. "May I see?"

"Sure."

She wiped her hands on a dry white towel and circled the island. I opened the book and began to slowly turn the pages. There were several of Lucio, a few landscapes, a couple of Ben, and a small one of her. I froze. I'd forgotten that I had drawn it. Her eyes were tight as they were the first day we'd met—not that they'd softened much in the week since.

It was a striking picture, a beautiful one, because Donata was beautiful, with her square jaw, straight strong nose, and umber eyes that flashed like topaz in delight and darkened to coal in an instant. I'd finished it late one night as I had sat in her kitchen.

I'd focused so fully on her I found myself forgetting time,

place, and even myself. At the end I'd been exhausted and finally ready to sleep. I'd reached her somehow—her vulnerability, her strength, her fierce loyalty, her fear—and revealed her. But it was only on paper. In life, I hadn't made that leap.

She touched the edge of the picture as if meeting herself for the first time. "I feel that way." She pulled back and twisted her hands within the dish towel. "Right now. That is what I feel."

Her breath exhaled weariness and disappointment, long held close and tight. Without another look, she flapped her hands, crossed back to the island, and buried them in her dough. "Go . . . Go . . . Lucio is in bed. This morning was too hard, but he will be happy to see you."

I headed up the stairs, tempted to turn left rather than right, and hide in my room. I tapped on Lucio's bedroom door.

"Such an exciting morning!" he called as I entered. "First Assisi, then such tension and drama. It seems she's now back safe and sound." He lifted an old flip phone from his bedside table and then waved it toward the chair opposite him. "Sit."

"I'm glad." I sank into the chair and a sigh emerged, almost as if it pushed out like air from the cushion beneath me. "Where I'm from, no one would've sounded such an alarm. Her boss would've left her a voice mail, maybe fired her, but . . ."

"No Mama calling? No brother chasing her down?" Lucio's voice was laced with laughter. "Probably best not. She is a grown woman."

"No new sister setting her up?" I told him the whole story. It was bound to come out soon.

Lucio smiled. "I didn't know you were such a romantic."

"Meddler." I hated saying the word, but it felt right.

"You wanted to fix something, and that felt good. It always does." Lucio pushed himself up farther against the pillows and

templed his long fingers in front of his face, tapping the tips together. "I'm sorry for your sake. But as for Francesca, I'm not entirely sorry it happened. Alessandro has tended to his wounds too long. That isn't a good thing. If he does have feelings for my daughter, she needs to rise within his priorities. This may turn out well in the end."

My phone beeped.

Francesca at work. Behind at Coccocino. Won't be home until late.

"Ben." I laid my phone back in my lap. Lucio watched me. "He's headed to the restaurant."

"See? This is all good. Come. Let us tell Donata." He glanced at me. "Perhaps not everything."

In the time I'd visited with Lucio, the kitchen had been transformed. Much of Donata's pasta hung from three wooden racks, and she'd started an extraordinary-smelling sauce. Garlic, tomatoes, basil, and something sweet wafted through the kitchen, mixing with the wild smell of the thyme growing on the windowsill. And the counters looked like Christmas, bowls of red tomatoes, chopped greens, and herbs lying in bunches.

"All is well. Your chicks are where they belong," Lucio announced.

"*Bene.*" She nodded.

I stopped in the doorway, but Lucio continued to the stove and stood behind his wife. Donata didn't turn or move. Rather, her body stiffened in recognition of his closeness. Yet at his slightest touch, she spun and melted into his arms. They stood, no lines of separation between them, unmoving, one. Her head tucked perfectly beneath his chin.

When I was upset or unsure, Ben held me the same way. I shook my head, remembering Francesca's story about her father. Books told stories. Books told us about ourselves. I now knew exactly why he had me reading *The Taming of the Shrew*.

Katharina, the main character, wasn't a "shrew" because it was enjoyable or fun, as I first thought. I'd immediately pegged her as a terror, Bianca as a brat, and Petruchio, her suitor, a bully. But as I read deeper into the story, I began to understand that Katharina reacted to those around her—family who constantly overlooked and diminished her. And once someone took her seriously, made an effort to reach her, she responded. At first I'd also thought Petruchio made the effort simply to secure her fortune, but then I figured out that he could have married anyone and worked far less. Something in Katharina, even simply hearing about her, had sparked his interest. From moment one, he felt she was worth pursuing.

Donata wasn't Katharina—I knew that. And even though I'd been ungracious enough in my head to think of her as one, she wasn't a shrew either. But she was someone who seemed to be reacting to everything around her—Lucio, Ben, Francesca, me. Joseph too. Simply because we didn't mention him didn't mean he wasn't ever-present. But to stop, be still, and strive to understand her. That might be something very worthwhile.

A soft laugh drew my focus to them again. Lucio held his wife close and smiled, not at me, but to her, even though she couldn't see it. "Okay now?"

"Sì," came the muffled voice lost in his chest. "*Non sarò in grado di respirare presto.*"

He chuckled softly. "If you can't breathe, you can't yell."

She unfolded from his embrace and swatted him, then stepped closer again, eyes fixed on his.

I left them alone and went to work on the ceiling.

❧

I rolled over in bed and stretched my arm into emptiness, glancing at the clock. Something had wakened me. I listened. The front door clicked shut.

Minutes later, Ben entered the room. Like a coward, I pretended to be asleep. Soon he climbed into bed, but he didn't pull me close as he usually did. He didn't whisper good night or kiss my hair.

And the absence of it, of him, was profound.

I whispered into the dark, "Did you get a rest at all today?"

He rolled over and touched my cheek. My gratitude and relief at this simple gesture swamped me. I lost my train of thought for a moment, feeling emptied and humbled—and equal parts humiliated that his rolling over, touching me, and implied willingness to talk meant so much.

I focused my thoughts. "I didn't know, Ben. About Alessandro. His wife. Any of it."

"I did not know to tell you. Part of me had forgotten as well. Francesca needed time to grow up, and Alessandro steadied her. Alessandro needed time too. I had always hoped."

"Don't be mad."

"I am not mad. I am tired and sad, for many reasons." His tone told me the chat was over, and I couldn't blame him.

There *were* many reasons to be both tired and sad.

Chapter 29

I overslept again.

"You have to wake me up."

Ben stood over me with a cappuccino. "Why?"

"Because it's Sunday and I'll get the stink eye if we miss church."

"We will go to San Biagio. Papa said you met Don Matteo."

"Yes, he . . ." I stalled. Lucio had specifically asked me not to mention the mural. Did that include Ben? Considering the Francesca fiasco, I decided it best to keep my mouth shut. "He introduced us last week."

After Mass, Don Matteo stood at the door shaking hands with his parishioners. He held on to mine.

"I hoped to see you again. I forgot to call Lucio back. Will you come see me?"

Ben looked between us.

"Of course. Tomorrow?"

He nodded, his glasses sliding down his nose with each dip of his head. "I'll be here all day."

As he walked to the car, Ben asked, "What is that about?"

"Doing some work there." The evasion felt wrong, but I was unsure how to navigate my way through these secrets. My own family held none—we didn't communicate enough to have any. But here? I tripped over them right and left.

Ben threw an arm around my shoulder. "The Stations of the Cross? That is *magnifico*."

"I hope so."

As we walked down the hill to the car, I realized that Sunday Family Dinner loomed ahead of us—an event now worthy of dread and capital letters. Donata had canceled the previous week's, as it was only days after our celebration dinner and the Piccolo disaster. But tonight there'd be talk too. Something about Francesca, Alessandro, and her flight to Florence was bound to come out— and who was responsible.

The dread grew palpable as we drove home. It rose to a choking point when I recognized Francesca's car already parked at the front door.

As we entered the house, Donata barked from the kitchen in stiff, clear English, "You took your time."

"Mama?" Ben strode to the kitchen, clearly surprised.

I rounded the corner to see her pointing a large knife at him. "Papa is in the library with Francesca. Go see your sister, then you help."

Ben raised his brows to me as he ducked back into the hallway. I glanced to Donata and found her eyes now trained on me.

In slow, sure English she said, "You go too. You may have more advice for my daughter?"

"About that . . . I'm sorry I said anything to her. I—"

She returned her gaze to the table before I could finish. Her hands moved back and forth with the knife, cutting the swath of dough in thin, sure strips. She then angled the knife and slid it

through the center, as if inserting it into a roll of paper towels, and lifted. Pasta unfolded like Rapunzel's hair down the tower in thin, even strands.

My breath caught. It was beautiful. It was art.

Donata flicked a glance at me, shocked, surprised, almost loving, before she remembered her anger. She tossed her head to the door. "Go find Francesca if your sorries you must say."

I trudged to the library. It was empty. Voices drifted in from the side door. I walked out into the warm afternoon and onto an olive tree–shaded patio. Lucio sat in a reclining chair tucked within a blanket as his children leaned on the stone wall in front of him.

All eyes found mine.

Ben reached out his hand. "Are you okay?"

"She is mad." I pulled *mad* long across several *a*'s.

Francesca laughed. "Of course she is. That's her default emotion."

"*Passerotta*," Lucio gently admonished.

"Papa, it's true and you know it. Emily didn't do anything. I never should have even told her about our conversation." She leaned across her brother to poke me in the arm. "Sorry about that. I wasn't thinking." She then faced Lucio again, her hands outstretched. "This is ridiculous, Papa. I—"

"You disrespect yourself chasing that boy." Donata blew onto the patio. She then narrowed her eyes at Ben. "He is a friend, but he plays with the heart. That is clear."

"Mama," Francesca whispered.

"There will be talk. Do you not care about this? About your family? Your . . . reputation?" She pronounced the final word slowly and carefully as if she had looked up the English translation specifically for this moment.

"I didn't do anything wrong," Francesca moaned. "He made me mad, that's all. Okay? And there's nothing to talk about. It's hardly worth any gossip. I told a friend that I wouldn't be around much. End of story. And now, believe me, I won't. So it's true."

"That is not true." Donata faced Ben. "You know they talk."

"What does she mean?" Francesca bumped her brother. "Who talks?"

"Nobody."

"That is not true," Donata repeated. "At the café, Andre shares all the news. There are no secrets."

"Mama, Andre is the same as he was twenty-five years ago. You know that." Ben lifted his palms as if begging her to understand. "Andre bullies Alessandro. There is nothing to it, and no one cares anymore. You say never to listen to gossip. We do not. Why does this upset you?"

"Talk is a beast easy to feed. Then it devours you." She stalked back into the library.

Francesca groaned. "She's insane. You do know that? This wasn't a big deal. Alessandro was a jerk and I got mad and went to Martine's. It's my business. My assistant covered with the kids at camp, and I apologized. What's her deal?"

Lucio chuckled within a sigh. "Your mother has very few hot buttons, but possibly harming your reputation, creating gossip . . . You hit two big ones."

"Then she's a hypocrite. She moved here alone, Papa—a young woman, showing up in the night, barely twenty. Are you kidding me? Talk about creating gossip. Even Nonna saw the hypocrisy in all her rules. Can't you talk to her?" Francesca pushed off the wall. "I won't come back. I don't need a free meal this badly."

The color drained from Lucio's already pale face. He set his hands on the armrests and pushed forward. "You go too far. You

will respect your mother, and if Sunday dinner with your family is only a free meal to you, by all means take time away. It is your choice. But don't you disrespect your mother in our home."

Francesca pressed her lips together as if stifling a protest, but she nodded. She then gave her father a light kiss on the cheek before walking off the patio and into the trees circling the house.

Moments later we heard her car tires crunch on the gravel drive. Lucio sighed and pushed himself up. Ben jumped to assist him. Lucio nodded his thanks, then drifted away. I assumed he was going to find Donata and tell her the news. One less for dinner.

Ben returned to his perch next to me and we sat in silence.

My dread had been pointless. Sunday Family Dinner never materialized. I didn't know if Donata sent word or everyone knew by osmosis, but not one person showed up.

Ben and I cooked a little of Donata's pasta, coated it in her sauce, and ate at the kitchen table alone.

"What happens now?" I carried our plates to the sink.

"I need to go see Alessandro."

"Now?" I turned off the tap and spun around.

"He hurts, but he also hurt her. It has been days, and as much as I do not want to get involved, I need to talk to him, as a friend." He pulled at his neck.

"It's not so different here, is it? I mean . . . your mom is overreacting, right? This isn't fodder for serious gossip. Does anyone really care?"

Ben leaned against the counter next to me. "Yes and no. It is a small town, traditional. At times, judgmental. People know

she went to talk to him. Mama was right; Andre has said as much. Gossip travels through the water." He paused.

I looked up, startled. *Osmosis.* How did he . . . ?

He smiled as if he'd read my thoughts, and I wasn't too sure he hadn't.

I smiled back.

He tugged at my waist, pulling me in front of him. "But no, it will not harm her reputation. Papa was right. Francesca was right. Mama has hot buttons. It will, though, give Andre ammunition. That animosity started when they were seven . . . Nothing new or unusual about that."

I clasped my hands behind his neck and kissed him. "I'll wait up."

He looked at me, almost questioning. "It could be late."

"I'll still wait up."

His eyes instantly cleared—as if we were no longer on opposite sides of a chasm. He pulled me tighter, kissed me good-bye, and headed out.

I spent the night painting. I'd set up my easel in Francesca's old bedroom. The posters and corkboards of friends' photos, postcards, and souvenirs still pinned to the walls reminded me of Brooke's room, or of Amy's when we were growing up. With each move, I would help Amy set up her half of our room on day one—pinning the same pictures and the same posters in apartment after apartment. She had teased me about my "blankie." I smiled, having only now recognized hers.

As I worked on Lucio's portrait, I wondered how well or how little I knew my sister. How well or how little I knew Ben.

Or Lucio? Francesca? My own parents? Amy had been right. I had carried my "blankie" with me, physically and mentally. I carried my perception of how things worked, how they should work, and how they could be fixed into every aspect of my life, every job and every relationship. And yet the important things held an intangible quality I was only now recognizing. I remembered mentally balking at Rachel's comment, as relayed through Brooke. But now I found a thread of disconcerting truth within it. *She says some things can't be fixed. We just have to endure them.*

. . . And perhaps share in them. Ben wasn't going to Alessandro's to fix things. Loss of trust? Could that be fixed? Certainly not by Ben. I suspected he was going to share it. That was Ben. That was what made him so attractive and also so inscrutable. I didn't fully understand him, yet so desperately wanted to.

I was so deep in thought and in the painting, I didn't see Ben until he stood beside me.

His short intake of breath brought me back to the present.

"How'd it . . ." My question died as I followed his gaze to the painting of his father before me.

Ben stepped forward. "That . . . I will remember him just like that."

I took a step back, stunned at what was before me. It was Lucio. He sat in his beloved library, light spilling around him, highlighting one side of his face. He was so vividly present. And his eyes . . . arresting. They revealed his soul, and tonight I felt the heartbreak within them.

We stared for a moment until Ben sighed and dropped onto the corner of Francesca's bed.

I ran my fingers through his hair.

"How was Alessandro?"

"He feels manipulated and he is very angry. He was not always so angry, but it is his first emotion now too. We talked . . . and I warned him that one can only be a victim for so long before it sinks too deep to rip away."

"You said that."

"He needed to hear it."

Too deep to rip away. His phrase caught my attention and niggled at something I knew or had seen, but couldn't quite grasp.

Chapter 30

The next morning I hauled an old Vespa out of the shed and headed to Francesca's school.

Her classroom was empty, so I wandered around until I found her watching the kids in a side playground. She was hard to spot at first among the trees and shadows. Kids laughed in bright sunshine atop a slide, then whizzed down into the shaded yard below. Francesca was hidden in this dappled light, eating an apple and frowning.

"Hey." I approached.

"Hi." She took another bite and watched the kids.

I dropped next to her. "I wanted to say again—"

She laid a hand on my knee. "Don't. It doesn't matter and it's done. I'm more mad at myself than at you." She shrugged slightly. "I wanted some great declaration; I could've waited or walked. Either would have been more honest." She thumped her fist against her heart. "It was my fault."

"I pushed you." I leaned against the bench's back. "And your mom . . ."

"None of that is new either. I'm only sorry for Papa's sake. I shouldn't have said what I did."

"Will you come over tonight?"

She slid me a glance, a smile playing on her lips. "Are you trying to fix this?"

"Probably," I conceded. "I only meant—"

"That now is not the time for petty family squabbles. Ben said the same thing. You probably come from that—all healthy communication—and I should come home tonight; I know I should." She watched the kids a few moments. "Yes, I'll be there for dinner."

"Good. But so you know, I don't come from any of that."

We sat in silence watching the kids, listening to their laughter.

"Can I come to your classroom today, play detective, like we planned?"

"Please. I've been too distracted to be a very good teacher." She threw me a glance, daring me to apologize again.

"I'll be one for you." I stood. "I strapped a few canvases to the back of a Vespa I found in the shed. I'll go get them and set up."

"You drove that old thing? Walking is faster."

"I loved it! Does no one use it? Because I got to see the countryside on my way here. It was so slow, I could actually smell flowers as I passed them. It was perfect."

Francesca laughed. "It's all yours. No one has driven that thing in years."

"I'm so glad. Now I can get places by myself. That puppy's my little bit of freedom, and you have no idea how much I need that right now."

"You sound just like Mama. She drove that stupid thing for years too."

∽

After an hour and well over a hundred cotton balls, I wandered out of the school yard. It was time to head to the church. Something about Lucio made me worry, feel urgency about his project and a desire to talk with Don Matteo.

Lucio had looked paler this morning, and his fingertips seemed to me more blue and yellow as he'd gripped his cup. And although no one would talk about it, there was something to his trip to Assisi. It all had the markings of a last good-bye.

I entered through a side door and stood, blinded by the darkness.

"Hello?" Don Matteo's voice and footsteps approached. He materialized directly in front of me dressed in black pants and a black shirt, the white of his clerical collar peeking out in the center.

"Ah . . . good, Emily. You've caught me dusting." He shook a white rag, then dropped it on the back of a pew and walked away down the aisle. "Follow me and we'll talk."

I followed. "May I help you?"

"Certainly." He pointed to a small pile of rags near me. I grabbed one, ran it along another pew next to him.

"Dusting helps me think. And call me Father Matt."

I tilted my head, questioning.

He stopped. "Yesterday during Mass, you looked like you needed a bit of home."

"How'd you catch that?"

Father Matt laughed, a deep, booming sound. "Everyone is so surprised when I say things like that, but it's quite natural. I'm looking at you all during the Mass. I see each one of you. It would be more surprising if I did not notice."

"I've never thought of that." I walked down another aisle and stopped at the end before one of the Stations of the Cross. Its

frame was warped. Moisture had buckled the wood along the seam lines and cracked the central work. I leaned forward and touched the upper edge. "I know I'm here to talk about the mural, but these pine frames are cracking because moisture got in somehow."

Father Matt came and stood beside me. "They've been on my list this year." He slowly looked around the church, his eyes trailing from the small rose window at the back across the transepts to the central altar. "There's a lot on my list. I've been here only three years, and the list grows rather than shrinks."

"Do you want help?" I tapped the painting's frame. "I can easily rebuild these, clean the paintings, and apply a new varnish. I can get you a portfolio of my work and references."

"Lucio is reference enough." He studied me, then the painting. "My notes say these are from 1914, and I doubt they've seen any refurbishment or care since then."

"I don't know. Joseph Vassallo worked here one summer." I tapped the bottom edge. "See here? Adhesive. Well applied too. I bet he worked on this."

"Yes, I've read all about Joseph this past week. Alberto Rodi kept detailed accounts. He was the caretaker from 1953 until his death last year, and his father held the post before him. They recorded everything around here." He paused and smiled. "In fact, I now know that a redheaded choirboy had a cold in September of '63."

"That's probably when the moisture got in this one." I kept my expression steady.

He looked startled, then chuckled. "You're joking."

"Yes." I smiled.

"The notebooks also told me more about that mural Lucio mentioned." He balled the rag in his hand and walked to the south transept. I followed.

He picked up a thick black book sitting on the last pew and opened it to a string page marker. "According to this, Don Pietro hired Joseph to refurbish items that summer and do odd jobs around the church. And . . ." He flipped several pages. "On June 23, Joseph asked Don Pietro if he could paint a mural. Alberto wrote here that Joseph was insistent—he used a word that translates close to *beg* in English. There's nothing about the subject, but Alberto recorded the proposed size."

Father Matt looked up at the wall and dragged his finger across the space, almost corner to corner.

"That big?"

He nodded. "It covered this entire wall from about a meter within the window to a meter off the edge." He flipped the pages, scanning. "And he came every day, sometimes asking Alberto if he could work late and lock up the church himself." The priest chuckled. "Alberto didn't like that." He turned more pages, his eyes scanning back and forth. "Then here. Lucio and Donata came to see it on September 8." He shut the book. "And that's the last reference."

"Nothing more?"

"There was one mention that Alberto repainted the wall on September 21 using leftover paint from the 1987 restoration."

"No mention of the subject? Why he painted it or why they covered it?" I ran my hand over the wall and could discern the slightest variance between two cream colors and two textures.

"That wasn't Alberto Rodi or the point of his diaries. The *who* or *why* rarely concerned him. Only the *what*." He waved the book before me. "I enjoyed reading these. It was like spending time with an old friend. I know how much petrol he purchased for his truck on a weekly basis, the cost of candles, and how he fixed the clogged pipes in the sacristy. But I don't know anything about the

heart of your brother-in-law or what compelled him to work so hard that summer." Father Matt pulled off his glasses. "Why does Lucio want this? Has he said anything?"

"Just that I'm to uncover it and not discuss it with anyone. I get the impression he's not ready for more questions."

Father Matt nodded as if none of this were a surprise. "I feel uncertain. But I've prayed about this and I do feel we should move forward. I sense Lucio needs this. Very badly."

"I do too."

"Then let us have a few conditions between us. We continue to pray about it, and if either of us feels the need to stop, we do. We can talk to Lucio then. And I ask you to cover it when you are not working on it. I do not want disruptions or talk." He pointed to a small side door. "You will find tarps in the closet off my office."

Chapter 31

$\mathcal{J}$ left the house early the next morning, Ben still sleeping, and arrived at the café before any of his friends had gathered. I stepped to the counter and laid down a euro with a quick *buongiorno* to Sandra. She smiled, nodded approvingly, and handed me my cup. I threw it back, trying not to react as the heat hit my throat, and returned the cup to the counter with a firm tap, mimicking Ben and his friends. Sandra's approving smile kept me grinning as I headed up the hill to the church.

"Hello?" I pulled open the huge wood door and walked the center aisle to the altar. The small door to the right, Father Matt's office door, was cracked open.

He had been hard at work. Upon leaving yesterday, he said he would clear space for me to work on the Stations of the Cross paintings.

And what had been a crowded and chaotic office the day before was now a clutter-free space with a large empty central table and a variety of lamps. I smiled, imagining him scouring the entire church and his rectory for every spare light. I especially appreciated the two mismatched reading lamps that arched over the table.

I laid down my toolbox and returned to the cool stone of the sanctuary. I pulled the first of the fourteen paintings off the wall, carried it back to the office, and began . . .

"Emily?"

I looked up and noted first the light, then Father Matt's drawn expression. "Hi. I hope you don't mind that I let myself in."

"That's fine. I didn't expect you so early." He looked at his watch. "Never mind, it is almost lunchtime. I was at the hospital this morning, and visits took longer than I expected. How are you doing?"

"I'm finishing a difficult seam line. It's got some debris in it, but I don't want to dig too much. The wood is soft. Then I'm using a superglue accelerator so that it'll latch more quickly. This should be stable by tomorrow." I pointed to the other end of the table. "The insides are right there."

He walked to the end of the table. The painting, depicting Jesus' condemnation, surrounded by soldiers and onlookers, rested on a cloth. The edges, protected from air behind the frame, looked bright compared to the yellowed central scene—like skin that'd been protected by a Band-Aid. He touched an outer edge. "Will it all look like this?"

"The tones will be even more clear. That, too, has experienced some discoloration."

"Remarkable." Father Matt walked to his desk and picked up the black leather book he'd shown me the day before. Today torn papers jutted from the pages.

He pulled at one of them. "I found more in here last night about those. They were a gift from the Cathedral of San Rufino in 1972. It does not say here why or what the connection was, but perhaps Alberto didn't know. He wrote that he drove to Assisi and picked them up himself, taking three trips so the paintings

wouldn't need to be stacked in the back of his truck. It took him eight hours and twenty-three liters of petrol."

"Nothing about the paintings?"

"No, but there's more about the petrol." He held it out to me. "Here, take this, and the others too. You may find something in them of interest to you." He gestured to the door. "Did you start on the mural?"

"Prep work. I mounted hooks to hang the tarp and tested solvents. I wanted to talk timing with you before I began."

"You can work every day after morning Mass—except Sundays."

That night when Ben came home he found me in the library. "You are up late."

"I got reading these after you went back to the restaurant this evening. They're fascinating."

He reached a hand down to me.

"What time is it?"

"After one." He pulled to draw me close.

"Why are you so late?" I traced a line at the corner of his eye. I thought of these as his laugh lines, but as they cut more deeply into his face, I knew exhaustion, not excessive laughter, to be the culprit.

"I am still catching up. Every night is so busy; there is no time. I feel like I am at Piccolo with our long lists of to-dos, but without you to organize it all."

"Do you want me to come help?"

"Thank you." He exhaled the words as if I'd offered a lifeline. He then squeezed me with what I understood to be a gentle refusal. "I need to do this on my own. This is my work now, and I

feel . . ." He looked over my head as if searching for the right word. "I feel I am failing."

I nodded against his chest. "I get that, but I doubt you are."

"How was the church?"

"Exciting. Can I tell you about it?" I pulled back and grabbed the notebook.

"Please. But upstairs?"

I curled into our bedroom's armchair while Ben moved in and out of the bathroom getting ready for bed.

"So I'm starting with the first painting of the Stations of the Cross, and it's got all the usual suspects. Oxidation, moisture, swelling, some warping and cracking. Alberto's diary fills in a little history, but he was more interested in the day-to-day than in the story behind the paintings before he picked them up."

"That does not surprise me."

"You knew him?"

He raised a brow. "Everyone did."

"I know. Small town. Everyone related . . ."

He waved a finger to the book. "You will soon find the incident of the honey in the chalice and the time two choirboys ate Don Pietro's chocolates before one of them, I will not say which, threw up all over the sacristy after rehearsal."

"I read something about honey. Wait—I didn't see your name."

"He called us something else . . . I cannot remember." Ben plopped on the bed.

"Here." I handed him the thick black journal.

He turned back through the pages. "Are you getting all the Italian?"

"More than I expected, or I'm making stuff up. But I've got a translator on my phone that helps too."

He kept turning pages. "Here. Nineteen ninety-two. I was

seven." He flipped the corners until he reached May. He dragged his finger down the page, translating far more quickly and smoothly than I had.

"'The Sons of Thunder ate Don Pietro's birthday chocolate. Two kilos. I saved the silver ribbon for a decoration, but couldn't save the box because the younger'—that's me—'vomited on it. The rug came clean with a mixture of water and vinegar.'"

I laid my hand across the page. "A man after my own heart. That's a good, safe way to clean chocolate."

Ben laughed. "Move your hand." He leaned over the page. "That is what he called us. 'The Sons of Thunder.' We fought all the time." He flipped through the pages. "I bet we are in here a lot. We got very good at the Sacrament of Reconciliation."

"Which is?"

"Confession." Ben grinned. "Do you want me to read you some?"

At my nod, he settled back against the headboard and lifted his arm. "Come here."

I tucked into his side as he started to read. Most of the journal told of daily work in a solid life, but there were glimpses of humor, grace, and care. There were also profound moments of great kindness toward Ben's family or someone else Ben knew that occasionally silenced him. Alberto Rodi may have been primarily concerned with the *what*, but he was most definitely motivated by the *who* and the *why*.

Ben would stall on such passages, sigh, smile down at me, and read on.

It was almost three thirty before we flipped off the light.

Chapter 32

We soon fell into a routine. Breakfast with Donata and Lucio, then Ben and I both headed to work. I climbed onto my slow, lime-green Vespa and followed behind his car down the drive, staying far enough back to avoid the jumping gravel. Soon he outdistanced me and I was left scooting along in the sunshine.

After a few days and several hundred cotton balls, the mural revealed color and texture, a draping of coarse brown fabric, layered facial tones, and one piercing eye. From these few visible glimpses, Father Matt and I could tell it was extraordinary.

"Have you updated Lucio?" The priest studied the one eye.

"He hasn't mentioned it, so I haven't either. Things are good at the house. Maybe because I'm gone most of the day, but I feel like bringing it up would rock our steady boat. He knows I'm here. Wouldn't he ask?"

"When more is uncovered, perhaps we should bring it up . . . but for now, find the other eye."

After work each afternoon I dropped by the Coccocino and stole a kiss and something yummy. I sat in the kitchen's corner

and watched everyone work with and around each other. It was like a dance. Everyone knew their place and how to step and when. I understood how things could go wrong within six weeks—the pace was frenetic, and Ben was the leader. Without him, the underlying melody, the backbone to everything, would be gone.

Then I scooted back to the house to paint and read some of Lucio's stories. While I spent mornings at the church, my father-in-law seemed to spend his mornings adding to the book pile next to my armchair.

"I left you a treat." Lucio walked into the room, his cane tapping beside him. He gestured to my pile of books.

"*The Flanders Panel*?" I picked up the new top book.

"Joseph liked that one, and you, like him, enjoy mysteries. That one is by a Spanish author, about a restorer who discovers a mystery in a famous fifteenth-century painting and finds herself in danger."

"Is it in Spanish?" I opened the cover to peer inside.

"English. I bought that on a trip to London."

"Excellent. I'll get to that next. I'm almost finished with *Emma*."

"I didn't suggest that." Lucio sat down across from me.

"Francesca mentioned it."

"Ah . . . And what do you make of it?"

"I'm not sure. Emma is a hard character to like, and yet I do. She is completely the opposite of me, and yet I see myself in her. Actually, I take that back. She's not the opposite; I just don't like our similarities. And yet, I *like* her."

"Good writers do that. They show us ourselves, but in a new light. What did you think of Shakespeare?"

"I've read Shakespeare." I smiled. "You mean specifically *The Taming of the Shrew*, and I'm still not so sure I'm happy with it." I

narrowed my eyes at him. "Am I the shrew?" I wasn't about to ask, *Is Donata?*

Lucio sat back and smiled. I knew he was trying to teach me a lesson but didn't want to spoon-feed me. And he knew I knew. Again, a dance. We were each waiting to see who would take the first step.

"Fine." I gave in. "It made me feel like I see things too black and white, jump too fast, and react too strongly—that I'm reactive rather than proactive." A few heated debates with Amy came to mind.

"You are a delight." Lucio laughed. "Literature teaches us empathy. But my children never approached it so willingly." He offered me a gentle smile. "But the lessons aren't so direct. I wasn't positing any theories about you."

"Then why'd you want me to read it?"

"It's fun. Shakespeare wrote bawdy comedy, and while the play has its problems in a modern context, it is still fun. I doubt he expected to be read four hundred years later, but I suspect he is because he speaks truth. We do push and pull against people. And however it comes about, we recognize when someone takes us to heart and strives to understand us, in here." He pointed to his own heart.

With that, Lucio seemed to drift away into his own thoughts, then into his own book. I picked up *Emma* and continued on with her misplaced matchmaking, all the while suspecting she was missing a match of her own with Mr. Knightley.

Eventually Lucio rose, headed to his shelves, then tapped his way out of the room. As he passed by my chair, he dropped a new book on my pile.

A Portrait of the Artist as a Young Man.

I could only smile and return to my reading.

⌒

It was at night Ben and I found each other. He'd crawl into bed beside me and drag me back against his chest, and I'd whisper the same question into the darkness, "How was your day?"

"There was an American family in tonight. They ate well and ordered all the best dishes. Their son reminded me of Joseph. Like the boy tonight, he was so sure of himself." Ben's chest rumbled against my back. "Like that night we first met. He was so arrogant and you were so adorable." He squeezed me tight. "I overheard this boy tell the next table that cholesterol forms in the body because of glass that is mixed with the salt in America."

"Glass?"

"I had to pause to listen as I rounded the tables. I could not believe it. Then he said your companies add it as filler to keep costs low, and then the body heals itself by oozing out cholesterol as a safety coating."

"I highly doubt that."

I felt Ben's chest move again with his chuckle. "I put extra salt in his gnocchi tonight. I could not stop myself."

"Ben."

"He is in Italy. We do not add glass here . . . Besides, the gnocchi was perfection. He devoured it."

⌒

"You just missed an American family," Father Matt called across the sanctuary as soon as I entered the next morning.

"Don't tell me. Glass in the salt? In the wine?"

"Glass?" He shook his head. "No. One of the kids scraped back your tarp. I was worried it might have damaged something."

I crossed through the pews. "It can't. The paint underneath is hard. I wipe off the solvent before any color comes up, so it's as tough as it's been for seventeen years." I dragged over the ladder and climbed to unhook the tarp's corners.

The first thing revealed was the man I'd uncovered the day before. The complexity of emotion in his face was breathtaking. There was anger, but also an aching sadness—the conflict fully realized in one clenched fist and the tension in his eyes. *Is that a rock peeking between his knuckles?* His other palm was spread against his breast.

Joseph was a true artist.

"Have you looked at the mural recently?" I called to Father Matt.

"Not for a few days . . . Oh . . ."

I glanced back in time to see his mouth drop open.

He stepped away as if trying to gain a wider view of the whole. "It's powerful, but . . . it's a mob, isn't it?"

I climbed down and stood beside him. "I think so. Look at that child. He's confused, and angry too. Almost like he's been told to be angry. And here . . . Is that a rock? How does he do that? Joseph captured so much conflict."

"He certainly did." Father Matt's voice lilted and lingered as if he were contemplating a different question. With a quick head-shake, he brought his attention back to me. "How much more do you have to uncover?"

"If it's as large as we think, there's enough room for at least ten more people. And these are so high I suspect they're in the

background, and there's something closer to the viewer down here." I tapped lower, waist level, on the wall. "But I'm working on a grid system, so we'll have to wait."

"I had no idea," was all Father Matt muttered as he walked away.

I stood there thinking the same thing.

⟡

That night I twisted slightly within Ben's arms. "I've restored about two-thirds of the hallway ceiling. Your dad is delighted. Have you seen it?"

"I walk through that hallway every day and have not looked up. I am sorry."

"Don't apologize. You've been slammed."

"He was already asleep when I came home this afternoon. Mama was at the kitchen table. She said something about colors?"

I rolled over fully to face him, all the breath leaving my body. "I didn't think she noticed . . . This morning after you left . . . We were sitting in the library and I was putting color to that new drawing I made. I didn't think . . . I just grabbed the colors I saw within him."

"And?"

"They were different. I caught your mom's expression and looked down at the pencils. I'd grabbed chalky colors, paler colors, nothing like the palette I selected even last week . . . She left the room."

"Did Papa see?"

"He didn't say anything, but I think he noticed before either of us did. He sees so much, Ben, more than any of us. Your mom called his doctor . . ."

"Dr. Salvai. Dario has been a family friend for years. What did he say?"

"I was leaving as he arrived, and your mom doesn't talk to me, not like that. Will you ask her? I want to know too."

"Tomorrow morning . . ." Ben let his words trail away in thought.

I had begun to drift to sleep when he whispered again. "We have been busier than usual. That is also so different this summer. Friends and family are coming by the restaurant. It is normal to stay away in favor of the tourists. We do that for each other in summer. Not now. They come to be close, but not burden Papa or Mama. I find it hard—so many questions in their eyes."

"How do you know they aren't coming for your pizza?"

A snuffled laugh caught the tail end of Ben's sigh. "I doubt it, but making extra now helps, working with the dough helps . . . Come tomorrow morning and cook with me? The rest of the crew can handle prep. No knives, and I will let you go by noon to get to your paintings. I want to be with you."

"I'd love that." I snuggled deeper within his arms.

No lines of separation between us.

Chapter 33

Despite entering the kitchen well before dawn, upon flipping the light switch we found Donata.

"Mama? What are you doing?"

She stretched her back and pushed up from the table, immediately moving to serve us something to eat and "open" her kitchen for the day.

Ben reached for her. "Wait. We are going early to Coccocino. Go back and rest."

She waved her hands as if trying to find something in the air, something solid she could hold. "I do not sleep. All night."

Ben folded her into a hug. "I am sorry, Mama. How can we help?"

She shook her head. "It is life." She then gently pushed him away. "You go. Go to work. Come home before service. We will eat an early supper."

"Okay. Please do not overdo it."

She raised a single brow.

Ben read the message and pushed out a laugh tinged with frustration. "We are going. Fine. Do what you must."

Ben and I spent the morning together, creating the different styles of breads and fashioning what felt like hundreds of dough balls for the night's pizza orders. We'd arrived early, long before the rest of the staff, and it reminded me of Lucio's stories about wooing Donata—the bread, the pasta, creation, and falling in love.

I almost mentioned it to Ben, but I wasn't sure if the image would bring him joy or pain. Everything felt so fleeting and tender—anything could ruin the illusion that all was well and that this was nothing more than a fun, and oddly romantic, morning.

But it wasn't.

Ben lifted a large tub of pizza dough and bumped into me. "Are you still with me?"

I stepped back from the table, more flour covering me than it. "I was just thinking about your parents, and your mom this morning."

"Me too." He set down the tub, lifted his towel, and wiped my cheek. "Flour." He then looked back to the table. "It is silly in some ways, that bread, this pizza, means so much to me. It is so basic. But it is also like life—built on the elements." He looked around the still-quiet kitchen. "The foundations are all here and when I work with it, I think of them too. I am with them."

He picked up the tub and carried it to a far counter. I began wiping down the wood worktable.

To Ben, it was all one. Life, bread, family, Coccocino, home—there was no commute from work to home, no separation, no fracture between where he went and who he was or what he did. He was right . . . Simple ingredients. Water. Yeast. Flour. Salt. Love. Made whole and beautiful.

As I pulled the tarp off the hook, still lost in my morning, Father Matt's voice startled me. "I've been reading about your husband."

"Mine?"

"Yes." He raised his brows and held up the diary. "'Benito Vassallo stole a dozen candles, which he immediately returned after trying to light a passage under the church for exploration. He will polish the candlesticks on Saturday.' I also found the honey-coating-the-chalice prank, which he wiped clean after the service, and there's something about hiding candy in the confessionals. There was barely a day for a while when he wasn't in Alberto's way."

Father Matt dropped into the pew. "But for all his antics, Alberto adored your husband. Joseph too. It's one of the few places in the journals where Alberto says why something was done, not just what was done. *To go exploring. To feed the birds. To make the wine sweeter.* And Ben seems to have cleaned up his act by about fourteen. He isn't mentioned again."

He flicked at the corners of the pages. "In fact, after that mural was painted over in 2000, there isn't another word about either him or Joseph."

"Joseph went to college that fall in Naples. Ben says he never came home after that. Then to the States for graduate school and on to Atlanta." I climbed down and stepped away from the painting. "So?"

Father Matt's head bounced up. "You've moved down your grid."

"You've been gone."

He'd been at the hospital with two elderly parishioners, dear friends, who were suffering.

I jabbed a finger to what I suspected was the painting's focal point. "What do you think this is?"

"It's the color of blood. Could it be a pool of it?"

"I thought so, too, at first, but see here . . ." I walked closer and ran my finger to the splotch's outer edge. "I think that's shadow, as if it's material catching the light. I'll get more uncovered today."

I only had another hour to give to the mural, and I felt Father Matt hover throughout. Both of us were becoming increasingly intrigued. I uncovered more red, which seemed to open to brown. *A cloak? A dress? A cloth over an animal?*

"Is it okay to confess something to you? We priests are unaccustomed to that, but I feel we are in this together." His soft voice crept into our silence.

I slipped the last corner of the tarp over its hook—unsure how to answer yet sure that we were, in fact, *in this together.* "Of course."

The pew creaked under his weight. Father Matt wasn't a heavy man, but it was old wood and it protested his thick frame. I climbed down the ladder and waited.

"Remember how I asked you to pray about this?"

I closed my eyes. I hadn't. I turned my head, feeling he deserved eye contact with my bit of honesty, when he continued.

"I've been praying, too, and I think I needed this painting, and you. I've been praying for years now, for a revelation. Not something epic. Just something in my heart. I've felt old and tired and joyless for too long."

I sat in the pew in front of him, twisting to face him. "You?" I didn't hide the surprise in my voice. "You're a priest."

He offered a heavy smile. "And I'm human. We all have doubts, fears, and we forget. We forget who we're called to be sometimes, and by whom."

"Isn't that life, though?" I thought back to my moment on the couch in Atlanta with Amy. *Life is hard.* I said it then because it

didn't feel like a unique moment; it felt like a continuation of a lifetime of them.

Father Matt's eyes widened in a flash before he could correct his surprise. "It's all there, yes, but that's not what you're to expect each and every day. Who taught you that?"

"Life," I said as if stating the obvious.

He nodded. "She is a convincing teacher."

"The best."

"That's where you're wrong." He waggled a finger at me. "But I've been listening to her, too, and now I'm remembering true life. And this . . ." He pointed to the mural. "Something about this is significant. It's a good thing. It somehow reminds me that joy isn't a feeling, it's a truth."

"Is it ever going to get easier?" I flopped back on the bed, spread my arms wide, and dangled my feet near the floor.

"You are doing great."

I bolted upright. "You liar!"

Ben held his finger to his lips. His parents had come up to their room only moments before. He didn't want them to hear me. I knew he was right, but I also wanted to be heard—by someone.

"Every woman in your family completely ignores me. And the men are no better. They either pretend I don't exist or treat me like a child. One actually patted me on the head tonight."

"Outsiders take some—"

"They need to get used to me? I'm the one alone, I'm the one with no support. They all have each other. Anne implied your mom might be tough, but Sophia, Gemma, Fina, Silvia, and who's that one with the thick glasses? They all shoo me away . . .

And they speak so fast I can't understand them. Or, what's worse, they sometimes slow down just so I can catch some of what they say."

Ben dropped beside me. "What do they say?"

"*Inetto*. Your mom said it to that glasses one. I am inept. But I'm not. She just has to show me what she wants done and I'll do it. I'm good at stuff like that. Give me a task and I'll get it done."

"Are you sure she didn't say *onesto*? They sound alike."

"What does that mean?"

"Honesty." Ben brushed a strand of hair behind my ear. "Genuine." He kissed my neck. "Sincere."

I bounced off the bed. "Don't even try that. She did not say that." I thought back and wavered. Had she said that instead? I pressed on. "And *bionda*. She called me that too."

Ben jumped up and reached for the doorknob. "I must go talk to her. That is not right; I draw your line."

"You mean you draw *the* line . . . Why? What does it mean?" I sat down again as my heart dropped. I'd been right the first time. *Inept.* And now . . . to have something truly awful said, to know there was something so wrong about me . . . "Just tell me."

"Blond." Ben crossed his arms and smiled at me.

"What?"

"Blond. You are blond. They were probably either complimenting your hair or they are jealous of it. If you have not noticed, there are no blondes in this family, and you have beautiful hair." He reached for a strand again, but it pulled through his fingers as I lay back on the bed and burst into tears.

"How can that make you cry?"

"Because there's no end. They don't even like my hair color!" It sounded ridiculous to my own ears, but I couldn't stop myself. "And you're laughing about it."

Ben lay next to me and pulled me on top of him, hugging me tight. "I am not laughing. Please, no crying."

I rolled to the side. "And my one ally wasn't there, because I ruined that too."

"I was there."

"You were with your dad, as you should be, but I mean in the kitchen . . . Francesca didn't come. Gemma and Silvia, they talk to me when she's around, but not tonight. No talking to the inept blond one tonight."

"Francesca is still mad at Mama. I gather Mama gave her another earful again about the Alessandro mistake."

"See? My fault again."

Ben rolled onto his side, facing me. "It is over." He kissed my hair. "Francesca and Mama are like oil and water. This is nothing new. Besides, she said Mama was not angry so much at what happened with Alessandro as she was about Francesca running off to Florence. Mama can be rough when it comes to poor choices."

"That doesn't surprise me. No wonder she hates me. I'm a poor choice."

"Are you done yet?"

I heard a smile in his voice.

"Yes." Even I couldn't keep it up, but I also couldn't smile about it because it was all true. Perhaps it didn't deserve the drama and tears, but the core was true. I was the outsider and, as far as Ben's family was concerned, I was inept. I certainly hadn't proven to be otherwise. Where it mattered, in the relationships, I only fumbled. And, face it, I was blond too.

Chapter 34

Father Matt! Are you busy?" I called across the church.

He opened his office door. "This is a sanctuary. Shh . . ."

"No one's in here."

"But still . . ."

"You've got to see this," I called in an exaggerated whisper. "Hurry."

"You cannot hurry a sixty-seven-year-old knee. Patience." He walked toward me, smiling. "What?" He stilled upon reaching the first point at which he could glimpse the mural. "It's a face."

"A beautiful one. A woman. I haven't finished it all, but this is a dress. And the red? It's a cloak." I dabbed another cotton ball in solvent. "I can't imagine covering this. Ever."

"It is absolutely stunning." He looked it over. "That young man had talent. Does he still paint?"

"Wouldn't you think? But I never saw that he did. So maybe not."

My comment struck me. Working in his studio, I never saw Joseph work. At all. On anything. He didn't use the worktables, and yet he was going to handle the painting on the Ming vases.

And I knew he'd done something spectacular on a Fabergé egg Lily mentioned. Did he work after-hours? Was that when he painted? *If* he painted? Lily said he had a workroom, but I'd never seen it.

Father Matt soon left to run some errands, and I covered the painting. I'd worked long enough and needed a break. Joseph had captured the tension so well it sat hard with me. There was such anger and condemnation in the faces, such vitriol, that I couldn't work on it too long or look at it too closely. Although its beauty was extraordinary, I wondered if Don Pietro had asked Alberto Rodi to paint over it due to its hostility. It was certainly not a welcoming vision.

I calmed my nerves with the fourth of the Stations paintings, the one in which Jesus meets his mother. Mary's face held some of the same characteristics of Lily's triptych back in Atlanta. I texted her a picture, and she replied immediately.

She's lovely. What's the medium?

I replied, Oil on wood. 1914.
She then sent me a picture of her work.

Nice Picasso. Way to make me feel inept.

I typed the word before realizing its significance. It had clearly made an impression on me. She replied again.

The Van Geld estate is proving great fun. I'll send you more pics later. Talk soon.

"Does Joseph still paint?" I snuggled against Ben in the darkness.

"What makes you ask that?"

I stilled. Ben didn't know about the mural. I felt caught and unsure—and instantly resolved to speak to Lucio, soon.

For now, I told the bare truth. "Father Matt said something today as I was working at the church."

"If he does, he never talks about it. Not that we talk much."

I moved to my next question. "You know those diaries? You two aren't mentioned after the summer Joseph worked there."

"That does not surprise me. We started going to Santa Maria that fall."

I lay still. It amazed me that I could hear him so well. Not what he said, but how he said it and what he chose not to say. The shades of his voice were becoming as distinct and discernible as the colors I chose for a painting. He had been blue, a soft blue, tired and yearning for peace and sleep, when we started talking. Then it twisted, like color fractured by oxygenation, as if a thread of fear or a dark question inked it.

I wondered myself at what had happened. Was it the mural?

"Are you okay?" I whispered.

"Everything changed that summer. Not just Joseph. When I came home from Anne's house, everything was different and no one talked about it. It is like the way you described last Sunday with the family. Something happened and someone must know, but they keep silent or talk among themselves and I am on the outside. To ask so often . . . It feels like I am beating my head against a wall."

I twisted in his arms to face him. "I'm sorry."

"It is not your fault, *mia bella bionda*." I could feel his smile as he kissed my forehead.

My beautiful blonde.

I kissed his lips.

Chapter 35

ould you all come to the library when you're finished?" I dried the last espresso cup as Donata put away the knives. Lucio still sat at the long farm table chatting with us as we cleared breakfast.

Ben smiled at me. He knew. "Come. Come, Mama." He bustled her from the kitchen and I hung back, wanting Lucio to follow them first.

As I trailed behind, the light from the library poured into the hallway. It was perfect, soft and yellow. I glanced up at the ceiling mural. That work was complete—I only needed time to varnish it.

A gasp brought my head back down as I reached the threshold to the library.

Donata's hand was clamped across her mouth. I couldn't tell if the portrait before us upset or delighted her.

"What do you think?" Ben asked.

Donata kept her hand on her mouth and then, with a small shake of her head, fled the room.

My eyes flashed to Ben. His widened with no answers. I turned my gaze to Lucio and saw tears in his eyes.

"Is it wrong?"

Lucio took a step and pulled me, first my hands, then by my shoulders, until I was folded tight against him. "It is perfect. What a gift you have given me. It is exactly how I want to be remembered."

He held me for a long moment, then stepped back and clasped my hands again. He raised them and kissed my knuckles. "You are such a blessing. Thank you. I will now go find my beautiful wife." He walked slowly from the room.

"It's okay?"

Ben stepped to the painting. "More than okay." He scrubbed at his chin, the gesture I recognized as something he did when he couldn't find words.

"I think I upset your mom."

"Because she will lose him. But this . . ." He tapped the edge of the portrait. "He is here. I can feel it in the eyes. You always said they were impossible for you." He faced me. "How did you do it?"

"Something has changed. I . . . I wanted it for him, not for me. I didn't even think, really." I laughed that the one aspect of painting that had always eluded me, eluded me still because I had no idea what I'd done to achieve it or how to replicate it. I'd found the windows to the soul. But had I left a path to follow? "I simply focused on him."

I crossed to the other side of the room, where I'd stacked a few more canvases in the corner. "I was going to show them these as well, but maybe another time." I spun around another portrait of Lucio and one of Donata.

Ben barked out a quick laugh. "You captured her too. There is fire in those eyes. It burns kind, most of the time, but it does burn."

I smiled. He was right. I had captured Donata's essence in her eyes. Again, I hadn't thought about it; I hadn't reached for it. It almost felt as if I'd reached beyond it and landed there.

Ben's voice cut through my thoughts. "Do you have other sketches? Paintings?"

"Lots."

Ben studied his father's portrait. "That show you wanted so much? It could be yours now."

"Do you think? Should I send Olivia Barton the pictures?"

"Right away." He pulled me close. "What have you to lose?"

Chapter 36

Another week passed, and bit by bit the scene became a story. The qualities of hostility, pain, and betrayal that Joseph had conveyed through paint, brushstrokes, and sheer brilliance astounded me. I finally dropped the last of the cotton batting into my bucket.

I stretched and, rather than yell, crossed the church to tap on Father Matt's office door. At his call I pushed it open a crack. "I'm finished."

"I thought it'd be today. I was waiting."

"Come on."

I led him back to the transept. Evening was approaching, and the light only hit the highest windows of the church. I'd twisted my lamp so that it shone directly on the mural's focal point—a woman, staring at the viewer in a three-quarters turn, only one eye visible. But what an eye! What emotion Joseph had captured— deep stress, fear, and even a flash of defiant anger as her body angled to the mob above her.

"You've been so busy the past couple days, we haven't talked about it. I think they're about to kill her." I reached up to touch the

faces. "It's so powerful. Look at this man. You can feel his intake of breath after a scream—angry and murderous. Maybe Don Pietro ordered it covered because they're going to kill her. It's horrible in some ways."

"Is this it?" Father Matt scanned the mural from window to corner. "There's nothing more?"

"I cleaned the entire wall. Why?"

"Because it's not finished. This isn't the story. Not the end. It is a mob, yes, but no one dies. They walk away in peace. Calm. No stone thrown."

"They walk away? Is it a Bible story? I think you must have the wrong one."

"There is only one. This is very clear . . . But not to finish it? What did Joseph mean?" Father Matt stood still, and I couldn't tell if he was speaking to me or to himself. "You find it in the gospel of John. The scribes and Pharisees bring an adulteress to Jesus, to trick him with the law and force him to condemn her. Instead, he stoops down, twice, to write in the sand of the temple floor. The accusers go away, stones and all, without another word. They leave in silence. Jesus then tells the woman to go and sin no more."

"What did he write?"

Father Matt flicked me the smallest glance before returning to the mural. I couldn't blame him; it was mesmerizing. Disturbing, but spectacular.

He continued. "Scholars have debated that for centuries. What matters is that he offered her, and them if they had not walked away, grace. He would have forgiven them as he forgave her. That is the story. The whole story. Grace."

"Where is he then?"

Father Matt pushed up his glasses. "Exactly. He is not there.

Joseph has left the story out of the story. He has not painted the true focal point. He has twisted it."

"Were they angry because she was pregnant?"

"She was not pregnant."

"She is here." I stepped to the painting. "Look at the fabric here and her hands. One balances her on the ground, but the other holds her stomach. In art, and in life, that's usually what that signifies."

"I wonder . . ." He didn't finish his sentence. "Cover it with the tarp for now. It is time to talk to Lucio."

"Lucio asked me not to say anything, but I feel I need to tell Ben. There's something about this. We were talking about that summer, the summer Joseph left, and this is part of it. It was a really painful time for their family."

"I can see why." Father Matt's dark tone confused me. "I will call and ask Lucio to come now. Please go see Ben."

I'd meant I'd talk to Ben tonight. But clearly something had upset Father Matt, and he meant right this minute.

He has not painted the true focal point. He has twisted it.

A returning sense of dread engulfed me as I wandered down the hill to Coccocino. It was early, but the restaurant was already bursting with activity. Tourists ate earlier than Italians.

I walked through the courtyard, listening to all the languages bounce off the stone walls. I passed through the dining room and into the kitchen.

"Emily!" Noemi called across the counter.

"You're better?" She had been out with a cold, stretching Ben all the thinner because of it.

"It was horrible; I couldn't shake it. How are you?"

"I'm fine. Is Ben around?"

She tilted her head, confused. "He's at the grill. You passed him."

"I did?" I walked back out. Sure enough, Ben stood at the grill pulling off one of his beloved *bistecca fiorentina*. His brow was furrowed in concentration. Mine felt the same.

I stood and watched a full minute before he glanced up. "Bella? Is all well?"

"I came to talk to you."

After he pulled three steaks from the grill, he stretched over and laid a quick kiss on my lips. "We are busy tonight. I have no time to talk."

"It won't take long. May I sit at the bar?"

That brought a smile and a nod. "Ask Luigi to fix you a Spritz."

A moment later Ben perched on the stool next to me. "Okay. I have *un momento*. Spill your beans."

I couldn't help but smile, and I couldn't bring myself to correct him. "What do you mean?"

"Do you think I can spend all this time at night talking with you and not know your voice? Something is very wrong. Tell me."

In that moment, I didn't feel alone. I was tempted to savor it, linger here . . .

"I haven't just been working on the paintings at the church. I've also been uncovering a mural that Joseph painted that last summer. Your father asked me to do it . . . and to not tell anyone."

"Does Don Matteo know?"

A small laugh escaped. "There's no way he couldn't. It's about twelve by twelve feet. It's huge."

"Joseph painted it?"

I pulled back, a little surprised. "Do you really know nothing about this? It had to have taken your brother months."

Ben raked his hand through his hair and shrugged. "I told you, I got sent down to Anne's. And then Joseph was gone and . . . When my family is silent, it is not good."

"Well . . . I finished uncovering it today, and it wasn't what I expected. It's a story, from the Bible."

"How is that surprising? It is in a church."

"True, but it's an angry, violent scene. No hope or light in this thing at all. And Father Matt says that the murder—that's what the mob's about to do, kill a woman—doesn't happen. He says Joseph purposely misrepresented the story. Didn't finish it. And he painted the woman pregnant, which was also inaccurate, but that he also—"

"Slow." Ben squeezed my knee. "Slow down. What does Papa say now?"

"I just finished it, not ten minutes ago. He hasn't seen it." I leaned forward. "And, Ben, I'm sorry I didn't tell you. Your father asked me not to and I wanted to honor his trust, but—"

"You did right, I think, if that is what he asked." Ben sighed and pushed himself off the stool. "I must get back to the kitchen."

"But—" I slid off the stool as well. "That's why I'm here. Father Matt is calling your parents now. I expect they're on their way."

Ben's eyes widened.

"Let me tell Noemi. I'm coming with you."

He disappeared into the kitchen briefly, and then we walked through the courtyard and started up the hill together.

"Start again from the beginning . . ."

Father Matt stood waiting for us. "Good. Good. You came." He stretched out his hand to Ben. "Your father was anxious to come too. They are on their way." He led us back into the nave. "He doesn't sound well."

"He is not," Ben whispered in reply before his voice resumed its usual tone. "Where is this picture?"

"Come see."

We rounded the corner and Ben stopped. After a few moments, he stepped deeper into the transept to see the entire mural straight on. I watched him scan every inch of the scene's approximate one hundred and fifty square feet.

"You see?" I said. "It's beautiful, but terrible too—"

Anything I was about to say fled as the huge front door scraped against hinges and stone. The sound magnified as it echoed through the church. Anything Ben was about to say morphed into a slow head shake as his mother's voice filled all the empty spaces.

"Why are we here?" It was sharp and cutting. Too loud, too strident for this place of quiet I'd come to enjoy.

Father Matt rushed out to meet them. Ben and I remained in the transept and, for the moment, out of view.

I peeked around the corner. Donata was paler than usual, almost matching Lucio's tones. Her eyes looked completely black. At first I thought she was holding Lucio up. Their arms were tightly linked. But as I stared it became clear—he was supporting her.

Father Matt led them to us. I glanced to Ben, who hadn't moved a muscle.

"What?" I whispered.

He only had time to glance at me before his parents rounded the corner.

Donata's eyes hit me first. "Why did you bring us here?"

I opened my mouth but no sound came. I looked to Lucio. His eyes were soft, but not focused on me. He was watching his wife.

Without waiting for me to find a reply, Donata faced the mural. She studied it, then stepped toward it. She reached up and touched the woman's face.

"Dopo tanti anni, non è mai va via." Her voice was low and felt

heavy, filled with heartbreak and something darker. It took me a moment to name it—despair.

"That's not true." Lucio stepped forward and put his arm around her shoulders. He spoke English, slowly and with great care. "It has gone away. This is in the past."

"Not for him. Or for me." She ground out the words, in English now as well, and withdrew her hand from the mural. She held her fingers to her lips. "Never."

Her spine stiffened, and I could see her shoulder blades drop down her back beneath her white blouse. She seemed to grow before me as she spun around. "How did you find this? How did you know? Why?"

"Donata," Lucio whispered. "This is not her fault. I asked her to do this."

Any remaining color drained from her face as her body slumped away from Lucio. "You told her?"

"No." Lucio reached out, but she stepped away. "I asked her to uncover the mural. You, we, need to see it, to face it. And she is skilled, like Joseph."

"Like Joseph." Donata repeated in a soft whisper, eyes on the stone floor.

We stood in paralyzed silence until she lifted her head and locked eyes on me. "Would you do what my son did? Which stone would you throw?"

"I . . . I don't understand."

She turned to the mural and ran her hand, almost lovingly, across the woman. "You did not see me? How could you not? I am here for all to see."

I heard Ben's sharp intake of breath; it matched my own.

But it was Lucio who spoke. "Father, could you tell Donata what you told me on the phone?"

All eyes turned to Father Matt. His eyes clouded in confusion. "You mean about the story not being over yet?" At Lucio's nod, he sighed, warming to his topic. "Joseph didn't finish—"

"No," Donata called out. "There can be no more. How long must I pay?"

"That's not what—" Father Matt stopped.

There was no reason to continue. Donata had fled, her feet making a soft scuffling noise as she dashed up the center aisle and out the door.

Lucio faced the three of us. After a moment he said, *"Mi dispiace." I'm sorry.* And he followed his wife from the church.

Chapter 37

Ben and I returned to the restaurant. There was much to say, but neither of us spoke until we reached the turn to Coccocino.

"Do you want to wait for me?" He squeezed me tight.

"Do you mind? I want to give them space. You can send food out to the bar like you used to in Atlanta."

"Only the best dishes." I could hear his smile.

As we entered Coccocino's small courtyard, I pulled him back. "Are you piecing it together now?"

"It all makes sense. You said it yourself, I look like Joseph and Papa, but they don't look like each other. And her fear makes sense too. I wonder about Maria, Vito, all Mama's family. It must have been . . . significant."

"Will she forgive me?"

"Will you forgive him?" Ben looked to the restaurant. "Papa is at his end, Bella, and I understand wanting to set things right, bring wholeness. But he hurt you. He put you where you should not be and I . . . I am having trouble with that."

I reached up and kissed his cheek.

He nodded and slid his hand down my arm to grasp my hand. "Come inside. I will feed you."

Hours later and well fed, I retreated to the dark stillness of Coccocino's courtyard to check e-mails and wait for Ben to emerge.

Dear Emily,

The photos you sent are staggering. Pictures never convey a piece's full potential, so I'm anxious to see your work firsthand—it is alive, daring, and yet so warm. You have a gift for translating the essence of a soul. The elderly man— touching and markedly different, yet recognizable in each of your three treatments—constitutes your focal point. The woman—I need to meet her. I feel the sting of her lectures in my ears.

A new artist, Ron Stratton, has underdelivered for his upcoming show. I have half a gallery available and no paintings. While I dislike dissipating the power of a solo show, I truly believe your work will complement Stratton's more austere ascetic. The interplay could be both dynamic and quantifiable. I can offer approximately eight hundred square feet of hanging space, the entire right portion of the gallery.

Let me know your color preferences and requests in your reply. We'll need to move quickly. I open Stratton—and you— on August 15.

Talk soon . . .
Olivia

"Hey." Ben laid his hand on my hair. "I would have missed you without your phone light." He looked up to the black sky. "No moon tonight."

I tapped it off and stood. "It was an e-mail from Olivia Barton. I got a show at her gallery, if I want it."

"Congratulations." He pulled me into a hug, but his voice and heart weren't in it. Neither were mine. "Will you take it?"

"I'd like to, someday." I shrugged. "But as you say, now is not the time."

"I was off all night in there." He glanced back to Coccocino's now dark doorway.

"None of it has left my mind either." I pressed into his side. "Do you think they're asleep?"

We stepped out into the small parking lot.

"I hope so. I want to let this settle before talking more." He glanced to my Vespa and gently nudged me away from it. "Let us leave your Vespa here and go home together. It is late."

As we neared the final feet to the house, Ben lifted his foot from the accelerator. No stone kicked up. No screech of the tires. We crept to the door on a slow roll.

We let ourselves in and shut the front door softly, and were met in the dark by a voice.

"I'm sorry."

I closed my eyes. I was tempted to take two steps to the stairs and let them talk. But before I could move, Ben's arm reached around my shoulders.

"Will you come to the kitchen? I made tea."

"Sì." Ben replied for us, but I stepped forward first.

Lucio clearly had been sitting at the kitchen table for a long time. There was a crumpled newspaper, the tin of tea, and the espresso machine's knock box—as if crossing the kitchen to empty the tea strainer for fresh leaves had been too arduous. There was even a small plate of nibbles. He gestured to the two spare cups.

He'd only turned on a small light by the stove, so we sat in semidarkness. The light caught only one side of his face such that every line was visible, the bags under his eye, the sagging around his chin and neck. He'd aged within a single evening.

"Please forgive me. I'm deeply sorry." He poured as we sat, and when he handed me my cup, he wrapped his hands around mine. "I have one great regret in my life, and in my haste, I tried to fix it in the wrong way. I should have told you both about the mural. You, Ben, long ago." He pressed his hands into mine. "And I should have told Donata that I asked you to uncover it."

"It is time to tell us everything. No more secrets." Ben's head dropped forward as if too heavy to hold up.

"I know. It needs to end. Joseph needs to come home. Now."

"Papa . . ." Ben's whispered reply told me, and Lucio, that he understood what wasn't being said.

"Donata's parents disowned her when she became pregnant. It sounds so old-fashioned, but it still happens today in many small villages. It was a shame her family condemned, and they abandoned her." He waved his hand as if rolling time along. "She made her way to Montevello and walked into Coccocino, so clearly alone and lost, and started making pasta. She barely spoke to me beyond telling me she needed a job. We fell into working together that first morning, and I was in love with her by the next. It took time, but she soon told me everything. She was brave, and so wounded . . . Still is in many ways."

Lucio caught himself as if he'd meant to keep the last words inside his head. He continued. "I wooed her, day in and day out, until she agreed to marry me. I suspected she thought I was motivated by pity, but I wasn't. From our first moment, I only ever felt love for your mother."

"How have I never heard this? Here?" Ben flicked his head to

the front door. The village was outside that door—the village in which everyone knew everything, almost before it happened.

"They all knew." Lucio gave a short, affectionate laugh. "And marrying silenced much of the talk. The men respected that . . . The women? They respected Nonna. Nonna was formidable and deeply loved. She declared your mama family and made it clear that children are innocents, to be cherished and protected. You remember Nonna."

"She was a force."

"Everyone loved her. Everyone obeyed her." Lucio chuckled, then sobered. "We were wed before Joseph was born, and that was the end of it. He was my son. He is my son."

Lucio leaned back and rubbed his chin. The gesture so similar to Ben's that I couldn't help glancing to him. Ben's eyes held a sad look of understanding, as if his entire childhood was coming into focus.

"That night at Coccocino, Joseph found a letter from Donata's father. She always kept it close. She had written to him about our marriage and Joseph's birth. And he had replied . . . with great cruelty. I have never asked her why she kept that letter, even keeps it now. Mortification? Penance? And then when her father died, her family reached out, through Maria, and Donata refused them. I think by that time she believed her father, even agreed with him."

"That she could not see her family?"

"That she was beyond forgiveness, receiving it or giving it. She could no longer bend. The wound cut too deep."

Too deep to rip away. Ben's words returned to me. He'd been talking of Alessandro, but even when he'd said them they'd reminded me of someone else, of something else. They'd reminded me of Katharina from *The Taming of the Shrew*; they'd reminded me of Donata and even of myself—reacting in the same ways we'd always

reacted because we didn't or couldn't see another way. Perhaps we'd cracked too far or not enough to let in something new, something different and unexpected.

Lucio stopped tracing a line in the wood tables and held his hands still. "Joseph is so like her. That letter, something that did not change his reality, changed everything. I suspect he always sensed her fear, even if he did not understand it, and then the fear became him." He caught Ben's eyes. "Do you remember that night?"

Ben nodded. He remembered.

"He went a little crazy in his anger and was arrested. Don Pietro stepped in and offered to hire him, take him on. If not, Joseph would have gone to jail. So he worked at the church and then he painted the mural, every day. He was like water freezing, clear and hard, beautiful in its strength."

"Why did you send me to Anne's house?"

"I wanted to protect you and your mother. Her shame was so deep." Lucio shook his head. "And no one knew what Joseph was painting."

"How could you not know?" Ben whispered.

"We gave him the privacy he requested. He painted at night, and we were delighted that he was working. Don Pietro believed creative work was good work, forgiving work." Lucio spread his palms across the table. "But you've seen it. A masterpiece of hate. Donata ran away."

Ben's head shot up again. "I remember that. You asked Uncle Vincenzo to keep me longer."

"Mama went to Florence to stay with friends, just as Francesca did with Martine." Lucio offered a small smile. "That was why she became so angry with her . . . We don't change, do we, son? Even across the generations."

Before Ben could reply, Lucio continued. "While she was gone, I asked Don Pietro and Alberto to cover it. I wanted her to forget it ever existed. I wanted Joseph to forget too. I denied him his pain. It was as if I told him that it didn't matter; he didn't matter. And I denied Donata her healing, as if that didn't matter either."

"And here we are," Ben whispered.

"Yes, here we are."

"How is Donata now?" I asked the question.

"As I said, she is like her firstborn son." He let a rueful sigh escape. "Sensitive. I asked her for forgiveness, and I expect she will get back to me soon." Lucio sat back and fixed his gaze on Ben. "I need to tell you something else. I called Joseph tonight. He's coming home."

Ben shook his head.

"It is time, and somehow, in some way, he needs to stay." Lucio tapped at his heart. "In here, he needs to stay."

"Papa . . ." Again, Ben's one word encompassed all that needed to be said.

Chapter 38

Joseph exited the airport in a linen shirt and twill pants. He'd traveled ten hours. Me? One. And he looked more cool and fresh. But perhaps I'd had less sleep and the more frenetic morning.

I'd insisted Ben let me come alone. Francesca had obligations at camp, but as soon as those ended she wanted to be with her father. Ben wanted the same. Although Noemi said she could handle Coccocino, Ben started the day racing back and forth.

This was the only way I could help—and stay out of the way. So I'd woken early, climbed into Ben's tiny car, scraped across the gears, lurched down the road, and merged onto the freeway. The most terrifying part had been exiting on the edge of Florence and making my way through the chaos of winding roads and traffic to the airport. I almost died twice and got yelled at three times before I finally pulled the car up to the arrivals curb, drenched and shredded.

I jumped out of the car at Joseph's approach.

After looking around and confirming that I was alone, he lifted his chin in greeting and kissed both my cheeks. "You're my advance team?"

"Everyone wanted to come, but Lucio . . . your father . . . They wanted to be with him too."

Joseph didn't reply. He simply dropped his leather duffel into the trunk and circled to the passenger door.

I chased after him. "Oh no you don't. You're driving."

He laughed and backpedaled. "Ben is as bad as you. Where do you people buy these dreadful cars?"

I heard myself defending the little beast. "It's a perfectly fine car; it does exactly what it needs to. It's the roads that are terrifying."

As we drove out of the airport, Joseph took a detour. The morning sun still cast a rose haze over the city, made all the more distinct as it bounced off the terra-cotta tiled roofs. In the near distance I could see the Duomo tower above us—nothing could touch it in presence or splendor.

Joseph tapped his window as we passed the Basilica di San Lorezo.

"I had no idea . . ." The Basilica was huge, a massive, heavy structure of brick and stone that spread across a city block.

He slammed on the brakes and pulled to the curb. "You haven't been here? How is that possible?"

"We've been busy."

He lifted a brow. "Yes, I've heard."

"Don't start."

His eyes softened as he gestured back out his window. "It's not as delicate as Il Duomo, but it's my favorite. Consecrated in 393; I find comfort in that longevity, that solidity. And Michelangelo's Laurentian Library is in there—an absolute marvel." He pulled away from the curb and darted back into traffic. "Come on. Let's take a tour. If you think this is good . . ." He zipped down a side street, which opened into a plaza and . . .

"Cattedrale di Santa Maria del Fiore." I let the words roll off my tongue, savoring the sight.

Joseph sent me a smile. "Il Duomo di Firenze. Nine hundred years old and remains the city's crowning jewel. Giotto's bell tower, to your left, is worth the climb. A friend handles restoration for the cathedral; I'll give you his name, he can take you up after-hours." I felt him glance my way. "And show you the restoration labs."

"I'd love that. It's all exquisite." I craned my neck to keep the cathedral and her bell tower in sight as Joseph darted around the next corner.

"Now over here, you'll—"

I gripped his forearm. "I can't tell you how much I want to see all this, but I was given one job—to bring you home."

"That's the Ponte Vecchio." He pointed out my window. The sun cast a perfect replica of the bridge's shops upon the mirror-smooth surface of the Arno below it. "Don't worry; this is the way out of the city."

"Thank you." I sank into my seat.

"I can't believe Ben hasn't brought you to Florence yet or you haven't stolen away yourself. There really is no excuse."

"If you'd been around these past weeks, you'd understand." I absorbed my own words and their biting delivery. "I didn't mean it like that. I just meant it's been a busy, tense time."

Joseph sped up a hill, took a sharp right, and we were on the highway. I turned my head to my window and focused on the scenery. It seemed the safest plan.

It took a good thirty minutes for him to break the silence. "Your questions are deafening."

"I haven't asked one."

"I noticed. At first I think you were scared, but about ten

kilometers ago you grew angry, and you're remarkably loud about it, so just ask." He glanced over at me and smirked. "You've huffed three times and sighed five."

I obeyed. "Why'd you paint it?"

"The truth?"

"Please. Because I can't figure it out. I get anger, believe me, but that was more than anger. Your father—your real father, Lucio—fell in love with your mother. You had, have, a wonderful family. You found a letter. I understand being upset, they lied to you, but you have a family that loves you—even I sensed that within days of being with them. Your absence is like an open wound. And that painting—which is spectacular, by the way—and an almost twenty-year exile—it's extreme. How long are you going to punish her?" I watched him, a new idea forming. "Or are you punishing yourself?"

"So you know, then?"

"Know what?"

"How I feel? How I *should* feel?" His voice had arced; now it dropped with disdain. "How I should have absorbed the realization that my mother's sadness, anger, depression, gripping fears—they are all about me. I am the embodiment of all she hates, about herself and her life. Looking at me each and every day kept her shame and her family's betrayal fresh, salt to that wound. And Papa? He chose to pretend and return to his bread and his books, his quiet comforts, rather than help me. You would know how to handle that? Each lie? Each daily deceit?"

"But hasn't it all gone on long enough?"

"Don't, Emily. Don't act like there was a whole that somehow broke, that I'm some object that merely needs a little glue, some drying time, and heat to cure before you can set me back on the shelf. Some things do not get restored, because they were never whole."

"But they can be if . . ." My next words evaporated. Lucio was right, it did feel good to fix things. But not here, not now. I had nothing to offer. "Fair enough."

Joseph exited the highway in a sharp turn and climbed the hill to Panzano.

I sat silent for a minute, thinking of Lucio and all he was trying to fix too. I couldn't help but appreciate the irony. Despite many members treating me like an outsider, I really did fit well within this family.

"What?" Joseph flicked me a glance.

"Nothing."

"You snorted."

"Sorry. I was just . . . It doesn't matter." I took a breath and started over. "Your father's dying, Joseph."

"That's why I'm here." The words came with the soft finality of a sigh.

As he navigated our way through the tiny hilltop town, minus a good wall, we remained silent, but as the road opened before us with a smooth, winding, downhill expanse, he glanced toward me again. "How is Mama?"

"Hurt. Scared, I think. I look in her eyes and I think disliking me helps her right now. Anger is the easiest of all emotions, really."

"True. But I'm sorry, for your sake."

He drove the final slope around the base of Montevello and into the valley beyond, turning at his parents' gravel road. He slid to a quick stop at the front door and, without another word, pulled the keys from the ignition, tossed them to me, and grabbed his bag from the trunk.

Joseph's homecoming was a full village affair. Everyone wanted to know what he'd been up to, how long he was staying, how he had stayed so young and handsome, when he was coming home for good . . .

The questions went on and on, and soon that slightly warm Joseph I'd seen glimpses of in Atlanta completely disappeared and a hard, fixed mask dropped firmly in place—as if each question, touch, and hug stung him. Rather than embrace them or even endure them, he retreated.

"Warm Joseph" reappeared slowly, late in the night. Only when extended family left did his eyes soften and a hint of a smile return to his lips. Ben and I cleared plates and glasses from throughout the house, enjoying the bits of laughter we caught from Joseph and Francesca as they cleaned the kitchen. Donata, hovering about him, but rarely in sight, soon went upstairs to be with Lucio. The four of us found our way to the back patio.

There the siblings began their stories. They started with tales of early childhood, then, as the candles burned low, moved to the lessons and memories of their teenage years.

"Do you remember when Papa took your door off its hinges to teach you not to slam it?" Ben poked Joseph's arm.

"How could I forget? He lost the bolts and Tito had to forge new ones. I grew so tired of that . . . All those lessons, then he'd forget what he wanted to teach and start something new."

"I always thought he did that on purpose." Francesca sighed. "He'd give me some book and then leave it, as if I was supposed to figure it out on my own. Usually I got it wrong, so I'd have to begin again."

Joseph reached out to his sister and whispered, "He got it wrong sometimes, too, Francesca. Don't take it all on."

"But he listened, you know? I'm going to miss that." Francesca hugged her arms around her shoulders.

"Me too." Ben rubbed at his chin.

"But then he'd try to fix it. How can you two not remember that?" Joseph faced his sister. "It didn't matter if you understood his lesson if you disagreed with him. If you missed his point, you got another. Again and again, until he fixed your thinking and you saw things the way he did, whether you wanted to or not. I don't think he ever listened, really listened. He used the time to prepare his next lesson."

"Joseph . . . ," Ben warned softly.

"I'm not saying it was bad. I love him. I'm simply saying to see him clearly." Joseph shook his head slowly. "That's all." He tilted his head up and watched the stars.

"What makes you think *you* see him clearly?"

It was the first time I'd ever heard true challenge in Ben's voice.

"I'm sure I don't," Joseph conceded.

Francesca stood, and I got the impression she wanted to cry. "I should head home." She glanced at Ben. "Will you call me if . . . I mean, he was waiting, right? And now that Joseph is home . . ." Her voice dwindled.

Ben nodded. Joseph looked away.

"Do you want to stay, Francesca?" I reached up to touch her hand. "I cleared my paints from your room. I thought maybe you'd want to."

"Yes." She squeezed my hand. "I'll bring some stuff by tomorrow. Thank you."

The next three days passed in a kind of half light, half world. The house was quiet. We were waiting and we knew it, but we couldn't discuss it. It would make it too real.

In the mornings I finished the Stations of the Cross paintings at the church, walking by the covered mural without glancing its direction or ever lifting the tarp. I noticed Father Matt did the same. We, too, were waiting, but for what we couldn't say.

I met Ben every afternoon at Coccocino. He'd hop on my Vespa and drive us home for his few hours' break between prep and service. We'd sit with his father or, if he was sleeping, with any family who happened to be around.

We chatted in soft voices. They told stories. I listened. But Ben had quit insisting on the family speaking English. Some moments required Italian.

Then he'd drive us back to Coccocino. I'd sit behind him with my arms wrapped around his waist and, in that warm, short drive, I could almost imagine this was the Italian paradise of my dreams. Almost.

"Are you okay?" I lowered my feet as Ben climbed off the Vespa.

"No." He stood next to me but looked over my head, beyond me, toward Coccocino's arched doorway. "Nothing feels right. It feels . . . it feels like it never will be."

I didn't reply; I couldn't. He was right. It felt like the world had tipped and nothing could right it, fix it, again.

I turned the Vespa around and headed out of the town's arch and onto the winding road down into the valley. I drove even more slowly than usual, but it was quieter than usual, as though everyone else was slowing down and waiting too. The height of tourist season, yet not a single car passed me.

Not ready to return home, I kept on, past the driveway up a new and unexplored road. I breathed in the evening sights and smells—sunbaked earth and stone, the dust kicking up on the dirt road, the bumps of rocks that had probably sat there since some Roman had found himself too tired to clear them—and let them soothe my soul. There was something about the land that did that to me. It invited me to stop struggling and rest.

A flash of black dancing in yellow caught my eye, and I pulled the Vespa over. *How . . . ?* The field of sunflowers faced me. Every single yellow-petaled, black-centered, stiff-stalked flower stared right at me—for the very first time.

"Aren't you all pretty? Finally decided to share yourselves, huh?" I sat for a few minutes, snapped a few pictures, then slowly turned the Vespa around.

When I entered the house I heard a soft "Emily?" drift down.

I trudged up the steps to the landing and poked my head into Lucio's room. He was propped up in bed—just as we'd left him not an hour before.

He flapped his hand at me, as if he had only the energy to move the wrist, and the rest swung on momentum. "Is Ben back at work?"

"He is, but he's not happy about it." I sat on the corner of the bed. "He'd rather be here."

"Work is good. We're just waiting, aren't we?"

"Don't say that."

Lucio fixed his gaze on the window. "I have a favor to ask." He let his sentence sit, and the silence gave it weight.

I began to dread what might come next.

"Don't paint over the mural."

I wrapped my arms around my shoulders and pulled at my shoulder blades as if trying to split myself apart, or make myself

tight and small. I wasn't sure which. I just knew I couldn't grant this favor. "I need to paint over it, and soon. Uncovering it only brought pain. You must see that, and now is not the time—"

He cut me off. "Emily, no. Covering it in the first place was the mistake. Donata never needed me to fix her pain. She needed me to share it. I never . . . I never did that well. You . . . you can let the story unfold."

"It's taken a turn for the worse."

"Don't all stories do that, before the beautiful ending?"

I slumped. "But it's not a story, Lucio. You must see that; it's your lives."

"That is where you are wrong. They are one and the same. I missed that they are meant to be shared." He reached for my hand, which was resting on the quilt between us. "Wait six months. If you and Don Matteo agree to paint over it then, you may."

"And if you disagree?"

"My darling daughter, I won't be here to protest."

Chapter 39

I sat in the library reading. I had long since finished *The Flanders Panel* and, other than being thoroughly annoyed that the conservator smoked like a chimney while trying to restore a painting, in a dust-filled room no less, I loved it.

I was now on to Lucio's latest selection, Joyce's *A Portrait of the Artist as a Young Man*. This one was hard for me. I had nothing in common with this young boy, becoming a man. It was a chaotic narrative that I failed to grasp, jumping through time and full of angst, religion, nannies, and prostitutes. And yet, I had to concede, my own thoughts, efforts, and concerns often felt as tortuous and weighted. The need to reach wholeness and clarity overwhelmed young Stephen Dedalus. It overwhelmed me.

Francesca, who had moved back into her room a few days before, opened the door and interrupted me.

"You need to call Ben."

That was all she said, but nothing more was needed. I nodded and tapped my phone. He answered on the first ring.

"I'm sorry to call."

"I am on my way."

I laid down my book, unsure what to do. I knew where everyone was, upstairs in Lucio and Donata's bedroom. When Lucio hadn't woken that afternoon during Ben's break, we knew. He had slept all yesterday. All night. His face was paler, his breathing more shallow.

Dario, their family doctor and distant cousin, had been in and out of the house more times than I could count in the past two days. Ben dashed back and forth between his father and his father's life's work. Joseph hovered. Francesca read in the chair by his bed. Donata cooked. I hid in the library.

We were prepared to be completely unprepared.

I walked outside and waited on the gravel drive for Ben. Soon dust flew up along the tree line.

He leapt from the car and, rather than walk straight into the house, pulled me into a hug and stood there for a few heartbeats. Then he nodded into my shoulder, and we walked hand in hand into the house and up the stairs.

Donata sat at the side of the bed, Francesca next to her with an arm draped around her mother's shoulders. Aunt Sophia and her husband, Lucio's youngest brother, whose name I still didn't know, sat in the armchairs. Joseph perched on the windowsill. His face was perfectly still, a mask, and I knew that even if he wanted to, Joseph had no idea how to cross that room—physically or figuratively.

I reached my hand out to draw him over, one outsider to another. He shook his head and dug his fingers into the sill.

Ben immediately dropped next to Francesca and reached a hand out to touch his father's leg, a small bump under several blankets.

Donata glanced at him and then returned her gaze to Lucio. She rested her hand on his forehead. *"Ora puoi andare. Siamo tutti qui e ti vogliamo bene."*

I understood, and her words brought tears to my eyes. She

loved him and we were here and he could go. She said more, but I could no longer catch her words as she lowered her face to his and whispered against his lips.

Within moments his shallow, rasping breath quieted. Donata tipped over and rested across his now-still chest.

Chapter 40

The next morning I woke early to bring coffee back to Ben. He'd barely slept. Neither of us had.

Considering I'd crept down the stairs before dawn, I expected the kitchen to be empty. Instead, I found myself in a sea of black. Already there was no room to breathe. Women in long skirts, thin cotton shawls over black blouses, loose and light in preparation for a hot day, filled all the space between the dining room to the back patio.

Men in black pants and dark shirts, T-shirts, broadcloth, or oxfords—all black—filled every other room. I hadn't known. I'd thrown on a printed blouse and simple beige cotton skirt because I thought we'd be alone, that the day would move slowly and we'd all have a moment to adjust.

I pulled two espresso shots and raced back upstairs. Ben was pulling on a black shirt. Without saying a word, I put the cups on the dresser and pulled him into a tight hug.

As we stepped apart, I gave him the lay of the land. "The house is full down there already and everyone's in black."

"Si."

I pulled the covers over the bed, hastily making it. "What am I to do? I don't have any black. I don't want to embarrass your family."

"It does not matter." He looked me over without expression. "Ask Mama or Francesca if you want something, but you look fine." He squeezed my arm and gave me a quick kiss on the top of my head. "You do, I promise."

"Okay." I nodded simply to end the conversation, not because I agreed.

Ben downed his espresso, then twisted the doorknob. "Are you ready?"

Again I only nodded.

I couldn't bring myself to ask Donata or Francesca for something black. This was not the time for them to worry about my wardrobe. So I skirted the gathering, as I usually did, and hoped no one would notice me.

It was clear that all the details had already been arranged. From snippets of conversation I learned the funeral had a time and location, a hearse ordered, flowers organized. It felt as if not only details had been arranged in advance, but everyone knew their role and fulfilled it before anyone thought to ask.

Now it was time to talk, remember, and eat—the dining room and kitchen overflowed with food, and the glorious and colorful display felt almost obscene. Red tomatoes sat against bright white fresh mozzarella, and that lay beneath bold green basil leaves; beef rolls in a thick red *pomodoro* sauce; fresh pasta dishes, some cold, some hot; and bread . . . *Panina gialla aretina*, *Bozza pratese*, *Ciaccino*, and *Ficattola*.

Lucio had taught me the names one day while we sat in the library—me sketching his portrait, he telling me stories of baking, Donata, and the trials and tribulations of running Coccocino. Ben had taught me how to recognize all the different varieties,

even how to make and mold them. I looked around for him, but he was nowhere to be found. He'd been absorbed by the sea of black.

I soon found myself sneaking off to the library.

The room was cool, shaded and empty. The wood shutters were almost fully pulled across the windows. I already missed the sunshine and my mornings with Lucio.

I shut the door behind me, pulled the shutters open, and sank into my usual chair. Donata's chair. Rather than pick up my sketch pad, I reached for my book. A slam brought me to my feet.

Donata raced across the room and yanked the shutters closed. One squealed on its hinges and another splintered with the force. The sound bounced off all the hard surfaces, even the soft ones.

"I shut these. There is no light now. It is gone." Her English was thick and slow, each consonant getting full attention and all the room's available oxygen.

I certainly wasn't getting any. I slid from the chair and backed away. "I . . . I'm sorry."

"No. I do not want that from you. He is gone and I am where I began. Alone." She looked around the room. "All I had . . . All my life . . ." She dropped into his chair and covered her face with her hands. There was no sobbing, no sound at all. Perfect stillness, and then she raised her head slowly. "I have lost . . . *ogni cosa*."

Everything. I understood. I had ruined everything.

Her voice dropped and her gaze trailed to her fingers. She was kneading them together, her knuckles white with the force. "What did he say? He asked for you. There is more I do not know."

It took only a moment to understand. "I'm not to paint over the mural for six months, if ever."

"He gives it to you." A single tear ran down her cheek. "And me?"

I stared at her.

"Please go."

I couldn't find Ben in the house. People said he was here, then someone would point to another room. "Over there."

Several minutes of frantic searching didn't produce him, but it did my Vespa. I hopped on and sped down the gravel road with no clue where I was headed.

About an hour later Ben found me. I'd pulled the Vespa off to the side of the road and was sitting on a rock watching the sunflowers turn.

"Give them time and they will face you." He walked up behind me.

"I doubt that. They've only done it once, and I don't think I get a second chance." We both knew my answer was illogical.

Ben sat down. As there wasn't room on my rock, he'd dropped to the ground next to it and looked up, his face several inches below mine.

"She blames me. For the mural. And that your dad asked me to leave it."

"She cannot blame you for all that."

"She does, in English too." I didn't turn my head. "She wants me gone, Ben, and I don't blame her. I don't think an apartment in the village is far enough right now." Suddenly I was sad I'd ever mentioned it. When I'd wanted to leave, it was one thing, but knowing that my presence was wounding Donata was another. Illogically it made me want to stay, help . . . do something.

Ben reached up and touched my knee. "She is grieving. She is angry. She acts like she is strong, stronger than Papa, but she never was. She leaned on him, tucked into him right here." He patted his chest at the base of his neck. The precise place I tucked into him. I couldn't help my small smile because I knew how safe Donata must have felt.

I looked back to the thick green backs of the flowers stretching

across the field and hill before me. "That doesn't change who she blames, how she feels."

"All the elements were here, simmering for years, long before you arrived." He laid his elbow on his knee and leaned into me. "I understand her better now, after Papa talked to us. She has always been so afraid, but I could never call it that because I did not know. She reminds me of your poppies, that painting you showed me in Atlanta."

"The stems that couldn't bend?"

"You said the wind would break them." Ben kept his eyes trained across the field. "I think Mama broke."

"We need to help her, Ben. Joseph would call me the salt to her wound now."

"That would be unkind of him."

I only shrugged because that didn't mean it wasn't true.

"Maybe, after the funeral, we could go to Atlanta together, stay a couple weeks for that show Olivia offered you. Give Mama time." Ben's voice dropped to a whisper.

"What?"

"Time may be all she needs."

I knew he was wrong, and it almost frightened me that he even suggested it.

Ben, who worked to bring people together, who went to the US to reach his brother, then stayed to help an aunt and uncle he'd never met. Ben, who'd learned to make spectacular pizza to honor his parents, and his craft and his restaurant . . . Ben felt it was best we go?

I glanced down at him. He wasn't looking at me, but across the field. I realized then that he understood. At least I suspected he did. Time wasn't going to help Donata. He was offering it to me. An out. A chance to breathe.

"Maybe that's a good idea."

Chapter 41

The funeral was to start at ten o'clock, but Santa Maria was packed by nine. Ben left me in the first pew before going through a small door to my left. I hadn't been in this church before, and I soon found myself assessing the paintings and what work they needed—anything to distract.

My eyes kept darting to Lucio, resting in his open casket before the altar. He looked much the same, yet completely different. It was true what they say, all warmth leaves in death. His face was chalky, white, with an odd transparency to his skin. My eyes pricked. I'd never called him Papa, and yet that was how I'd come to think of him. It now felt like I'd withheld something precious from us both.

As people entered, they kissed his forehead or cheek before finding a seat. Although everyone looked the same, dressed in black, the tone felt markedly different from the house. There people had bustled about, and although a palpable sadness hovered, a sense of celebration over Lucio's life permeated the atmosphere. Not here. Here Lucio's loss felt like a crashing tidal wave. Sniffles and an occasional sob echoed off the stones.

Someone tapped my shoulder, and I spun around to find Father Matt staring at me. "I didn't see you come in."

"You were lost in thought." He squeezed my shoulder and looked past me to the altar. "Lucio called a couple days ago and asked me not to paint over the mural. I gather he asked the same of you."

"He did and I said I wouldn't, but it's a mistake."

"I'm not so sure. Have you prayed about it?"

"No."

"I wondered. Because if you had, we were hearing very different messages." He leaned closer and dropped his voice to a whisper. "I agree with Lucio and feel a peace about it, though I have no idea why. Donata is formidable when angry." He chuckled softly and pressed his fist against his heart. "But I feel it here. The mural must stay, for now."

Speechless, I swung back around.

He tapped me again. "I'm sorry that upsets you."

"She's not angry so much as devastated, and leaving it there is a cruel reminder of her past. It wasn't only the pregnancy. She lost her family, her parents, siblings . . . everything. And I uncovered it for the world to see and judge all over again. She won't forget it—no one will now."

"You did not remind her of something she had forgotten, Emily. She had never forgotten it, covered or not."

When I didn't turn back to him, he tapped me again. "Will you come see me tomorrow?"

I shrugged. "Now that the paintings are finished, even walking into the church feels like a betrayal."

"Walking into church is never a betrayal." He squeezed my shoulder one last time, then retreated through the same small door to my left.

As the music began, Ben reemerged from it, paused at his father's casket, kissed his cheeks, and shut the lid. He escorted his mother inside and then reached for my hand as he sat between us.

I caught few words as Don Giorgio's deep and aging voice broke across the congregation with heartfelt love. It was a full and formal Mass. The priest swung the thurible full of incense at the crucifix and the paschal candle, and at the final commendation, Father Matt incensed Lucio's coffin as well. I'd studied the practice when I'd restored a thurible for a Catholic church in Chicago.

We soon shuffled down the center aisle and out like a row of ants—dark clothes and dark cars. Following the hearse, we trailed a long line deep into the countryside. I'd never ventured far in the direction we headed and realized that I didn't know what lay beyond the farthest hill. I'd painted that very one from Lucio's bedroom window.

We crossed over it and another, and another, before we finally arrived at a cemetery packed with mausoleums. Tucked within the center, and surrounded by flowers, was one for *Vassallo* and *Gagliardi*, Lucio's mother's family.

Don Giorgio spoke a few words in both Italian and Latin, then everyone filed by, laid a quick kiss on their hand, and touched it to the wood.

Cars dispersed, and Ben and I were among the last standing.

"Home?" I asked.

"This is only the beginning." He clasped my hand. "How are you doing?"

I squeezed his tight. "How are you?"

He shook his head but did not reply.

As soon as we crossed the threshold, Ben was again swept into a sea of black. I skirted the tide and, unthinking, made my way to the library. But what had been my warm yellow sanctuary now

held Donata's anger—and it felt as real as a living entity, one I could reach out and touch, but would rather avoid.

Today, even though shutters still covered the windows, the double doors stood wide open. I walked straight through the room, out onto the small patio, and into the trees beyond. I wove in and out until I found a path. A little farther on, I found a bench.

A snapped twig swung me around, and I saw Francesca before she saw me.

"What are you doing out here?"

"Alessandro just arrived." She dropped next to me. "I don't feel like facing him today."

"He may want to say he's sorry or offer support. You were . . . are . . . friends."

She tucked her knees under her skirt. "Let me be immature for a sec, then I'll be a big girl and do my duty."

I laughed. "Don't be mature on my account."

She nudged me. "We've lived in the same house lately and I've barely seen you."

"I've been lurking on the edges. I'm not needed close."

"But you're family." She nudged me harder, and I tipped away.

"Debatable . . . I don't feel like family."

"And what does family feel like?" She shot me a quick smile. She didn't expect an answer. Her tone was slightly sarcastic, bold—American—and spot-on.

"No clue."

She laughed. "We probably exhibit a little more than standard dysfunctionality. Did you know Joseph called for a car and is leaving in about an hour?"

"Today?"

Francesca pressed her lips in a firm, straight line, keeping her criticism tucked safely inside.

"I'm sorry . . . Did you hear about the mural?" I hadn't had the courage or the chance to talk to her about it in the past few days.

"I went to the church and saw it yesterday."

"You did?"

"Yes . . . It's amazing. I remember it, you know." She caught my expression and offered a slight nod. "Yeah. Ben was gone, but I was only eight. I was here . . . I was actually with Mama and Papa that evening. Of course I didn't understand the significance, and until Papa told me the story a few days ago I'd forgotten all about it, even about Mama leaving. Now it's all back."

"I am so sorry."

"Why?" She grabbed my arm. "Everything makes sense now. There was so much that was wrong for so long. Mama is so rigid, always has been, and I understand it now. Everyone talks about how Joseph hasn't forgiven her for years for who knows what, but she never forgave herself. She hasn't finished the story any more than he failed to do. I feel like I finally get why it's so hard to be here. Why I sometimes hate it."

Francesca stopped as if remembering the day, and why she was sitting out on a bench, with me. "I shouldn't say all that. Not now. I just wish I'd known why she was always so angry and afraid. I wouldn't have poked at her so . . . I might've actually tried to understand her, even make pasta if that would've helped." She snorted. "Forget that. I still wouldn't have made the pasta." She dropped her head to her hands. "For all Joseph's criticisms, Papa was our glue. I don't know how we'll be without him. No one expected Joseph to stay, but will he come back? How will we ever be a family now?"

"You will. Ben's kinda glue-like." I nudged her. "I think you all sticking together is very important to him."

"It is." Francesca nudged me back. "I'm glad you married my brother. He's a keeper."

When I didn't reply, she bumped my shoulder again. "Hey . . . I agree." I looked back to the house. "What will happen to you and Alessandro?"

"I'll learn to let him go."

"That's my fault. I tried to fix something that wasn't broken."

"It is now." Francesca tried to laugh, perhaps for my sake. "But it will all be okay. We couldn't have gone on much longer like we were, despite the fact I may have wanted to. You do reach moments, you know? Turning points. We were close to one."

"Speaking of turning points." I stretched my back. "I was offered a show in Atlanta, and Ben suggested we both go. Give your mother a break from me."

Francesca shot straight, genuinely surprised. "He did?"

"She's hurting, and lest anyone forget, I am the one who barged into her home, disrupted everything, and then uncovered the mural."

"You have been busy."

"Very."

"But to leave now?" Francesca shook her head. "It doesn't feel . . . I mean, you'd come back, right?"

Now I pulled up, surprised. It hadn't occurred to me that I wouldn't . . . And yet . . . "Of course. It's just for a gallery show. Ben offered up a couple weeks, but we both know that's not possible."

Chapter 42

The next week held much of the same. Each day the house filled with people, with food, with stories and laughter, with tears and drama. I skirted it all, tired of not fitting in and weary of Aunt Sophia's overt humor at my discomfort and Donata's palpable antipathy.

Ben began working more, finally returning full time for service on the fourth night. And Francesca moved back into her apartment. So rather than escaping into the countryside on my scooter, I hid in her room and painted. Ben and I had decided to accept Olivia Barton's offer, and in a week we planned to head back to the States, him for three days, as that was all he felt he could afford away from Coccocino, and me for ten.

But as the day drew close, a black certainty crept over me. I needed to go alone—for myself and for Ben. Each morning when I came down to breakfast, he was already there chatting with his mom. Each afternoon when he joined us during his quiet time between prep and service, she brightened and offered her only smiles of the day.

Donata was drowning. She was tighter, thinner, angrier, and slowly filling with despair. She needed Ben.

Each night he'd pull me close and it would again, for a moment, feel like magic—like the mornings Lucio described as he fell in love with Donata at Coccocino. Like our own nights in Atlanta when we'd stay up talking, holding hands, flicking paint on each other—not able to say enough, share enough, get close enough. Like the nights only weeks ago, when Ben would hold me close and we'd share our days, laughing about Lucio's latest literary lesson or Donata's best passive-aggressive barb. We were on the same side, and sharing it all made it sweeter and more golden. But not now. I couldn't say if it was me or him—I just knew the magic was gone.

The night before our trip, he still hadn't packed. He came home at one in the morning and, like his father so many nights ago, I stood waiting in the front hall.

"Can we talk?"

"Bella? You scared me. Why are you awake?"

"I couldn't sleep." I led him back to the kitchen.

I smiled when I looked down at the table. So like Lucio and I hadn't realized it—the table now showed evidence of my long waiting night: the tea tin, a small plate of food, a book, and the espresso machine's knock box—because it really was too far to the bin to dump the cold tea leaves.

I sat down and passed a cup between my hands.

Ben sat across from me. "Emily?"

"I don't think you should come to Atlanta with me tomorrow."

"Why?"

His tone surprised me. He wasn't questioning the fact, just my reasoning—as if he already had his own.

"Because you're needed here. Even three days, and that's not counting travel, is too long."

"You are my wife."

The declaration almost made me smile. I knew he meant *I go where you go*, but it fell flat to my ears. He might have said *You are a cheese sandwich* and it would've evoked the same emotion. I needed to be out from under the pressure, and taking Ben away from Coccocino and Donata simply added more pressure.

"I'll be back soon." I looked up. "Please let me do this. Let me go, and then I'll be back. You do what you need to do and I'll do the same."

"What does that mean?"

"It means I need a break. I . . . I think I've been trying to pretend I'm someone I'm not—a member of this family." I waved my hands around the kitchen. "But all I do is knock into things, and right now is not the time to be knocking into things. I feel like if I get back to what I know, being who I know, then this will all sort itself out."

Ben reached for my hands and stilled them around the cup. "What are you talking about?"

"I'm talking about being comfortable, understanding how things work, fit together. You say I like puzzles, and I do—but this is not one that fits for me and it clearly doesn't fit for Donata, and she's the more important one right now. Please. I just need to go—"

I stopped. There was an unexpected tinge within my voice, an irritation, a burr—anger. From Ben's expression, I knew it surprised him too. His eyes widened, then softened, then dimmed.

"You have decided."

"Yes."

He wiped a thumb under my eye. "Has it been that bad?"

"Don't ask that. You know it hasn't." I scrunched my nose to stopper my emotions. We were going off script . . . I took a deep breath and said what I'd rehearsed, all that I'd meant to say in the first place. "Let me head back for a few days and see this show

through in Atlanta. I committed to it. I'll even get some of my stuff out of storage in Chicago and check in with Amy. It'll be good to take care of all that."

Ben nodded. Up. Down. Up. Down. He agreed, but not because he felt the same. He agreed because I gave him no option. I'd seen Amy do the same thing.

⸻

Joseph surprised me outside customs and baggage claim.

"So you're my advance team?"

He caught my tone and grinned. "I am your only team. Ben texted your flight information and asked me to meet you." He grabbed my bag and headed to parking. "He didn't have to ask. I would've come. You're staying with me, by the way."

"I thought I'd get a hotel, now that Ben's not with me."

"What does Ben have to do with anything?" Joseph threw me a glance. "You make me wonder if this trip signifies more. You are my sister. Yes?"

"Yes." I nodded.

"Then don't act like family isn't family."

I smiled. This from the one who hadn't gone home in seventeen years and left the day of his father's funeral.

Joseph pulled into ACI's parking lot before I realized we weren't headed to his apartment.

"We're going to the studio?" I stifled a yawn.

"We've got three days, and you don't get over jet lag by sleeping too soon. Let's get a few of your paintings back into frames."

We entered to find Lily with her face pressed into her scope, scraping at something on a small modernist piece. I leaned against her table and asked, "Anything I can do to help?"

She whacked her eye, jumping up to hug me. "You're here. I figured I wouldn't see you until tomorrow." She waved her hand at my bag. "This is so exciting. Let me see your work. The pictures you sent weren't lit well at all."

"Later. Let me frame them so they look good."

She pointed to my worktable, questioning.

"Not there. We're framing in my workroom." Joseph's voice cut across the room.

Lily raised a brow at me.

"They'll create too much dust, and you don't need the noise. You're under a tight deadline, Lily, remember?"

Lily saluted a "Yes, sir" as Joseph grabbed the duffel and headed to his office.

"I'd better go." I tapped her table. "Dinner tonight? Piccolo?"

"Yes, please. I haven't been there since you and Ben left."

"It's a date." I smiled and followed Joseph, calling to him, "Piccolo tonight?"

"I may be busy, but you go with Lily. I haven't caught up from the trip. The Van Geld estate goes up for auction next week."

Joseph does work. I remembered wondering about it . . . In fact, there was a lot I wondered about Joseph. In the couple weeks I'd spent in Atlanta before, I'd never seen him work, barely stepped into his office, and had no idea where his apartment was, despite the fact that Ben had stayed with him. And I learned little new in Montevello. I read about what he did, mostly from Alberto Rodi's journals, but still knew virtually nothing about who he was, then or now.

Joseph opened the door behind his desk.

"Lily said you had a work—" I froze.

Nothing could have prepared me for the room behind his office. This was no stark and sterile lab. This was a sanctuary.

Antique lamps and objets d'art; bookshelves lined with classics; a beautiful Italian Renaissance table stretching three feet by six feet, with huge thick legs and detailed carvings along its flanks; a reading chair covered in bright red velvet, worn on the arms, pillows pushed deep within its corners; and the most beautiful rug I'd ever seen, boasting a cacophony of color in swirling patterns. And yellow. The walls were the exact yellow of Lucio's library.

He followed my gaze, which rested again on the rug. "And they say all the quality is out of Persia. I bought that in Milan a few years ago, woven in Lombardy."

His voice was light, playful, and rather than tilting his accent for his advantage, he seemed lost in his country's culture, heritage, and beauty.

I scanned the room again, absorbing my first glimpse of the true man. My gaze settled on an easel with tubes of paint filling its tray. "You still paint."

"Could you stop? Would you want to?"

I laughed and shook my head. I loved painting, and there was no way I would stop. It was there I felt most alive. *Not only there.* I mentally conceded that I felt that way with Ben too. Rachel's words over coffee that long ago day flowed through me. *You can feel just that alive every day—as long as you don't forget.*

Joseph crossed over to the easel. "Olivia has actually hosted several shows of mine. I paint under the name Luca Bellotto and I'm quite popular with Russian buyers."

"Why hide it? I even asked Ben if you still painted. He said he didn't know."

"No one does. Hence Luca." He spread his palm across his chest. "It's too raw for me. I paint from here."

I envisioned the mural and realized, again, how truly

remarkable it was, how devastating—made all the more powerful when I recalled he was eighteen when he painted it.

"Someday, if you'll let me, I'd like to see your work."

"Someday." Joseph rolled a freestanding tool chest over to the table. "Time to get to *your* work. Spread them out and let's see what we're dealing with."

I pulled over some cloth-covered weights to hold down the edges and started unrolling each canvas, now embarrassed. I knew how talented he was, but to learn he still painted, sold works, and had a Russian following—it was intimidating.

I glanced up as I spread out the first, the second, the third . . . He said nothing.

"Say it. No good?"

He didn't lift his eyes from his father's face. *"Magnifico."*

Chapter 43

The next morning I dropped Joseph at ACI and headed across town to Gallery Barton. I hauled in the three paintings we'd already framed and found Olivia pacing.

"Good. You're finally here."

"Am I late?" I set them down and kissed both her cheeks, wondering when I'd appropriated the custom.

"Not at all, but until I actually have something in hand, I don't trust it." She tipped through the three paintings. "Such aching beauty." She then threw her arms out. "What do you think of the space? Is this what you imagined?"

I walked around. I'd sent her a color number for the walls, a deep Tuscan yellow. I called it Lucio's yellow. "It's brighter than I expected."

"The color you picked was deeper, so I lightened it a touch. I wanted that sweet spot between taxicabs and Tuscany." She ran one jet-black nail along the wall. "A designer out of Chicago swears by taxicab-yellow walls and I can't say I disagree, especially with your work."

She crossed the gallery, her heels clicking like gunshots. "You've captured the Tuscan sensibility in such a short time.

Unbelievable, really; it's like your heart was looking for a home."
She spread her hand as if presenting a marquee sign. "Let me
show you how I envision this, but feel free to disagree. It's your
show. Dune—what a name—will be here tomorrow. He's working
as handler, but he's not your caliber, so you may find yourself
hanging your own pieces." She glanced back at me. "You're the talent and the crew. I've got a good feeling about this collaboration."

She flicked her finger here and there, pointing out the lighting and other details of the space—all of which would need to be
taken into account when installing the show.

"And here is the dividing line between you and Stratton. He
gets fully black walls. His work is an entirely white-on-white
experience. I think you'll play well off each other. Possibly to your
advantage, but don't tell him that."

"I won't." I circled my portion again. "And if I won't get in the
way of your painters, I'll hang first thing tomorrow."

"This was supposed to be done by last week, but that's the way
it always goes. The painters should wrap up Stratton's side today."

"Good. I'll walk the space, then get back to Joseph's and finish
framing."

"Glad to have you here, darling." She waved her hand and disappeared. Just. That. Fast.

I took my three paintings—one of Lucio, one of Donata, and one
of my sunflower field, and positioned them side by side. I pulled out
my phone and took a picture of the sunflower painting. And as Ben's
voice echoed in my memory, I stored it as my home screen. *My own
girasole. Please, Bella, only turn toward me.* I missed him.

I then stared at Donata. Joseph had framed her picture alone.
Without even discussing it with me, he'd moved it to his side of the
table and set to work. He'd chosen birch and a clean framing style,
simple and unconventional, and then added a wash to the finish,

laying on a subtle white patina. It was incongruent with the classic style of the picture, but highlighted the deep tones and broader strokes I'd used to form the background. It captured the painting as well as the painting had captured Donata.

I felt a sense of loss looking at her now—one I hadn't expected. I reached for my phone to e-mail Ben. I'd already called three times and sent a couple texts, but hadn't gotten through or received a reply. Cellular service within Coccocino's kitchen was sketchy at best. An e-mail seemed my next-best option.

Dear Ben,

I'm standing in the gallery right now. Olivia painted the walls "taxicab yellow." You might not know that color, since your cabs are white. But you were here awhile; you must have seen a few. Anyway, it's a shocking, wonderful color.

I sent her my interpretation of a Tuscan yellow, but I have to admit, hers is better. It will play well against my work. The sunflowers will pop, and the glint on the bookshelves behind your father will come to life. There is no yellow to call out within the painting of your mother, but I think its absence will be striking too.

I guess that's it for now. Please call. I've tried a couple times but can't get a connection. You're probably in the kitchen.

I love you.
Emily

I walked the space, measured the walls, and made a thorough list of dimensions, lighting changes, mounting requirements,

and placement. And one last time, before heading back to the studio, I tapped my phone to check messages. No missed calls. No missed texts. I tapped on e-mails. There was one—from Ben.

Dear Emily,

I am sorry I missed your calls.

I filleted an *orate* today. It is a tender whitefish; I am not certain if you have it in the States or what you call it. I envied that fish. One flick of the knife, one swipe of my hand, and it was clean. I wish life were that easy.

Alessandro came by the café this morning. Andre teased him so badly that he asked me to take a walk rather than sit. Andre will never let that go, but I doubt Alessandro cares. He came to ask my permission to court Francesca. Our word, *corteggiamento*, feels more active than your words—it is a wooing, enfolding, and embracing. Think of our nights in Atlanta. If you did not know, that was what I was about.

It was sad he had to ask me. A father should grant that honor. I did not tell Francesca. There is no need until he comes to ask for her hand in marriage, and I know that will be soon. He comes to see her every day since Papa died, wanting to be near.

I brought Mama a pizza during my break yesterday. She laughed and grumbled, as is her way. We ate in silence, but she looks better. I helped her move some of Papa's things and I put away your book pile. I hope you do not mind. As I slid yours away, I pulled down one of Papa's favorites. He loved Dante. I borrowed his *Vita Nuova* and read too late into the night. My dreams were full of dark halls and endless tunnels.

I must go back in the kitchen. *Caio*, Bella.

Vita Nuova? His dream bothered me. *Dark halls and endless tunnels?* Lucio never read anything by accident, and I suspected Ben was the same. I Googled the title. It was a mix of poetry and verse, one of Dante's few Italian rather than Latin works, and was his reconstruction of courtly love. A romance, autobiographical in nature, of his unrequited love for Beatrice Portinari—a woman he desperately loved but never "caught." A work of beauty, of longing, of letting go . . .

Ah . . . Lucio . . . Did he never understand and truly find Donata? And . . . Ben . . . What have I done?

I tapped my phone again.

"Emily?"

My heart glowed at the long trail of *e*'s, then dimmed with its next beat. Ben's tone did not hold the notes of expectant surprise, but rather the sorrow of longing.

"Hi. I've been calling. I just read your e-mail."

"I miss you." His voice was still, without lilt or inflection.

"I miss you too. Are you busy?"

"We are. Two freezers broke. We are hurrying meats to Andre's freezers."

"Oh no, that's not good. I . . . I wish I could help."

He didn't reply.

"You need to go, don't you?"

He hesitated, and I loved him the more for it.

"I do. I wish I did not. I miss your voice."

"I will call later. I love you."

"Ciao."

I tapped another number and listened to the ring.

"Hey, Emily. Why are you calling?" Amy's voice sounded harried. Everyone seemed to have something pressing.

"Does something have to be up for me to call you?"

She didn't answer for a beat. Two beats. "Well . . . yes."

"That's probably true . . . I'm in Atlanta for a couple weeks."

"Why are you in Atlanta?" I heard a shuffling noise, as if she was pulling out a chair.

"Remember that gallery we drove by? They're having a show of my work, oils on canvas, opening tomorrow."

Her brief pause ended with a happy squeal. "Congratulations! How could you not tell me this? You should have texted; I could've come."

"Don't worry about it."

"Hey . . . I'm sorry about Ben's dad. Is he with you? Ben. Not his dad."

"No." I smiled. Amy always had a quick and easy way about her. "He stayed in Italy. Ben. Not his dad. Well, actually . . ." I stopped. It didn't feel funny. "You never texted me, by the way. What job did you take?"

"I got the job with that party planner."

"And?" I cringed and closed my eyes. My tone was too harsh. What had Amy called it? Patronizing?

"Ems, please. I'm not five."

"Yeah, I caught that too. Sorry. Tell me about the job."

"I'm good at it. Really good. In the past month I've managed three weddings and taken on more new projects than anyone here. It's a staff of seven. And I love it. Listen . . ." Her voice came soft, coaxing, across the line. "I'm doing well, Emily. Be happy for me. I shouldn't have blamed you; I never stuck up for myself. It was easier, you always making everything right, and that was on me. But I'm okay now."

She sounded as if she'd rehearsed that speech a few times, maybe over a few years. I shook my head, as if she could see me, and so much became clear with each shake. "I *am* happy for you,

and I think I got more in your way than I ever should have. That was my fault." I swiped at my eyes, surprised to find the back of my hand come away wet. "I need to go, Amy. I have a bunch of paintings left to frame today. I'll call in a few days when things are quieter. Okay?"

"When do you go home?" When I failed to give a quick reply, she called out, "Italy? Hello?"

"In a couple weeks, when the show winds down."

"Can you come up here before you go?"

"I thought about it. It'd be good to clear out the storage locker." I stood and looked around the empty gallery. "I really do need to go now."

"Okay. We'll talk soon . . . I love you, sis." Her voice sounded like she was throwing out a line. Fishing.

Maybe for the first time ever, I caught it. "I love you too."

Chapter 44

I hoisted Lucio's portrait above my head and aimed for the three hooks I'd secured moments before. Dune, Olivia's handler, had offered to help, but as I felt he'd hung the entire Stratton show at least five inches too high, I politely refused. Besides, there was something comfortable, elemental and tactile, about doing it myself.

Olivia was right. Stratton's austere white-on-white works played well off mine. I disagreed that mine shone brighter—not like at some art shows when the velvet dogs next door make one's painting look like newly discovered Rembrandts—but we certainly didn't cheapen each other.

A soft shuffling noise turned me. Joseph approached, his eyes fixed on my centerpiece. Lucio standing in his beloved library.

"There's a red dot. Have you already sold it?"

"It's not for sale. It's for your mother." I stepped back, assessed it, and then straightened it.

"I didn't get the impression you two were close."

"True, but it's still hers. The first time I showed it to her she

ran from the room. I thought she hated it, but then your father said he wanted to be remembered that way, and I figured maybe she saw that too."

"I expect she did." Joseph nodded, still fixated on the painting. "Will you take it or ship it?"

His question surprised me. And yet it didn't. I knew what he was really asking, and I had no ready answer. I loved Ben. But I hadn't found my place within Montevello, within Ben's family, and I wasn't sure I would or could. The way I viewed the world and how things worked didn't come close to the swirling sense of life there. I felt displaced and didn't know if I could survive that for ten, twenty, fifty years . . .

Joseph left the gallery before I answered his question—before I even tried. I watched as his car rounded the corner before I pulled my phone from my back pocket and slid down the wall to the floor. The *girasole* picture on my home screen didn't generate its usual smile.

I tapped Ben's picture. No answer. I waited for voice mail. "Hey, Ben—just calling to say hi. You're probably starting service right now. I'll try later."

I tapped off the call and onto e-mail.

Hey Ben,

I just left you a message. I miss you. More than you
know. I've attached a picture of your father's portrait. It's the
show's centerpiece. You can see the yellow wall behind it and
the red dot on the card, lower left. Joseph thought it strange
I was saving it for your mother. But it belongs to her. I know
Lucio would want that.

I've been staring at it all morning. You have his eyes. His heart too. You and he are the two best men I've ever known. Please call.

I love you.
Emily

A few hours later, with still no call from Ben, I cleaned the last of the debris and mess from Joseph's worktable and headed toward ACI's front door.

"Wear something beautiful tonight." Joseph saw me leaving and called out. "Tonight is about art, but art is about beauty and desire. The art and the artist are both on display."

With only an answering nod, I pushed out the studio doors. As much as I didn't want to be on display, even chafed that I would be, he was right. Artist and art, in many ways, became one. That was one reason Joseph used an alias, and the reason my own paintings almost brought me to tears. I still felt as if every time I looked at them—Ben, Lucio, Donata—I was trying to reach them, and failing.

As I drove to the gallery, I realized that Joseph had pegged only part of the equation. Art is about beauty and desire, yes, but it's also about truth. That's what pricked my eyes, not the paintings, but what they conveyed. Truth.

And when art touched the soul, it was because it spoke to something beyond ourselves and the temporal; it called out to our deepest understandings and dreams. It reached higher. It meant more. I saw that in Ben's, Lucio's, and Donata's portraits—in their eyes. I saw them.

With a head full of musings and questions, but no answers, I pulled up to the gallery. I caught Olivia in the window, looking

pristine in white linen. She'd dressed with cool confidence, but her quick steps betrayed serious nerves.

Soon I was as jumpy as she was—especially when her seemingly disembodied head popped out from Stratton's white-on-white world and barked at Dune.

"Did you do that on purpose?" I flicked my finger to the painting behind her.

She looked back at Stratton's ten-by-ten-foot "blizzard" behind her and laughed. "I like to share in the experience, but this isn't working, is it?"

I shook my head.

"I should've dressed for your show. I have just the blouse to get lost in those flowers your husband sent."

"What flowers?" I spun, searching.

She pointed to a table just on the edge of Stratton's black walls. *Girasoli.*

The massive crystal vase was filled with over twenty large sunflowers standing at least thirty-six inches high. I fingered one and tried to gently twist it. Packed too tight, it wouldn't turn. "They're gorgeous."

"They are. They set just the right tone." She swayed side to side, taking in the gallery. "I love this moment. Right before flight. Can you feel it?"

Flight. I released the flower and stepped back. "Olivia, I . . . I'm all set up, but I need to go. I'll be back before opening . . . but . . . I'll see you soon." I backed toward the door.

A Portrait of the Artist as a Young Man.

I finally knew why Lucio had laid it on my stack of books.

And it broke my heart . . .

I drove back to Joseph's apartment, refusing to think, refusing to feel. I needed to be alone and motionless to work through this one. I pulled into the parking space in front of his town house and froze. *Amy?*

She saw me before I turned off the engine and was by the door as I opened it. "Surprise!"

I climbed out and hugged her. "What are you doing here?"

"I came to celebrate with you. Ben's not here; you need family to share with. Joseph knows, obviously. He gave me his address." She trailed me up the walk and through the front door. "This is your big moment. Are you okay?"

I dropped my bag on the floor and flopped on Joseph's couch. "I read this book and I finally get it, but now you're here." I looked up at her. "You came."

Amy said nothing. She shot me a strange look but stayed silent and dropped next to me.

"It was a puzzle, a collage of emotion and turmoil along with musings on art, religion, politics, and the nature of true beauty. The hero, Stephen Dedalus, was trying to figure out how to be a man and, in the end, an artist." I leaned back and took a long, deep breath. "Maybe that's why I hated it. He kept trying to define himself. I do that too. I mean, isn't that what *The Way Things Work* is all about? Even when you teased me about it, I didn't see it. We both know what I'm tying to fix."

Rather than reply, Amy simply reached for my hand. I covered it with my other one and kept on.

"But it was harder than Stephen Dedalus thought. It's harder than I thought. He had to leave everything behind, like that Greek myth of Daedalus where he makes his beautiful wings and flies away. That was his name, too, in the book. And that's what he was

telling me. He knew I'd need to leave, that I'd never fit in and understand. He was giving me permission to leave."

"The author?" Amy tilted her head, clearly not following me. I couldn't blame her. I wasn't following me.

"Lucio."

"Lucio wrote the book?"

"You're not listening." I moaned and covered my face.

Amy pulled my hands away and held them in my lap. "I'm listening; you're not making sense."

"I'm saying I fell in love with Ben and I thought it'd be enough. He was the dream. And, like you said, marriage is for life and I thought once I married him, that's how it would work. Not for Mom and Dad, but for me. It would all be fixed, finished. But when I got into it . . . I can't fix all I got wrong, and Lucio knew that. He knew I would need to get back to a place I understood and was comfortable. He knew I'd have to stop trying to be something I'm not."

"But I was here, Ems. I saw you . . . You were the best *you* I've ever known. You weren't pretending anything." She flopped back against the cushion next to me. "Do you remember the night Dad left?"

"No."

"I do. It's actually my first memory. I was six, so I should have some before that, but I can't dig any up . . . Anyway, Mom and Dad were yelling, and we both woke up. I said I was scared, and do you remember what you did?"

"Gave you a lecture? Built you headphones from Barbie hair and paper clips?"

"No. You climbed down from your bunk and crawled into bed beside me and held my hand. You didn't say anything. I woke the next morning still holding your hand."

"Why are you telling me this now?"

"Because that's the sister I saw when I was last here. That's the sister who shared the longest night of my life with me and the sister who brought me down here today. And I don't believe she got it all wrong then, and I don't believe she is trying to be something she's not now."

"You don't?" I swung my head toward her. "Then what went wrong?"

"Nothing. You just don't want to get hurt anymore."

Chapter 45

She says some things can't be fixed. We just have to endure them. Wisdom relayed by a fourteen-year-old girl, but I hadn't listened.

My taxi pulled into the airport as my phone rang. *Joseph.* I'd completely forgotten about him. I was tempted not to answer, but I tapped the phone anyway.

"Where are you?" came across the line in a furious faux-whisper.

"I'm going home." I rustled through my bag for my credit card and handed it to the driver. "My cab is pulling up to the airport right now, and Amy is headed to the gallery to meet you."

"You're leaving your sister with me?"

"You can handle her." I smiled at his dry tone. "And it's pretty incredible that she came, so be nice to her. Can you believe she did that?"

"I'm having less trouble believing that than the fact that you're at the airport and not on your way here. What are you doing? Are you trying to end your career before it starts?"

"I'm not. Sincerely. Amy can handle all the details. You said yourself art is about beauty and desire. Amy's gorgeous and poised; she'll handle it all perfectly."

"She's not the artist."

"True." I got my card back and rolled my bag into the airport. "Hang on . . ." I stepped into a quiet corner by the door. Planes passed overhead. I was about to be on one of those.

"Are you still there?" Joseph barked.

"Yes, sorry. I was getting out of the cab . . . Listen, I am the artist, Joseph, I do know that, but my art doesn't come from a place like yours. You've found a home in Atlanta and it works for you, but my art came from screwing up on a daily basis within your family. Mine came from not knowing most of the conversations swirling around me and getting slighted by your aunt Sophia; from every story your father told and every book, good or bad, he passed my way; and from every nasty look your mother sent me. It came from watching her dote on your father, adore Ben, and even send you achingly painful looks whenever you crossed her line of sight a couple weeks ago."

I heard a slight intake of breath, but I couldn't stop. I couldn't risk his opinion, his advice, or his disdain. I needed to finish this.

"It came from sharing their lives, Joseph, when I forgot about trying to fix them. I don't need to fly away to be free and find my art; I need to tuck in and let go of trying to control it. If I don't go home right now, I'll lose it all—everything that matters to me. And for once I have no plan, nothing to do or fix. I just need to be there and . . . I don't know how else to say it, but I need their mess and to accept and forgive my own. And in the end, I think that's what your father was trying to do, too, but he couldn't see it clearly. Just like you said, he got it wrong sometimes."

I waited, expecting Joseph to launch at me. He didn't.

"Joseph? Are you still there?"

"You're so dramatic I was afraid to interrupt. Are you finished yet?" He added an Italian lilt to his dry sarcasm.

"You're such a jerk." I laughed. "I want the show to be a success tonight, Joseph, but I can't come back . . . Will you help?"

"Of course." He sighed. "I'll even escort Amy around the gallery and weave a sense of mystery and romance around your absence. Olivia will eat it up."

"Good, 'cause I've got a surprise for you someday soon."

"What?"

"Nothing yet. Just an idea. I've got a plane to catch. *Arrivederci*, Joseph."

"Wait, Em—"

I clicked off my phone and headed to the ticket counter. It was time to catch a plane; Joseph's questions could wait.

Chapter 46

The plane touched down, and I grabbed my phone to call Ben. No answer. Again.

I vacillated between hurt, annoyance, pure anger, fright, and anticipation—emotions overlapping, crashing into one another, and churning in my stomach.

I grabbed my chocolate, hurried my way through customs, seized my bag, ran to *Autonoleggio*, and rented my own tiny car. I set my GPS to Montevello and was on my way home like a true Italian—darting in and out of traffic like a crazy woman, too tired to be scared.

I accelerated as I merged onto the highway leaving Florence and sped down the hill, racing in and out of shadow into the valley below, buildings soon giving way to piney woods, olive trees, and cultivated fields and farmhouses. Outside Panzano, I waved hello to the small trattorias, the *emporio* where Clara the shopkeeper ordered my cleaners, solvents, and a few hard-to-find glues, and drove past my favorite field of sunflowers. My *girasoli*.

I slowed to take them in. At present they faced away from me, but they'd turn. They were smarter than I'd been. They always followed the light.

I stomped the accelerator again and turned onto the Vassalloses gravel drive. The quarter mile gave me time to form words . . . any words. None came.

I slowed at the front door and, setting one foot down, realized that none of the words I imagined could quite work. I wasn't sure what I was chasing myself; I just had a feeling about it. There was something wonderful, expectant, and glorious ahead. *Joy.* But I had no idea how to articulate it.

The door opened, and there she stood. "I heard noise" were Donata's only words, but at least she said them in English so I could understand.

"*Buongiorno,*" I offered.

She raised an eyebrow and left it arched high. "Why are you here?"

"*Sono a casa.*" *I'm home.*

"He is not here."

I'd imagined our chat over coffee, maybe even a bite of pasta, but it was going to take place here, standing face-to-face in the late-morning sun on a gravel drive, without Ben's support.

"I'll find him at Coccocino, but first I wanted to talk to you. I'm sorry it needs to be in English, but I don't know how to say it in Italian."

Donata nodded.

I tried to take a deep breath, but my chest was too tight. "I never meant to bring you pain, in so many ways, and I hope you will forgive me. And I want to share something with you . . . Would you let me . . ."

My pulse filled my head and ears. This was going to be either the start or the end of us. Donata didn't seem to allow for much waffling in the middle.

"Would you . . . let me finish the mural? In the church? Joseph

didn't finish the story, and we need it. We, all of us, need the fact and the reminder of grace and forgiveness. Maybe that's what Lucio wanted, but even he didn't understand how to tell us . . . And maybe I don't either, but this feels like the place to start. The only place to start." I noticed my hands flapping in front of me and I clasped them together to quiet them, to quiet me.

I continued more slowly, hoping she could understand. "I need to stop feeling like if I don't put it back together, I'll never be whole. And I need Ben and I need you. And Joseph too. I need him as a brother, but he needs us. Maybe he never knew, or he forgot. But I think, through the mural, we can reach him too."

Donata didn't speak, but she wasn't yelling either, and that gave me courage.

"If we finish the story, as it is supposed to end, we'll better understand. I know we will . . . And I thought together, you and I might . . ."

I dropped my hands. I didn't know how to say it in English. How could I possibly expect her to understand it? I simply knew that to stay and share life, we needed to finish that story because, unlike all the others, that one was ours. Life and story were, in fact, one.

"*Sì.*"

"Yes," I repeated. "Yes? Are you sure? I mean, did you understand? Because I was asking—"

She held up a hand, and I noticed her knuckles were just beginning to bend with age. "I understand and I agree. It is not right to leave out the vital part, but"—she tapped her heart with a bent finger—"for so many years, it has hurt. I am tired of hurting so. I am weak with it." She used that same finger to point within the house. "Come. I am making the pasta."

"I . . ." My lips parted. "I would love that, but I need to go find Ben. I don't think he thought I was coming back and . . ." I shrugged.

"I wasn't sure myself, until yesterday, but I am. I mean, I'm sure, not that I'm back. You can see I'm back. I mean I'm sure I'm staying."

I stopped talking, way too late.

Donata stared at me like I wasn't making sense—and I wasn't. She repeated her first words. "He is not here."

"I know. I'll go to Coccocino now." I pointed down the drive as if that clarified everything.

She shook her head. "He left yesterday, to go for you. He said he would move there, for you."

"But I'm here!"

"*Sì*. I see that." Her eyes lit with a beautiful smile. It was her first to me and I reciprocated with, probably, my first to her. "Call him."

"I've tried. He doesn't answer."

She waved me to follow her into the house. "He had three stops. Maybe he is not landed."

"I had four." I laughed and pressed my lips together. Tears were next.

I followed her through the hallway and back to the kitchen. It smelled of tomatoes and basil. Not cooked, but clean and raw and infinitely Italian.

"When he lands, he will call."

I smiled, because of course he would. A good Italian boy will always call his mama. Donata's smile told me she knew it too.

She pointed to the huge wood island, dusted with flour. "Wash your hands and I will show you."

Hours later, I washed my hands again and walked out onto the patio. The sun had warmed the flagstones and heat came from

above and below—it warmed my skin and bones on its way to my soul. But the sun wasn't high now; it was moving toward the hills and would soon set. Day was ending, and I still hadn't heard from Ben.

I tapped his smiling face on my phone and prayed he would answer.

On the third ring . . . "Emily?" One word, filled with a few *e*'s and endless hope.

I felt my eyes prick again. "I'm—I'm home and you're not."

"I missed your show last night. But I am here, and Joseph is not home. Are you close? Can you let me in?"

Donata stepped next to me and angled her face to my phone. "Tell him he wastes good money." As she pulled away, a smile curled the tiniest corner of her lip. She was so like her elder son—light with the compliments. At least I thought it was a compliment.

Ben's shout brought me back. "Is that Mama?"

I nodded and then realized he couldn't see me. "She said to tell you—Oh, never mind. I'm standing on the back patio having just ruined an entire batch of pasta, but your mother's not yelling, so there's hope, but you're not here and—"

"Bella. Shhh . . ."

I sucked in a deep breath and whispered, "I know what you thought, and I'm sorry." Silence met me. The sun crept behind the hill, taking the heat with it. "Ben?"

"Do not move," he whispered in reply. "Not a muscle."

I smiled because he was so unlike his mother and brother in that way. Ben savored moments, brought them forward to recapture and linger over them. He also laid on the compliments thick, like his *Bistecca alla pizzaiola*—a sauce so thick it could almost stand. I heard his promise, his love, and I understood him. I barely contained my excitement. Barely.

"Can I get a bite to eat? I ruined mine, but your mother's pasta came out really well. She might give me some. And perhaps I could take a short nap?"

He chuckled as a breeze sent the olive leaves dancing. "Only because it will take me some time. I *am* coming for you."

"Good, because I love you."

"That is all I need to know. *Ciao, Bella. Ti amo.*" He sighed across the line. "I will be home soon."

Chapter 47

Six months later

It took Ben sixteen hours . . .

    It took Joseph . . . until today . . .

"What are you doing out here?" Ben whispered as his arms slid around my waist.

I kept my eyes on the farthest hill. "I came to see the sunset. It's different now. Winter doesn't shoot off the same colors." I snuggled deeper into his sweater that I'd grabbed from the back of a chair.

"They'll be back." Ben pulled me against him and rested his chin on the top of my head.

"Are you watching?"

"*Sì*. It's the most beautiful moment of the day. It reminds me of Papa."

"Is he here?"

"Dust just kicked up on the drive. It will be any minute. Do you want to come up and say hello?"

"Not yet." I shook my head. "Your mother asked everyone to

wait until at least nine to come over tonight. She's nervous. Let's give them a moment. This has been a long time coming."

Eighteen years and six months.

And the last six months alone had been staggering . . .

After Father Matt's first exclamation of surprise, he welcomed me into the church each morning and read aloud as I painted. Each and every day. He said I needed to better know this man I was about to add to the church walls. And he was right. It took me time to understand even the smallest fraction of the grace, wisdom, and unconditional love I sought to convey through the mural.

Some I learned from Donata. We were changing together, and although we scraped and bumped occasionally, she no longer shooed me from her kitchen. She didn't purse her lips when she spoke English. And she even slowed her words, inviting me to understand and learn her Italian.

And when Olivia finally sent Lucio's portrait back, Donata had reached for my hand with both her own and clasped it tight. Now the portrait hung above the fireplace in the library and often, when I looked up from working on a painting or reading a book, I found Donata curled in Lucio's chair across from me, reading or simply staring at her husband.

Some I learned from Francesca. No longer trying to manage or "fix" her, I listened to her—as she planned her wedding, whined about Alessandro's taciturn nature, or daydreamed about married life. Those last musings always made me smile. Rachel's words came back to me often as Francesca chatted. *You can feel just that alive every day . . . After all, you get to be with that one guy who lights up your world and shares it with you.* Francesca was going to have a wonderful time. I was having a wonderful time.

Those "sisterly" moments also made me realize what I'd missed with my own sister. We were only now beginning to share

like that, and as Amy would say, it was "on me" that we'd missed so much.

I felt Ben smile against the top of my head. "Look."

We watched as the sun's last rays ignited the white under-bellies of the olive leaves. It looked like silver flashing within gold. It was beautiful and never failed to thrill me. Within seconds, it was gone and the hillside shaded and cooled.

I turned in Ben's arms. "We should go now."

"Are you going to be okay?"

I loved the hint of concern in his voice and kissed him. His eyes widened in surprise.

"You once told me that Piccolo was never about the restaurant. It was always about Maria and Vito. I won't be sad about the mural either, even if Joseph scrubs the wall, paints over my work, and starts afresh. I truly don't believe it all could've happened any other way."

I'd sent Joseph a picture of the completed mural only days before. Within seconds, I received a five-word text.

You lack the necessary skill.

My next text was from Lily asking me what I'd done to get Joseph on a plane home so fast. He was leaving ACI in her care to "restore a ruined beauty" back home.

"Okay, forget all that." I shook my head. "I'm not as mature as you. It'll kill me. It was some of my best work."

"I disagree." Ben chuckled. "I think the eyes ended up a little freaky." His tone captured my Midwestern notes perfectly.

Sarcasm. I smiled, kissed him again, and pulled him up the hill.

The kitchen lights spilled into the darkening evening. Candles

lit the farm table on the patio, and Ben had lit a fire in the stone fireplace at the patio's edge.

Ten places were set, but I knew Donata had planned and cooked for at least sixty. Her son was home. And laughter from the kitchen confirmed it. No one had obeyed her—family had arrived early.

Ben reached his arm around me and kissed my temple. "And that, my dear, was our last moment of peace. Shall we join the others? I suspect dinner is about to begin."

A Peek Behind the Curtain . . .

This page is great fun. Yes, there is the risk of forgetting some- one who has helped shaped the journey, the story, and that would be bad . . . But there is also the joy of remembering—and the delight of introducing them to you . . .

I'll begin by introducing the fiction within my fiction. First, Montevello. It's the one and only fictional town I've created and I hope you enjoyed it. Think Montepulciano meets Montefalco meets Vitigliano and you're getting close. Throw in a bit of my "research trip" truffle hunting, wine tasting, olive oil tasting, eating, walking, and more eating, and you are there. I hope you savored Montevello's steep, narrow streets and sunbaked walls— and the espresso. Second, my Italian. It was important to me to use, in many ways, "incorrect" Italian—a learner's Italian with words, verbs, and conjugations occasionally wrong as it is what Emily heard and interpreted. I hope these constructions didn't prove too jarring to my fluent Italian-speaking friends.

Now you must meet some extraordinary people. Daisy Hutton, editor, publisher, and friend, is a daily inspiration. She gives the best of herself to every project and every writer—with an

amazingly contagious smile. I hope never to take her faith in me, or in these stories, for granted. Thank you, Daisy.

The incredible team at HCCP is next—Jodi Hughes, Kristen Ingebretson, Paul Fisher, Becky Monds, Stephen Tindal, and the amazing Sales Team who work tirelessly to make these stories beautiful and get them into your hands. Kristen Golden gets a special shout-out and introduction. She shares her publicist acumen, excellent taste in books, and extraordinary glow and glitter with me—and I'm the better for it.

And now meet The Home Team:

Claudia Cross brings literary knowledge, diplomacy, my kind of humor, and great generosity as my agent, mentor, and friend. Elizabeth Lane dreams up the "events" with me, and is my first, last, and all-stages-in-the-middle reader. She is also my beloved sister. The three MMRs always play an important role . . . Three generations of Joy Seekers: Meet my mother, my cousin, and my younger daughter.

And though you've met them before . . . the entirety of Team Reay is ever-present and deserves mention. The kids are growing older, but we parents have decided to stop *all* growing for a time. We'd like to savor these last years before they're out of the house and not weighing in on stories or dinner plans and fighting us for control of the music.

Last, but never least . . . meet you. You are a vast set of wonderfulness full of readers, bloggers, reviewers, and now friends who have generously read these novels, joined in this journey, and reached out, meeting me on social media or in person. Thank you.

Again and again, *thank you* to everyone in this beloved cast. I'm beyond grateful to share *A Portrait of Emily Price* with you. Let's join together for something new this time next year . . .

Discussion Questions

1. Emily believes all can be fixed at the beginning of her story. Whether you believe it's true or not, can you see yourself acting in this way or have you seen others doing so? Is it a common belief? Do we have control over anything/ everything or is Emily deceiving herself?

2. At Ammazza, Emily looks at Ben and realizes he might "find a sense of wonder, a sense of wholeness or delight" in her. Why do you think she finds that disconcerting? Would you?

3. Everything Emily touches she tries to fix. What drives that? Have you ever felt such compulsion? Are we naturally wired that way or is it fairly unique?

4. Emily wonders, *What if I'm trying to be someone I can be?* Have you ever felt like that? More comfortable in a new aspect of you, while afraid it may not be real?

5. At her wedding, fears plague Emily. Do you feel she's stepped too far too fast? How realistic is it that someone

could find something so special she is ready to leap that fast? Have you ever done something so bold?

6. Amy tells Emily that marriage within two weeks is "for lust, not love." She then withdraws the statement. Was she right the first or the second time? Can someone find "true love" in only a matter of weeks? What does "true love" even mean?

7. Francesca calls Emily an "Emma." Is Emily meddling or innocently helping a friend? Or asked another way . . . Is she helping Francesca or herself?

8. We all have a lens through which we see the world. What are some of them you see in these characters? Do you see any within yourself?

9. In watching Donata, how easy or hard is it to become trapped in one's mistakes or what others tell us about ourselves?

10. Lucio teaches and shares through books. Do you think he was trying to teach Emily about herself through his choices or simply sharing something about himself?

11. The changes in Emily's art surprise her as it develops from "freaky" eyes to capturing the essence of the person she paints. What does she discover within her art, and what brought about that change?

12. Why did Emily ask Ben not to come with her to Atlanta? Was she running to or away from something? Can they be the same thing?

13. Do you think Lucio gave Emily *A Portrait of the Artist as a Young Man* as an escape hatch like Emily thought, or could he have had another purpose in mind? Or no purpose at all?

14. The author brings Emily and Donata together before Emily finds Ben. Why do you think that was important to her?

15. In finishing the mural, what was Emily chasing? Did she find it?

16. Do you think Joseph will "stay," emotionally if not physically? Why or why not?

An Excerpt from
Dear Mr. Knightley

April 2

Dear Sir,

It has been a year since I turned down your generous offer. Father John warned me at the time that I was making a terrible mistake, but I wouldn't listen. He felt that by dismissing that opportunity I was injuring not only myself, but all the foster children helped by your foundation.

I hope any perceived ingratitude on my part didn't harm anyone else's dreams. I wasn't ungrateful; I just wanted to leave Grace House. A group home is a difficult place to live, and I'd been there for eight years. And even though I knew graduate school meant more education and better job prospects, it also meant living at Grace House another two years. At the time I couldn't face that prospect.

My heart has always been in my books and writing, but I couldn't risk losing a paying job to pursue a dream. Now I'm ready to try. Not because I failed, but because this degree gives me the chance to link my passion with my livelihood.

Please let me know if the grant is still available. I will understand if you have selected another candidate.

Sincerely,

Samantha Moore

April 7

Dear Ms. Moore,

The grant for full tuition to the master's program at Northwestern University's Medill School of Journalism remains available. At the strong recommendation of Father John, and due to the confidence he has in you, the director of the Dover Foundation has agreed to give you this second chance. There is, however, one stipulation. The director wants to receive personal progress letters from you as reassurance that this decision was the right one. You may write to him as you would to a journal, letting him know how your studies are going. He has opened a post office box for this purpose so you won't feel the added pressure of an immediate connection to him or to the foundation. Additionally, he will not write back, but asks that you write to him regularly about "things that matter."

He recognizes that this is an unusual requirement, but the foundation needs to know that its resources are being used in the best way possible. Given your sudden change of heart, he feels it is not too much to ask. To make this easier for you, he will also remain anonymous. You may write to him at this address under the name George Knightley.

Sincerely,
Laura Temper
Personal Assistant to Mr.
G. Knightley

April 12

Dear Mr. Knightley,

Thank you so much for giving me this opportunity. I submitted my application to Medill this morning. I had to use a couple papers on Dickens and Austen in place of the journalism samples requested. While that may count against me, I felt the rest of my application was strong.

If you will allow, I want to honor Father John's trust and yours by explaining my "sudden change of heart," as Ms. Temper described it. When I graduated college last spring, I had two opportunities: your grant to fund graduate school or a job at Ernst & Young. In my eagerness to leave Grace House and conquer the world, I chose the job. Six weeks ago I was fired. At the exit meeting my boss claimed I was "unengaged," especially with regard to peer and client interactions. I did good work there, Mr. Knightley. Good solid work. But "relating" in the workplace is important too, I gather. That's where I failed.

I'm guessing from your literary choice of pseudonym that you are very likely acquainted with another admirable character from fiction—Elizabeth Bennet, Jane Austen's complex and enchanting heroine. At Ernst & Young I tried to project Lizzy's boldness and spirit, but clearly she had a confidence and charm that was more than I could sustain on a daily basis. So now here I am, back at Grace House, taking advantage of the state's willingness to provide a home for me till I'm twenty-five if I stay in school.

Nevertheless, Father John still doubts me and couldn't resist

a lecture this morning. I tried to listen, but my eyes wandered around his office: photographs of all the children who have passed through Grace House cover every space that isn't taken up with books. He loves murder mysteries: Agatha Christie, James Patterson, Alex Powell, P. D. James, Patricia Cornwell . . . I've read most of them. The first day we met, right before I turned fifteen, he challenged me to stretch beyond the classics.

"Are you listening, Sam?" Father John finally noticed my wandering eyes. "The Medill program is straight up your alley. You're a great reader and writer."

"'I deserve neither such praise nor such censure. I am not a great reader, and I have pleasure in many things.'" Elizabeth Bennet has a useful reply for every situation.

Father John gave a small smile, and I flinched. "What if I can't do this?" I asked. "Maybe it's a mistake."

He sat back in his chair and took a slow breath. Eyebrows down, mouth in a line.

"Then turn this down—again—and find another job. Pound the pavement quickly, though. I can give you a couple weeks here to get on your feet, then my hands are tied." He leaned forward. "Sam, I'll always help you. But after this, if you're not in school, Grace House is closed to you. This foundation helps a lot of kids here, and I won't jeopardize that support because you can't commit. So decide right now."

A tear rolled down my cheek. Father John never gets charged up, but I deserved it. I should only be grateful to you both, and here I was questioning your help. But help is hard, Mr. Knightley—even when I desperately need it. Every foster placement of my childhood was intended to help me; every new social worker tried to help my case; when I was sent back home at twelve, the judge meant to help my life too . . . I'm so tired of help.

"I'm sorry, Father John, you're right. I want this grant and I asked for it again. I must seem so ungrateful to you, to be questioning again."

"You don't, Sam, and I can understand wanting to stand alone. Even in the best of times and circumstances, it's hard to accept help—"

In the end, Father John believed my commitment. I hope you do too. Here is our agreement: you will pay for graduate school, and I will write you letters that give an honest accounting of my life and school—and you will never write back. That simple, right?

Thank you for that, Mr. Knightley—your anonymity. Honesty is easier when you have no face and no real name. And honesty, for me, is very easy on paper.

I also want to assure you that while I may not relate well to people in the real world, I shine in school. It's paper-based. I will do your grant justice, Mr. Knightley. I'll shine at Medill.

I know I've said more than was necessary in this letter, but I need you to know who I am. We need to have an honest beginning, even if it's less impressive than Lizzy Bennet's.

Sincerely,
Samantha Moore

April 21

Dear Mr. Knightley,

Each and every moment things change. For the most part, I loathe it. Change never works in my favor—as evidenced by so many foster placements, a holdup at a Chicago White Hen, getting fired from Ernst & Young, and so many other changes in my life I'd like to forget. But I needed one more—a change of my own making—so I pursued your grant again.

But it's not of my own making, is it?

Father John told me this morning that he was the one who proposed journalism for me—it was not an original requirement for your grant. I wouldn't have chosen it myself. My professor at Roosevelt College said I produced some of the best work on Austen, Dickens, and the Brontes he'd ever read. I'm *good* at fiction, Mr. Knightley. And I don't think it's right that Father John took away my choice. I'm twenty-three years old; I should be the author of the changes in my life.

I went to Father John and explained all this. I feel he has arbitrarily forced me into journalism—a field I don't know and don't write. "You need to undo that," I pleaded. "They'll listen to you."

Father John closed his eyes. One might think he'd fallen asleep, but I knew better. He was praying. He does that—a lot.

Minutes passed. He opened his eyes and zeroed in on me. Sometimes I feel his eyes are tired, but not at that moment. They were piercing and direct. I knew his answer before he opened his mouth.

"Sam, I won't . . . but you can. Write the foundation's director and ask." Father John stared into my eyes, measuring his words. "Don't lie. Don't tell them I've changed my mind. I have not. I am wholly against a change in program."

"How can you say that?" My own shrill voice surprised me.

"I've known you for eight years, Sam. I've watched you grow, I've watched you succeed, and I've watched you retreat. I want the best for you, and with every fiber of my being, I am convinced that 'the best' is not more fiction, but finding your way around in the real world and its people."

I opened my mouth to protest, but he held up his hand. "Consider carefully. If the foundation is unwilling to alter your grant, you may accept or you may walk away. You always have a choice."

"That's not fair."

Father John's eyes clouded. "My dear, what in your life has ever come close to fair? That's not how this life works." He leaned forward and stretched his hands out across the desk. "I'm sorry, Sam. If I could protect you from any more pain, I would. But I can only pray and do the very best God calls me to do. If I'm wrong about this, I hope that someday you will forgive me."

"'My temper would perhaps be called resentful.—My good opinion once lost is lost forever.'" When Elizabeth Bennet doesn't come through, one can always count on Mr. Darcy to provide the right response. I shook my head and, quoting no one, said, "I won't forgive you, Father John. I don't forgive." And I walked out.

I don't care if that was ungenerous, Mr. Knightley. He overstepped, and he's wrong. So now I'm asking you: Will you let me decide?

Sincerely,
Samantha Moore

April 25

Dear Ms. Moore,

Please forgive me for violating our agreement already, but I felt your question warranted a personal reply.

I understand your anger. It is hard when others hold power over you. Rest assured, your situation is not unique. There is very little any of us chooses in isolation.

Through my foundation, Father John has helped five young adults from Grace House. One attended junior college; another, trade school; one graduated from cosmetology school; and two successfully completed residential treatment programs. Each individual has grown closer to whole.

Father John not only fulfilled all the grant requirements for your application, but wrote me an additional five pages outlining your writing abilities, your gifts, and your determination. His decision to recommend journalism school was not made lightly, as you well know. Remember that, and remember what he has meant in your life. Don't throw away friends and mentors carelessly. They are rare.

I trust Father John's prayerful counsel and judgment, and stand with his original recommendation. My foundation will only award the grant for Medill's master's program.

The choice to accept it or not is yours, Ms. Moore.

Sincerely,

G. Knightley

May 10

Dear Mr. Knightley,

I didn't withdraw my application. I made my choice and now I sit, waiting for Medill to accept or reject me.

In the meantime I've settled into my old ways and my old jobs: I resumed tutoring at Buckhorn Cottage (Grace House's cottage for 8-to 13-year-old boys) and I picked up a few shifts at the public library. I've been working at that library for a decade now, even before I moved to Grace House for the first time.

I was about fifteen when I first arrived at Grace House. Father John took me to his office and invited me to sit. No one had ever done that—invited me to do anything. He chatted for a few minutes, then handed me an Anne Perry novel.

"Detective Huber got your file for me, Sam, and it's full of references to *Pride and Prejudice*, *Jane Eyre*, *Oliver Twist*, and other great classics. I think you must like to read. So until I get some of your favorites, would you like to read one of mine?"

The thick hardback had a picture of a Victorian house on the cover. I slowly turned the pages, hoping if I feigned interest in his book, he'd take me to wherever I'd be staying and leave me alone.

He didn't. "This is one of the first mysteries I ever read. Now I'm hooked. I've got about a hundred titles over there." Father John pointed to his bookcase and waited.

I looked up.

"Come to my office anytime you want a new one. I picked that

for you because it takes place in England in the nineteenth century, about the same time as your favorites."

I put the book down, never breaking eye contact. A show of strength, I thought.

He sighed and leaned back in his chair. "Your choice. I'm sure I can get some classics this week. Or you can go to the public library; it's on the corner of State and Van Buren."

I wanted to say I knew exactly where the library was, but that would require speaking to him, so I simply slid the book into my lap. I wasn't going to admit, even to myself, that I liked the man—and still do. In spite of how angry I am with him at the moment, I know that Father John has always been on my side.

He welcomed me at fifteen and again at eighteen, after I tried to move out. And now at twenty-three, despite my heated words, he's opened Grace House's door once more. So while I'm here, I will listen to his lectures and I will try to do what he asks. I owe him that much.

I'll even try to play nice with Morgan, my new roommate in Independence Cottage . . .

"She's had a rough time, Sam. She turned eighteen a couple days ago and her foster family ended the placement."

"She can go on her own. Isn't that a good thing?"

"Not without her GED . You know how important that is. She's testing next month, then joining the army." Father John stared right through me.

"Why are you telling me this?"

"I'm asking you to be kind. Morgan's defense mechanisms are different from yours, and it may be rough going. Please don't make waves."

"I make waves?"

"Like the ocean, kiddo. Then you retreat before they hit the sand."

Ouch.

So I'm being kind, but Morgan isn't making it easy. We were cleaning the kitchen the other day and I told her about your grant. I was trying to be friendly. She was not.

"You're selling yourself for school? I can't believe you'd give it up for tuition. At least get some money or clothes from the deal."

"Morgan, shut up. You're disgusting. It isn't like that. I write letters to an address in New York and I get my tuition paid to graduate school."

"I bet a lot of girls start out that way." Morgan stopped washing her dishes and stared at me. She smiled slowly, almost cruelly. "Letters will be worse for you anyway. Good luck with that."

"What do you mean 'worse for me'? I can write a few letters, Morgan. That's what I do. I write."

"Honesty will kill you. You're a coward, and you'll lie. That makes the whole deal a lie." She put her plate down and walked away.

She's not right. I'm not a coward, and I will be honest in these letters. Simply because I don't blab my business to the world like Mrs. Bennet doesn't mean I'm a coward. I'm prudent when dealing with people. That's smart. Wouldn't you agree?

But Morgan brings up a good point—her only one so far. Have you read *Jane Eyre*? There's a part when Mr. Rochester meets Jane and asks if she expects a present. Adele, his ward, believes everyone should receive presents, daily. Jane isn't so sure. She replies, "They are generally thought pleasant things . . . a present has many faces to it, has it not? And one should consider all before pronouncing an opinion as to its nature."

You've led me to believe your gift has one face, Mr. Knightley. I'll leave it at that.

Sincerely,
Samantha Moore

P.S. Okay, I can't leave it . . .

If you are truly a "Mr. Knightley," I can do this. I can write these letters. I trust you chose that name as a reflection of your own character. George Knightley is a good and honorable man—even better than Fitzwilliam Darcy, and few women put anyone above Mr. Darcy.

Yes, Darcy's got the tempestuous masculinity and brooding looks, but Knightley is a kinder, softer man with no pretense or dissimilation. Yes, he's a gentleman. And I can write with candor to a silent gentleman, and I can believe that he will not violate this trust.

I admit that if you had a face and a real name—or a nefarious name—it might be different. Morgan might be right. But as I sit here and think about this, I feel comfortable. See what power a name holds?

The story continues in *Dear Mr. Knightley* by Katherine Reay.

About the Author

Katherine Reay has enjoyed a lifelong affair with the works of Jane Austen and her contemporaries. After earning degrees in history and marketing from Northwestern University, she worked in not-for-profit development before returning to school to pursue her MTS. Katherine lives with her husband and three children in Chicago, Illinois.

Visit her website at www.katherinereay.com
Twitter: @Katherine_Reay
Facebook: katherinereaybooks